THE VOLATILITY COURSE

George A. Fontanills
Tom Gentile

JOHN WILEY & SONS, INC.

Published by John Wiley & Sons, Inc., Hoboken, New Jersey.
Published simultaneously in Canada.

For general information on our other products and services, or technical support, please contact our Customer Care Department within the United States at 800-762-2974, outside the United States at 317-572-3993 or fax 317-572-4002.

Wiley also publishes its books in a variety of electronic formats. Some content that appears in print may not be available in electronic books.

Library of Congress Cataloging-in-Publication Data:

Fontanills, George.
    The volatility course / George A. Fontanills & Tom Gentile.
      p. cm.—(The Wiley trading series)
    Includes index.
    ISBN 0-471-39816-0 (cloth : alk. paper)
    1. Speculation. 2. Options (Finance) I. Gentile, Tom, 1965– II. Title. III. Series.
  HG6015 .F597   2002
  332.64'5—dc21
                                               2002034203

Printed in the United States of America.

10 9 8 7 6 5 4 3 2 1

It is with great love and respect
that we dedicate this book to
Traci Gentile

Preface

All serious daring starts from within.
—Eudora Welty

The phrase "simple pleasures are the best" describes what has become a very popular approach to living. In these highly precarious times, many of us seek to enrich our lives by trying to make them a little less volatile. While teenagers may crave excitement and wild adventure, the majority of us prefer a more stable, consistent existence with very little uncertainty. After all, it is the rare few that volunteer to become police officers—one minute sipping coffee and the next moment chasing criminals, wheels screaming in high-speed pursuit. Too much volatility for me, I'm afraid. Rapid change may be exciting, but it also stimulates the growth of gray hairs and high blood pressure.

Throughout my many years of trading, as well as life, I have noticed that very few things are consistent enough not to exhibit "volatility." What is volatility? It is best described as a rapid change from one time period or condition to another. A patient in the hospital is in a state of high volatility if their condition changes rapidly from one moment to the next. In the stock market, volatility exists when rapid change occurs in the price of a stock due to some known or unknown factors. Volatility is in essence the explosive nature inherent in all things—from your child's erratic behavior to your neighbor's hot temper. It simply means that a change has occurred that could be significant, or not.

Let me give you an example that may be close to your heart. Let's say two drivers go into an insurance agency to insure their brand-new sports cars. The first driver is an 18-year-old whose record already includes accidents and moving violations. The second driver is a 55-year-old who hasn't had an accident or ticket in 20 years. Which driver has more potential "volatility"? I hope you answered the 18-year-old. The insurance company would undoubtedly also look at it this way. Now, the computers have to come up with the premium for the insurance policy. The computer calculates $5,000 per year for driver 1, the 18-year-old, and $1,000 per year for driver 2, the 55-year-old with a great driving record. Statistically, the computers see a much greater probability that driver 1 will be more volatile; therefore the insurance premiums are significantly higher. Driver 2 has proven to be a consistently safe driver, so her "volatility premium" is significantly lower. Insurance premiums are very similar to the premiums created when stock options are priced. It only makes sense that the more volatile the stock, the higher its options premiums.

Let's take one more example that may also hit home. Let's say you're one of those individuals who diets, loses weight, and then gains it all back—again and again. Sometimes you gain way too much and then have trouble losing it; the next time it's even harder to get back to your original weight. You are simply unable to maintain a consistent weight that fits your frame. This kind of dilemma can be thought of as a high-volatility weight issue for today's calorie-challenged baby boomers.

In the marketplace, the volatility of a stock, also referred to as an underlying asset, contributes significantly to the price of an option. For a moment, pretend you're in the shoes of a trader on the floor of an options exchange. Many investors do not realize that options exchanges exist so investors like you can take risk or hedge risk. The "floor trader" is there to make a market through the use of financial instruments called options. Floor traders are, in essence, very much like the computer of the insurance company. They look at the many pieces of the puzzle in order to determine prices at which they feel confident they can buy and sell options and not be hurt. Volatility is one of the major components of this puzzle.

Let's look at an example using the stock of a very stable company, ABC. Over the past year, the price fluctuated between a low price of $20 per share and a high price of $25. ABC just seems to trade between these numbers and never threatens to break out of its trading range. It constantly stays between the lower range, also referred to as "support," and the upper range, which is called the "resistance." ABC is not exhibiting a hint of volatility. This would make it an easy one for the floor trader to price. It appears to be a pretty boring stock, so the floor traders would feel comfortable in keeping the volatility premium low. They would look at all the factors that go into the price of the options, and since the volatility component would be low, the price of ABC's options would also be lower than those of a company that has more uncertainty.

Now all of a sudden some bad news comes out on an important issue such as earnings or accounting problems. This may very well drive the stock much lower; the trading range, which looked unbreakable, is now just a thing of the past. As investors panic and drive the stock down to levels that have not been seen for a while, historical volatility increases to levels it may have never seen before. This, in turn, creates a panic in the purchasing of options, which creates its own momentum. This volatility, which is the volatility placed into the price of an option, is also referred to as implied volatility. In general, it is what today's options trader looks at as the "risk premium." And thanks to volatility, that premium is much higher than it was before.

I have always found volatility's elasticity fascinating. It's like a stretched rubber band. As soon as it is let go, it'll snap back to where it's used to being. In effect, volatility usually has a comfort zone, and you can typically see it in a chart of volatility (yes, you can chart volatility just like a stock price chart). When volatility gets too high, you can bet it will come down. If it gets too low, you can almost bet it will get higher. You just have to look at the charts.

As an options trader, I just love the fact that I have such a large array of trading strategies to wield in almost infinite combinations. This is the real challenge—looking for that gem hiding among all the potential strategies we can employ. Once you have accurately succeeded in identifying the market conditions—including looking at present volatility by assessing the stock's historical volatility—you can use the right tool from your arsenal of trading strategies to find that gem and profit from it.

The distilled truth of volatility investing can be summed up in four little words: *Buy low, sell high.* This is undoubtedly the easiest way to explain when you should "buy" or "sell" volatility. Just like a stock, you want to buy it at a lower price and sell it at a higher price. The trick is to figure out when low is low and when high is high. It's too bad that the world makes it so hard to pinpoint these opportunities. Volatility you think is high can become higher. On the flip side, volatility you think is low can always become lower. It's never black and white, folks. Astute traders operate in a world of grays. This book is designed to show you how volatility works and how it can work for you.

Tom Gentile and I have taught and written together for 10 years now. I attribute our success to our emphasis on risk management and a lot of hard work. I sincerely believe that the most important element of becoming a good trader is learning to manage risk. Alas, it may be the gospel for the professional floor trader; but unfortunately, it is one of the last lessons learned by most individual traders who trade for themselves. I challenge you to integrate risk management into your trading approach starting today.

This book was written to teach you the secrets of volatility and how it helps traders attain greater trading success. Take your time and absorb its teachings; the lessons learned may very well change your life for the better or at least give you a chance to succeed where others may have failed due to lack of knowledge. Sit back and get ready to learn about one of the most valuable secret weapons available to option traders: volatility.

My best wishes to everyone, and good luck in these volatile times.

GEORGE A. FONTANILLS
President Emeritus
Optionetics

Acknowledgments

After cowriting *The Stock Market Course*, we were approached about writing a comprehensive book on how to use volatility to gain a competitive edge in the markets. As far as we're concerned, volatility is the most important phenomenon a trader can master to trade successfully. We were thrilled at the prospect of sharing the knowledge we have gained over the years, especially in these volatile times.

Although this book is written from a first-person perspective, please note that it is the work of two authors. We've spent a tremendous amount of time and energy researching, designing, and writing every aspect of this book. It has been a very rewarding experience to share our extensive experience and insightful trading knowledge in its creation. But there's no way we could have written this book without the help and support of the Optionetics staff and research team that helped us to pull it all together. We would now like to take the time to acknowledge each and every one of these brilliant people.

At the top of the list, we want to thank Frederic Ruffy. As a Senior Writer at Optionetics.com, Fred is one of the most brilliant writers and traders we know. To his credit, Fred put in a phenomenal amount of time and energy researching every aspect of this book while sharing his extensive experience and insightful trading knowledge. Thank you, Fred Ruffy, for your supreme effort in the completion of this book.

There are also a host of excellent writers on our research team that deserve a big round of applause. Without them, we would not have been able to write such a comprehensive book or finish it on time. Specifically, we would like to thank Kevin Lund, Andrew Neyens, Jody Osborne, and Shelley Souza for their timely commentary and market expertise. Special thanks also go to Kim Diehl for her last-minute edits and overall assistance in the completion of this book.

Optionetics would not be what it is without the innovative leadership and tireless efforts of Richard Cawood, our CEO, and Tony Clemendor, our Chief Operating Officer. Thanks for everything you do each day to make Optionetics a thriving business. We salute you both for your excellent ideas and dedication to providing comprehensive options trading education all over the world.

Finally, let us express our deep appreciation to Kym Trippsmith, Editor-in-Chief of Optionetics.com and Senior Editor for this project. As usual, she's done an excellent job coordinating the development of this book as well as editing every inch of it. Kym's consistency, attention to detail, and can-do attitude make her the best editor we can imagine. Thank you, Kym!

If the tragic events of September 11th have taught us anything, they have reminded all of us of the supreme importance of security. As far as we're concerned, financial security is a vital part of protecting your family. But volatility seems to just keep on rocking the markets. Just when you think there is no more room to the downside, the markets start to tumble once again. Even money managers are scrambling to find something that works in this choppy environment. We believe that learning to integrate volatility into your trading approach may be the most important step you can take toward becoming a financially secure trader. The trading strategies discussed in this book will teach you how to take advantage of various volatility levels and help you to maintain consistent trading account growth. It is our utmost hope that this book provides a solid foundation for you to grow as a trader, as well as grow your trading account exponentially.

Good luck and great trading.

GEORGE A. FONTANILLS
TOM GENTILE

About the Authors

George A. Fontanills

Optionetics was pioneered in the early 1990s by super-trader George Fontanills. The development of this innovative trading approach is a testament to human will and perseverance. Fontanills' journey was not an easy one. Having struggled to overcome a life-threatening illness as a young man, George Fontanills received his MBA from Harvard Business School and went out to conquer the world. His first business failed. Undaunted, he started a second business that never left the starting gate. Running low on money, George became a real estate investor and did quite well until the bottom fell out of the real estate market. George's next move was to begin 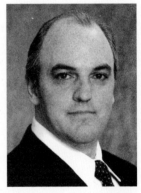 trading. Rather than concentrate on his losses, he began studying successful traders to see what they were doing differently. Using the analysis skills he learned at Harvard, George conducted a comprehensive investigation to determine what differentiated the winners from the losers. Risking the money he made in real estate, George tested his conclusions and eventually developed a creative approach that used options to mathematically control risk every time a trade is placed, thereby consistently producing income without the stress of unbridled losses. He called this trading style Optionetics.

As his net worth soared, he gained a reputation as an expert in nondirectional, managed-risk trading and has become a well-respected teacher and speaker at trading conferences all over the world. Today, the Optionetics Seminar series is one of the best-attended courses in the world of finance. George's straightforward and insightful approach to trading has enable thousands of people to learn how to limit their risks and maximize their trading successes.

These days, Fontanills is the President Emeritus of Optionetics and President of Pinnacle Investments of America. He actively trades equity options and stock and is a registered investment adviser and hedge fund manager with a number of offshore trading organizations, professional trading firms, and large financial institutions.

George's reputation as "the dean of options trading" has led to numerous guest appearances on television and radio shows across the United States. Most recently he has been quoted in the *Wall Street Journal*, *Barron's*, *Research* magazine, CBS MarketWatch, and TheStreet.com. He also appears on CNBC, Bloomberg, and CNN, as well as a number of radio stations across the country. In addition, George Fontanills has three best-selling hardback releases, *The Options Course*, *Trade Options Online*, and *The Stock Market Course*. These "definitive guides to trading" have added to his critical acclaim as one of the best trading instructors in the country.

Tom Gentile

From his humble childhood as the son of a steelworking family, Optionetics cofounder Tom Gentile has become not only a very successful trader, but a renowned educator, author, and businessman as well. Like many before him, he sought the opportunities Wall Street had to offer and headed to New York at an early age in search of his niche trading the markets. A stroke of luck afforded him the opportunity to connect with and work alongside famed trader and author George Fontanills. Through that relationship, Optionetics was born in 1993. Since then, Tom has developed a unique style of trading that could be described as fundamentally contrarian, yet 100 percent technical.

Born in Pittsburgh, Pennsylvania, in 1965, Tom moved around the country as his family worked on various state government projects. Early on, winding up in a different school each year, he dubbed himself the "professional new kid." Gentile excelled as a distance runner, and during 1982 and 1983 was rated one of the top distance runners in the state of Georgia. In 1984, Tom went to work for the Home Depot, and by 1987 had become one of the youngest managers in the company. By 1990, Gentile progressed to become a regional coordinator in information services. His responsibilities included training executive, regional, and district managers over the entire northeastern United States.

Gentile began his trading career in 1986 and made the jump to full-time trading in 1994, landing a job at the American Stock Exchange. During his tenure on the floor, he met George Fontanills and began teaching the Optionetics Seminars, which are among the most successful options seminars in the markets today. Gentile also played a key role in the development of the "synthetic straddle," a strategy developed as an off-the-floor trading approach to rebalance a position.

Currently, Gentile serves as the Chief Options Strategist for the Global Investment Research Corp. and Optionetics. He has been featured and quoted in numerous publications, including *Fortune* magazine, *Barron's*, and *The Wall Street Journal*, as well as many other magazines and publications. Online appearances have been numerous, with regular spots and articles at RadioWallStreet.com, TheStreet.com, Barrons.com, Bloomberg, Reuters, and a host of others. Tom Gentile also cowrote *The Stock Market Course* with George Fontanills, published by

John Wiley & Sons in 2001. According to Francis Gagnon (Quote.com and Active Traders), *The Stock Market Course* is "the best stock market introduction ever written for traders and investors searching for a path of trading success."

Tom Gentile is also a very popular speaker in the United Kingdom, where he is building a well-deserved reputation as the "option guru" for U.K. option traders. As an up-and-coming market wizard, Gentile's passion for trading and down-to-earth style are both refreshing and sensible in these volatile times.

Contents

Introduction: Volatility versus Risk   1

1   Crisis and Chaos in Financial Markets   8

2   Volatility in the Stock Market   23

3   Historical Volatility   38

4   Trading Historical Volatility   52

5   The World of Stock Options   70

6   Implied Volatility   91

7   VIX and Other Sentiment Indicators   110

8   Exploiting Low Volatility   130

9   Exploiting High Volatility   161

10 Volatility Skews   187

11 Final Summary   213

Appendixes
A. Studying the Market   217
B. Stock Charts and Technical Tools   228

C. Statistical and Implied Volatility   249

D. Sentiment Indicators   253

E. Using Risk Graphs   265

F. Option Reviews   268

G. Paper Trading Your Way to Success   309

Index   323

Introduction:
Volatility versus Risk

> Knowledge increases in proportion to its use—
> that is, the more we teach the more we learn.
> —H. P. Blavatsky

Human nature is a fascinating mystery. Trying to understand why people do what they do reduces many of us to a simple shake of the head and a roll of the eyes. For instance, why do people take risks? What could possibly motivate sky divers to jump from airplanes while traveling at high speeds, tens of thousands of feet above the ground? For some people, thrill-seeking behavior is apparently quite satisfying. Perhaps they become addicted to the adrenaline rush associated with fear and danger. Perhaps that's why roller coasters, snowboarding, and horror movies are so commonplace in today's society. Ultimately, however, in most risk-taking activity there is a safety net. For the sky diver, it is a parachute.

In financial markets, too many traders jump out of airplanes without a parachute. There seems to be some kind of innate human desire to take on risk by placing money on the line in the hope of making more money. For example, gambling or playing the lottery are both popular ways of deriving gratification from speculating or wagering money in an effort to obtain a large reward. Ultimately, the type of trading activity that seeks large rewards generally leads to miscalculated bets and financial losses. Speculators lack safety nets to protect them from placing ill-timed risky trades. Trading with a parachute is one of the biggest distinctions between successful option strategists, or investors, and speculators. Thus, learning to identify and mitigate trading risks separates successful investors from speculators.

Chances are that you have picked up this book because you want to become a better investor. Perhaps you want to find ways to build up your retirement account or increase the value of a portfolio earmarked for your children's educations. Maybe you simply want to build wealth to pursue other dreams—buying a new

1

home, driving a luxury car, or spending six months lounging on a beach in the Caribbean. Or perhaps you are reading this book in an effort to become a full-time, professional trader. Regardless of your individual motivation, this book is designed to help you integrate the use of volatility into your trading approach, which will ultimately empower you to become a more successful trader.

I opened my first trading account in 1986. Investing was not foreign to me because I had owned stocks before that, but I hadn't involved myself in trading them for profit. Like many people, I started trading after receiving something in the mail that spelled out all of the rewards that trading had to offer: the flexible hours, the independence, no customers, no inventory, and so forth. The literature immediately sparked my interest; but I must admit, I never once thought about what might happen if I were to actually fail. But that's exactly what happened. I failed. It didn't happen right off the bat. In fact, at first I did everything right. I traded very boring markets, which didn't move much at all. I was prudent. I placed my orders in a way that limited my potential risk, and basically treated everything as if I were running a tight business.

As time passed and I started enjoying some success, my head grew faster than my wallet. The peak of my initial trading career came to a screeching halt on October 20, 1987. That's right: one day after the market crashed. That's the day I learned what a margin call was, and how I couldn't meet it. That's the day I learned what holding a position overnight can do to you if you are overleveraged. That's the day that I found out that a "stop" order doesn't guarantee that you will get out of an asset at an expected loss, or "stop" potential losses. That's the day I found out about a word that very few people knew how to spell, much less comprehend: volatility.

My next year was spent doing two things: paying back my debt to the brokerage firm (I officially consider it my tuition for attending the market's school of hard knocks), and deciding whether to continue beating myself financially senseless. I wanted to take another shot at the markets; only this time, I was determined to do it right. During the year, I ferociously studied the markets—both the fundamental and technical aspects. I bought nearly every book I could get my hands on that mentioned the markets, and became a permanent fixture at the local library. Slowly, I developed systems that enabled me to take my emotion out of the marketplace. I learned how to treat trading like a business, paying strict attention to all the responsibilities that go along with running a business. But the one thing I couldn't seem to get a handle on was market volatility.

I started out by following the trading philosophers who talk of hedging stock with other stock, and looking at bonds to determine where the price of a given stock was likely to go. I realized that some instruments move together or opposite the stock you are looking at in the short term, but over the long term there are no guarantees. I soon found out that if you are trading a stock, there is no way to completely hedge that stock using a positively or negatively correlated stock. That's when I discovered options.

I remember asking a friend what an "option" was, and he told me, "It's just like a stock, but cheaper." That friend couldn't have been more wrong. When I first started trading options, I did immediately notice how much cheaper they were in comparison to stock, but the pricing that went into the premiums was new to me. It wasn't until later that I grew to understand how volatility affected the price of an option. In the beginning, I created my first system for options trading—which is adopted by many novice options traders—that consisted of buying options on a stock I expected to go up the day before the release of an earnings announcement. Once the announcement came out, I would wait for the big move and cash out. Most of the time the big move never came, and even if it did, it never seemed to outrun the price I paid for the option in the first place. Little did I know that volatility played a big role in determining whether I made a profit.

After years of trading experience, it is clear to me that there are basically three dimensions to successful trading: price, time, and volatility. Most traders who enter the arena pay attention to only the price of an asset, a derivative, or an option. They recognize that understanding price is essential; price determines profit. At the same time, only on the exit will the profit be ultimately determined. Since selling at the right price makes money, most traders get lazy; they adopt the traditional "buy low/sell high" theory of trading. Obviously, in 2000 and 2001, since most fallen stocks have only moved lower, this has not been the best approach. As a result, many traders are actually buying low and selling lower, which ultimately leaves them with a dwindling account and higher stress as they try to tackle the tough times.

Prices in options can be deceiving, too. Often, traders view a premium, or price, of an option as what the buyer is willing to risk. This is technically true. But in the year 2000, some stocks had options with no real value trading at ridiculous price levels, indicating a lot of volatility risk in them.

Focusing on price can lead to a variety of additional problems, including risk management. For example, in late March 2000, Micro Strategy (MSTR) was trading in wild ranges, even closing over $300 per share at one point (see Figure I.1). Three weeks later the stock was below $50 per share—an 83 percent swoon. Imagine buying Micro Strategy stock when it fell from $300 to $225 and getting 1,000 shares at $225 per share. Say that you decided to cap your risk and place a stop order (an order designed to get you out of the market if a certain price is hit) at a price of $200. Now, theoretically, if the price goes below $200, you are out of the position with a $25 loss, right? Wrong! If the stock opens the next day at 100, down 50 percent, your order is then executed and you are lucky to be out at $100 per share— a 50 percent loss. Even worse, imagine for a minute that you margined this trade, or borrowed money to pay for the stock. If you put all your money on this one trade, your capital would be dry in one week—a pretty quick end to what could have been a lucrative trading career.

Time is the second dimension in trading. Time interacts with a whole bunch of important trading factors, including the time someone decides to hold onto a particular stock. This is one of the main differences between investors and traders. Investors think of time in terms of a lifetime; traders think of time in seconds, hours, days, and weeks. Some traders trade only the first and last hours of each day—that

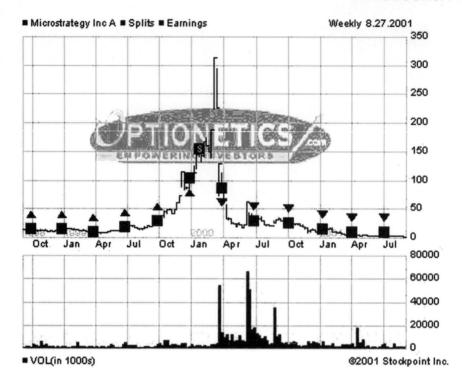

Figure I.1 MSTR Volume/Price Chart with Splits and Earnings (Courtesy of Optionetics.com)

is simply their trading style. Others place trades in relation to earnings reports; the levels of volume increase and decrease as these reports come and go. Still others trade just major report days such as the labor statistics report day—generally the first Friday of the month. I have a friend who does this, and trades only one day a month. Actually, he trades for only *5 minutes* one day a month; that's the full extent of his trading system!

Thus, you have to look at time from many perspectives. Just like in a poker game, there's a time to put your money on the table and a time to sit out a hand or two. It all comes down to how you choose to approach the business of trading. Most professional stock traders rely on some sort of pattern recognition—fundamentally, technically, or mechanically—only taking trades that have a better than average chance of success. Options traders see time in a much different light than pure stock traders. To an option buyer, the passage of time is always against you because options are "wasting assets" that sooner or later expire. This means that options traders have a unique set of questions that come with the territory: How much time should I buy? Is there such a thing as too much time? What is considered too little time? Should I be an options seller instead of a buyer? All of these questions seek answers that offer important clues as to the nature of the overall puzzle. To trade successfully, it is vital to know how to use time to make the best of a variety of market situations.

Volatility is the third and final trading dimension. Up until recently, this word hadn't been bandied about much. In the old days, when people asked what I did for a living, I used to have a lot of fun telling them I was a "volatility trader." It was almost like saying you were an insurance salesperson or that you worked in the funeral business; the conversation inevitably faltered and then shifted to someone else. Not that I minded, as I take great pride in being an expert at doing something most people consider esoteric. Bottom line—volatility is a market instrument that, when used properly, can increase your trading profits substantially and reduce your risks dramatically as well. Unfortunately, many people simply don't understand what volatility is; they are vaguely aware that volatility means "confusion in the marketplace."

Usually if you don't understand something you tend to be fearful of it; and it can easily become your enemy. Volatility, if understood and used properly, can become a great ally in the trading environment. But it is much more than confusion, or the potential for movement, in the market. To begin with, there are several types of volatility. This book explains both historical and implied volatility in great detail. It introduces certain volatility indicators that are designed to help you get a grasp of volatility and be able to use it to predict future market movement. We will explore VIX and VXN, two indexes that provide footprints to where the index markets are likely to go in the short term. We will also investigate the volatility of option premiums to determine whether an option is overpriced or underpriced, as well as review several important aspects of volatility to enable you to integrate them into your own trading approach.

Do you want to learn how to trade successfully in any type of market environment? If so, you have picked up the right book. *The Volatility Course* is designed to teach the ins and outs of trading: whether it is a period of extreme market turbulence, or when the market appears to be moving nowhere, and anything in between. After reading this book, you will understand the different types of volatility and how to measure and anticipate changes in volatility, and then be able to adapt your strategies to fit the current environment.

Learning to trade in three dimensions is equally important as you combine strategies with probability or expected outcome. One of our traders has an interesting parallel to trading in three dimensions, and it has to do with his animals at home. He has a dog and a cat. The dog is the pedigreed kind that you invest time into and select from a breeder or a pet store. The cat is the kind of animal that introduces itself at your front door, and the moment you feed her, she is there to stay. The cat can leap up to another surface far above the floor and out of the sight of the dog. But it took a long time for the dog to even figure out what stairs are for. The dog can see in only two dimensions; while the cat, high above the ground, can survey her surroundings in three dimensions. That's why we encourage our students to "trade like a cat." This means we are always looking at how volatility impacts our positions.

As an investor, you want to make money regardless of market conditions. The traditional buy-and-hold philosophy teaches that the most profitable investor is the one who buys stocks over the long haul. Under this approach, the investor buys shares of XYZ company in anticipation of a rise in the share prices' value. Historically, stocks have appreciated and delivered handsome returns to the investor with a long-term horizon and the ability to weather short-term market volatility.

While the long-term buy-and-hold philosophy is a highly popular approach to the market, it is not the subject of our discussions here. Personally, I don't like seeing the value of my trading account fall, regardless of the time horizon. Passively waiting for the market to turn around is not my idea of fun. Instead, my approach is proactive. Rather than waiting for the market to move higher, I actively develop and implement trading strategies that will foster an increase in the value of my account. This is possible to do, even when stocks head south.

More often than not, the trades I choose to place deliver consistent profits. They offer low risk and I don't have to be right about market direction. That's right: Many of my favorite approaches are designed to be profitable regardless of whether the stock market moves higher or lower. These strategies are easy enough to learn, but require a thorough understanding of volatility; and that's the aim of this book.

On the surface, a book about volatility might seem like a complex discussion of quantum physics. Luckily it isn't; but there are many misconceptions about what volatility means and how hard it is to learn about and fully understand. In order to understand volatility, and how to profit from it, one first must grasp the basics of investing in stocks and options. To make sure you have a strong foundation, our discussion begins with the basics. To be specific, the first few chapters answer some elementary questions: What is the stock market? How are stock prices determined? What causes them to fluctuate from day to day? The second half of the book introduces more complex strategies that focus on successfully trading volatility using options. By reading this book, even traders with limited experience will gain the knowledge and resources to successfully trade volatility.

It is vital to your survival as a trader to know how to take advantage of the wide range of opportunities that various states of volatility present. When stock prices dive and mayhem greets the markets, many investors simply move to the sidelines. If you find yourself sitting idle when markets become volatile, it's high time you got in on the action. Periods of high volatility offer terrific trading opportunities! But in order to profit, you have to know how to implement successful strategies that manage your risk. Low-risk trading and volatile markets are not mutually exclusive; high-volatility trading does not necessarily mean high risk.

Although they teach how to make money in high volatility situations, the trading strategies outlined in this book are not for thrill seekers. The ultimate objective in trading is to make profits in the market—regardless of whether stocks are skyrocketing, in a tailspin, or moving sideways. Rather than seeking an adrenaline rush by putting money at risk by trading wildly fluctuating investments, sometimes it is prudent to trade downright boring markets that offer smaller, but more consistent, profit-making opportunities. Since there are always risks involved, it is essential to be aware of those risks and to make sure that a safety net is in place before entering a trade. Trading volatility doesn't have to involve great risk taking; it is not a speculative activity. There are always techniques that can be employed to mitigate risk.

Throughout the history of the stock market, there have been times when uncontrollable events have caused stock prices to spiral out of control. Since many investors use stocks as investment vehicles, when the stock market tumbles there can be a vast destruction of wealth. For that reason, many investors who have been burned by the market consider it a risky and volatile place. History has shown that it is such a place on occasion. Over the longer term, however, the stock market has endured each recession, war, and political crisis. In that respect, the market is batting 1,000. But volatility is *not* the same thing as risk. To gain a clear understanding of the current market setting, the first chapter examines several historical periods that exhibited the greatest volatility.

Investors encounter the term *volatility* often when dealing with financial markets. But what does it mean if a stock, option, or other asset is *volatile*? Merriam Webster offers this definition: *characterized by or subject to rapid or unexpected change*. Therefore, if an object is volatile, it is also unstable, unpredictable, and uncontrollable. Volatility, then, is an asset's tendency to change in a random, erratic, and extreme manner. However, for investors in today's complex financial markets, volatility doesn't necessarily mean chaos. In fact, volatility falls along a spectrum: There are episodes of high volatility, as well as periods of low volatility. An asset's price can fluctuate wildly over the course of several months, but then remain stable over an ensuing time period.

Although high volatility is associated with falling stock prices and lost wealth, I do not treat periods of high volatility as holding any less profit potential than periods of low volatility. Let's put it in perspective for a moment: Volatility is traditionally associated with chaos and instability. This helps to explain why many investors choose to disengage from the market when stock prices fluctuate wildly. When the markets seem chaotic, investors sell their holdings and move to the sidelines. But through the years, I have found a multitude of profit opportunities regardless of overall levels of volatility. Bottom line, volatility changes, and as it does traders—especially options strategists—can adjust their strategies to meet the current market environment. That last sentence spells out the aim of this book: to demystify volatility and to teach how to successfully apply it in your trading. Upon understanding these concepts, hopefully you will be able to avoid the pitfalls that I faced as a novice. Consider this book a shortcut to successful volatility trading.

TOM GENTILE
Chief Options Strategist
Optionetics

1

Crisis and Chaos in Financial Markets

Recent tragic events highlight the uncertain and unpredictable nature of financial markets. I was working on this book about stock market volatility on September 11, 2001, when terrorists attacked the heart of the financial world by devastating the World Trade Center towers in lower Manhattan. Prior to that, the stock market was already in peril. Between March 2000 and September 2001 many stocks had lost more than 90 percent of their value. One measure of the stock market, the Dow Jones Industrial Average, had fallen 15 percent in the four months prior to the terrorist attacks. On the first trading day after September 11, Monday, September 17 (the market was forced to close for several days following the attack), the Dow Jones Industrial Average tumbled 684 points—its worst decline in history.

The difference between what happened before and after the terrorist attacks demonstrates how political, instead of economic, events can impact financial markets. Prior to September 11, stocks were falling. This is quite normal; there have been many episodes in stock market history that have witnessed declines of 15 percent or more in the Dow Jones Industrial Average. The market's tumble after the attacks, however, was owed to extraordinary events investors rarely face. Of course, there were specific economic repercussions stemming from the attack; but the event also served to stir up investor anxiety. It raised concerns about the financial system and triggered widespread political and military uncertainty. Consequently, there was a general fear that swept the country regarding the soundness of the U.S. financial and social system.

Turning back the pages of the history books reveals that the decline in the stock market in 2001–2002 was not extraordinary. There have been at least 11 episodes since the Great Depression of the 1930s that have seen similar declines. Some of these periods were the result of a normal cycle in the stock market in which so-

---

What Is the Stock Market?

Today's U.S. stock market includes the trading in shares of more than 5,000 different companies on several different exchanges. Trying to make sense of which stocks are rising or falling on a daily basis is best accomplished by viewing stocks collectively. Market averages serve this purpose. A detailed analysis of market averages can be found in Chapter 2, including how they are calculated and constructed. For now, let's consider two of the more popular indexes:

- **Dow Jones Industrial Average ($INDU):** Subject of nightly commentary on the six o'clock news, the Dow Jones Industrial Average, or Dow, dates back to the late nineteenth century. Charles Dow first published the average closing prices of 12 industrial companies in 1896. The Dow was the first index to offer investors a means of seeing the performance of stocks as a whole. Today the index consists of 30 stocks; it is still considered the most widely followed barometer of the stock market. General Electric is the only company of the first 12 that remains part of the Dow Jones Industrial Average.

- **S&P 500 ($SPX):** Standard & Poor's created this barometer of stock market performance in the late 1920s. While it is not quite as familiar to the investing public as the Dow, most professionals consider it a better gauge of the stock market. Why? As the name implies, it measures the performance of 500 stocks in comparison to only 30 on the Dow.

---

called fundamental factors such as falling corporate profits, rising interest rates, a spike in energy prices, or other economic events have traditionally caused stock prices to move lower. Others have been the result of external events, or crises.

The period of greatest stock market volatility began in the late 1920s. The bear market that preceded the Great Depression of the early 1930s began on September 7, 1929. On October 29, 1929, what is now known as Black Tuesday, the stock market crashed and paved the way for a three-year bear market that ended in June 1932. Over the course of those three years, the Standard & Poor's index lost 86.2 percent of its value! That means, on average, investors saw their portfolios lose almost 90 percent of their values.

So, what events led up to the dramatic downturn in the market during the great bear market of the early 1930s? Prior to the great crash of 1929, the stock market was rewarding investors with exceptional returns. Throughout the 1920s, the United States enjoyed economic prosperity, and investing in stocks became a national pastime. The growing popularity of stocks was owed to a number of factors. In 1924, Edgar Lawrence Smith's book *Common Stocks as Long-Term Investments* challenged the conventional view that buying stocks was a speculative endeavor and that true investors bought only high-grade bonds. Smith put forth stock market data that covered the period from the Civil War until the 1920s. The book achieved a wide audience, and investing in the stock market, which prior to the 1920s was considered a highly speculative endeavor, received legitimacy.

Bull and Bear Markets

- **Bull market:** Bulls buck upward with their horns. An extended period of time (months, years, decades) of rising prices is considered a bull market. This can relate to gold, bonds, stocks, or any group of investment vehicles. Because there are periods of time within the bull market that see prices fall, it is sometimes difficult to tell whether it is or isn't a bull market. The general rule is a 20 percent rise from a low in the Dow Jones Industrial Average or other measure of the market is considered a bull market.

- **Bear market:** Bears swat down with their claws. An extended period of time that sees the Dow Jones Industrial Average or other market average fall is considered a bear market. Again, the rule of thumb is a 20 percent decline from a previous high.

In the late 1920s, thanks to surging stock prices and a growing propensity for investors to take on risk, investing in the stock market became more commonplace. In fact, by the middle of 1928, stock prices were surging sometimes 10 or 15 points in one day. Investors simply couldn't curb their enthusiasm for shares, and many were buying stocks with borrowed money. Brokerage firms allowed margin up to 90 percent! That is, for every $10 of stock investors purchased, they could borrow $90 from their brokerage firms. From 1921 until 1929, margin loans (or money borrowed to buy stocks) increased from $1 billion to $9 billion—a huge sum of money at that time. Indeed, speculative fever engulfed the stock market.

In the fall of 1929, the rapid rise in stock prices proved unsustainable, the floor caved in, and stocks tumbled. Table 1.1 shows the rise and fall of some of the companies that traded during the 1929–1932 bear market that are still trading today. Throughout the 18 months leading up to Black Tuesday, some stocks surged between 150 to 200 percent. Three years later, stocks traded for fractions of their 1928 highs. As noted earlier, from the fall of 1929 until the summer 1932, the Standard & Poor's 500 index plunged nearly 90 percent. In short, during those three years, stock market investors swallowed hefty doses of both volatility and risk. According to David Blitzer, the Chief Investment Strategist at Standard & Poor's, it took until 1954 for the S&P 500 to return to its September 1929 highs, or 25 years!

WHAT CAUSES BEAR MARKETS?

Since World War II, there have been 11 more bear markets—including the one facing investors as I write these words. Table 1.2 lists those market slides in chronological order. Astute observers will notice that two of the last three periods did not witness a 20 percent decline, and therefore do not technically fall into the bear market category. For the purposes of putting today's events into the broader discussion of volatility, however, let us define a bear market as a decline of 19 percent or more.

Table 1.1 Rise and Fall

Company	Stock Price 3/3/28	High Price 9/3/29	Low Price 1932
American Telephone & Telegraph (T)	179.50	335.63	70.25
Bethlehem Steel (BS)	56.88	140.38	7.25
General Electric (GE)	128.75	396.25	8.50

Table 1.2 Bear Markets Since World War II

Start	End	Duration (Months)	Percent Loss in S&P 500
5/29/46	6/13/49	36.4	−29.6
8/5/56	10/22/57	14.6	−21.6
12/12/61	6/27/62	6.5	−27.9
2/9/66	10/7/66	7.9	−22.2
11/29/68	5/26/70	17.8	−36.1
1/11/73	10/3/74	20.7	−48.2
11/28/80	8/12/82	20.4	−27.1
8/25/87	12/4/87	3.3	−33.5
7/16/90	10/11/90	2.9	−19.9
7/17/98	8/31/98	1.5	−19.3
3/24/00	—	18+	—

Source: "The S&P 500," Speech at the Indexing & ETFs Summit, by David Blitzer, Ph.D., Managing Director and Chief Executive Strategist of Standard & Poor's, March 26, 2001.

What Is Margin Debt?

A margin account allows investors to buy stock on credit or borrow based on the value of stocks, or other investments, already held in the brokerage account. Buying on credit and borrowing are regulated by standards set by the U.S. Federal Reserve and the brokerage firm holding the account. As with any loan, interest is charged on the loan. "Following the stock market crash in 1929, Congress and the public became concerned that personal debt used to finance purchases of common stock had caused or exacerbated the magnitude of the crash. The 1934 Securities Exchange Act gave the Federal Reserve Board the responsibility to set the minimum levels of margin for purchasing common stock. The Fed has not changed its minimum levels of margin requirement since 1974."—G. William, Shwert, "Stock Market Volatility," *Financial Analysts Journal* (May–June 1990): 23–34.

Margin Call: A call for additional funds in a brokerage account triggered by either a drop in the value of investments in a margin account or the purchase of additional securities on margin.

So what causes bear markets? Of course there are no simple answers; bear markets are often impossible to predict. Perhaps only in hindsight can analysts clearly see the factors that contribute to create a major market decline. For example, the Standard & Poor's 500 index tumbled 36 percent between March 2000 and September 2001—its second largest drop since World War II. The decline can be attributed to four key factors. First, similar to the 1920s, stock prices soared during the 1990s. Over the course of a decade, the S&P 500 surged more than 300 percent! Early in the year 2000, margin debt, or borrowed money used to buy stocks, reached record highs and investor interest in stock ownership reached a feverish pitch. Just like the late 1920s, speculation overcame the market.

Indeed, 70 years after the bubble that preceded the Great Depression and bear market of the early 1930s, history repeated itself. Stock prices rose exponentially throughout the 1990s. Investing became a national pastime as investors added a substantial amount of borrowed money to the market. At its height, in March 2000, margin debt—the money borrowed to buy stocks—reached $278.5 billion. Shortly thereafter, on April 4, 2000, the stock market went into a tailspin. Sitting in a San Mateo, California, office with a number of colleagues, we all watched in awe as shares in some of America's best companies fell 15 to 20 percent that morning. Later, there were reports of portfolio liquidations; those investors who had borrowed heavily to finance stock purchases were faced with margin calls. After nearly a decade of soaring stock prices, the slide in the market that started on March 24, 2000, triggered a series of margin calls in early April that helped to fuel the decline. From its high to its low on April 4, the S&P 500 fell 6 percent in just a few hours. From there, the market recovered somewhat, but began a steep descent beginning in late September 2000.

One of the chief reasons for the market slide from September 2000 until September 2001 was the impact of rising interest rates. Seventy years earlier, during the collapse of the stock market bubble in the summer of 1929, the Federal Reserve began raising interest rates to cool the red-hot stock market. At the time, the Federal Reserve was only 16 years old, but its tools for controlling the economy and fighting the forces of inflation were the same—the raising of interest rates. That's exactly what the Fed did in the late 1920s, and some blame their actions for the collapse of the stock market beginning in September 1929. By January 1931, stocks were down 58 percent. As noted earlier, the S&P 500 eventually lost nearly 90 percent of its value. The destruction of wealth drained the capital of many individuals and financial institutions through colossal margin calls. Bank failures wiped out the savings of families and corporations. It was the worst liquidity drain in modern economic history.

Seventy years later, in order to slow a red-hot U.S. economy, the Federal Reserve raised interest rates on six occasions from June 1999 until May 2000. Again, although not as significant as prior to the Great Depression, rising interest rates pulled liquidity out of the system and that, in turn, spelled trouble for the stock market. Third, as the economy started to slow, so did corporate profits. And, as earnings began to deteriorate, the attractiveness of stock ownership started to wane (we will discuss this in detail later). Finally, as noted earlier, the terrorist attack on September 11 caused a great deal of uncertainty and anxiety among market investors. In

Why Rising Interest Rates Hurt Stock Market Investors

The most common cause of bear markets throughout the history of the stock market has been ascribed to actions of the Federal Reserve. Economists refer to it as "restrictive monetary policy" when the Federal Reserve, or Fed, sets out on a campaign to raise interest rates. Most often, the Fed increases interest rates to slow the economy. Why? When economic growth becomes too robust, it can trigger the forces of inflation, or a period of rising prices. The Fed has a mandate to curb the forces of inflation but, at the same time, keep the economy stable. Historically, rising interest rates can cause havoc on the stock market because they make alternative investments—bonds—more attractive. In other words, investors are less apt to buy stocks when interest rates are rising; alternative investments become more appealing.

In addition, falling interest rates add liquidity to the economy. For instance, when the Federal Reserve lowers the federal funds rate, banks follow suit by lowering prime rate, which will lead to lower mortgage rates. Lower mortgage rates, in turn, lead to refinancing of loans and frees up cash in the hands of the consumer. That cash, in turn, can be used to finance purchases or invest in the stock market. Lower interest rates, therefore, serve to spur the economy by making low-interest loans more available and adding liquidity to the system. In the stock market, many consider the Fed to be a powerful force behind bull and bear markets. There is an old adage that says when the Federal Reserve is lowering interest rates, investors shouldn't bet against the market. Hence the saying, "Don't fight the Fed."

Federal Reserve System: A U.S. system established by the Federal Reserve Act of 1913 to regulate the U.S. monetary and banking system. The primary goals of the Federal Reserve are to stabilize prices, to promote economic growth, and to strive for full employment. These goals are accomplished through managing monetary policy, which is implemented by the Federal Open Market Committee (FOMC). In addition, the Federal Reserve supervises the printing of currency, regulates the national money supply, sets reserve requirements, examines member banks to ensure they meet various regulations, and acts as a clearinghouse for the transfer of funds throughout the banking system.

sum, bear markets can result from a number of factors. During 2000 and 2001, investors had to deal with four of the most significant: the collapse of a speculative bubble, rising interest rates, deteriorating corporate profits, and war.

Turning back the pages of the economic history books reveals that bear markets are generally caused by the same factors that wreaked havoc during 2000–2001. One of the longest periods of falling stock prices occurred after World War II. From May 1946 until June 1949, the S&P 500 dropped nearly 40 percent. While the United States was cheering an important military victory, the economic situation was marked by a fair amount of anxiety. The Great Depression left a psychological impact on Americans, and the end of the war signaled a return to the prewar sense of economic distress. Predictions of gloom and doom surfaced as 12 million World War II veterans returned home to find unemployment lines and an anemic U.S. economy.

Harry S. Truman was in charge of leading the nation through this period of economic malaise. He proposed tax cuts and instituted other measures to help stimulate the economy. The net result proved to be rampant inflation. In 1946 the rate of inflation soared to 18.2 percent! With the memory of the Great Depression and the 1929–1932 bear market still fresh, the prospect of a slowing economy and rising interest rates curbed any investor enthusiasm for the stock market. The result was a 36-month-long bear market that wiped out nearly one-half the value of the stock market.

The next bear market started in the fall of 1956 and lasted a little over a year. During that time, once again, the stock market suffered as the economy began to falter. Beginning in September 1957, the U.S. economy fell into a seven-month recession. The stock market faired even worse. From August 1956 until October 1957, a 15-month bear market wiped out almost 22 percent of the value of the S&P 500.

The next bear market occurred between December 1961 and June 1962. This time economic worries were not the chief culprit. During that time, investors were fretting over the Cold War and the failed Bay of Pigs invasion in April 1961 stoked fears over the possibility of a nuclear attack. Even though the economy was beginning a decade-long expansion, uncertainty over the political and military outlook posed problems for stock market investors. During that six-and-one-half-month bear market, the S&P 500 tumbled almost 28 percent.

After the market slide in 1961–1962, stocks moved higher until the next bear market began in February 1966. Shortly prior to the market peak, the Federal Reserve instituted a series of interest rate increases in late 1965 due to concern about a rapidly expanding economy and accelerating inflation. By 1967, economic activity in the United States screeched to a halt. The Fed moved swiftly to cut interest rates; but the damage to the stock market had already been done. This resulting bear market lasted slightly less than eight months with the S&P 500 losing 22.2 percent of its

---

Why a Slowing Economy Punishes the Stock Market

A slowdown in the business activity in the United States generally has a negative impact on the stock market. When the economy slows, profits of many U.S. corporations fall. Shareholders are more inclined to buy stocks when profits are robust and growing. For instance, investors are more disposed to buy stock in a company that is making a lot of money than one that is struggling. Therefore, if there is a perception that profits are deteriorating, the crowd is more likely to sell than buy stocks. Indeed, profits are one of the key drivers of stock prices; and the strength of the overall economy is an important factor that determines the strength of corporate profits. Concerns over the state of the economy and falling corporate earnings often lead to increased market volatility. Today's rampant accounting irregularities continue to increase investors' fears and further fuel the current bear market.

value. The stock market fell again less than two years later. From November 1968 until May 1970, the Standard & Poor's tumbled 36.1 percent. Again, concern over an overheating U.S. economy and the forces of inflation put the Federal Reserve into action. Rising interest rates once again punished stock market investors.

One of the nastiest bear markets in history began shortly after incumbent Richard Nixon defeated George McGovern in a landslide victory. Three months after the election, in January 1973, stocks went into a precipitous free fall. The slide gathered momentum as the Watergate scandal triggered increased uncertainty. Top Nixon advisers resigned on charges of obstruction of justice toward the end of April. By August, the market had tumbled nearly 20 percent. Meanwhile, rampant inflation forced interest rates higher and that, too, was taking a toll on the U.S. economy and stock market. By 1974, the economy fell deep into recession and the rate of unemployment skyrocketed. All this, of course, spelled trouble for investors, and from January 1973 until October 1974 the S&P 500 lost 48.2 percent in value. In less than 21 months, the S&P was nearly cut in half!

As inflation began to subside and political uncertainty waned, the stock market recovered and began to move higher until November 1980. At that time, Ronald Reagan defeated incumbent Jimmy Carter and Republicans took control of the Senate. In April 1981, even after the assassination attempt on Reagan and in the face of a significant increase in interest rates on the part of the Federal Reserve, investors remained fairly optimistic and the bear had not officially paid the markets a visit.

As the Federal Reserve increased interest rates to all-time highs in May 1981, however, the floor began to crack. By July, the S&P 500 was trading at its lowest levels of the year. At the same time, a series of international events started to erode investor confidence beginning in early 1982. A major conflict erupted between Britain and Argentina over the Falkland Islands. Tensions in the Middle East escalated as Israeli troops invaded Lebanon. When Syria became involved, concern about a full-out war in the Middle East rattled the markets. Skyrocketing inflation and the impact of record-high interest rates sank the U.S. economy deep into recession. Beginning in November 1981, the Federal Reserve responded to the worsening economic situation by lowering interest rates. The Fed continued to cut rates

---

Who Were the Nifty Fifty?

Although higher interest rates and political uncertainty were important factors causing the bear market of the early 1970s, the downdraft was also the result of a speculative bubble. At that time, stocks of major companies—the largest U.S. concerns with shares listed for trading on the stock exchanges—received enormous investor interest. Shares of Avon Products, Eastman Kodak, Walt Disney, and Hewlett Packard rose dramatically in value. The investment crowd fell in love with roughly four dozen companies that became known as the Nifty Fifty. These stocks later suffered enormous losses during the 1973–1974 bear market.

throughout 1982. During the month of August, the Fed lowered the rates on three separate occasions, which finally restored investor confidence. August 12, 1982, marked the end of the 20.4-month bear market that drove the S&P 500 index 27.1 percent lower.

The next bear market stands out in the minds of many investors as one of the most volatile in history, but the duration of the decline was among the shortest. From August 1987 until December of that same year, the S&P 500 declined 33.5 percent. The violent downturn can be traced to a number of factors. Once again, the Fed was vigilant and interest rates were on the rise. There were also political events causing uncertainty in the marketplace. Burton Malkiel wrote an insightful assessment of these events in his book, *A Random Walk Down Wall Street* (W. W. Norton & Company, 1990):

> In addition [to rising interest rates], a number of events created significantly increased risk perceptions in the market. In early October, Congress threatened to impose a "merger tax" that would have made merger activity prohibitively expensive and could well have ended the merger boom. . . . The risk that merger activity might be curtailed increased risks throughout the stock market by weakening the discipline over corporate management that potential takeovers provide. Also James Baker, then secretary of the Treasury, had threatened in October to encourage a further fall in the price of the dollar, increasing risks for all foreign investors and thereby frightening domestic investors as well.

The net culmination of these events triggered the market slide that saw the S&P 500 shed 20.5 percent on Monday, October 19, 1987. The bear market lasted from August 25, 1987, until December 4 of that same year and saw the S&P 500 decline 33.5 percent in a little over three months.

The next bear market occurred roughly three years later. The market decline was brought about largely by three events. First, Iraq's invasion of Kuwait triggered a renewed bout of concern surrounding a larger war in the Middle East. The subsequent Persian Gulf War also led to a sharp rise in crude oil prices and caused concern over the prospect of rising inflation. Finally, economic activity in the United States was faltering and the economy entered a recession during the mid-1990s. War, rising inflation, and a slowing economy all served to rattle investors, and from July until October 1990 the market suffered a three-month, nearly 20 percent decline.

WHAT MAKES TODAY'S MARKET DIFFERENT?

A recent period of market volatility serves to highlight the changing nature of financial markets today as well as the new risks investors face. Although the decline spanned only one and a half months and the S&P 500 didn't officially enter a bear market (because the index fell only 19.3 percent instead of 20 percent), the events from July 17 through August 1998 serve to illustrate how global financial events can trigger extreme bouts of stock market volatility in the United States.

Events started to unfold in midsummer 1997 when South Asian currency markets collapsed. The uncertainty from the impact of the crisis eventually caused a 6.2 percent six-day drop in the S&P 500 beginning on August 6, 1997. The index recovered, but once again volatility struck the market roughly one year later when it became known that Russia along with countries in Latin America and parts of Asia were no longer paying their debts. The Global Financial Crisis, as it has become known, triggered the collapse of a prominent U.S. hedge fund, Long Term Capital Management, which owed billions of dollars to various investors around the world. The collapse of that fund threatened the solvency of major U.S. banks. A bailout of the fund through a special committee formed by the U.S. Federal Reserve, banks, and major brokerage firms helped avert a major financial catastrophe.

The Global Financial Crisis served to highlight the impact that international events can have on the U.S. stock market. In less than two months, from July until September 1998, the S&P 500 lost almost 20 percent of its value. At the same time, a global financial crisis has been happening with near regularity over the past dozen years. There was, of course, the crash of 1987 that sent not only U.S., but global financial stock markets into a tailspin. Two years later, the Japanese stock market collapsed. When the exchange rate system collapsed in 1992–1993, Europe's currency troubles also caused mayhem throughout the global financial community. In 1994, a collapse in the U.S. bond market and the Mexican peso catastrophe occurred. Crises in Asia, Latin America, and Russia rattled markets in the United States in 1998. All of these events serve as reminders that, besides speculative bubbles that have existed since the history of humankind, interest rate increases by the Federal Reserve, war, and economic recessions, today's investors have to contend with a relatively new force that can trigger market volatility: contagion.

CORPORATE MISCONDUCT

A few years after dealing with the forces of contagion that emerged during the Global Financial Crisis of 1998, investors had to grapple with yet another risk that threatened to completely undermine investor confidence—corporate malfeasance. The S&P 500 had managed to recapture the losses recorded immediately following

---

What Is Contagion?

Contagion is a term popularized during the Global Financial Crisis of 1998. It refers to the idea that events in one economic system can cause repercussions throughout other nations. Like the spread of a disease, volatility in one financial market finds itself infesting others.

the terrorist attacks of September 11 with a 20 percent advance, but in mid-March 2002 another decline ensued. A host of uncertainties already weighed on investor confidence. Some stemmed from worries regarding the U.S. economy. Others were related to corporate profits and a relatively bleak earnings outlook. Yet nothing could prepare for the wave of systemic corporate accounting scandals that shook investor confidence in the first half of 2002.

The chain of events related to corporate misconduct started with the high-profile collapse of energy giant Enron. Problems began to arise in July 2001 when Enron warned investors that it would post a large loss in its quarterly earnings report. The energy trader cited the effects of the California energy crisis and mistimed investments in India and South America for its surprisingly poor results. Later, in August, CEO Jeffrey Skilling resigned after holding the position for only six months. The news was completely unexpected. Skilling said the departure was for "personal reasons." Nevertheless, the news shocked investors and raised questions about the stability of Enron.

In the fall of 2001, the Securities and Exchange Commission began a formal inquiry into Enron's massive losses. In October, Enron said that losses on its broadband division, its partnerships, and international subsidiaries would force the company to cut shareholder value by $1.2 billion. Two weeks later, Enron fired chief financial officer Andrew Fastow. The company alleged that the CFO arranged deceptive partnerships that were being used to hide millions of dollars in losses. The SEC investigation intensified.

Enron told investors in November that it had overstated profits by nearly 16 percent, or $600 million. The company's auditor, Arthur Andersen, warned investors not to rely on any of the company's financial statements issued prior to June 2001. Shareholders panicked on the news, and sent the stock into a tailspin. The company's market value plunged and its credit rating was reduced. Consequently, the company was forced to pay back millions of dollars of debt immediately, but couldn't attain additional financing due to its lowered credit rating. Faced with the prospect of insurmountable debt, corporate executives agreed to file for Chapter 11 bankruptcy in December 2001. In less than six months, from the time the company issued its earnings warning in July 2001 until December when the company filed for bankruptcy, Enron completely collapsed and left shareholders and employees with no recourse whatsoever.

From that point forward, investors had to navigate through a meteor shower of corporate accounting scandals. While some high-profile companies such as Global Crossing and Adelphia also shocked investors by filing for bankruptcy, SEC probes into corporate accounting practices began to mount. In 2002, Bristol-Myers, Tyco International, Xerox, and a host of other high-profile companies were being scrutinized regarding accounting issues. As news related to accounting misstatements surfaced seemingly daily, investors were left stunned and wondering whether they could any longer trust the financial statements that served as the foundation for so many investment decisions.

If investors were growing uneasy in early 2002, WorldCom completely shattered investor confidence in June of that year. On June 25, 2002, WorldCom admitted that it had misreported nearly $4 billion in expenses in 2001. The shocking admission meant that, instead of recording a profit, the second largest U.S. long distance company actually lost money for the year. Just like Enron and many other companies, WorldCom had violated accounting rules and was likely to head down the road to bankruptcy. The news sent shares of WorldCom as well as stocks around the globe into a freefall.

On July 21, 2002, the *Wall Street Journal* reported that WorldCom, which faced $41 billion of debt and an accounting scandal that destroyed its access to capital, filed for bankruptcy court protection. Prior to the announcement, the market, as measured by the S&P 500, had suffered a two-week 14.5 percent decline—one of its swiftest drops in history. On Monday, July 22, 2002, when the markets opened for trading immediately after the news, the S&P 500 dropped another 3 percent. Consequently, July 2002 proved to be one of the most volatile periods of trading in stock market history.

Obviously, the bankruptcies of both WorldCom and Enron, concerns over accounting scandals, and tumbling stock prices weighed heavily on investor confidence in the first half of 2002. Angst in the stock market was already high for a variety of other reasons. Wall Street analysts were under fire for not warning clients of pending troubles and, in some cases, making unsuitable investment recommendations. Mutual fund managers were being questioned for taking on large positions in troubled companies just before their collapse. Scandals and systemic corporate fraud seemed to permeate every sector of U.S. business activity. Even Martha Stewart was being investigated for insider trading after she coincidentally sold 40,000 shares of ImClone the day before the Food and Drug Administration refused to consider an application for the company's cancer-fighting drug. There was also ongoing uncertainty regarding the impact of plunging stock prices on an already frail U.S. economy. All of the events served to cast a dark cloud over the stock market and the U.S. economy. The subsequent volatility turned Wall Street into a minefield for investors.

BUY AND HOLD?

Ultimately, the stock market rises more than it falls. In other words, there are more bull markets than bear markets. If not, there would be few reasons to want to own a portfolio of stocks. In fact, since its inception during the mid 1920s, the S&P 500 has risen at an average annual rate of roughly 11 percent. Over the course of 75 years, the average has risen 54 times and posted losses on only 21 occasions. Given the long history of growing ever higher, some investors naturally consider stocks to be the best vehicles for long-term investment funds. While there are inevitably bear markets, corrections, and pullbacks, stocks are ultimately the best vehicles for building wealth.

Yet, while stocks have historically offered the best returns, the investor, or owner of stocks, must be prepared to withstand periods of declining stock prices. As noted earlier, the S&P 500 has moved lower 21 times in the past 75 years, or roughly one-third of the time. Given that historically the stock market eventually recovers from the bite of the growling bear, some financial advisers recommend building a portfolio for the long haul by investing in not one or two stocks, but the entire market.

Indeed, the notion of simply buying the market has developed widespread appeal among investors. For that reason, the growth and increasing popularity of mutual funds have been exceptional during the recent past. Thanks to a surging bull market in the 1990s, which produced generous average annual returns in excess of 18 percent for the S&P 500, the notion of simply buying the market seemed to be a no-lose proposition. Investors piled into mutual fund shares. As of September 2001, there were more than 3,600 mutual funds investing in the stock market, with combined assets of $3 trillion. According to the Investment Company Institute, in 1983 42.4 million Americans owned stocks through mutual funds. By 1999, that number had mushroomed to 78.7 million—an 86 percent increase!

In fact, one of the largest mutual funds today tracks the performance of the S&P 500. As of this writing, the Vanguard S&P 500 mutual fund is the second largest mutual fund and commands a whopping $66 billion worth of assets. While it is not the only mutual fund that attempts to mirror the performance of the U.S. stock market (in this case the Standard & Poor's 500 index), it is by far the largest. The fund is also among the oldest, and its origins can be traced back to 1976 and the inception of a fund known as the First Index Investment Trust. Its recent performance speaks for itself. During the decade ending December 2000, the fund boasted an average annual return in excess of 17 percent—not bad when one considers the 2 percent return paid by most bank accounts during that time.

Despite the superior performance of the S&P 500 during the 1990s, I do not advocate the buy-and-hold philosophy of investing. Shares of mutual funds are not immune to the forces of volatility. Indeed, a stock mutual fund represents a basket of stocks. For instance, buying shares of an index fund is the same thing as owning the S&P 500 index, which has been in 21 bear markets during the past 75 years. When the market feels the bite of the bear, the psychological damage to passive investors can prove severe. For me, bear markets are simply too painful to ride out. In addition, there are times when stocks move sideways for prolonged periods. In that case, the investor doesn't lose money but doesn't profit, either.

Bear Market Terminology

- **Normal decline or pullback:** A 5 percent loss in the major averages. Expect, on average, three per year.

- **Correction:** A drop of 10 percent, which occurs roughly once a year during a bull market. A "severe" correction takes the market down 15 percent. Since World War II, there have been 15 corrections—eight of which led to a bear market.

- **Bear market:** A 20 percent fall in the Dow Jones Industrial Average or Standard & Poor's 500. Since the inception of the Dow in 1896, there have been 32 bear markets—including the one we are experiencing at the start of the new millennium. The average duration is roughly 13 months.

What Is a Mutual Fund?

Mutual funds are investment vehicles that allow investors to participate in the stock market. In essence, mutual fund investors are pooling their money with other investors. That pool of money, in turn, is invested in a variety of stocks, bonds, and other securities. Mutual funds are extraordinarily popular today, but they cannot be used to trade volatility, and therefore, with the exception of this discussion, are not covered throughout this book.

BEAR MARKETS DO NOT MEAN LOST WEALTH

Ultimately, while I don't recommend riding out periods of high market volatility, bear markets inevitably surface and must be acknowledged as part of any long-term investment plan. History has shown that bear markets are a part of the investment world; while some investors view them as risky periods to ride out or a reason not to keep money safe in certificates of deposit at the local bank, my trading approach will keep you invested and making profits.

Ultimately, I'm bullish on our financial markets. Like the buy-and-hold advocates, I believe stock prices will move higher over the long term and that the U.S. financial system remains sound. Since stocks began trading under the buttonwood tree at 68 Wall Street, the size of the stock market has grown exponentially. For instance, on December 15, 1886, the New York Stock Exchange saw its first one million share day—the number of shares bought and sold exceeded one million for the first time! During the great stock market crash on October 29, 1929, 16,410,000 shares traded hands, which was enormous by the standards of the day. The first 100 million share day occurred in August 1982. Today, it is not unusual to see trading volume on the New York Stock Exchange top 1.5 billion shares.

Since the creation of the Philadelphia Stock Exchange in 1790, a number of new stock and options exchanges have emerged. In 1971, the Nasdaq Stock Market was created and today sees more trading activity than the New York Stock Exchange. The first organized options exchange—the Chicago Board Options Exchange—emerged in 1973. Today, there are five different exchanges that offer options trading and an even larger number of stock exchanges. In brief, trading of stocks and options has mushroomed, and the buy-and-hold investor can rest assured that 20 or 30 years from now, the stock market will be larger and more active than it is today.

My trading approach is practically the polar opposite to the traditional buy-and-hold approach to the market. Trading volatility doesn't offer investors the luxury of sitting passively and awaiting the bull to drive stock prices higher. Thus, the strategies reviewed in this book, while enabling investors to make money in rising, falling, or sideways-moving markets, also force investors to actively make decisions on an ongoing basis. However, during periods of rising market volatility, falling prices do not necessarily put capital at risk. In fact, a number of strategies actually benefit from rising market volatility enabling investors to make additional profits as volatility rises. Bottom line, volatility does not equal risk.

CONCLUSION

History has shown that periods of uncertainty, although quite serious, are also the reality of the game. It shows that the stock market can absorb shocks and persevere. As traders, our aim is to detach ourselves from the emotional responses triggered by unexpected events and shift the focus back to trading. Throughout history, that has been the key to long-term success in the financial markets. Since the inception of stock trading in the United States, it has never been profitable to bet against the financial system over the long term. The U.S. stock market is batting 1,000.

There have been episodes in history that have clearly left their mark on investors. Periods of extreme market volatility—like the crash of 1987, fall 1998, spring 2000, September 2001, and others—serve as memorable events with wide-reaching consequences. For instance, on one day the Dow Jones Industrial Average plunged from 2,247 to 1,739: 22.6 percent! That, of course, was Monday, October 19, 1987, when the stock market crash wiped out a vast number of trading accounts. Unfortunately, I was one of the victims of Bloody Monday. These kind of turbulent times not only make headlines, but for many investors can also prove ruinous.

Periods of high volatility, however, are the exception. More often than not, financial markets swing, but do not collapse. While occasional spikes in volatility can destroy the trading accounts of novice investors, they also serve as profit opportunities for the astute trader. At the same time, there are also prolonged periods of low volatility. Stock prices can move sideways as well as trend gradually higher or lower for periods of months, even years. While the periods of high volatility make the newspaper headlines, the periods of low volatility generally do not. The fact of the matter is: panic, chaos, and mayhem sell newspapers and drive advertising revenues. The financial press makes a living by reporting on the unusual and sensational events. Most of the time, however, there is no crisis to report. Successful traders must make an effort to generate profits in both environments. One of the important elements in doing so is being able to measure and quantify volatility. When volatility is high, your trading strategy will differ greatly from when volatility is low.

As stated earlier, our aim in writing this book is twofold. The first task is to teach readers what volatility is and how it affects the market. Our second goal is to teach the reader how to trade it. In later chapters, the reader will learn how to incorporate volatility into his or her own trading strategies and how to use past prices to identify trading opportunities.

Before launching our discussion on volatility, however, the reader must have a thorough understanding of stocks and indexes. While our discussion of volatility can be applied to commodities and futures markets, the focus of discussion within this book is the stock market, which includes stocks, or equities, indexes, exchange-traded funds, and options. The next few chapters serve that purpose.

2

Volatility in the Stock Market

Over the years, I've traded a number of different markets including commodities, futures, and stocks. Ultimately, I found my niche trading stock and index options. Since the value of an option is derived from another investment vehicle, options are derivative instruments. In the case of stock options, their value is derived from the value of a stock. Therefore, in order to understand stock options, it is first necessary to have an in-depth understanding of stocks. The same can be said about index options. Thus, a comprehensive understanding of the stocks, indexes, and the stock market as a whole is paramount to successfully trading volatility. In this chapter, we seek to identify the factors that cause volatility in individual stocks.

Have you ever heard a news reporter comment about stock market volatility? For instance, "The Dow Jones Industrial Average recovered from early losses to close up 50 points today in another volatile session." What exactly does that mean? First, when reporters comment on the performance of the stock market, it is usually in reference to one of three averages: The Dow Jones Industrial Average (the Dow), the Nasdaq Composite, or the Standard & Poor's 500. All three can be used to gauge trends within the stock market—whether the bull is driving the market higher or the bear is pressing stocks lower.

Indeed, the stock market has a rich and interesting history that dates back centuries. As the words "stock" and "market" imply, it is essentially a market where investors meet to buy and sell stocks. Although much of it is done electronically these days, the concept is the same today as it was in 1792 when traders met under the buttonwood tree in lower Manhattan to exchange cash for shares. The stock market is an arena for buying and selling different individual stocks. Similar to an auction, the prices of individual stocks are determined by the buying and selling of those individual shares. At the same time, each stock and every index is unique in its own respect.

What causes stocks to exhibit price volatility? Chapter 1 presented a number of events that have caused the collapse of the entire market: rising interest rates, bursting of a speculative bubble, war. But there are also factors that can cause volatility in shares of just one company. In other words, why do shares in one company exhibit greater volatility than shares in a similar one? Outside of the events that can cause the collapse of the entire market, what factors can trigger a slide in just one stock? This chapter identifies some of the causes. But first, let's explore what a stock represents.

WHAT IS A STOCK?

Let's get back to basics for a moment. Throughout this book, the reader will be presented with a variety of examples that require an understanding of the stock market. Specifically, to trade volatility it is important to have an in-depth understanding of stocks, indexes, and options. Options will be covered in detail in later chapters. In this chapter, stocks and index basics will be discussed. While for some readers the following review may seem a bit too elementary, a comprehensive discussion of volatility requires a solid understanding of stocks and stock quotes.

What is a stock? By recent estimates, today 50 million or 50 percent of all American households own stocks in one form or another. Some individuals have exposure to stocks through their retirement funds at work. Other investors have been persuaded to buy shares in individual stocks by a broker or colleague. Others may have acquired stock through an inheritance or a gift. However, as I travel throughout the country presenting options trading seminars, I am constantly surprised to hear some of the misconceptions people have, despite widespread stock ownership.

When an investor buys a particular stock, he or she is investing in the partial ownership of a company. A company that has stock trading in the marketplace is known as a public company because the public has access to its shares. Not all companies are public and have shares available for purchase. Companies that choose not to go public are known as private companies.

Most large, successful companies issue stock in order to raise money to expand operations. This can be accomplished by hiring an investment bank to sell shares of the company's stock. The investment bank brings the company's shares, or stock, to the market through something known as an initial public offering (IPO). In this manner, the bank makes ownership shares available to the public for purchase. Since not all companies choose this avenue, not all companies have shares available for purchase. Our discussion centers on public companies, or those with shares trading on the stock markets. Therefore, in discussing volatility, it is with respect to the volatility of the share price in the marketplace, and not the volatility of a firm's business cycle, revenue, or other company-specific factors.

In the United States, after a company goes public, the shares are listed on one of the three principal stock exchanges: the American Stock Exchange (AMEX), the New York Stock Exchange (NYSE), or the Nasdaq stock market. After hiring an

Initial Public Offering

The initial public offering (IPO) is the company's initial sale of stock to the public. Most often, shares offered through an IPO are those of a relatively new, smaller company that is attempting to obtain outside equity capital. After an IPO, shares become available to the public and trade on one of the stock exchanges. The company hires an investment bank to orchestrate the initial public offering. The investment bank determines the price and number of shares and how much the IPO is likely to fetch. In the following example, Liquidmetal Technologies undertook an initial public offering and hired investment bank Merrill Lynch to launch its shares.

Liquidmetal Tech Files for $120 Mln IPO
Tuesday, November 20, 2001
Alloy developer Liquidmetal Technologies filed with U.S. regulators on Tuesday to raise up to $120 million in its initial public offering. Details of the price or how many shares of common stock will be offered are expected in subsequent Securities and Exchange Commission filings. The Tampa, Florida–based firm, which develops products from amorphous alloys, said it plans to use proceeds from the IPO to repay debt and for general corporate purposes that may include acquisitions or joint ventures. Merrill Lynch is underwriting the offering, according to the prospectus. Liquidmetal said it has applied to list on the Nasdaq under the symbol "LQMT" (LQMT.O).
Source: IPO.com.

investment bank to distribute shares to the public, the company will decide on what exchange the shares will be listed. In other words, the company must not only decide on an investment bank to issue shares, but also on which exchange its shares will trade. Each exchange has different requirements for having a company's stock trade on that exchange.

Before the stock begins trading on one of the exchanges, it is assigned a symbol. For instance, the stock symbol for Microsoft is MSFT, Intel is INTC, and Motorola is MOT. Most stocks that are listed on the Nasdaq have symbols with four letters. For that reason, when talking about the Nasdaq some traders refer to "four-letter stocks." Stocks that trade on the AMEX or NYSE, on the other hand, are assigned symbols with either two or three letters. Some even have only one letter. For instance, the ticker symbol for AT&T is simply T.

Investors looking to buy or sell shares of a public company listed on any of the exchanges will have to pay the current market price for the stock. These days, the current market price is relatively easy to find. In the past, investors had two primary sources of information concerning stock prices. The financial newspapers, such as *The Wall Street Journal*, publish tables with closing prices at the end of the trading day—so investors can open the newspaper each morning to find out what yesterday's

Listing Requirements by Stock Exchange

- **NYSE:** The New York Stock Exchange (NYSE), sometimes called the Big Board, has the most stringent restrictions on the companies that seek to list their stock on the exchange. The publicly held stock must have a minimum market value (shares traded times market price) of $18 million. The company's net income in the latest year must be over $2.5 million before federal income tax and $2 million in the preceding two years. A company is also asked to pay an initial and annual fee to be listed on the NYSE. Complete details of the listing requirements are available at www.nyse.com.

- **AMEX:** Today, the American Stock Exchange (AMEX) lists over 700 companies and is the world's second largest auction marketplace. To have a stock listed on the AMEX, the company must have pretax income of $750,000 in the latest fiscal year or two of most recent three years, a market value (shares traded times market price) of at least $3 million, a minimum stock price of $3, and minimum stockholders' equity of $4 million. In 1998, the National Association of Securities Dealers (NASD), the parent company of the Nasdaq, and the AMEX agreed to add the AMEX to the NASD family of companies. This strategic alliance enables the AMEX and the Nasdaq to share resources and certain facilities, yet continue to operate as separate subsidiaries of the NASD. The complete listing requirements for the American Stock Exchange are available at www.amex.com.

- **Nasdaq:** The Nasdaq Stock Market is the newest of the three stock exchanges. Founded in 1971, it is not a floor-based exchange like the AMEX or Big Board. Instead, it is an electronic network of market makers and securities dealers. To become listed on the Nasdaq, a company must have a market value of at least $8 million, pretax income of $1 million, and a stock price of $5 or greater. Visit www.nasdaq.com for the latest listing requirements.

- **Regional exchanges:** There are six regional exchanges—in Boston, Chicago, Cincinnati, Philadelphia, Los Angeles, and San Francisco. Some of these exchanges use an open outcry auction-style system where buyers and sellers come together to trade shares of stocks and option contracts. Others are evolving into fully automated systems that electronically match buyers and sellers.

closing prices were. Investors looking for current prices, or intraday quotes, would call a brokerage firm and ask for a quote on the stock.

Today, however, the process of finding intraday stock prices is quite simple. For instance, if you go to the www.optionetics.com home page, you will find a feature that allows you to obtain stock quotes. At the top of the home page, you will see an empty box with the words "quotes/options" to the left and the word "GO" to the right. If you type in the symbol INTC, for example, you will obtain a quote for shares of Intel Corp.

Using the information from Figure 2.1, the last trade on INTC was $18.52. This means that the last time Intel stock traded (shares were bought or sold), the stock price was $18.52. Since this was written during market hours on July 22, 2002, that price does not represent the closing price, or the last price of the trading session. On that day, the opening price, or "open" in Figure 2.1, was $18.47. As an off-floor trader, you will usually buy at the ask price and sell at the bid price. The last price is usually somewhere within the bid-ask spread. The highest and lowest prices of the day are also included in the stock quote. As we will see, the closing, opening, high, and low prices can all be used to compute historical volatility. You should now have an understanding of what those terms mean. (See Table 2.1 for a complete description of all the fields.)

INDEXES

When investors discuss the stock market, it is not in reference to the performance of one or two stocks, but rather to stocks as a whole. One common way to discuss the performance of stocks as a whole is through the Dow Jones Industrial Average. The Dow is actually a stock index, and it is also an average or market average. Since the term "index" is used more often with respect to options, it is used throughout this book. Furthermore, while the Dow Jones Industrial Average is one of the oldest and most widely followed indexes, today it is one among many. The box entitled "The Mighty Dow" offers a more detailed discussion of the evolution of the Dow Jones Industrial Average.

To put it quite simply, an index is a group of stocks. Originally, the price of an index was computed by taking the average stock price of a group of stocks. For example, when Charles Dow created the first index in 1884, the Dow Jones Rail Average, he simply took the average stock price of 12 railroad companies. Today, the methods for computing an index are somewhat more complicated but the purpose is the same: to measure the performance of not one or two stocks, but an entire group.

Detailed Quote/News

Symbol: |INTC | |Detailed Quote/News ▼| **get info** Symbol Lookup

Intel Corp (INTC)

Delayed Quote as of JUL 22, 2002 2:58:03 PM
(E.T.)

Last	18.520	Change	⬇ -0.130
Open	18.470	% Change	⬇ -0.70%
High	19.200	Low	18.350
Bid	18.510	Ask	18.520
52 Week High	36.780	52 Week Low	16.260
Earnings Per Share	0.26	Volume	62.29M
Shares Outstanding	6.69B	Market Cap	123.82B
P/E Ratio	71.73	Exchange	NASDAQ

Figure 2.1 Detailed INTC Quote (Courtesy of Optionetics.com)

Table 2.1 Understanding Stock Quotes

Data	Definition
Last	The last price that the option traded for at the exchange. For delayed quotes, this price may not reflect the actual price of the option at the time you view the quote.
Open	The price of the first transaction of the current trading day.
Change	The amount the last sale differs from the previous trading day's closing price.
% Change	The percentage the price has changed since the previous day's closing price.
High	The high price for the current trading day.
Low	The low price for the current trading day.
Bid	The highest price a prospective buyer (floor trader) is prepared to pay for a specified time for a trading unit of a specified security. If there is a high demand for the underlying asset, the prices are bid up to a higher level. Off-floor traders buy at the ask price.
Ask	The lowest price acceptable to a prospective seller (floor trader) of the same security. A low demand for a stock translates to the market being offered down to the lowest price at which a person is willing to sell. Off-floor traders sell at the bid price. Together, the bid and ask prices constitute a quotation or quote, and the difference between the two prices is the bid-ask spread. The bid and asked dynamic is common to all stocks and options.
52-Week High	The highest price the stock traded at in the past 52-week period.
52-Week Low	The lowest price the stock traded at in the past 52-week period.
Earnings per Share	The company's bottom line (net pretax profit) divided by the number of shares outstanding.
Volume	The total number of shares traded that day.
Shares Outstanding	The total number of shares the company has issued.
Market Cap	Shares outstanding multiplied by the closing stock price.
P/E Ratio	Stock price divided by the earnings per share; P = Price/E = Earnings per share.
Exchange	Where a company lists or registers its shares (e.g., the New York Stock Exchange).

There are events that trigger a rise or fall in a majority of stocks. Sometimes stock-specific news—earnings reports, management changes, or new product announcements—can cause investors to buy or sell the stock in question. Other times, breaking news events cause a move in a majority of stocks. For example, rising interest rates, uncertain political developments, or increasing energy prices can all serve to drive stocks lower. Of course, there are exceptions and not *all* stocks fall,

---

The Mighty Dow

The Dow Jones Industrial Average dates back more than 100 years. Created in 1896 by Charles Dow, then editor of *The Wall Street Journal* and cofounder of Dow Jones & Company, the average was intended to help investors view the price changes of stocks collectively, rather than piecemeal. To compute the average, Dow took 12 of the most popular stocks trading on the New York Stock Exchange and took the simple mean or average of those 12 stocks. Since that time, the index has changed, and there are now 30 components, which are occasionally adjusted to reflect the constantly changing market environment.

---

but in certain circumstances a majority of stocks will fall or rise together. This tendency for stocks to behave in a similar manner is known as comovement.

In Chapter 1, the factors that have triggered bear markets were covered. In that discussion, the performance of the stock market was considered in terms of the price changes of the S&P 500 index. In addition to the S&P 500, there are a number of other indexes designed to measure the performance of the entire stock market (see Table 2.2). These so-called broad market indexes or averages are the subject of daily market commentary in the financial press. The Dow Jones Industrial Average has already been mentioned. Some investors, however, do not like the fact that the Dow consists of only 30 stocks. After all, there are thousands of companies with stocks trading on the exchanges. The S&P 500 is often considered a better gauge because it includes 500 stocks instead of only 30. Other major averages include the following:

- *New York Stock Exchange Composite Index ($NYA):* The NYSE Composite index measures the aggregate performance of all stocks trading on the New York Stock Exchange.

- *Nasdaq Composite Index ($COMPQ):* The Nasdaq Composite measures the performance of all stocks trading on the Nasdaq.

Table 2.2   Broad Market Indexes

Index Name	Symbol	Number of Constituents
Dow Jones Industrial Average	$INDU	30
S&P 500	$SPX	500
Wilshire 5000	$TMW	7,000
New York Stock Exchange Composite index	$NYA	All Big Board stocks
Nasdaq Composite index	$COMPQ	All Nasdaq stocks
S&P 100	$OEX	100
Russell 3000	$RUA	3,000

- *Wilshire 5000 Index ($TMW):* One of the broadest measures of U.S. stocks, the Wilshire 5000 was created in 1974. Since that time, the number of stocks within the index has increased from 5,000 to 7,000.

- *U.S. Total Market Index:* In February 2000, Dow Jones & Co. launched this new index designed to represent a fixed percentage (95 percent) of all U.S. stocks.

- *Russell 2000 Small Cap Index ($RUT):* Often referred to as "the Russell," the Russell 2000 is one of many indexes created by the Frank Russell Group in Tacoma, Washington. It is a measure of the 3,000 most actively traded stocks on the New York Stock Exchange, the Nasdaq, and the American Stock Exchange with the 1,000 largest companies removed. It is the most widely followed gauge of small-cap stock performance.

- *S&P MidCap 400 Index ($MID):* The Standard & Poor's MidCap index consists of 400 (mostly industrial) companies. Selection is based on market size and popularity (measured by liquidity or trading volume) and is a widely followed barometer for the performance of mid-cap stocks.

- *Wilshire 4500 Index:* This index includes all of the companies of the Wilshire 5000 with the components of the S&P 500 removed. Therefore, it provides a measure of both small- and mid-cap stocks.

- *Nasdaq 100 Index ($NDX):* The Nasdaq 100, or NDX, is a measure of the 100 largest nonfinancial companies trading on the Nasdaq. Given that most are technology companies, the index offers an accurate gauge of the technology sector.

While the Dow, S&P 500, and Wilshire 5000 are used to gauge trends within the stock market, some indexes are designed to measure the price changes of specific industry groups. For instance, when Charles Dow created the first index, the Dow Jones Rail Index, he was attempting to gauge stock prices within the most important industry during the late nineteenth century: railroads.

The PHLX Semiconductor Index is a popular index that represents the aggregate performance of slightly more than one dozen chip stocks, including Intel, Texas Instruments, LSI Logic, and others. Certain events can trigger a rise or fall in the entire chip sector. For instance, the monthly report from the Semiconductor Industry Association or the book-to-bill ratio from the Semiconductor Equipment and Materials International. In fact, some investors consider industry-related news the major driver behind a stock's performance. In short, stocks within the same industry tend to exhibit a great deal of comovement; with a group of developments with respect to an industry, the factors underlying an individual company's stock price become easier to understand. Some of the more important industry, or sector, indexes and the factors that can lead to price swings appear in Table 2.3. This list is not meant to be exhaustive. In fact, there are sector indexes to track the performance of virtually any industry group, including forest and paper stocks, defense, chemical, wireless, transportation, utility, pharmaceutical, natural gas, oil, networking, computer software, and a variety of others. (A comprehensive list of indexes can be found in Appendix A).

Table 2.3   Sector Indexes

Name	Symbol	What Causes the Greatest Increase in Volatility?
PHLX Semiconductor Index	$SOX	Monthly book-to-bill ratio, statistics from the Semiconductor Industry Association
PHLX Bank Index	$BKX	Changes in interest rates
PHLX Oil Service Index	$OSX	Oil prices and changes in the number of active drilling rigs
AMEX Biotechnology Index	$BTK	New discoveries or approval of drugs by the Food and Drug Administration
CBOE Internet Index	$INX	Trends regarding online advertising revenues and online sales
AMEX Airline Index	$XAL	Jet fuel prices and passenger traffic
PHLX Gold Index	$XAU	Gold prices and rising inflation

In addition, indexes also exist that track stocks by their relative size. For instance, the Russell 2000 Small Cap Index (symbol: $RUT) measures the performance of smaller companies. "Small" in this case refers to a company's market capitalization, which equals the number of shares of stock outstanding times the current market price of each share. Similarly, there are indexes that measure the performance of medium-sized companies. The S&P MidCap index (symbol: $MID) is an example.

Finding a quote for an index can be done in the same fashion as a stock, but there is one important difference between the two. As we saw earlier, there is an important difference between the price at which a stock can be bought (offer or asking price) and the price at which it can be sold (the bid). Indexes do not have bids and offers because they cannot be bought or sold. An index is used as a gauge and not an investment.

Although investors cannot buy an index itself, there are two ways to trade them. The first is through index options, which are covered in detail throughout this book. The other means of participating in the rise and fall of an index is through exchange-traded funds, (ETFs), as well as Holding Company Depository Receipts. These types of investments emerged in the late 1990s and have since proliferated in

---

Book-to-bill ratio: The Semiconductor Equipment and Materials International (SEMI) book-to-bill is a gauge for the business activity of the North American semiconductor equipment industry. It is a ratio computed as the three-month moving average bookings (i.e., new orders) divided by the three-month moving average billings. For instance, on July 19, 2002, SEMI reported that the North America–based manufacturers of semiconductor capital equipment recorded $1.16 billion in orders in June 2002 (three-month average basis), $906 million in billings, and a book-to-bill ratio of 1.28 (or 1,160/906).

the investment scene. Put simply, an ETF is an index that trades like a stock. Each share represents a fractional interest in a group of stocks. Those stocks, in turn, are the same ones that comprise a given index.

The most popular ETF is the Nasdaq 100 Index Trust. Known also by its ticker symbol, QQQ, and referred to simply as the Qs, it is one of the most actively traded securities on the U.S. stock market (see Figure 2.2). Investors can buy and sell the QQQ as they would a stock. Each share, in turn, represents ownership in a trust, which holds the same stocks as the Nasdaq 100. As noted earlier, the NDX is an index comprised of 100 of the largest stocks trading in the Nasdaq Stock Market. Therefore, the Nasdaq 100 includes such familiar names as Microsoft, Intel, and Oracle. As of this writing, 75 percent of the index consists of technology companies.

Therefore, investors seeking to own a basket of mostly technology stocks can buy shares of the QQQ. In addition, much like a stock, the shares can be purchased throughout the day. Also like a stock, exchange-traded funds represent an ownership interest. Shares can be purchased (at the asking price) and sold (at the bid). A list of ETFs and the index each is designed to represent appears in Table 2.4. There is also a wide array of industry, sector, as well as broad market index exchange-traded funds.

Holding Company Depository Receipts, or HOLDRs, are very similar to exchange-traded funds. That is, while HOLDRs are structured as a trust and represent beneficial ownership interest in a portfolio, shares trade like stocks and can be purchased throughout the trading day. Unlike ETFs, however, HOLDRs do not mirror the performance of a specific index. Instead, Merrill Lynch—the investment firm that has developed HOLDRs—determines what stocks are included within each trust.

In addition, Holding Company Depository Receipts have been designed to offer investors a means of owning shares of companies within specific industry groups. For instance, there are holders that include stocks within the biotechnology sector and holders of Internet stocks. Like exchange-traded funds, holders allow investors to buy and sell entire baskets in a single transaction. Table 2.5 lists the various HOLDRs available to investors today.

Whether trading stocks, indexes, ETFs, or HOLDRs, each one has a current

---

Exchange-Traded Funds

Exchange-traded funds (ETFs) are relatively new investment vehicles. Like a traditional mutual fund, an exchange-traded fund is a pool of money that is used to purchase a basket of stocks. Most often the exchange-traded funds are designed to track the performance of a specific index—such as the Nasdaq 100, or $NDX. Investors can then take an ownership interest in that pool by buying shares. Unlike a mutual fund, however, shares are not purchased through a mutual fund company. Instead, shares trade like stocks on the organized stock exchanges.

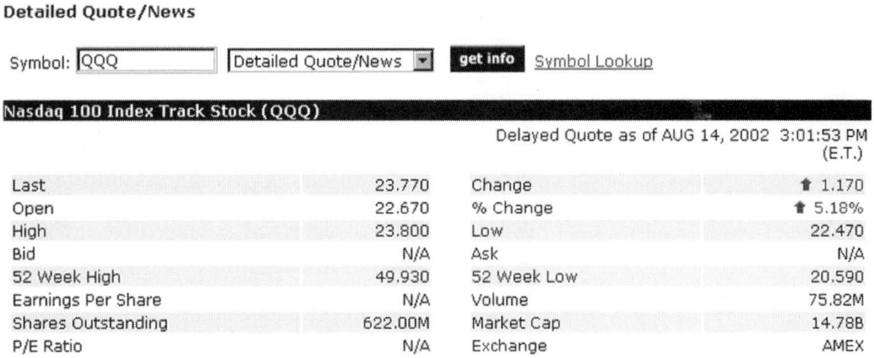

Detailed Quote/News

Symbol: |QQQ | |Detailed Quote/News ▼| **get info**   Symbol Lookup

Nasdaq 100 Index Track Stock (QQQ)

Delayed Quote as of AUG 14, 2002 3:01:53 PM
(E.T.)

Last	23.770	Change	↑ 1.170
Open	22.670	% Change	↑ 5.18%
High	23.800	Low	22.470
Bid	N/A	Ask	N/A
52 Week High	49.930	52 Week Low	20.590
Earnings Per Share	N/A	Volume	75.82M
Shares Outstanding	622.00M	Market Cap	14.78B
P/E Ratio	N/A	Exchange	AMEX

Figure 2.2   QQQ Quote (Courtesy of Optionetics.com)

Table 2.4   Examples of Exchange-Traded Funds

Name	Symbol	Index Tracked
DIAMONDS	DIA	Dow Jones Industrial Average
SPDRs	SPY	S&P 500
Nasdaq 100 Index Trust	QQQ	Nasdaq 100
MidCap SPDR	MDY	S&P MidCap 400
iShares Russell 2000 Index Fund	IWM	Russell 2000

price that is quoted in the market. The price of the stock or index in question is the most important factor in determining an asset's volatility. If the price of a stock is $50 one day, $50.10 a week later, then $50 in two weeks, it has exhibited low volatility. The price of the stock is just not moving a great deal. But if a stock jumps from $50 to $60 in a week, and then back down to $40 two weeks later, then it is experiencing high volatility, which changes the kind of strategies investors employ to make money on it.

As investors, it is important to understand that shares can be purchased at the ask (offering) price and sold at the bid, but for measuring volatility it becomes essential to understand how prices change. The closing price, or the final trade of the day, is the most common price for computing volatility. At the same time, investors must also understand the differences between the open, the high, and the low. Stock prices change throughout the trading day; some computations incorporate the day's highs and lows, or intraday prices, into measuring volatility.

At this point, the reader should have an understanding of the four different investment vehicles discussed in this book—stocks, indexes, exchange-traded funds, and HOLDRs—and also know that there are six different price quotes for each: bid, ask, open, close, high, and low.

Table 2.5 Examples of HOLDRs

Name	Symbol
Biotech HOLDRs	BBH
Broadband HOLDRs	BDH
B2B Internet HOLDRs	BHH
Europe 2001 HOLDRs	EKH
Internet HOLDRs	HHH
Internet Architecture HOLDRs	IAH
Internet Infrastructure HOLDRs	IIH
Market 2000+ HOLDRs	MKH
Oil Service HOLDRs	OIH
Pharmaceutical HOLDRs	PPH
Regional Bank HOLDRs	RKH
Retail HOLDRs	RTH
Semiconductor HOLDRs	SMH
Software HOLDRs	SWH
Telecom HOLDRs	TTH
Utilities HOLDRs	UTH
Wireless HOLDRs	WMH

SPOTTING VOLATILITY

In later chapters, the math required to compute historical and implied volatility will be examined in detail. For now, let's take a graphical look at the concept of volatility. First, let us consider a chart of the Dow Jones Industrial Average six months after the October 1987 crash, on April 19, 1988 (see Figure 2.3). Notice the sharp drop in the Dow in October 1987. The vertical bars on the chart are rather long, which suggests a wide gap between the highest and lowest prices of the day. When there are long bars between high and low prices on a stock chart, it is safe to assume that volatility is high.

Consider, however, the period from February until April 1988. The vertical bars are short, the Dow Jones Industrial Average is moving sideways, and volatility is low. Now, notice Figure 2.4, which shows the long-term chart of the Dow Jones Industrial Average. The stock market crash appears much less dramatic. Indeed, as noted earlier, an important factor to consider when looking at volatility is time. Is it minutes, days, weeks, or months? We will see that extreme periods of market volatility, like the stock market crash in October 1987, are the exception. Trading volatility involves taking the possibility of a sharp fall like the 1987 crash into account, but not focusing too closely on the chances of that happening on a regular basis.

For almost any stock or index, there are times when volatility will be high and other times it will be low. Actual levels of volatility tend to increase during periods when important and relevant new information arrives in the market. If that new information causes investors to aggressively buy or sell, the result can be an increase in volatility. Human emotion can then serve to drive volatility to extremes. During times of little or

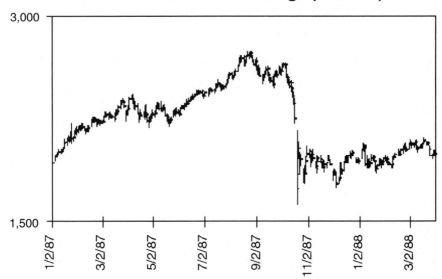

Figure 2.3   Two-Year Chart of Dow Jones Industrial Average

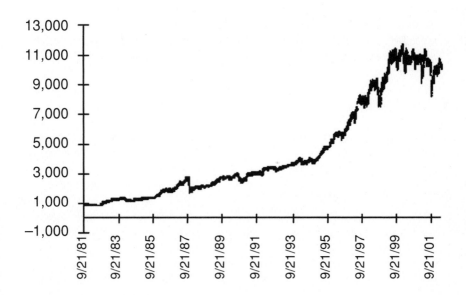

Figure 2.4   Long-Term Chart of the Dow Industrial Average

no new information, however, stock and index prices may exhibit low levels of volatility. In that case, human emotion will not have a major impact on volatility.

While volatility is often associated with chaos, falling stock prices, and lost wealth, it should not be feared. Periods of high volatility and times of low volatility are the natural ebb and flow of the market. For example, the crash of 1987 was an episode of high volatility followed by a prolonged period of lower volatility and gradually climbing stock prices. Luckily, profit opportunities exist in both market environments. But simply being cognizant of the fact that volatility changes through time—periods of high volatility are followed by times of low volatility—is not enough. Strategists also need a way to measure it beyond looking at prices or pulling up stock charts.

There are two ways of measuring volatility: historical and implied volatility. In basic terms, historical volatility gauges price movement in terms of past performance, while implied volatility approximates how much the marketplace thinks prices will move. Historical volatility is akin to looking in the rearview mirror to measure a stock's actual volatility by using the standard deviation of a stock's price changes from close to close of trading going back a specific number of days. Implied volatility is also a measure of a stock or index's volatility, but one that is computed using an option pricing model. The most familiar model is the one developed by Fischer Black and Myron Scholes (i.e., the Black-Scholes option pricing model). Implied volatility is such an important, yet complex, topic that an entire chapter of this book is devoted to the subject. For now, the reader should simply be aware that implied volatility is computed using current option prices and an option pricing model. Therefore, unlike historical volatility, which is computed using past prices, implied volatility is derived using current prices. It reflects market expectations of the type of volatility the stock or index is likely to exhibit in the future.

Both implied and historical volatility are equally important and, once understood, equip any trader with the tools necessary for excavating profits from the marketplace. These types of measurements will be discussed in great detail in later chapters.

CONCLUSION

Volatility has become the most important factor in my trading life. I've been a professional trader for almost two decades, and when I first started the concept was completely foreign to me. But it didn't take long for me to find out that a lack of

---

Historical volatility: Also known as statistical volatility, historical volatility measures a stock's propensity for price movement based on the stock's past price action during a specific time period.

Implied volatility: A computed value that measures an option's volatility, rather than the underlying asset. It matches the theoretical option price with the current market price of the option.

understanding of volatility can wipe out a trading account in a short amount of time. It took much longer to learn how to appreciate volatility and recognize it as a valuable tool. Once understood, it can offer not only monetary rewards, but also increased enjoyment in day-to-day trading. This book is designed to help you avoid the potentially damaging impact of volatility while helping you to wield it in order to derive both personal and financial rewards.

Volatility generally stems from the arrival of new information. When investors receive fresh news concerning corporate profits, interest rates, or the economy, they use that information to make buying and selling decisions. Collectively, this stimulates the potential for aggressive buying and selling, which leads to increasing volatility. When investors receive unexpected, breaking news, they are forced to reassess their market expectations, which can cause aggressive buying and selling. Furthermore, when emotions begin driving those decisions—such as the panic in October 1987—volatility can skyrocket.

For example, the most common reason for a stock to fall precipitously is concern over earnings. Sometimes a company will report earnings that are less than the market expects. When it comes as a nasty surprise, the stock usually falls on the news. Other times, a company's management tells investors that earnings will be better than were expected, and the stock will rise sharply on the news. That is, the stock rises due to the positive surprise. Suffice to say, earnings are a major driver behind stock prices. As information pertaining to a company's profits reaches the market, investors will buy and sell on the news. These days, accounting irregularities have driven the market to multiyear lows and extreme volatility. Big surprises lead to increasing volatility, which can move the market in either direction. Volatility cannot help you to predict the market's future direction—just the magnitude of the move.

Nevertheless, whether stocks are responding to earnings news, oil prices, the full moon, or anything else that might cause investors to react emotionally, the result can be a surge in market volatility. During such times, many investors will panic, move out of the market, or simply make poor emotionally driven decisions. This happens to everyone at one time or another. Over the years, however, I have learned to control my emotions when the market becomes volatile—especially greed and fear—in order to be able to make profits in the market in a systematic way. The strategies outlined in this book are designed to help you keep sane when the rest of the market is gripped with panic and mayhem.

Before launching into a discussion of specific strategies, however, it is first necessary to explore volatility a bit further. So far, the reader should have an understanding of stocks, indexes, exchange-traded funds and HOLDRs, as well as how to interpret price quotes. You should also understand that volatility is part of the stock market and always has been. Finally, stock charts can provide a quick and easy way to get a sense of the volatility of a stock or index. However, charts do not provide enough information to trade volatility. The options strategist must also be able to measure volatility by employing two tools, historical and implied volatility—the subjects of the next two chapters and Chapter 6.

3

Historical Volatility

When dealing with financial instruments, certain forces trigger volatility, and emotion is one of the key drivers. In a nutshell, when prices are rising and the majority of investors are making money, optimism and greed drive prices higher. When prices are falling, fear and panic can overwhelm investors, driving prices lower. The less certainty and predictability associated with an asset, the greater the probability that greed and fear will drive prices to extremes to create greater volatility. This book seeks to explore this dynamic between fear and greed by looking at the two main types of volatility: historical and implied.

Historical volatility, also referred to as actual volatility, is computed using past stock prices. Remember the words "past" and "stock" make up the meaning of historical volatility. It can be calculated by using the standard deviation of a stock's price changes from close to close of trading going back a specified number of days, although 10, 20, or 90 days are often used. Since statistical volatility measures a stock's propensity for movement, it is an important variable that also helps to determine an option's worth. High or low historical volatility also gives traders a clue as to the type of strategy that can best be implemented to optimize profits in a specific market. Instead of computing statistical volatility, a variety of indicators, such as Bollinger bands, can be used to create historical volatility computations that are graphed on a chart.

Implied volatility (IV) is a measure of an underlying asset's volatility as reflected in an option's price. It is the volatility *implied* by the option's current price. Later we will see that an actual IV percentage can be derived using a model; the most common is the Black-Scholes option pricing model (but there are others). For now, it is sufficient to understand that by plugging in different variables (the stock or index price, time until the option expires, the price of the option, etc.) the volatility implied by the option can be determined.

Therefore, while historical volatility measures an asset's price change in the past, implied volatility is priced into an option's value in the present. Thus, it represents the market's perception of volatility. Implied volatility is also forward-looking. For that reason, when market participants expect greater volatility going forward, the price of an option has a tendency to increase due to a rise in implied volatility. It is similar to the owner of a high-volatility property demanding a larger down payment than the low-volatility property owner because there is a greater probability that the high-risk property will rise sharply in value before the term of the agreement expires.

In short, learning how to use volatility involves developing a solid understanding of historical volatility as well as implied volatility. Let's try to put it in perspective: Historical volatility is a measure of an asset's past price changes, while implied volatility is derived from an option's price and reflects market perceptions of volatility. If market participants expect an underlying asset to exhibit high volatility going forward, options premiums (implied volatility) will be high. If, however, an asset is expected to show little volatility going forward, implied volatility will fall to reflect those expectations. If this is somewhat unclear at this point, do not fret; you are only at the beginning. Keep reading.

Historical volatility is a relatively straightforward concept to grasp. Put simply, it is a measure of prices that have existed in the past. For instance, if you visit the grocery store once every week for a period of six months and notice that the price of a loaf of bread rises from 50 cents to $2.50, goes down to $1.25, and then goes up to $3, you would say that the historical price volatility of a loaf of bread is quite high. At the same time, if the price of a carton of eggs remains between $1.50 and $1.60 during that time period, it has exhibited relatively low levels of historical volatility.

In the stock market, the concept is the same. If a stock or an index fluctuates wildly in price, it is said to have high historical volatility. On the other hand, if the chart shows a long period of sideways movement on the chart, the stock or index is exhibiting low levels of historical volatility. The stock market is like a storm; there are times when it exhibits high volatility and others when it remains relatively calm—but like the wind it never stops moving entirely.

According to the New York Stock Exchange, the year 2000 was among the most volatile in history. The Dow Jones Industrial Average changed in value in excess of 1 percent during 40 percent of all trading days. Since the crash of 1987, the only year to witness levels of volatility anywhere near that was 1998, when the Dow moved up or down in excess of 1 percent on 34.5 percent of that year's trading days.

Does this mean that volatility is higher today than in the past? Well, computing the number of days within the year in which the Dow Jones Industrial Average increased or decreased in excess of 1 percent is, indeed, a way to measure historical volatility. Yet it is not a practical one. Instead, traders need a more effective way of computing historical volatility, and this chapter introduces the reader to four such techniques: historical or statistical volatility, Average True Range (ATR), beta, and Bollinger bands.

MEASURING HISTORICAL VOLATILITY

In order to develop a measure of volatility using a stock or index's past prices, and determine a number that is also relatively easy to work with, one must use a bit of mathematics. For example, the most widely used measure of historical volatility involves computing the standard deviation of closing stock prices over a period of time. Consequently, calculating historical volatility requires an elementary understanding of statistics. All measures of historical volatility are derived using statistical mathematical formulas.

Yet, while most measures of historical volatility involve mathematic calculations, not all traders know the precise formulas. In fact, armed with a computer, the trader can quickly obtain historical volatility on any stock or index with the click of a mouse. Some measures, such as statistical volatility, can be obtained merely by plugging in a ticker symbol within the appropriate area of the Optionetics.com Platinum site. Other indicators, such as Bollinger bands, are viewed visually alongside a stock chart. The point is, not all traders know how to compute the historical volatility, and instead prefer to let the computer do the work for them—and there's nothing wrong with that.

At the same time, although traders often simplify the process of measuring volatility through the use of a computer, in order to understand the differences and unique character of each measure, a basic understanding of how each measure is computed can be helpful in developing trading strategies. For instance, how does the information concerning past volatility using beta differ from Bollinger bands? In other words, how is each indicator unique? And, importantly, which is more useful? The answers to those questions become clear once the trader understands the mathematics underlying each indicator.

STATISTICAL VOLATILITY

In volatility, as in life, change is the only constant. While you can be 100 percent sure that the volatility of a stock or index will change over time, there is no way of knowing with absolute certainty what the volatility will be like in the future. However, it is easy to determine what the volatility has been in the past. The question is: How does one take the past prices and compute a number that is useful and easy to interpret? There are a number of tools for doing so.

One tool for gauging and measuring the volatility associated with a stock or index is the standard deviation of past stock prices. In Chapter 1, we reviewed four different prices with respect to stock or index quotes: open, high, low, and close. Statistical volatility is derived from the closing price of the stock or index over a fixed number of trading days.

A common method of computing historical volatility uses an annualized measure—the standard deviation of the stock or index price over the past year. Standard deviation, in turn, is defined as the variability of the distribution of stock or index prices (see Figure 3.1). High standard deviations are generally associated with

---

Computing the Standard Deviation

$$\sigma^2 = \frac{\sum\limits_{i=1}^{n} (P_i - P)^2}{n-1}$$

$$v = \frac{v}{P}$$

Where:
P_i = the stock price over a range of n days
P = the average stock price over n days
n = number of days
v = volatility

Figure 3.1   Standard Deviation of Stock Prices

higher-risk or higher-volatility investments; a higher standard deviation reflects a higher level of variability in the distribution of stock prices.

Note: If you are not determined to compute historical volatility on your own, do not worry about understanding the details underpinning the computations here. They are included to help shed light on how statistical volatility is computed on the Optionetics.com web site and for programmers interested in constructing their own analysis tools.

In practice, however, most computations of statistical volatility use the lognormal distribution of stock returns rather than the simple standard deviation. In financial theory, it is assumed that the logarithms of stock prices are normally distributed, and not the prices themselves. Therefore, to compute historical volatility, the logarithm of prices will take the place of P and P_i. The most common way of computing statistical volatility, then, is found in Figure 3.2

As an example, let us consider 11 trading days of the S&P 100 index, or as it is more often called, the OEX (see Table 3.1). During the 11 days ended June 5, 2001, the index fell from 678.60 to 662.10—a 2.4 percent decline. Notice that the average logarithm of the closing prices—the last row of the fourth column—equals –0.00246. The fifth column shows the difference between each logarithm and the average or mean (–0.00246); the sum of the differences is presented in the last row of that final column.

Since we are calculating historical volatility using the changes in closing prices,

---

Standard deviation: A statistical measure of the variation of a set of values over time. Standard deviation is commonly used to compute the statistical or historical volatility of a stock price over a period of 10, 20, or more days. Generally expressed as a percentage, the higher the standard deviation, the greater the volatility of the stock or index.

Computing Statistical Volatility

$$\nu = \sqrt{\frac{\sum_{n=1}^{n}(X_i - X)^2}{n-1}}$$

Where:
X_i = lognormal $(\ln)(P_i/P_{i-1})$
X = average of X_i over a period of n days
n = number of days
ν = volatility

Figure 3.2   Statistical (Historical) Volatility

Table 3.1   Computing Historical Volatility Using 11 Days of OEX Trading

Date	OEX Closing Price	P_i/P_{i-1}	$X_i = ln(P_i/P_{i-1})$	$(X_i-X)^2$
5/21/01	$678.60			
5/22/01	676.06	0.996257	–0.003750023	0.000002
5/23/01	665.20	0.9839363	–0.016194082	0.000189
5/24/01	668.30	1.0046603	0.0046494270	0.000051
5/25/01	658.30	0.9850367	–0.01507642	0.000159
5/29/01	652.90	0.9917971	–0.008236776	0.000033
5/30/01	642.96	0.9847756	–0.015341464	0.000166
5/31/01	646.24	1.0051014	0.005088438	0.000057
6/1/01	649.62	1.0052303	0.005216625	0.000059
6/4/01	654.48	1.0074813	0.007453451	0.000098
6/5/01	662.10	1.0116428	0.011575575	0.000197
			Average = –0.00246	Sum = 0.0010105

to compute the 10-day volatility we need 11 days of data. In this example, the final two steps for computing the 10-day statistical volatility are relatively straightforward. Specifically, the sum of the differences between the natural log of each price change—$(X_i - X)^2$—is divided by the number of days of observation minus 1, or $n - 1$. In this case, the formula yields: $\nu = \sqrt{0.0010105 / 9}$ or .0106.

The final step involves converting the 10-day volatility into an annual figure. To do so, the number is multiplied by the square root of the total number of trading days in the year. In this case, the strategist will use 253 days. Therefore, the OEX 10-day historical volatility for the period ended June 5, 2001, equals: .0106 × $\sqrt{253}$ or 16.9 percent.

Obviously, the historical volatility of a stock or index will change and vary over time. A stock or index can become quite volatile at certain times. Then, suddenly, that same investment can fall flat and trade sideways. For example, the 20-day historical volatility of TheStreet.com Internet Index ($DOT) reached 100 percent in April 2001; but by the end of July of that year, it had fallen by almost half to 54 percent.

The trader must understand that every measure of volatility covered in this book is always in a state of flux. This is true of statistical volatility. For example, the 10-day historical volatility of the OEX has at times been as high as 30 percent, and at other times has been, closer to 10 percent. In addition, the historical volatility on one stock or index does not necessarily provide information concerning the volatility of another stock or index. Thus, assuming that market volatility is falling merely because the statistical volatility of IBM or AOL has been trending lower could prove to be a mistake.

In sum, when looking at historical volatility, the strategist must view each stock or index individually. A large spike in the statistical volatility of, for example, the stock of America Online (AOL) might be owed to events related only to that company. Therefore, in studying statistical volatility it is important to consider it in light of (1) other stocks or indexes, (2) past levels of historical volatility associated with that stock or index, and (3) historical volatility along different time frames.

VIEWING STOCK CHARTS

Although it is possible in today's world to trade without a computer, we strongly discourage it. With all of the capabilities offered by trading software and the vast amount of information available on the Internet, there really is simply no reason to trade without one. Computers just make trading so much easier and much more interesting, too. For example, to obtain historical volatility information without doing the math, the trader can simply turn to the Optionetics.com Platinum site. This service enables users to get historical volatility at a click of a button, over different time periods, and even create a graphical representation of volatility. Computers not only simplify the process of doing cumbersome calculations, they also provide traders with the ability to view volatility graphically, on a chart.

At the same time, it is vital to understand how to read and interpret a stock chart. Learning to make accurate assessments of charts simply comes from practical experience. In the long run, it makes trading easier and more interesting and exciting. In fact, some traders base all their investment decisions on the appearance of stock prices on a graph, or a stock chart. These so-called "technical analysts" are looking for patterns on the chart and trying to predict the stock's future movement. Although I refer to charts, I do not rely on them to predict the future direction of a stock or an index. Instead, I use charting to see the activity of a stock or index in the past along with its volatility.

In order to effectively use volatility graphs in your trading, it is important to understand basic charting tools and techniques. Many of you probably understand this already. Still, it is such an important factor that, before continuing our discussion of volatility, let's examine the most useful types of stock charts and graphs.

Computers have made stock charting as easy as flipping on a light switch. Most of the charting examples in this chapter are taken from the Optionetics.com web site. Recall that finding stock quotes was a simple matter of punching a ticker symbol into the quote box at the top of the home page. Retrieving a stock chart is the same process, except you can select "chart" rather than "quotes" immediately to the left of the quote box. After doing so, a line chart showing the price of a stock will appear on your screen.

A line chart is the simplest type of stock chart. Similar to computing historical volatility, the line chart considers only closing prices, or the last trades of the day. The line chart is also a common way of viewing stock prices graphically. For instance, Figure 3.3 (taken from the Optionetics.com site) shows the past prices of AOL Time Warner. By punching the ticker symbol AOL into the stock quote box and selecting "chart," you can create a similar graph at any time. On the right-hand side of the chart, or the vertical axis, the stock price is displayed. This is known as the price label. At the time the chart was created, the stock price was near $40 a share. Along the bottom of the chart, on the horizontal axis, the dates are displayed (the time label). In this case, the months are listed.

The price line generated in a stock chart connects the closing prices of the stock through time and offers traders a visual sense of the stock's historical volatility. Therefore, a stock like AOL that has fairly sharp price swings will have a chart with significant peaks and valleys. Compare Figure 3.3 to the chart of General Motors (GM) shown in Figure 3.4. Notice that the price fluctuations are less dramatic on the GM chart. At the time these charts were drawn, the statistical volatility on AOL was nearly 50 percent while the stock price of General Motors was only 22 percent, or less than half.

Line charts are useful for viewing the performance of stock prices over time, but

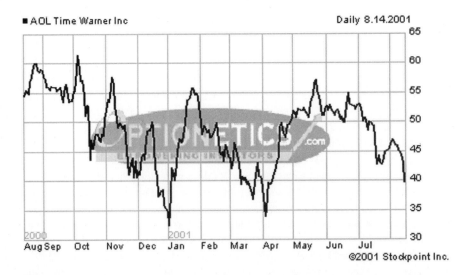

Figure 3.3   AOL One-Year Line Chart (Courtesy of Optionetics.com)

Figure 3.4   GM One-Year Line Chart (Courtesy of Optionetics.com)

are limited in that the closing prices are the only ones included on the graph. Recall that throughout the trading day a stock has an open, a high, a low, and a close. To view each graphically, the trader can create an OHLC chart, which incorporates all four pieces of data. On the Optionetics.com web site, this is referred to as a range bar chart.

The advantage of the range bar chart over the line chart is it allows one to see the price ranges of a stock throughout the trading day. When the vertical bars on the price chart are quite long, this suggests that the stock price has exhibited relatively high levels of volatility throughout the trading day. When the vertical bars are short, however, it suggests a fairly narrow intraday trading range. Compare the OHLC chart in Figure 3.5 of AOL Time Warner to that of Colgate-Palmolive (CL) (Figure 3.6). A stock exhibiting high volatility will have greater peaks and valleys on the stock chart and also longer vertical bars on the range bar chart.

AVERAGE TRUE RANGE

When measuring volatility, some traders consider the distance between the high and low prices of a stock throughout the day to be just as important as closing prices. Thus, OHLC charts are sometimes considered superior to line charts. In keeping with this line of thinking, J. Welles Wilder Jr. created an indicator called Average True Range (ATR). Average True Range separates itself from statistical volatility in that it also considers the open, high, and low prices of a stock or index.

Wilder introduced the ATR system in his 1978 book, *New Concepts in Technical Trading Systems*. Rather than simply taking the closing price of a stock over a period

Figure 3.5   AOL One-Year Range Bar Chart (Courtesy of Optionetics.com)

Figure 3.6   CL One-Year Price Chart (Courtesy of Optionetics.com)

of time, he defined ATR as the greatest of either: (1) the current high minus the current low, (2) the current high minus the previous close, or (3) the current low minus the previous close. In general, if the difference between the high and low of the day is large, it will be used as the true range (TR). In instances when the difference between the high and low is relatively small, one of the other two methods will typically be the TR. The Average True Range is simply an average of the TRs over time. Fourteen days is a common time frame to use when averaging the true ranges. Obviously, computing ATR would be a cumbersome task without the aid of computer.

The best way to view ATR is over a period of time alongside a stock price chart. An example of ATR with a stock price chart of AOL is shown in Figure 3.7. Notice that during periods of high volatility—seen as long vertical bars and a fluctuating price chart—ATR rises. During periods of sideways trading, ATR moves lower. The next chapter will explore ways to use ATR to trade historical volatility.

BOLLINGER BANDS

Bollinger bands have become one of the most widely used measures of volatility among traders today. Developed by John Bollinger, this innovative indicator uses a moving average as an input along with the standard deviation (defined earlier). As with Average True Range, Bollinger bands are best viewed graphically and are not practical to compute by hand.

Just to make sure we're all on the same page, let's define a moving average.

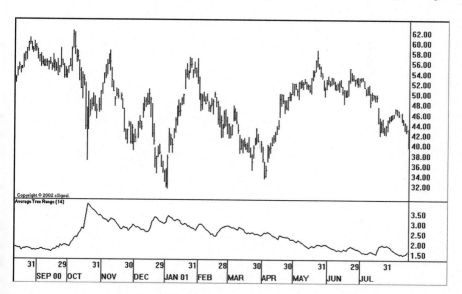

Figure 3.7   One-Year Chart of AOL with ATR Indicator (*Source:* eSignal)

Moving averages are simply the average of a stock price over a set period of time. For instance, if a stock closes at $40, $44, $50, $48, $50, and $52 at the end of six trading days, the four-day moving average at the end of the fifth day is $48, or [($44 + $50 + $48 + $50)/4 = $48]. Importantly, as each new day is added to the moving average, the earliest price is removed. So, in the previous example, the four-day moving average at the end of the sixth day equals $50 [($50 + $48 + $50 + $52)/4 = $50]. Moving averages are most often used over a period of 20, 50, or 200 days.

Moving averages are commonly plotted alongside a stock's price chart. For example, Figure 3.8 shows a daily stock chart of J. P. Morgan Chase with a 20-day moving average. Individual traders, professionals, and institutional investors often use the 50- and 200-day moving average (MA) as a method of timing buys and sells, as well as locating key support levels. For example, when a shorter moving average like the 50-day crosses above a longer one like the 200-day it is a major buy signal. This technique is often used to determine overbought or oversold conditions in the market.

Bollinger bands are moving standard deviations. What this means is that the chart plots the two standard deviations above and below the last price bar each day, taking into account the mean of the previous 20 days' prices. After each new trading day, the price data from the first day is dropped off and replaced with the new data (hence, the "moving" average). As this occurs, you can see that the bands will converge and diverge as movement in the stock (volatility) increases or decreases over time. This is what makes the Bollinger bands a unique visual gauge of a stock's volatility. When movement in the stock is less volatile, the bands come together. When the movement of the stock becomes more hyperactive and volatile, the bands will diverge or widen.

Now, in statistical jargon, the first standard deviation will contain roughly 68 percent of the price data of the stock, and two standard deviations contain 95 percent of the price data. To better understand this concept, consider the bell curve in Figure 3.9. This chart represents the grades received on a high school history exam. The first standard deviation of grades will fall somewhere around a grade of C, which is the average or mean; 68 percent of the grades fall between C– and C+. The next standard deviation contains Bs and Ds. Between a D– and a B+ is where 95 percent of the grades given on the exam fall (two standard deviations from both sides of the mean, or C). Finally, there are only a couple of As and one or two Fs.

An important difference between the Bollinger bands and the history test example is that Bollinger bands are moving standard deviations. In other words, the indicator considers the two standard deviations above and below the last 20-day

---

Moving average: One of the most popular lagging indicators, moving averages are used to analyze price action over a specified period of time on an average basis. Moving averages can be simple averages of a stock's closing prices or they can be weighted or smoothed in various ways.

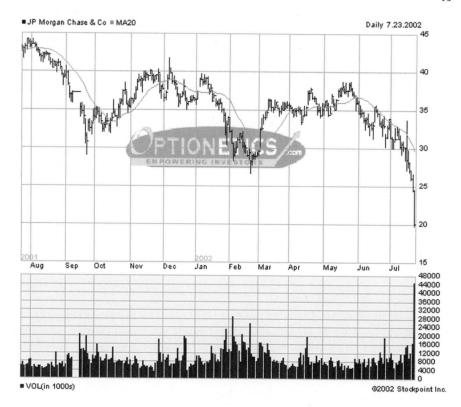

Figure 3.8   JPM Bar Chart with Moving Average (Courtesy of Optionetics.com)

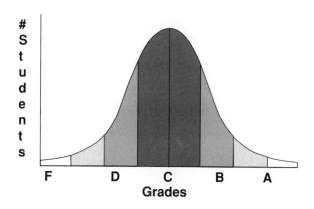

Figure 3.9   Bell Curve with Standard Deviations (Courtesy of Optionetics.com)

moving average. After each new trading day, the earliest price is dropped and replaced with the new data.

As the stock price changes through time, the bands will become wider and narrower, indicating an increase or decrease in the stock's volatility over time. This is what makes the Bollinger bands a unique visual gauge of a stock's volatility. When movement in the stock is less volatile, the bands come together. When the movement of the stock becomes more hyperactive and volatile, the bands will diverge or widen. The next chapter will consider how to make predictions concerning a stock price's future movement using Bollinger bands.

BETA

The final measure of historical volatility is beta. Although I don't personally find beta quite as useful as other historical volatility indicators, it is highly regarded by others in the financial community. Beta is an indicator of a stock's volatility relative to the market as a whole. It gauges how a stock's price movement correlates to the changes in the entire stock market.

To calculate beta, one first assigns the value of 1.00 to a broad market average: for instance, the S&P 500. A stock with a beta of 2.00 will see price swings twice as great as the market. For instance, if the S&P 500 rises 5 percent, the stock will increase by 10 percent. In contrast, a stock with a low beta will be more stable than the market; when the S&P 500 declines by 20 percent, a stock with a beta of .5 will fall only 10 percent. In Street talk, a high-beta stock is a high-volatility stock and a riskier investment.

Through the years, financial theory has held that high-beta or more volatile stocks have a better chance of moving higher than low-volatility stocks. This is the familiar risk/reward trade-off that students of finance learn early in their studies. For instance, a certificate of deposit (CD) at the local bank carries much less risk than a speculative investment in a start-up Internet company. At the same time, the potential reward is far less as well. As you move up the risk echelon, the potential reward also becomes higher. It is important to note, however, that trading volatility has little to do with the traditional risk/reward equation depicted in Figure 3.10. Stocks will vary in terms of levels of volatility and beta. What is more important is that traders understand how to measure the overall levels of volatility and structure trading strategies around that information. In that respect, beta offers little relevant information.

CONCLUSION

As a lecturer and an instructor, my methods of teaching new traders have always started at the basic level. This chapter has covered a lot of ground. Consequently, for some, much of the information reviewed so far is not new. Still, in order to understand historical volatility, the reader must first understand the mechanics of stock

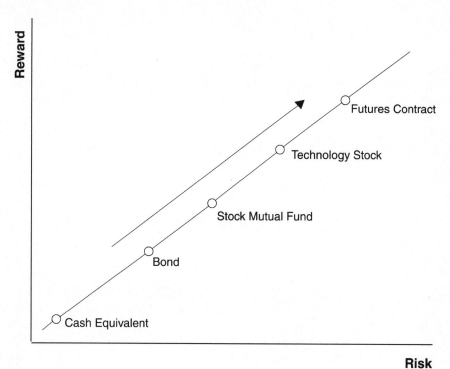

Figure 3.10   Risk/Reward Chart

trading and obtaining price quotes. Armed with a computer and an Internet connection, this is fairly easy to do.

To trade volatility, the trader must also make a distinction between two types of volatility. On the one hand, there is implied volatility—which is covered in later chapters and is derived through the price of an option. On the other hand, there is the subject of this chapter: historical volatility. Historical volatility simply means volatility that is computed using historical prices. Statistical volatility falls into this category. Some of the other measures of volatility discussed in this chapter also use historical, or past, prices. The examples are Average True Range, Bollinger bands, and beta. However, most people use the terms historical volatility and statistical volatility interchangeably. While the math is not extraordinarily difficult to understand, it is not necessary to compute by hand. All of the information is available at the Optionetics.com Platinum site.

This chapter also offered an introduction to stock charts and indicators. Both are invaluable tools to the volatility trader. Stock charts provide a graphical look at a stock price's performance and can give the trader a quick sense of the volatility associated with a specific investment. Meanwhile, indicators such as Bollinger bands can help you to pinpoint trading opportunities in anticipation of changes in volatility. The next chapter is designed to show you exactly how.

4

Trading Historical Volatility

Throughout history, there have been several episodes of extreme market volatility. In the spring of 2000, concerns over corporate profitability within the technology sector sent the Nasdaq Composite index into a nosedive. In the fall of 1998, concerns over the state of the global financial system triggered mass selling and spiraling stock prices. The years 1991, 1989, 1987, and 2002 all saw periods of high volatility. Turning back the pages of the financial history books brings forth numerous examples of panic, mayhem, and chaos.

As traders, we have learned to understand and appreciate that the stock market is not always an oasis of tranquility. In fact, it is more like a manic-depressive beast capable of turning on a dime. Given its unpredictable nature, our trading strategies can not depend solely on a never-ending climb skyward in stock prices. The simple fact is that the stock market moves lower at times; those periods can seem like an eternity for the investor simply looking to make money by trading stocks to the upside.

For more than 15 years, I have searched for profit-making opportunities in the financial markets. This is what I do for a living; I can't afford to be on the sidelines—even during periods of falling stock prices. In all honestly, there have been times when I've wished I was a baker or a cattle rancher in Montana instead of a trader, but those difficult times taught me some valuable lessons. I have learned to appreciate and understand that there is no way to predict with certainty what the market will do next. I've also realized that, although stock prices fall at times, it does not mean that there won't be profit-making opportunities when it happens. The final lesson, which is one of the most important and the subject of detailed discussion throughout this book, is risk management. Given that I am a professional trader, these lessons have changed my approach to the market and made it quite different from the way the majority of people choose to trade.

In the previous chapter, the reader was introduced to a number of ways of measuring past volatility—historical or statistical volatility, Average True Range (ATR), Bollinger bands, and beta. Each measure provides a unique look at volatility. For instance, statistical volatility uses the standard deviation of past stock prices over a period of time. When a stock or index swings wildly, its statistical volatility will rise. On the other hand, there are times that stocks or indexes move sideways and exhibit low levels of statistical volatility. Therefore, statistical volatility (and other measures of historical volatility) can be used to gauge whether a stock has been trading quietly and in a narrow range, or erratically with wide swings and large price movements.

In this chapter, we'll be looking at each measure of volatility and how it can be used to develop effective trading strategies. Now that the reader understands how to compute historical volatility, view it on a chart, and interpret it, how can that information help to create trading strategies that make healthy profits? In later chapters, the reader will learn to structure specific option strategies using historical volatility.

TRADING HISTORICAL VOLATILITY IN THE STOCK MARKET

Regardless of whether a trader is using Bollinger bands, statistical volatility, or ATR to view historical volatility, it is important to remember that using these indicators is like trying to drive forward while looking in the rearview mirror. Thus, as historical volatility measures past prices, it offers little information about what will happen in the future. In addition, it is important to keep in mind that volatility is always in a state of flux. Although it is possible to assign a value to the past behavior of a stock or index, it is impossible to predict whether the same levels will recur in the future.

Given the dynamic and changing nature of statistical volatility, the trader must also take into account unusual events. For instance, if a trader studied the historical volatility of the Dow Jones Industrial Average in late-September 1987, he or she would be grossly underestimating volatility because it only includes closing prices through September of that year. In other words, the stock market crash, or Bloody Monday, led to a sharp and instantaneous increase in volatility.

At the same time, that event was unusual and unlikely to recur. When there is a unique and usual event, it can cause a spike in historical volatility that is not sustainable. Therefore, in looking at statistical volatility it is also important to consider different time frames and acknowledge the impact of unusual occurrences, such as panics, earnings surprises, and other unexpected events.

Traders, therefore, must consider historical volatility over different time frames and make a determination as to what is normal for that particular stock or index. By considering an average value of historical volatility over a period of time, unusual periods of high or low volatility become more obvious. If, for instance, the average volatility of AOL over the past 90 days is 35 percent, but over the past 10 days it rises to 75 percent, the large increase warrants investigation. What caused the large increase in volatility? Perhaps it was earnings news, a takeover attempt, or some other one-time event.

In trading historical volatility, there is an important concept to understand: reversion to the mean. That is, although historical volatility is always in a state of change, most stocks or indexes can be assigned a "normal" or average value. When volatility diverges greatly from that normal range, there is a tendency for it to revert back to that average, or mean. Historical volatility enables traders to approximate the normal range and to find deviations from the mean for developing profit-making trading opportunities.

MORE ON MOVING AVERAGES

Before we discuss various ways to trade historical volatility, let's first take a closer look at moving averages. There are two reasons for doing so. First, moving averages are often used in conjunction with volatility indicators. For instance, Bollinger bands are computed using standard deviations of the moving average. In addition, many of the strategies I teach will utilize moving averages as indicators. Second, moving averages are useful in understanding trends with respect to the market and individual stocks. They offer a way of smoothing out stock prices over time to gain a visual sense of what is happening with a stock or index over a predefined period. Moving averages give the trader a feel for whether buyers (bulls) or sellers (bears) are in control of the market in question.

The stock market is a place where people go to invest, trade, or speculate. Sometimes buyers who have a bullish or favorable outlook on a stock take control and drive prices higher. Other times, sellers dominate trading, which sends prices lower. The masses of buyers and sellers in the market are sometimes called "the crowd." Stocks and indexes change over time because the crowd buys and sells shares. When the crowd is dominated by bulls, stock prices move higher; but when bears control trading, the disproportional amount of selling takes the market lower.

Periods of high volatility generally occur when investors become driven by emotion. For instance, market crashes are created out of fear: mob psychology reigns, the crowd panics, shares are sold, and prices spiral downward. Other times, out of greed, investors buy aggressively, chase stocks ever higher, and drive prices too high. During such episodes of extreme fear or greed, there is a tendency for the crowd to overreact and push stock prices way too high or low. This can happen with indexes (the market) or individual stocks. Savvy traders do not get caught up in the periods of panic or euphoria, but rely on market indicators to keep a bearing on reality.

Technical traders often use the terms "overbought" and "oversold" to describe the situation when a stock or index price has been driven to an extreme. Overbought conditions exist when prices have been driven too far to the upside. In other words, relative to normal conditions, a stock or index has moved upward considerably and unsustainably. This can occur in very short time frames or over long periods of time. However, regardless of the duration, when stocks are over-bought they have a natural tendency to revert back to toward their historical norms. When stocks or indexes fall from overbought levels back towards normal levels, it is referred to as a "correction." An oversold stock has fallen too far and will have a tendency to revert back to its mean by moving higher. The question is: How does one gauge what normal or average levels are? There are a number of indicators for doing so; one of the most commonly used is the moving average. Later in the book, I'll discuss ways that Bollinger bands can be used to identify over-bought and oversold market conditions.

Moving averages are a common tool for studying stock prices over a period of time and gauging levels of market psychology. The moving average indicator is not a measure of volatility, but of average stock prices. Recall that the moving average is computed as the average price of a stock or index over a fixed number of trading days. There are only two factors under consideration when computing moving averages: the stock price and the time frame (generally, measured as n number of days). The formula is straightforward:

$$MA = \frac{P_1 + P + \ldots P_n}{n}$$

Where:
P = price
n = the number of days in the moving average

Few traders compute moving averages by hand, but rely on stock charting software to create a moving average for them. The moving average is generally plotted along with the stock price on a chart. For instance, a 50-day moving average for Eastman Kodak (EK) appears alongside its stock price chart in Figure 4.1. The number of days used in the moving average depends on the trader's objectives. Short-term traders generally use fewer days: for instance, 5, 10, or 13. Longer-term investors often work with longer time periods. Fifty- or 200-day moving averages are commonly used for studying long-term trends with regard to a stock or an index.

Moving averages provide a number of ways to assess market performance. The first is to consider its direction. When a stock is strong and moving higher, the moving average will take on an upward slope. Therefore, when investors are predominantly bullish on a stock and drive it higher, the moving average will take on an upward slope. It is generally a healthy sign when a moving average is trending higher. Conversely, when the chart is downward sloping, bears have seized control and are driving stock or market lower.

The traditional method for using moving averages to trade is fairly simple. A "buy" signal is triggered when the moving average begins an upward slope and the stock price closes above it. For example, Figure 4.2 uses a chart of the oil drilling giant Halliburton Co. (HAL) and the 20-day moving average. In April 2001, a bullish signal was triggered once the moving average began an upward slope and HAL closed above that line. It is not enough simply to have a crossover of the stock price

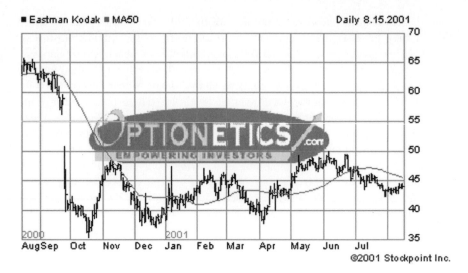

Figure 4.1   EK Price Chart with 50-Day Moving Average (Courtesy of
Optionetics.com)

Figure 4.2   HAL Price Chart with 20-Day Moving Average (Courtesy of
Optionetics.com)

and the moving average. The average must take on an upward slope. Similarly, "sell" signals are generated when the moving average takes on a downward slope and the price closes below the line. For instance, using the HAL example, see how the moving average crossed above the price line triggering a sell signal in June 2001. Generally, the shorter the time period used in the moving average, the greater the number of buy and sell signals.

Some traders dislike using moving averages to determine entry and exit points for a position because of the whipsaw nature of the trading signals; there is often a quick reversal from "buy" to "sell." To remedy this problem, some traders use two or three moving averages simultaneously. In this case, signals are generated when all of the moving averages move in the same direction. Figure 4.3 shows HAL along with 20- and 9-day moving averages. As you can see, the buy and sell signals—which occur when both moving averages move in the same direction—are less frequent.

Moving averages can also be used to identify areas of support or resistance. In technical analysis, *support* is the price at which a stock attracts a significant amount of demand—the type of buying that can stop a downward slide in a stock price. Alternately, *resistance* is a price level where a stock or index has witnessed great amounts of supply, which can stop any move higher. An upward-sloping moving average can serve as a floor when a stock is rising. Falling moving averages often serve as resistance during periods of falling prices. Notice in Figure 4.3, the 9-day moving average rides along the top and the bottom of the stock chart.

Figure 4.3 HAL Price Chart with 20- and 9-Day Moving Average (Courtesy of Optionetics.com)

For that reason, traders often buy near an upward-sloping moving average and sell as prices move upward toward a falling moving average.

The traditional methods for using moving averages are relatively straightforward, but I have a unique way of using them. First of all, you do not want to use the 9-day or 18-day moving averages or those in conjunction with one another. It is common for software programs to have these set as defaults in their systems, so many traders use them because they think they are the right ones. This is simply not the case, as most of the time the defaults have been set by programmers at these particular software companies who have never bought or sold a stock in their lives. Two moving averages that I do like are the 50- and 200-day moving averages. These are used by institutional traders and are highly regarded as trend averages, especially the 200-day MA. If the market is above the 200-day moving average, it seems that trading systems have better luck with their buy signals than their sell signals; conversely, when the market is below the 200-day MA, sell signals are more accurate.

Another way to use moving averages is to use two moving averages in conjunction with one another. This is another popular system, but I add a unique twist to the traditional crossover system. During periods of high volatility, as a market pulls back from a trend, using a shorter-term average to time your buys and sells makes great sense. For instance, if the 50-day moving average pulls back to the 200-day moving average, this sets up a nice buy signal for the stock. The same holds true for the reverse, creating a sell signal.

TRADING WITH BOLLINGER BANDS

When John Bollinger developed the ideas underlying the technical indicator that is his namesake, he probably had no idea just how popular it would become. Everybody from day traders to sophisticated financial institutions use Bollinger bands to analyze the overbought and oversold conditions relative to a stock or index. Bollinger bands are definitely one of the most useful indicators available to traders today.

Bollinger bands are based on the laws of statistics and a phenomenon known as the "normal distribution." In this case, the distribution refers to prices over a period of time, or the same information displayed on a stock chart. Normal distribution tells us that a set of data (i.e., stock prices) over a period of time will lie close to an average or mean. The moving average can be considered the mean. At any given time, prices will rise above, move below, or fall along the moving average, which represents the average price of a stock over a fixed number of days. For example, as we have already seen, the 50-day moving average is the average closing price of a stock over the course of 50 days.

Bollinger bands are computed as the standard deviations of the moving averages. The indicator consists of two bands; each lies two standard deviations away from the moving average—one above and the other below. Just as with moving averages, after each new trading day the price data from the first day is dropped off and the new data is added. As this occurs, the bands will converge and diverge as the movement in the stock (volatility) increases or decreases over time.

The tendency for Bollinger bands to converge and diverge gives the trader a sense of volatility with respect to the stock or index. In that respect, it is a unique indicator. When movement in the stock is steady and less volatile, the bands come together and become narrow; when the movement of the stock or index begins to swing wildly and volatility rises, the bands will diverge or widen.

To understand how Bollinger bands are used, recall the concept discussed earlier about reversion to the mean: Stock prices have a tendency to revert back to average or normal levels. So if a stock price moves above two standard deviations of its normal range, it is due to correct and fall back toward its moving average. The stock is considered overbought at the band two standard deviations above the moving average and oversold at two standard deviations below it.

To put it quantitatively, recall that two standard deviations encompass 95 percent of all the prices of a stock or an index over a period of time. Therefore, it is natural to assume that, since the Bollinger bands contain 95 percent of the price data between the two bands, a piercing of one of them occurs only 5 percent of the time— a rare occurrence. Since the next move of the stock is fairly predictable—it's going to fall back into the 95 percent group and head toward the moving average once again—rare events increase the possibility of profitable trades. Therefore, it is logical to expect a profit opportunity by positioning a trade based on the overbought or oversold extremes reflected in the Bollinger bands.

Now that we understand what Bollinger bands are telling us about a stock's price action, there are obvious ways to trade using the indicator. A penetration of the upper band suggests overbought conditions, and reversion to the mean tells us that the stock or index is set to head south. Conversely, when the price falls below the lower band, it is a sign that the stock has been oversold and the trader can expect a bounce back toward the mean (see Figure 4.4). Winning trades can be placed accordingly.

Bollinger bands, and technical analysis in general, can overload the brain and result in "analysis paralysis." So before moving on, let's do a little inventory to specify what makes Bollinger bands an important part of the volatility puzzle. Bollinger bands are lines around the stock price that depict the stock's historical volatility. Tops and bottoms made outside the bands indicate a trend reversal. A move originating at one band tends to go to the other band. These indicators work well for the disciplined option trader, but what about traders who don't have the discipline to go long or short when the bands line up? How about going both ways?

I look for Bollinger bands that are contracting to a point where the daily range of the market is close to touching both the upper bands and lower bands. This tells me that the market is tightening, much like the coiling of a spring. When a spring is coiled and then released, it propels itself into one direction. The market acts much the way a spring does after consolidating for several days. News may be the

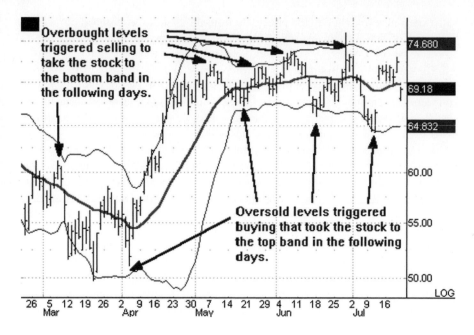

Figure 4.4 Overbought and Oversold Levels Using Bollinger Bands (Courtesy of Optionetics.com)

catalyst for the impending move, but often it's the quiet stocks that jump to big highs or lows.

Breakout moves from narrow Bollinger bands are great for options traders who know how to play the move using neutral option strategies that can potentially make a profit whether the stock moves higher or lower. For those who don't want the hassle of trying to figure out which way the market may move, a straddle—the purchase of a long call and long put at the same strike and expiration—is a great way to take advantage of this kind of scenario. The straddle is discussed at length in Chapter 8.

UNDERSTANDING STATISTICAL VOLATILITY OVER DIFFERENT TIME FRAMES

Like a moving average, statistical or actual volatility is a measure of price changes over a period of time. Unlike moving averages, however, computing statistical volatility involves more than calculating an average or mean. As discussed in Chapter 2, the measure is calculated as an annualized standard deviation of stock prices over a period of days—10, 30, 90, etc.—and is viewed in terms of a percentage. It is the most important measure of historical volatility that options traders look at.

As an options trader, I primarily use statistical volatility in two ways: to gauge whether an option is cheap or expensive and as a trading tool that helps traders understand a stock's current price in relation to past trends. In Chapter 6, we will see exactly how statistical volatility is used to compute the "fair value" of an option. This enables traders to determine whether an option is a bargain or too rich to buy. For now, however, we will look at statistical volatility in terms of how it supplies information on a given stock or index's price with respect to past trends.

In order to trade historical volatility, the trader must first consider it over different time frames. Each stock or index has a unique statistical volatility. For instance, computing the historical volatility for AOL says absolutely nothing about HAL. Each stock or index has a unique statistical volatility that can be computed over different time frames. A common way to view statistical volatility over time is by looking at the 20-, 30-, and 50-day time frames. By viewing volatility over different time frames, traders can gain insights into a stock or index's trends with respect to its volatility pattern. Table 4.1 shows various levels of actual volatility using several differing time periods (20-, 30-, and 50-day) for a number of indexes. Notice, for instance, that the AMEX Biotechnology Index has a 50-day volatility that is significantly higher than its 20-day. In other words, volatility has been trending lower. In contrast, the last index on the table—the PHLX Gold Mining Index—saw an increase in volatility during that period. In other words, the 20-day volatility is much higher than the 50-day.

Computing historical volatility over different time frames can be a cumbersome task. Luckily, a number of trading programs and web sites enable traders to view the same information graphically. For example, consider what happened to Ciena Corporation (CIEN), a maker of networking equipment, on August 16, 2001. Figure 4.5 shows a price chart of CIEN with its 20-day moving average. Notice at the end of the chart that the stock price drops precipitously. In fact, on August 16 the stock dropped 30 percent after the company told investors that it would show a sharp drop in revenues and earnings going into the year 2002.

Now take a look at Figure 4.6 and you'll see that CIEN shares experienced a high level of volatility during the first half of 2001. Each line in the chart reflects a different time frame. The darkest line is a measure of statistical volatility over the longest period of time—i.e., 100 days. It is by far the smoothest and fluctuates the

Table 4.1 Statistical Volatility Table

Index	50-Day	30-Day	20-Day	Trend
AMEX Biotechnology Index	62.0%	58.0%	56.0%	Lower
Dow Jones Industrial Average	22.0	16.0	16.0	Lower
TheStreet.com Internet Index	84.0	67.0	64.0	Lower
S&P MidCap index	27.0	21.0	22.0	Lower/higher
Nasdaq 100 index	66.0	52.0	50.0	Lower
AMEX Networking Index	76.0	58.0	51.0	Lower
S&P 100 index	27.0	18.0	17.0	Lower
PHLX Gold Mining Index	39.0	45.0	47.0	Higher

Figure 4.5   CIEN Price Chart with 20-Day Moving Average (Courtesy of Optionetics.com)

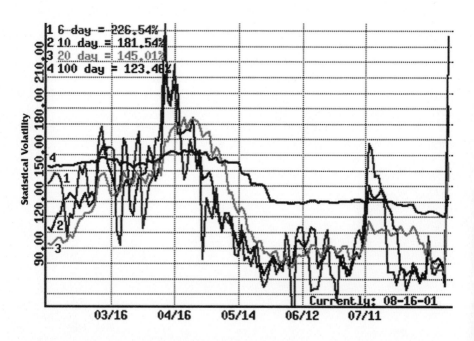

Figure 4.6   Statistical Volatility Chart of CIEN Using 6, 10, 20, and 100 Days (Courtesy of Optionetics.com)

least. When the chart was created, on the same day that shares plunged 30 percent on August 16, 2001, the 100-day historical volatility was 123.5 percent. By most measures, the 100-day statistical volatility on CIEN was quite high.

Now let's consider what the additional time periods of statistical volatility have to say. The other lines on the chart reflect Ciena's statistical volatility over shorter time frames: 20, 10, and 6 days. Notice that the shorter the time frame, the greater the fluctuations in the statistical volatility. Also, when volatility spikes higher, the 6-day statistical volatility reacts the most. On August 16, 2001, it surged to over 200 percent! That is extreme volatility.

Finally, there is an obvious tendency for statistical volatility to revert to the mean. In other words, the longer-term volatility (the 100-day) remains relatively flat compared to the others. At the same time, the other measures rise and fall above and below the longer-term measure, which can be considered a better gauge of average or normal levels. Therefore, short-term spikes in statistical volatility are often followed by a move lower (in volatility), and periods of extremely low volatility often anticipate a spike in statistical volatility. In short, by looking at statistical volatility over different time frames, the trader will be in a better position to assess whether it has reached extremes.

Although historical volatility can be used to measure the past movement of a stock, I also like to use it to gauge when a stock is likely to get quiet or explosive. One way that I have found to do this involves looking at two periods of volatility: a short-term average and a long-term average. I call this the 10/90 Volatility System, and it's pretty easy to learn.

First, I take a 10-day period historical volatility reading—basically the last 10 days of historical volatility annualized. Then I do the exact same thing using the 90-day historical volatility. The 10-day is considered a short-term reading, while the 90-day is considered a longer-term reading. I measure the ratio between these two volatilities. A very low 10/90 ratio suggests that the underlying stock is consolidating. What is so special about a volatility indicator telling you that a stock is quiet? Well, quiet stocks can become explosive stocks in a matter of time.

Let's create an example using the Optionetics.com Platinum site. Figure 4.7 provides a reading taken on April 5, 2002. Here we simply choose to evaluate the 10-day over the 90-day statistical (historical) volatility. By clicking on the Quiet button, we will be shown only stocks whose ratios are lowest when looking at the entire stock list.

Figure 4.8 details the top 10 stocks with a ratio of 10-day to 90-day volatility of

Figure 4.7   10/90 Volatility Search (Courtesy of Optionetics.com)

Rk	Stock Symbol	Stock Name	Stock Price ↑ ↓	6 day SV ↑ ↓	10 day SV ↑ ↓	20 day SV ↑ ↓	90 day SV ↑ ↓
1	JPM	J.P. Morgan Chase & Co.	34.44	15.25	15.3	28.07	42.04
2	TYC	Tyco International Ltd.	32.25	35.49	37.35	33.79	84.17
3	YHOO	Yahoo! Inc.	17.66	37.55	35.05	52.78	75.78
4	MRK	Merck & Co., Inc.	55.8	17.17	14.1	25.38	27.52
5	HWP	Hewlett-Packard Company	17.25	19.37	20.25	28.31	37.38
6	JNJ	Johnson & Johnson	63.48	8.44	9.05	12.11	16.59
7	NOK	Nokia Corporation ADR	20.03	36.29	30.26	35.79	54.79
8	NVLS	Novellus Systems, Inc.	51.07	44.95	37	45.44	66.66
9	NTAP	Network Appliance Corp.	19.69	61.24	58.29	52.52	100.01
10	GNSS	Genesis Microchip, Inc.	23	64.17	77.28	71.29	127.41

Figure 4.8   10/90 Volatility System—Top 10 Stocks (Courtesy of Optionetics.com)

approximately 0.6 or lower. These stocks have had much lower volatility in the past 10 days than they have had over the past 90 days. Let's look at a chart to visualize this "quietness" that is going on in Yahoo! Inc., the third stock on the list (see Figure 4.9).

Ratios of 0.5 or less indicate that the last 10 trading days saw less than half the volatility of the last 90 trading days. This kind of reading is a signal for a possible volatility breakout, which is a great system for trading straddles. If the market is likely to explode, but we are not sure where, then applying a neutral strategy that offers the possibility of making money in either direction can be very profitable.

USING ATR

The Average True Range (ATR) is a measure of historical volatility that, unlike statistical volatility, encompasses more than just the closing prices of a stock. In Chapter 2, we defined ATR and how it is computed. Recall that the measure can be used to gauge the past volatility of a stock or index over a period of time. Generally, ATR is a 14-day average of the true range (TR), where TR is defined as the greatest of the following:

- The current high minus the current low.

- The absolute value of the current high minus the previous close.

- The absolute value of the current low minus the previous close.

The advantage of the ATR over statistical volatility is that it accounts for not only the closing price of a stock or option, but also the highs and lows. Welles Wilder, who was using the indicator relative to commodity prices, was attempting to create a measure of volatility that would account for gaps and limit moves. A

Figure 4.9 Yahoo! Price and Volume Chart (Courtesy of Optionetics. com)

limit move occurs when a commodity opens sharply higher or lower and then does not trade again that day. It transpires when the price change at the open reaches the allowable limit. Limit moves do not apply to stocks or indexes.

Gaps are more common with stocks. A gap occurs when a stock opens sharply higher or lower relative to the previous close. If a stock opens significantly above the previous day's closing levels, it is known as a "gap up." If the first trade of the day is significantly below the previous session's close, it is called a "gap down." Figure 4.5 shows a gap down at the very end of the CIEN chart.

The Average True Range is the average of the true ranges over a period of time. If the span between a stock price's high and low is large, then, in all likelihood, the difference between the high and low will be used to compute the TR. If the range between the high and low is small, then one of the other two methods is more likely to be used. Generally, the last two methods are used when there is a sharp gap up or gap down. For instance, if the stock gaps down, the previous close would be greater than the current high. Then the TR would be the previous close minus the day's low, instead of the difference between the high and low of the day.

ATR is most often viewed graphically along the bottom of a stock chart, as in Figure 4.10. This chart includes a range bar chart of IBM along with ATR from

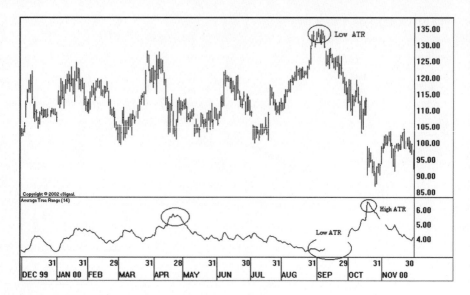

Figure 4.10   Chart of IBM with ATR (*Source:* eSignal)

December 1999 through November 2000. When IBM fell precipitously and gapped down in October, the Average True Range spiked higher. But, when the stock price was moving steadily upward in an orderly manner in August and September, ATR was giving off low readings.

Trading signals occur when ATR reaches extreme highs and lows. For instance, when IBM hit a peak on the chart and the Average True Range was at extreme lows, it forewarned of an impending move lower. That is, IBM made a move higher in a steady fashion, and volatility, measured by ATR, fell to abnormally low levels. This could be because of an absence of news or market-moving events. These periods of quiet trading, however, do not generally last, and the trader should expect volatility to rise. Unusually large spikes in ATR often result from sharp, sudden moves higher or lower that are not likely to last. For example, when shares of IBM fell precipitously in October 2000, ATR spiked higher and marked a temporary bottom in the stock price. From there, the Average True Range started to move toward its historical levels and the volatility in IBM shares subsided.

When dealing with Average True Range, just as with most other indicators discussed in this book, the trader is looking at extremes. In order to do so, the first step is to identify a "normal" level. Charting tools offer a visual way of doing so (see Figure 4.10). When ATR rises to extreme highs, the path of least resistance is to the downside, and chances are the stock will reverse course. Conversely, when the Average True Range is abnormally low there will be a tendency for it to rise, which can mean a significant move higher or lower in the stock or index.

STANDARD DEVIATION VERSUS ATR

Both standard deviation and Average True Range can be used to measure historical volatility. Each measures the volatility of a stock or index in the past over a fixed period of time. Although they are sometimes used interchangeably, they are different tools. ATR is sometimes considered superior because it encompasses more information (i.e., Average True Range includes highs and lows as well as closes, whereas statistical volatility considers only closing prices). But which is better: standard deviation or ATR?

The idea when trading any measure of historical volatility—statistical volatility, moving averages, Bollinger bands, or ATR—is that there is a normal range that the stock prices will gravitate toward. Traders look for deviations to determine whether the price of a stock or index has been driven beyond what is normal. For instance, using Bollinger bands, when a stock price penetrates the upper or lower band it has moved two standard deviations away from the moving average. Since two standard deviations encompass 95 percent of the stock prices under consideration, the penetration of the band represents an extreme departure from what is normal—in other words, it occurs only 5 percent of the time. From that point, the trader can expect the stock price to revert to its average levels.

Therefore, a superior indicator of historical volatility will offer a reliable gauge of what is normal and allow fewer false buy and sell signals. A false signal would occur if, for instance, a stock price penetrates the upper Bollinger band and, instead of moving back toward its moving average, continues to move higher. The trader depends on extreme divergences from what is considered normal to trigger trading signals.

An interesting study comparing Average True Range with standard deviation appeared in *Technical Analysis of Stocks & Commodities* (June 2001, pp. 46–50). In the article, the author, Gordon Gustafson, tested the effectiveness of trading signals generated by both indicators on the S&P 500 from March 8, 1991, until December 2, 2000 (2,500 days). The two indicators under observation included the ATR and the 20-day moving average with bands at two standard deviations above and below. The first test was designed to measure which indicator allowed, in the words of the author, "fewer price excursions." Again the idea is that the superior indicator will consider only the closes outside the normal range that trigger valid trading signals. Over the course of the study, "For the STDEV [standard deviation] bands, 173 closes fell outside the two standard deviation range. The bands captured 93.1 percent of the closes. This is about what you'd expect given the mathematical theory behind STDEV. . . . The ATR, however, let 330 closes fall outside of the range: it captured only 86.8 percent of the closes." Therefore, the Average True Range generated more trading signals than the standard deviation.

The study then looked at the number of times that the indicators fell outside the normal ranges simultaneously. The goal was to determine the degree of correlation between the two indicators. If two sets of data are highly correlated, then they behave similarly. For instance, if the two indicators have a correlation of +1, they are giving the exact same information. This is called a perfect positive correlation, while a correlation of –1 is a perfect negative correlation and tells us that the two sets of data behave in an opposite manner. According to Gustafson:

> Surprisingly, the correlation analysis showed that there was significant difference between the two indicators. The coefficient ranged between –.56 and .32 over the test, showing that each indicator, while measuring volatility in its own way, did so differently than the other. . . . In other words, each indicator showed a particular period more or less volatile than the other, and sometimes one even measured the volatility as increasing while the other showed it as decreasing. The average value over the whole test was –.05, indicating that there was no correlation whatsoever between the two indicators. This test clearly shows that there are significant differences in the way these two indicators measure volatility. They are not interchangeable.

CONCLUSION

There are a number of different ways to measure historical volatility, and each is unique. Rarely can one be substituted for another. In this chapter, the reader was introduced to possible trading signals generated by a number of different indicators like Bollinger bands, statistical volatility, moving averages, and Average True Range (ATR). Used alone, each can be valuable by providing a specific look at a stock or the market's past price movement. Used together, the indicators can be powerful tools for identifying specific trading opportunities.

Although not a measure of volatility, moving averages are the first indicators discussed in this chapter. Generally plotted along with the stock or index price, a moving average can be used in any number of ways. First, traders often consider its slope. When the moving average takes on an upward slope, it is a sign of a healthy trend in the stock or index. Conversely, when the MA begins moving lower, it is a sign of downward momentum. In addition, some traders use crossovers between the moving average and stock price to generate buy and sell signals. When the MA begins an upward slope and the stock price closes above it, a buy signal is triggered. In contrast, when the stock closes below a downward-sloping moving average, it gives a sell signal. Using crossovers between two moving averages with different time frames (e.g., the 50-day and 200-day) can also provide trading signals. Finally, moving averages can also be used to identify areas of support and resistance on a stock chart.

The tendency for Bollinger bands to converge and diverge gives the trader a sense of volatility with respect to the stock or index. The indicator consists of two lines, or bands. When a stock is trading quietly or in a narrow range, the bands come together and become narrow. Conversely, when the movement of the stock or index begins to swing wildly and volatility rises, the bands will diverge or widen. Therefore, Bollinger bands give a visual sense of a stock's volatility. Also, the indicator can be used to identify overbought and oversold conditions. A penetration of the upper band suggests overbought conditions and reversion to the mean tells us that the stock or index is set to head south. However, when the price falls below the lower band, it is a sign that the stock has been oversold and the trader can expect a bounce back toward the mean.

Statistical volatility is one of the most important tools to the options trader. It is computed as the annualized standard deviation of a stock price over a period of days. When looking at statistical volatility, the trader wants to consider it over time. For example, using the charting tools at the Optionetics.com Platinum site, it is possible to chart the 20-day statistical volatility for almost any stock or index. Doing so will reveal whether the volatility of a stock is rising or falling. In addition, it is sometimes useful to consider statistical volatility over different time frames. For instance, is the 90-day statistical volatility of a stock substantially different from the 10-day volatility? There is a tendency for statistical volatility to revert to the mean. The longer-term volatility (90-day) remains relatively flat compared to the others. Shorter-term measures (e.g., 10-day) often rise above and fall below the longer-term measure. However, the long-term volatility is a better gauge of the stock's true volatility. Therefore, short-term spikes in statistical volatility are often followed by a move lower (in volatility), and periods of extremely low volatility often occur prior to a spike in statistical volatility. In sum, by looking at statistical volatility over different time frames, the trader will be in a better position to assess whether it has reached extremes.

Average True Range (ATR) is another useful indicator that provides a look at a stock or market's historical volatility. It is most often viewed on a stock chart below the price data. Trading signals occur when ATR reaches extremes. When it rises to abnormal highs, it suggests that the stock or market is oversold and due to bounce higher. On the other hand, when it falls to extreme lows, it indicates overbought conditions and that the stock is at risk of heading south.

When looking at the past price action of a stock and its historical volatility using the indicators in this chapter, there are a number of important factors to keep in mind. First, each stock will have a unique level of volatility. Therefore, the volatility of IBM shares will tell us almost nothing about Microsoft. Second, the tools and indicators in this chapter look at past stock prices and do not necessarily give information about a stock or market's future price movements or volatility. Third, looking at historical volatility requires recognizing unusual events. For example, if a stock plunges because the CEO absconds with millions, that event is probably not going to happen again. The volatility associated with the event is likely to pass. Fourth, it is important to consider historical volatility over different time frames. For example, comparing the 10-day statistical volatility to a stock's 90-day statistical volatility can give information regarding short-term and long-term trends. Finally, reversion to the mean is central to successfully trading historical volatility. Reversion to the mean simply tells us that a stock or index will have a normal or average level of volatility, and when volatility rises well above or falls well below that normal range, we can expect it to revert back toward its average. It is one of the most important concepts for the volatility trader to understand.

5

The World of Stock Options

If you are serious about learning to trade volatility, developing an in-depth understanding of the options market is a must. The first part of this chapter, then, is a refresher course on options. Those with an understanding of stock options, index options, and other derivatives might simply wish to skim through this chapter. But remember: A basic understanding of options is essential to your success. What is the difference between a put and a call? How do you find an options chain? Where are options traded? What is involved in the buying and selling of an option? How are option spreads created and why? And, most importantly, how are option prices derived?

Having traded various types of investments over the years, I've found that stock and index options offer the greatest degree of versatility. For example, strategies can be created to do just about anything—from limiting risk to embarking on wild speculation. Furthermore, options can be tailored to create scenarios with extremely high rewards but with limited risk of capital losses. Consider some of the situations an option strategist can create:

• Generate an income stream.

• Protect an existing stock position.

• Speculate on the move higher or lower in a stock.

• Position a trade to profit on a big swing in a stock, regardless of market direction.

• Profit from a move sideways in a stock.

Like stocks, options trade on exchanges and can be bought and sold. Unlike stocks, however, option prices are derived from a variety of factors, and one of the most important is implied volatility (IV). Up to this point, the discussion of volatility has centered on historical measures. As we have seen in the past two chapters, historical volatility is a measure of stock prices that have existed in the past over a certain period of time. The options trader, however, is concerned with not only the overall levels of volatility that existed in the past, but, more importantly, the level of volatility that will exist in the future. There is, of course, no way to know for sure, but sophisticated options strategists are continually looking forward and attempting to make an assessment of what the future volatility of a stock or index might be.

Options provide a constant stream of information about volatility. As derivatives, options derive value from the price of another asset. For instance, AOL options are a function of, or are derived from, the stock price of AOL Time Warner. The volatility of that asset, in this case AOL shares, is an important factor in determining the price of the option. In short, the price of an option is derived from another asset—not only the price of that stock or index, but also its volatility. Option prices on a high-volatility stock will be higher than those on the equivalent option on a low volatility stock (with the same price). In conclusion, the option price at any given point in time implies a level of volatility for the asset from which it derives its value.

UNDERSTANDING STOCK OPTIONS

Before launching into our discussion of implied volatility, a discussion of options is in order. As noted earlier, options are among the most versatile and exciting investment vehicles available for trading today. Unfortunately, sometimes it seems that they have received a bad rap. Due to a few high-profile disasters stemming from poorly timed option trades, many investors associate options with high risk and speculative trading. Yet nothing could be further from the truth. While there are times when options are used purely for speculation, sophisticated traders also use them to create attractive risk and reward scenarios. In fact, in later chapters I'll show you how to develop strategies with the potential for unlimited profits—but virtually no risk of capital loss.

But first, what is an option? Outside of finance, an option is simply a choice. For instance, when buying a new car, you can have the option of air conditioning, leather seats, a sunroof, and other features. When dealing with financial instruments, options also give you a choice. For example, a stock that you own can be protected from a downside move or provide leverage in the case of a sharp move higher in a stock. Options can also be used to offer opportunities to make profits regardless of whether the stock or index moves in either direction. Savvy investors use options to create a consistent income stream in a wide variety of markets and market scenarios.

Learning how to profit in the exciting world of options trading requires a basic understanding of options and the options market, as well as the various options strategies that can be employed. While there's a seemingly infinite number of things to learn and understand related to options, it isn't necessary to know everything. But it is important to always remain open to learning more as you progress up the learning curve. I have been trading options for 15 years, and I still find myself learning new techniques and integrating innovative information.

While options in the financial marketplace have existed for several decades, formalized trading has existed only for roughly three decades. Prior to the early 1970s, options trading was relatively unorganized. In 1973, however, the Chicago Board Options Exchange (CBOE) formalized the trading of option contracts. Since then, in addition to the CBOE, four other exchanges have started listing options. The proliferation of options has resulted in a vibrant marketplace that offers investors a host of choices when developing investment strategies.

Options are created out of a financial agreement between two parties. It is a contract with specific and precise terms. An option gives the trader the right, but not the obligation, to buy (call) or sell (put) a stock or index at a specific predetermined price during a specified period of time. The stock, or index, is known as an underlying security. For instance, options to buy or sell shares of International Business Machines (IBM) have IBM as the underlying asset. In other words, the value of the option is derived from the stock price of IBM.

Options fall into one of two categories: puts and calls. The call option gives the owner, or the buyer, the right, but not the obligation, to *buy* the underlying security at a specific price during a specific period of time. The option contract specifies a price, known as the strike price, at which the stock can be bought, and a fixed date, called the expiration date, by which the transaction must take place. A put option gives the buyer the right to *sell* a specific stock (underlying asset) at a specific price over a predetermined period of time. When puts and calls trade on one of the organized exchanges, they are referred to as listed options, which, as noted earlier, have existed only since the early 1970s. This book deals only with listed options.

Option contracts are created only through buying and selling: For every buyer of an option, there is a seller. A seller is also known as a "writer." The option writer receives a payment, or premium, from the option buyer. In exchange, the seller gives the option buyer, or owner, certain rights. The writer of a call option gives the buyer the right, but not the obligation, to buy, or call, the stock at a specified price during a specific time period. The seller of a put option gives the owner the right, but not the obligation, to sell the underlying asset at a specific price during a specified period of time. In other words, the call writer agrees to deliver the underlying stock to the option owner at the strike price if the assigned owner exercises the call; the put writer agrees to buy the underlying stock from the option owner for the strike price if the assigned owner exercises the put.

Therefore, any option contract can be discussed in terms of four specifications:

1. The type: put or call.

2. The underlying stock or index: for instance, IBM or QQQ.

3. The strike price.

4. The expiration date.

In options parlance, an option is described in terms of those four variables. For instance, the IBM December 90 put provides the owner with the right to sell IBM shares for $90 until the third Friday in December. (The expiration date is always the Friday

---

Why Purchase a Call at All?

Buying a call (going long) is one of the most basic options strategies. A long call gives the owner the right, but not the obligation, to buy a stock for a certain price during a specified period of time. Speculators will buy call options because doing so provides a great deal of leverage and makes money in a bullish or rising market. They can either exercise the option and sell the stock at a profit or close the option position at a profit.

Example: Coca-Cola (KO) calls (assuming the stock price rises and other factors remain the same). In December, with KO trading for $47, a speculator buys one KO January 50 call for 70 cents.

Stock Price (KO)	Option Price	Stock Return	Option Return
$47.00	$0.70	0.00%	0.00%
$50.00	$1.90	6.40%	171.00%
$53.00	$3.85	12.80%	222.00%
$56.00	$6.35	19.20%	800.00%

---

before the third Saturday of the expiration month.) The IBM December 90 call gives the buyer the right to buy IBM for $90 up until the third Friday in December.

In order to decide which expiration months to use, you have to know which months are available. All stock options have available expiration months for the current month and the next month. When the front month options expire, the following month options become the front month and the next month options become available, and so on. In addition to the front and following months, each stock is assigned to one of three quarterly cycles: cycle 1, cycle 2, and cycle 3.

Cycle 1: January, April, July, October.

Cycle 2: February, May, August, November.

Cycle 3: March, June, September, December.

Expiration months generally do not exist beyond nine months, except for a type of option known as a long-term equity anticipation security (LEAPS—discussed later). Option buyers do not have to hold the option until it expires. Alternatively, the option can be sold at the current market price. In other words, once purchased, there is no obligation to hold an option until expiration.

It is vital to remember that an option has a limited shelf life. Every option contract is good up to a certain month and year. If you buy one call option on a stock, you can exercise your right to buy 100 shares of the underlying stock at any time until the Friday before the third Saturday of the option's expiration month. If you do not exercise an option or sell it to another option buyer before its deadline, the option expires worthless and you have gained nothing for the premium you paid for it—game over. Since options are contracts with a fixed expiration date, their value will diminish over time. This phenomenon is known as "time decay," and options are often referred to as "wasting assets." As time passes, their value will decline. In fact, many options do expire worthless. This is the primary difference between stocks and options: Unlike stocks, options come with a deadline. When you buy options, you pay money, and time decay is not on your side. When you sell options, you receive a credit, and time decay *is* on your side.

MONEYNESS

When is it better to sell an option, rather than hold it until expiration? To make this determination, traders often look at an option's "moneyness," which provides important information regarding the value of an option and the chances of that option holding value at expiration. Moneyness is expressed in terms of in-the-money, at-the-money, or out-of-the-money options. It describes the relationship between the price of an underlying asset relative to the strike price of an option on that same underlying asset. For instance, if the stock of XYZ company is trading for $50 a share, the XYZ December 50 call, with its strike price equal to the underlying asset's price, is at-the-money. Both the strike price and the stock price are equal with an at-the-money option. In this case, both equal 50. If, however, the stock price is within one or two dollars of the underlying stock's price, the options are near-the-money. In this case, the stock price is approximate, or near, to the strike price of the option contract.

Exercise and assignment: The option owner can exercise the right granted by the term of the options contract—by either calling the stock or putting the stock. The option writer, or seller, can be assigned (called or put the stock) based on the terms of the contract until the option expires. To exercise an option, the owner will instruct their broker to do so. When assigned, the brokerage firm will notify the client—who must then either sell the stock (in the case of a call) or buy the stock (in the case of the put) at the strike price of the option. If the brokerage firm notifies the client that he or she has been assigned, it is too late to try to sell the option in the market. He or she must then honor the terms of the option contract. The chances of assignment increase as expiration approaches. As a general rule, options that are in-the-money with little or no time left until expiration have the greatest chances of being assigned.

American versus European style options: In the United States, stock options settle American style, which means that exercise can take place at any time prior to expiration. European style options, however, can be exercised only at expiration (the Friday before the third Saturday of the expiration month). Most index options settle European style.

Time Decay: Part of the premium paid for an option is known as time value, and this amount is nothing more than a payment to the seller of the option to tie up the stock for the requisite time period—the longer until expiration, the higher the premium. This time value will decay, or disappear, as the option approaches the expiration date.

An in-the-money call option has a strike price below the stock price. For instance, if the option strategist buys the XYZ December 50 call, and XYZ rises in price to $55 a share, the call is in-the-money $5 (the stock price, $55, minus the strike price, 50). It's in-the-money because the 50 call gives the buyer the right to purchase XYZ at $50—a savings of $5 per share. Therefore, the higher the stock price relative to the call option's strike price, the more the call option is in-the-money.

The difference between the strike price and the underlying asset's price is known as intrinsic value. When call options have a large amount of intrinsic value and the stock price is considerably above the strike price, it is said to be deep-in-the-money. For put options, when the stock price is *below* the strike price, the put option has intrinsic value and is in-the-money. An out-of-the-money call option will have a strike price above the underlying stock's price, and an out-of-the-money put will have a strike price below the stock price. Therefore, out-of-the-money options have zero intrinsic value. When the strike price of a call option is considerably above the stock price, it is considered deep-out-of-the-money. Similarly, when the strike price on a put option is considerably below the underlying asset's price, the option is considered deep-out-of-the-money.

Knowing whether an option is in-the-money, at-the-money, or out-of-the-money will help you determine whether the option is likely to be profitable at expiration. Near expiration, an option that is in-the-money will have a greater chance of being profitable. For instance, say you purchased shares of XYZ stock for $50 a share and sold a December 50 call (i.e., a covered call on XYZ using an at-the-money call). If at expiration (the third Friday in December) the stock has risen to $55 a share, the call has an intrinsic value of $5. It is likely to be exercised and the stock will be called away from you for $50. Exercise is all but assured when an option is in-the-money at expiration. In fact, the Options Clearing Corporation (OCC) automatically exercises any option that has intrinsic value of three-quarters of a point or more at expiration—whether the option holder requests it or not.

What happens to in-the-money options before expiration? When there is a considerable amount of time left before the option expires, the chances are less that an in-the-money option will be exercised. The reason that an option with intrinsic value will probably not be exercised ahead of expiration is due to the fact that the option also has a different type of value—time value. The time value of an in-the-money call is computed as:

$$\text{Call time value} = \text{Call option price} + \text{strike price} - \text{stock price}$$
$$= \text{Call option price} - \text{intrinsic value}$$

The greater the amount of time value in the option, the less likely the option will be exercised. But time value falls as time passes. At expiration, time value will equal zero. At that time, if there is no intrinsic value (i.e., the option is not in-the-money), it becomes worthless and will not be exercised. Therefore, the odds of exercise increase as (1) the option becomes in-the-money and (2) the time value of the option diminishes.

Determining Moneyness

- **Call Options:** The time value of an option erodes as the time to expiration gets closer, whereas the intrinsic value does not erode (provided the stock price remains the same). For a call option, the stock price must be higher than the strike price for the option to have any intrinsic value.

  Option Strike Price < Stock Price　ITM Option　Intrinsic Value + Time Value

  Option Strike Price = Stock Price　ATM Option　Time Value Only

  Option Strike Price > Stock Price　OTM Option　Time Value Only

- **Put Options:** For puts, the relationship is just the opposite: the stock price must be lower than the strike price for the option to have any intrinsic value.

  Option Strike Price < Stock Price　OTM Option　Time Value Only

  Option Strike Price = Stock Price　ATM Option　Time Value Only

  Option Strike Price > Stock Price　ITM Option　Intrinsic Value + Time Value

Example

Let's calculate the intrinsic value and time value of a call option using the available option price shown in the following example for stock XYZ.

XYZ Stock = $68

Call Option Price = 9.75

Strike Price = 60

45 Days to Expiration

- **Intrinsic value** = Stock price − Strike price / Intrinsic value = 68 − 8 = **60**

- **Time value** = Call price − Intrinsic value / Time value = 9.75 − 8 = **1.75**

In the XYZ example, the $60 option was ITM with an intrinsic value of $8. The time value as derived from the example was $1.75. As the expiration day approaches (just 45 days away), the time value evaporates.

An OTM (out-of-the-money) option gets cheaper as you get further out-of-the-money. That's because an OTM option consists of nothing but time value; the more out-of-the-money an option is, the less chance it has of moving in-the-money by expiration. If the option remains OTM by expiration the option expires worthless. Many inexperienced traders see OTM options as great opportunities because of their inexpensive prices. However, the probability that an extremely OTM option will turn profitable is quite slim. The deeper ITM (in-the-money) a call or put is, the less time value and more intrinsic value the option has. Since you are paying less for time, an in-the-money option's premium moves more like the price of the underlying asset. This is also referred to as the *delta* of an option. Delta is the amount by which the price of an option changes for every dollar move in the underlying asset. Understanding delta is the key to creating delta neutral strategies, which are the foundation for many options strategies we at Optionetics teach and use daily.

What Is the OCC?

Founded in 1973, the Options Clearing Corporation (OCC) is the issuer and clearing facility for all U.S. exchange-listed options. OCC issues puts and calls on different types of underlying assets including stocks and indexes. The major options exchanges—the American Stock Exchange, the Chicago Board Options Exchange, the Pacific Exchange, the Philadelphia Stock Exchange, and the International Securities Exchange—share equal ownership in the Options Clearing Corporation.

According to the OCC, "The Options Clearing Corporation is dedicated to promoting stability and financial integrity in the options markets by focusing on effective risk management. In its role as guarantor, OCC ensures that the obligations of options contracts are fulfilled for the selling and purchasing clearing firms, regardless of the financial condition of the contra party. OCC provides substantial credit risk protection, even in times of significant market volatility. In 1993, OCC sought a credit rating from the Standard & Poor's Corporation (S&P) to establish a third party recognition of its 'AAA' rating. After reviewing OCC's operational capabilities and three-tiered backup system of financial safeguards, S&P awarded OCC with its highest 'AAA' rating. OCC's three-tiered backup system includes rigorous initial and ongoing membership standards, prudent margin requirements, and its substantial clearing fund. S&P reviews its ratings annually, and continues to consistently award the OCC a 'AAA' rating."

The OCC, then, is the safety net behind the options market and ensures that investors are not at risk from a financial collapse on the part of a broker, an exchange, or any other options market participant.

WHAT HAPPENS AT EXPIRATION?

All options expire at one point or another. Expiration occurs on the third Saturday of the expiration month. Most traders, however, refer to the Friday before the official expiration as the expiration date because that is the last business day to trade the options before they expire. For instance, the March 2002 call and put options expire on Saturday, March 16, 2002, but the last day to trade them is on Friday, March 15, 2002 (until 5:30 P.M. eastern time). So, what happens to an option at expiration? After expiration, the option ceases to exist. Prior to expiration, the owner will either (1) let it expire worthless or (2) exercise the option.

If an owner of an option has not exercised his or her right to buy (in the case of a call) or sell (in the case of a put) the underlying asset at expiration, one of two things can happen. If the option has no intrinsic value, the option expires worthless and essentially nothing happens to the trader's account (except the entire premium paid for the option is debited). But if the option has intrinsic value and the trader has not exercised the right to buy or sell a stock at expiration, there is a chance that it will be automatically exercised. The Options Clearing Corporation automatically exercises options that have intrinsic value of three-quarters of a point or more.

Many traders do not anticipate holding American options until expiration at all. Instead, the option is closed out before expiration. Anytime an option is purchased—a put or a call—it can then be sold before expiration. For instance, a call that is purchased for $3 and then increases in value to $4, has risen $1 in value. In this case, rather than waiting until expiration, the trader can sell the option and make a $1 profit. When the option is purchased, it is known as an opening transaction; when it is sold, it is a closing transaction.

MORE ON TIME DECAY

If you have been trading options for a while, you've probably heard the statistic that 75 percent or more of all option contracts expire worthless. Because options suffer from a phenomenon known as time decay, with each passing day an option decreases in value. At the same time, some options see more rapid time decay than others. In order to avoid holding worthless options at expiration, strategists must consider how time is impacting their particular options.

Stock options have fixed expiration dates. A call option gives the owner the right to buy the stock, and the put option gives the owner the right to sell a stock—but only until a certain day. An option is only valid until expiration, which is the Friday before the third Saturday of the expiration month. The time left until the option expires is known as the life of the option. As expiration approaches, the life and the value of the option will decline. Recall that options have time value premium; all else being equal, the greater the amount of time left until the option expires, the greater the time value afforded to that option.

At the same time, the rate of time decay is not linear. As an option approaches expiration, the rate of decay will increase. Therefore, an option with only three weeks remaining in its life will see a much faster rate of time decay than an equivalent option with 12 months of life remaining. Interestingly, the rate of time decay is related to the square root of the life of the option. For instance, an option with two months of life left will decay twice as fast as an option with four months left (because the square root of four equals two). Similarly, an option with four months left will decay at twice the rate of an option with 16 months left.

Opening and closing transactions: An opening transaction is the first, or initial, buy or sell option trade. For instance, if a trader buys one AOL January 40 call in anticipation of a price rise in shares of AOL Time Warner, the trade is considered an opening transaction. As we will see later, the sale of an option can also be an opening transaction. If AOL rises in price and the trader later sells that same AOL January 40 call option at a profit, it is considered a closing transaction. In short, the initial transaction is an opening transaction, and when that order is later closed out or nullified, that is a closing transaction.

DETERMINING OPTION PRICES

Time is not the only factor that determines the price of an option. In fact, as we have seen, there are four variables that define any option: type of option (put or call), the underlying asset, the strike price, and the expiration month, which reflects the time element. In addition, three other factors also help to determine an option's price: the underlying asset's volatility, the prevailing interest rate, and whether the underlying asset pays a dividend.

The price of the underlying asset is the most important factor in determining the value of an option. When the stock price is well above or below the strike price, other factors have little impact on the option price. Consider an option that is in-the-money $10 at expiration. At that point, the other factors will have no bearing on the value of the option. The value is determined solely by the value of the underlying asset and its relationship to the strike price. Thus, the price of the option at expiration is equal to its intrinsic value.

When the option has life remaining, the price reflects intrinsic value plus the time premium. Time is the second most important factor in determining an option's value. An at-the-money option will have the greatest amount of time value, while a deep-in-the-money option will have little time value and will trade near its intrinsic value. As expiration approaches, the time value premium diminishes and the option price approaches its intrinsic value. Again, the value of an option is equal to its intrinsic value at expiration. If it is not in-the-money at that time, the option has no intrinsic value and expires worthless.

The volatility of the underlying asset also has an important bearing on the price of an option: The higher the volatility of the underlying asset, the higher the option

---

What Is the Theoretical Value of an Option?

The theoretical value of an option is derived from an option pricing model and uses an assumption about what type of volatility the underlying asset will exhibit going forward. It generally does not equal the actual price of the option in the marketplace because there is often a difference between what the options market expects regarding volatility (i.e., the implied volatility currently reflected in the marketplace) and the volatility used in computing the theoretical value of the option (often based on the underlying asset's statistical volatility). For example, if the strategist computes the theoretical value of XYZ July 50 call option under the assumption that XYZ will exhibit low levels of volatility (say 10 percent) and plugs that number (10 percent) into an option pricing model, that theoretical value will be low if the current implied volatility of the same option is 30 percent. In this case, the market price of the option will reflect a higher level of volatility and the option price will be higher than the theoretical price. In short, when implied volatility is higher than the volatility used to compute the theoretical value of the option, premiums will seem high or overpriced.

premium. To understand this, consider the purchase of a call option during January to buy stock of XYZ company for $50 by July (the XYZ July 50 call). If the stock has been trading for between $40 and $45 for the past six years, the odds of the stock price rising above $50 by July are relatively slim. That option will not carry much value. But if XYZ has been trading between $40 and $80 during the past six months, it has exhibited relatively high volatility. In this case, the stock has a better chance of rising above $50 by July, and the option will be worth more and carry a higher premium. Therefore, the probability of the option being in-the-money at expiration is higher for the asset with relatively high levels of volatility than it is with the low-volatility asset.

Given the time until expiration, the strike price, the underlying asset's price, the dividend, and the interest rate, it is possible to find a theoretical value for any option. In order to do so, the inputs are plugged into an option pricing model. Since the beginning of organized options trading in the early 1970s, a number of formulas have been developed to compute option prices. Most of these models are based on the Black-Scholes option pricing model, which was introduced at roughly the same time as the establishment of the Chicago Board Options Exchange (1973). By plugging in the various inputs, it is possible to develop a theoretical value of any given option. For the less mathematically inclined, the formula may seem cumbersome. In actuality, however, it is relatively easy to compute and can be created in most programmable calculators. The simplest way to compute the formula is through the use of computer, which can handle the computation with ease. In addition, other option pricing models have been created. The one used on the Optionetics.com Platinum site is known as the Bjerksund Stensland American option model. It is a variant of the original Black-Scholes model.

The theoretical value of an option derived from any option pricing model will not always be equal to its value in the marketplace. In other words, options will not always trade at their theoretical values. The main reason that options do not always trade at their theoretical values is because theoretical prices are computed using historical volatility, or past stock prices. Volatilities, however, change over time. In fact, they are always in a state of flux. The value of an option tends to reflect market expectations regarding future volatility.

In order to determine what volatility the market is implying in an options contract, the option pricing model can also be used to solve for volatility. As we have seen in earlier chapters, the volatility of an asset can increase for a number of reasons. For instance, if a company has just surprised investors by announcing a stellar and unexpected profit, chances are the stock price will rise suddenly. The sharp move higher will cause the historical volatility to jump higher also. Options traders, however, may see the earnings announcement as a one-time event. If so, the option prices will reflect the anticipation of lower volatility going forward. When using the current market price of an option as an input into an option pricing model and solving for volatility, the result is known as implied volatility, which is the subject of the next chapter.

The Black-Scholes Option Pricing Model

The elements in the Black-Scholes formula represent uncertainty—and its solution. It was a problem that Myron Scholes, Fischer Black, and Robert Merton took years to solve. Their work later earned Scholes and Merton the Nobel prize (after Black's death). The economists calculated that in betting risk against risk, two uncertainties could, in effect, cancel each other out to produce a positive result. In 1973, the Black-Scholes model began being implemented on the newly opened Chicago Board Options Exchange, and for options traders even the sky was no longer the limit. Virtually all option pricing models today are derived from the Black-Scholes model. For those seeking to use the formula, it is as follows:

$$\text{Call option} = p_1 N(d_1) - p_2 e^{-rt} N(d_2)$$

Where:

$$d_1 = \frac{\ln\left(\frac{p_1}{p_2}\right) + \left(r + \frac{v^2}{2}\right)t}{v\sqrt{t}}$$

$$d_1 = d_2 - v\sqrt{t}$$

p_1 = stock price
p_2 = strike price
t = time remaining until expiration
N = cumulative normal distribution function
r = risk-free interest rate
$\ln$ = natural log
v = volatility measurement
e = logarithmic function

If you are interested in the mathematics behind the option model, a good book on the subject is *Option Volatility and Pricing*, by S. Natenburg, (Irwin Professional Publishing, 1994). A book on options without the math is *Trade Options Online*, by George Fontanills (John Wiley & Sons, 1999). The Bjerksund Stensland American option model is discussed in *The Complete Guide to Option Pricing Formulas*, by E. Haug (McGraw-Hill, 1998).

OPTION QUOTES AND OPEN INTEREST

Option quotes are not much different from stock quotes. Just as with stock quotes, there is a last or closing price, bid, offer (ask), high, and low on almost any option quote screen. There is also a variable that seems to get fairly little attention from option strategists. It is known as open interest. In fact, some traders ignore open interest altogether. Yet, while it is generally considered less important than the option's actual price and volume data, open interest does provide important information and should be considered before establishing any option position.

If you pull up an option quote on most data services, you will see a variety of information pertaining to that option. For example, if you take the symbol for the Microsoft (MSFT) October 2002 55 call (see box) and plug it into the quote box on the home page of Optionetics.com, you will be presented with a quote screen similar to the one in Table 5.1. (although if you are reading this after October 18, 2002, the option will have expired and no quote will be available).

Most of the variables within the quote box are easily recognizable. Indeed, "last" is the price of the last trade: The Microsoft October 55 call last traded for $4.30.

Table 5.1   Option Quote Box for MSFT October 2002 55 Call

MSFT Oct 2002 55.00 Call (O:MSQJK)			April 30, 2002, 3:47 P.M.
Last	4.30	Open interest	2,055
Bid	4.20	Ask	4.40
High	4.80	Low	4.10
Change	↑0.30	% Change	↑7.5%
Open	4.10	Volume	14.88K

Understanding Option Symbols

Just as stocks have ticker symbols, so do options. Option symbols consist of three different elements.

1. The root symbol, consisting of one to three letters, is derived from the underlying asset. For instance, the root symbol for International Business Machines is straightforward. It is the same as the stock symbol: IBM. Four-letter stocks, however, always have root symbols different from their stock symbols. For instance, while the stock symbol for Microsoft is MSFT, the option symbol is MSQ.

2. The second part of an option symbol represents the month and defines whether it is a put or a call. For instance, a January call uses the letter A after the root symbol; the IBM January call will have the root symbol IBM and then A, or IBMA. The February call is B, March C, and on and on until December, which is the letter L. Rather than starting at the letter A, puts begin at the letter M; thus the IBM February put will have the letter N following the root symbol, or IBMN.

3. The final element of an option symbol reflects the strike price. Generally, the number 5 is assigned the letter A, 10 the letter B, 15 the letter C, and so on until 100, which is given the letter T. Therefore, the IBM January 95 call will have the symbol IBMAS.

Tables of the option code symbols for months and strikes can be found in Appendix F.

The bid of $4.20 is the price at which the call can be sold. It can be purchased at the asking price of $4.40, which is the same as the offering price. On Thursday, April 30, 2002, the day this quote was captured, the call traded at a high of $4.80 and a low of $4.10. On the day, the MSFT October 55 call added 30 cents, or the "change" was $.30. In percentage terms that represented a 7.5 percent move higher. The opening price, or the first trade of the day, was $4.10. The volume, or the number of Microsoft October 55 calls traded on that day, equals 14,880. Indeed, most of the variables in the option quote table are the same as in most stock quotes, which were covered in detail in Chapter 2.

In order to own the Microsoft October 55 call, the buyer will pay $4.40, the ask price. In this case, it is possible that a buy order can be entered at a lower price (e.g., $4.25) and the option purchased below $4.40, but for this example, assume that one Microsoft October 55 call was purchased at the offering price of $4.40. Does this mean that the one contract costs $4.40? No. Actually, the trade will cost $440. The cost of a stock option is equal to the premium of the option times 100. In options parlance, 100 is known as the multiplier. The multiplier is almost always equal to 100 with stock and index options.

One item that appears in an option quote box and not a stock quote box is open interest. In this case, the open interest on the Microsoft 55 call is 2,055. What does this mean? It tells us that there have been 2,055 options opened on the Microsoft October 55 call. Were they bought? Sold? There is no way to know for sure. Recall that, when buying or selling options, the transaction is considered either an opening or a closing transaction. If you buy the MSFT October 55 call, you buy it to open. The buy to open adds one point to open interest. If you then want to get out of that position, you can sell that same option. In this case, you sell to close, and open interest will fall by one.

Selling can also add to open interest. For instance, if you establish a covered call on Microsoft using 500 shares of stock and then selling five MSFT October 55 calls (a covered call is the purchase of stock along with the sale of calls; this strategy will be discussed in detail later), then the options are sold to open. It is an opening transaction. In that case, the selling adds 5 to the open interest. On the other hand, if the position is closed and the options repurchased, the MSFT October 55 calls are bought to close. Options are bought to close, and open interest decreases. Therefore, in looking at the total open interest of any option, there is no way to know whether the options were bought or sold. For that reason, many option strategists choose to ignore open interest altogether.

Does this mean that open interest provides no relevant information to the option trader? Consider this passage from a November 5, 2001, Dow Jones Newswire story ("Tech Calls Fly as Nasdaq Tests 1,800," by Kopin Tan): "At the International Securities Exchange, the [Cisco Systems (CSCO)] November 17.50 puts were at 90 cents, down 20 cents, on volume of 15,566 contracts, compared with open interest of 10,580. Another 13,158 contracts traded at other exchanges."

In this case, the journalist made note of the open interest relative to the volume. On that day, the volume far exceeded the existing open interest and suggested that trading of Cisco Systems November 17.5 puts was exceptionally high on that day. Therefore, open interest can provide a gauge to help determine whether there is unusually high or low volume with respect to any particular option. In addition, open interest offers information regarding the liquidity of a given option. When there is no open interest on a particular option, there is no secondary market for the option. On options with high open interest, there are a large number of buyers and sellers. An active secondary market, in turn, will increase the odds of getting option orders filled at better prices (or in between the bid and ask prices). Therefore, all else being equal, the larger the open interest, the more attractive the option.

WHERE DO OPTIONS TRADE?

The beginnings of organized options trading can be traced back to the early 1970s. Prior to that time, options quotes were simply listed in newspapers by put and call

---

Liquidity

Liquidity can be defined as the ease with which an asset can be converted to cash in the marketplace. Liquidity is supply and demand for a stock or an option. ATM (at-the-money) options usually have the highest supply and demand (volume) because they are less expensive than ITM (in-the-money) options and have a better chance of becoming profitable by expiration than OTM (out-of-the-money) options. ATM options also have the greatest liquidity. A large number of buyers and sellers and a high volume of trading activity provide high liquidity.

Liquidity gives traders the opportunity to move in and out of a market with ease, buying and selling positions without difficulty. As stated, ATM options usually have excellent liquidity because they have a better chance of being profitable than OTM options. An option that is very far out-of-the-money is not going to have a lot of liquidity. Most of the strategies taught at Optionetics must be applied in specific market conditions to be moneymakers. Liquidity is one of these market conditions. Liquidity is the ease with which a market can be traded. A plentiful number of buyers and sellers boosts the volume of trading, producing a liquid market. Liquidity allows traders to get their orders filled easily as well as to quickly exit a position.

How do you avoid illiquid markets? An option's liquidity can be determined by ascertaining its open interest. A stock's liquidity can be monitored by reviewing the market's volume to see how many shares have been bought and sold in one day. As a rule of thumb, avoid markets with a trading volume of less than 300,000 shares a day, although one million shares a day is even better. It is also vital to ascertain whether trading volume is increasing or decreasing. This kind of volume movement is studied to indicate turning points in market price action. You can also monitor liquidity by noting the buying and selling of block trades—orders of 5,000 shares at a time—by institutional traders; or simply look at the "Volume Leaders" list in the "Market Data" section at Optionetics.com.

dealers. It was an unorganized, unregulated, and inefficient system. In 1973, however, the Chicago Board Options Exchange (CBOE) developed the first organized marketplace for stock options. Since the inception of that first exchange, four others have entered the scene, and the number of options traded each year has skyrocketed. For instance, in 1974 a total of 5.7 million option contracts traded during that entire year. According to the Options Clearing Corporation (OCC), in the year 2000 more than 700 million puts and calls changed hands.

Indeed, since the inception of the first options exchange in 1973, a lot has changed. Today there are five separate exchanges that actively match buyers and sellers. Although the CBOE is the oldest, and still the largest, four other options exchanges are in competition with it. The American Stock Exchange (AMEX), the Philadelphia Stock Exchange (PHLX), the Pacific Exchange (PCX), and the International Securities Exchange (ISE) also offer options trading.

Launched in May 2000, the International Securities Exchange was the first new U.S.-based exchange in more than 25 years. In addition, unlike the other exchanges, ISE is the first all-electronic options market. Therefore, instead of matching buy and sell orders on the trading floor of an exchange, buyers and sellers are matched via computer terminals. The exchange has been growing steadily since its inception. In fact, during the month of October 2001, ISE saw average trading volume of 380,299 contracts a day, making it the third largest options exchange behind the CBOE and AMEX.

Prior to August 1999 specific stock options traded on only one exchange. For example, the option strategist looking to buy calls on Dell Computer would have no choice but to send the order (through a broker) to the Chicago Board Options Exchange. From that point forward, however, stock options started trading on multiple exchanges. Today, options on Dell Computer trade on all five exchanges.

Options Trading Exchanges

There are several options trading exchanges that you can visit on the Web:

Chicago Board Options Exchange	(www.cboe.com)
American Stock Exchange	(www.amex.com)
Philadelphia Stock Exchange	(www.phlx.com/index.stm)
Pacific Exchange (San Francisco)	(www.pacificex.com)
International Securities Exchange	(www.iseoptions.com)

International Securities Exchange (ISE): A fully electronic exchange for trading stock options. Unlike the other options exchanges, it does not have a trading floor, but rather offers members screen-based trading.

When options on a particular stock trade on more than one options exchange, it is said to have "multiple listing."

Ultimately, option strategists have no contact with the options exchanges. Once an order is submitted to the broker, it is out of the options trader's hands. Instead, the broker selects where to send the order. At the same time, however, since an option can trade on as many as five separate exchanges, one option contract can have five different price quotes. For instance, the bids and offers for Dell options might be different on the American Stock Exchange than on the PHLX.

THE ROLE OF THE BROKER

While options trade on five different exchanges, the options trader does not have contact with any of the exchanges directly. Instead, all option orders are placed through a brokerage firm. Therefore, in order to trade options, one must first open an account and obtain approval to trade options. The business of buying and selling options for customers is under strict supervision of federal regulatory agencies. For that reason, brokerage firms must ensure that trading options is suitable for each customer by assessing the trader's total financial situation. Therefore, in addition to a new account form, the aspiring options traders must also complete an options approval form, which helps the brokerage firm determine whether options are an appropriate financial instrument for each particular individual to trade.

Just as with stocks, the first step to trading options is to open an account with a broker. This can be done using an online broker, over the telephone, or visiting a full-service brokerage. Whether it is an online or off-line brokerage firm, the first document is the new account form, which is important for two reasons: Like a doctor examining a patient, the new account form enables the brokerage firm to evaluate your financial condition and resources, including your assets, liabilities, income, net worth, and so on. The new account form also spells out the terms and conditions that the broker imposes on you, including commission rates. Therefore, while not particularly interesting, the new account agreement is your first look at the broker and, because it stipulates the terms of your relationship with that firm, it is worth reading in detail.

The next step is to fill out and complete the options approval form. The form asks questions regarding your experience as an investor and the amount of trading you do within a period of time. Many beginning options traders are frustrated by the fact that, although they have a comprehensive understanding of options, brokerage firms will not allow them to trade options or will allow them to trade only certain types of strategies (see the "Option Approval Levels" box). I have found that the best way to handle that situation is to open up a verbal dialogue with the broker, explain exactly what strategies you plan on trading, and say that you are willing to assume the risk of any losses. The brokerage firm may require a written letter stating so. But, if you show a clear understanding of options, the brokerage firm will, in most cases, allow you to trade them.

After the new account and option approval forms are reviewed and approved by the brokerage firm, trading can begin. Then, all of your orders are placed through the broker, who then sends them to the options exchange for execution. Some traders prefer online brokers, while others like the old-fashioned way of picking up the phone to place orders. Generally, the online brokers charge lower commissions and the cost of trading will therefore be less.

For more information about the different types of brokers, consider reading *Trade Options Online* by George Fontanills or visit the "Broker Review" pages at www.optionetics.com.

INDEX OPTIONS

Even if an investor has never traded options, the concept of an index is probably familiar. After all, the Dow Jones Industrial Average ($INDU) and the Nasdaq Composite index ($COMPQ) are often the subject of commentary in the financial press and on the evening news. In that respect, both the Dow and the Nasdaq Composite are market averages used as barometers, or gauges, for the performance of the U.S. stock market. However, in addition to serving as a window into the performance of the stock market, indexes can also be used as tools for the options trader. That is, options are listed on a host of different market averages and sector indexes that allow the trader to participate in the rise and fall of not just one stock, but an entire

---

Option Approval Levels

Brokerage firms vary in what they will allow and not allow customers to do in their brokerage accounts. However, there are six basic levels of options trading that are more or less used throughout the industry (see Table 5.2). As we will see in later chapters, each has a different objective and risk characteristic. Most of the trading strategies discussed in this book require Level III trading approval.

Table 5.2   Options Trading Approval Levels

Level	Strategy	Objective	Risk
I	Covered call writing	Conservative/generate income	Limited
II	Put/call buying	Speculation	Limited
III	Spreads	Various (speculation, income, hedging, etc.)	Limited
IV	Put selling (stock options)	Speculation/aggressive income	Limited
V	Call selling (stock options)	Speculation/aggressive income	Unlimited
VI	Index option selling	Speculation/aggressive income	Unlimited

basket of stocks. In fact, some traders find index options to be the best vehicles for making directional, neutral, and hedged bets.

There are a large number of different index options to choose from today. Since 1983, when the Chicago Board Options Exchange listed the first index options on the S&P 100 index ($OEX), the major options exchanges have each developed options trading on competing index products. For example, today the CBOE lists options on the S&P 500 index ($SPX), the Nasdaq 100 index ($NDX), and the Russell 2000 Small Cap Index ($RUT). Meanwhile, the American Stock Exchange lists options on the Major Market Index ($XMI) and the S&P MidCap 400 index ($MID).

In addition to market indexes, the major options exchanges also provide trading on sector indexes. For example, the Philadelphia Stock Exchange lists options on roughly a dozen different sector indexes, such as options on the PHLX Semiconductor Index ($SOX), the PHLX Bank Sector Index ($BKX), and the PHLX Gold and Silver Mining Index ($XAU). The CBOE also lists options on a number of sector indexes as well, including the CBOE Internet Index ($INX), the Morgan Stanley Retail Index ($RLX), and the GSTI Computer Software Index ($GSO). The American Stock Exchange lists options on the AMEX Biotechnology Index ($BTK), the Natural Gas Index ($XNG), the Airline Index ($XAL), and a handful of other industry-specific indexes. For a complete list of all sector indexes listed on the various exchanges, visit the web sites of the PHLX (www.phlx.com), the CBOE (www.cboe.com), and the AMEX (www.amex.com). A list of 72 of the top indexes can be found in Appendix A.

Whether trading options on a market average or on a specific industry, placing orders for index options is similar to trading stock options. Basically, the investor opens an account with a brokerage firm, completes the option approval document, and places orders online or over the phone through a broker. In short, unlike futures and futures options, trading index options does not require that an account be established with a futures firm. Almost any brokerage firm that provides stock and options trading on the U.S. exchanges also offers index options trading.

While the process of trading index options is similar to that of trading stock options, there are some important differences. First, index options settle for cash and not shares. When a stock option contract is exercised, settlement involves the transfer of shares. When index options contracts are exercised, there is a transfer of cash (equal to the difference between the strike price of the option and the current value of the index). In addition, with only a few exceptions, index options settle European style. Most stock options settle American style and can be exercised at any time prior to expiration. European-style options can be exercised only at expiration.

Index options, therefore, are not the same as exchange-traded funds such as the Nasdaq 100 (QQQ). Recall that the Nasdaq QQQ is one of the most actively traded options contracts in the marketplace today. The vehicle is an exchange-traded fund that is designed to equal one-fortieth of the value of the popular Nasdaq 100 index. However, since QQQ shares can be bought and sold like a stock, it is not an index. It is not possible to buy and sell shares of an index. Consequently, the QQQ settles for shares and not cash. In addition, options on the Nasdaq 100 QQQ settle American style.

When index options trading started in the early 1980s, they were largely the domain of professional traders. Through the years, however, the options exchanges have launched a number of unique indexes designed to attract the attention of smaller investors. For example, the Chicago Board Options Exchange launched options trading on the Mini-Nasdaq 100 index ($MNX), which is equal to one-tenth of the value of the Nasdaq 100 index. In addition, the CBOE also lists options trading on the Dow Jones Industrial Average ($DJX). The DJX is equal to one-hundredth of the value of the more familiar Dow Jones Industrial Average. Making the MNX a fraction of the NDX and the DJX one-hundredth of the Dow lowers their option premiums and makes them more appealing to smaller investors.

The major option exchanges are continually launching new indexes that are designed to attract investor interest. For example, in 2001 the Philadelphia Stock Exchange listed options on a new Fiber Optics Index ($FOP). In response to growing investor interest in military defense stocks, both the AMEX and the PHLX launched trading on defense sector indexes in late 2001. In fact, there are a host of unique indexes to choose from today, including the Dogs of the Dow Index ($MUT), the European-style OEX ($XEO), and the CBS MarketWatch 75 ($MWX). Again, all the specifications and details regarding these indexes can be found on the home pages of the AMEX, CBOE, or PHLX.

Therefore, while indexes are often used as barometers for the performance of the stock market today, they also offer the options trader a wide array of different methods for trading both the major averages or specific industry groups. Not all indexes have received an equal amount of investor interest, however. In fact, some indexes rarely see any trading activity. Consequently, the wide spreads on the index options quotes and the lack of liquidity make them sometimes unattractive for the options trader. Nevertheless, many indexes do have actively traded options and, consequently, provide the strategist with reliable means of participating in the rise or fall of not just one stock, but an entire market or industry group. In that respect, index options can be great tools for making directional, neutral, or hedged bets.

CONCLUSION

Trading volatility requires an in-depth understanding of options. At this point, the reader should understand the following issues:

- The difference between a put and a call.

- The main determinants of an option's price.

- How to find an option quote.

- How to use an option pricing model to solve for both an option's price as well as its volatility.

- The roles of the various stock exchanges.

- The function of the OCC.

- The role of the brokerage firms when it comes to options trading.

- The basics of index options.

The options market is one of the most exciting trading arenas in the world. The options market includes five different U.S. exchanges, with more than 725 million listed options contracts traded in the year 2000. Each options trader has his or her specific reason for deciding to trade options. Some traders want to use leverage and speculate on the rise or fall of a certain stock or index. Others use options to create an income stream. Many large financial institutions use options to hedge a large portfolio. Indeed, options are among the most versatile trading instruments available to investors today. The flexibility of these vehicles helps explain the growing size and popularity of the options market.

There are almost an unlimited number of ways to use options and structure trades to profit in a variety of situations. Many traders begin trading by aggressively buying calls on stocks that they expect to go up. Obviously, the leverage offered by options is one of the most compelling reasons to trade them. But leveraging works both ways. During more than 10 years as a speaker at investment seminars I have heard countless tales of how options have destroyed individual trading accounts. In short, while there are a large number of ways to use options, there are no get-rich-quick strategies. Using options for the sole purpose of speculation generally results in financial losses. My approach is designed to get rich slowly, but surely—which is why I'm dedicated to utilizing options to manage risk and maximize profits.

But first things first: Trading volatility is at the heart of my investment approach. As we saw in earlier chapters, one way to measure volatility is by using past prices, which includes statistical volatility and indicators such as Bollinger bands and moving averages. In this chapter, we touched on a different kind of volatility: implied volatility (i.e., the measure of volatility that is derived from option prices using an option pricing model). Implied volatility is one of the most important factors underlying the price of an option, and it is always in a state of flux. As it changes, the value of an option will change. For instance, all else being equal, the value of a call will drop if the implied volatility falls. So before trading options, it is imperative to understand how implied volatility will influence your positions. How do you know ahead of time how implied volatility can impact your options? That question is answered in Chapter 6.

6

Implied Volatility

Options are an excellent financial tool because they provide investors with leverage—that is, the means to control a large number of stock shares with relatively little capital. This attribute often encourages novice traders to turn to the options market in pursuit of instant riches. The potential for large returns in a short period of time is just one of the reasons options have become so popular, especially with speculators. Unfortunately, most speculators eventually crash and burn in the options market. These failures can often be traced back to a lack of understanding of exactly how options work.

As previously discussed, options are derivative instruments. Their value is derived from a variety of factors and, while many traders understand that the most important factor is the price of underlying stock (or the asset from which the option derives its value), they may not give enough attention to the other factors that influence the value of an option. For example, time decay is extremely important to understand. Significant financial losses can occur if traders do not fully understand that options, unlike stock, gradually waste away until they expire.

Implied volatility (IV) is another important factor. Implied volatility indicates to the options strategist whether options are cheap or expensive. For that reason, it can dictate whether the strategist is best served by purchasing or selling an option. Furthermore, changes in implied volatility can be a reason why an option fails to increase in value, even though the speculator correctly predicted the direction of the stock. In fact, IV is so important that this entire chapter is devoted to the topic.

WHAT IS IMPLIED VOLATILITY?

It is not an exaggeration to say that a solid understanding of implied volatility is paramount to success in options trading. In turn, there are a number of important factors to consider when analyzing IV. The first is how it is computed. Recall from the last chapter that implied volatility is derived using an option pricing model such as the one developed by Fischer Black and Myron Scholes and published in 1973. Second, each option contract will have a unique implied volatility. Not only will the implied volatility of IBM options be different from the implied volatility of Microsoft options, but also the July IBM options might have a radically different implied volatility than the December IBM options. When two options on the same stock have different implied volatilities, it is known as a volatility skew. In later chapters, the reader will learn how to structure attractive option trades that take advantage of volatility skews.

The third factor to consider when studying implied volatility is that it is always in a state of flux. That is, volatilities change over time. Why? Market expectations regarding future volatility of a stock are reflected in the price of its options. As investor expectations concerning the volatility of a stock change, the prices of the options on that stock change as well. For example, when the market expects a stock to exhibit high volatility, the prices of options tend to rise; if investors expect the stock to show low levels of volatility, the prices of the options on that stock will generally fall.

As previously noted, an option pricing model can be used to determine what volatility the market is implying in an options contract (thus the term "implied volatility"). When doing so, the following inputs are required:

- The stock price.

- The strike price of the option.

- The option price.

- The time remaining until expiration.

- The prevailing interest rate.

- In certain circumstances, any dividends paid by the stock.

All of these factors can have an influence on the option price. When all the other factors stay the same and the option premium increases, the change in price can be

---

Factors to Consider When Studying Implied Volatility

- Implied volatility is a product of an option pricing model such as the Black-Scholes pricing model and is expressed as a percentage.

- Each option has a unique implied volatility. Even two options on the same stock with different expiration dates and/or strike prices will not necessarily have the same levels of implied volatility.

- Implied volatility is always in a state of change: Simply because the implied volatility of XYZ was 25 percent last week does not mean that it will be 25 percent next week.

attributed to changes in implied volatility. As we have seen in earlier chapters, the volatility of an asset can increase for a number of reasons: a stellar and unexpected profit announcement, news of a takeover, a change in management, and so forth.

Unusual events often result in a flurry of option buying (or selling), which can cause market expectations regarding the volatility of a stock to change over time. For example, when speculators hear of a takeover rumor, they sometimes aggressively buy calls in the takeover candidate in anticipation of a sharp rise in the stock price. Conversely, when large professional investors fear volatility in the stock market, they sometimes buy puts on the major averages to hedge their portfolios. In either case, whether speculators are buying calls out of greed or investors buying puts as a hedge, the result is often fluctuations in the implied volatility of the options on the stock or index. In addition, all else being equal, when implied volatility rises, options become more expensive; when implied volatility falls, the option premiums also drop. Therefore, options that have low levels of implied volatility are sometimes said to be cheap and those with high IV are expensive.

However, if you want to determine whether options on a stock or index are cheap or expensive, you have to do more than just look at whether implied volatility is rising or falling. The options strategist must place the current levels of implied volatility in a broader context. How is this done? When does the options strategist know whether options are cheap and ready for purchase or expensive and worthy of sale? To find answers to these important questions, we will take an in-depth look at the following two tests:

1. Comparing implied volatility to the stock or index's historical volatility.

2. Looking at the implied volatility of an option over time.

GAUGING IMPLIED VOLATILITY AND OPTION PREMIUMS

Just as with any other product or commodity, the forces of supply and demand sometimes influence the price of an option. During times of unusually high demand,

---

Implied volatility reflects the market's expectations concerning the future volatility of the underlying stock or index. In order to compute implied volatility, the following five variables must be plugged into the Black-Scholes or other option pricing model:

1. The option's market price—generally (bid + ask)/2.
2. The stock or index price.
3. The time left until expiration.
4. The interest rate.
5. Any dividends paid out by the stock.

Why Dividends Impact Option Prices

Dividends are periodic payments a company makes to its shareholders. They can be extremely important to the options strategist because the dividend is one of the determinants of a stock option's price. Obviously, if the stock pays no dividend, it has no effect. However, the call options of high-yielding stocks will be lower than the call options of low-yielding stocks. In addition, the larger the dividend, the lower the price of the corresponding call options. Therefore, stocks with high dividend yields will have low call option premiums. To see why, let's consider an extreme example.

Example: Shares of ABC Company trade for $20 a share, and the company pays a large dividend of $2 a share annually. As is generally the case, the dividend is paid quarterly. Therefore, each dividend payment is 50 cents and paid every three months. Each time a dividend is paid, the stock is said to go "ex-dividend" and the share price falls by the amount of the dividend. Now, suppose a call buyer is considering buying the June 2002 ABC 20 call in mid-December 2001. Since there are six months remaining until the option expires, the call buyer must take into account two dividend payments. In other words, ABC Company will pay $1 in dividends and the share price will be reduced by that amount when it goes ex-dividend during that time. Therefore, all else being equal, the stock price will fall by $1 during that time. Since the call buyer is not entitled to the dividends, the value of the ABC June 20 call will be less than if the company paid no dividend at all. So, although the stock is trading for $20 a share, the strategist must assume the price is actually $19 because of the dividends.

The impact of dividends will not be equal on all call options. Generally, the near-term dividends will be discounted in the option price to a greater degree than dividends paid out at a much later date. In addition, low-volatility stocks with high dividend payout ratios will have lower-priced calls than high-volatility stocks with low payouts.

Why Interest Rates Impact Option Prices

While dividends clearly influence the prices of call options, it is uncertain what, if any, impact interest rates have on option prices. Nevertheless, the current interest rate is an input into most pricing models. Generally, the rate used is the current 90-day Treasury bill (T-bill) interest rate. Higher interest rates mean higher option prices, and lower interest rates mean lower premiums.

the market makers—those responsible for buying and selling a specific option contract—will raise prices. Strong interest in an option contract will force prices higher because investors are willing to pay more. However, when there is very little or no interest in an options contract, market makers cannot afford to raise prices because investors are not willing to pay up for an options contract.

When buying and selling causes option prices to rise or fall, mathematically the price changes are attributed to changes in implied volatility. Since implied volatility can fluctuate during short periods of time—even minutes—option prices can rise and fall without any meaningful changes in the actual volatility or price of the stock. In short, implied volatility is a key factor that causes the value of an option to fluctuate over time.

To understand why option prices sometimes change without meaningful changes in the stock price, recall that there are basically two types of volatility: historical and implied. Like their names suggest, historical volatility is the average volatility shown by the underlying security *in the past*. Implied volatility, in contrast, is computed by using an option pricing model. Implied volatility gives a sense of what traders and market makers believe the volatility of the stock will be *in the future*. As expectations change regarding the stock's volatility going forward, so will the implied volatility change.

In sum, implied volatility is always in a state of flux. Sometimes the implied volatility on a stock option becomes quite high, which causes the option premiums to increase in value. Other times, implied volatility will fall and cause option premiums to decrease in value. For that reason, when traders say premiums are high or low, cheap or expensive, for a particular option, they are talking about implied volatility. Therefore, the first step in determining whether options are cheap or expensive is to compare implied volatility over time.

Charting implied volatility on a specific stock or index is relatively straightforward. In the next chapter, the reader will be introduced to a measure of marketwide levels of volatility known as the CBOE Volatility Index, or VIX, which provides real-time information regarding the implied volatility of S&P 100 index options. In order to determine whether the implied volatility of a specific index or stock option is low or high relative to past levels of implied volatility, it is necessary to create a chart. Figure 6.1 provides a look at the implied volatility of at-the-money Sprint PCS options during six months ended March 2002. The chart was created using Optionetics.com Platinum software. Notice the chart has four lines. Each line, in turn, corresponds with a different set of options. For example, the top line shows the options contracts that are expiring in 7 to 30 days, and the bottom line shows the longer-term options that expire in 90 days or more.

In Figure 6.1, the implied volatility of Sprint PCS fluctuates between 40 percent and 125 percent. Notice the sharp rise in implied volatility of Sprint PCS options in early 2002 when rumors surfaced that the company was a potential takeover target. The sharp rise was unusual because it is rare to see the implied volatility of an option triple over the course of a few months. Nevertheless, there are events that can trigger abnormal surges in the IV of a stock or index option (see box). In the case of Sprint PCS, it was a takeover rumor.

THEORETICAL VALUES VERSUS MARKET PRICES

In the preceding chapter, we saw that it is possible to arrive at the theoretical value of an option through the use of an option pricing model. That is, assuming a given level of volatility, we can estimate what the option price should be. When options

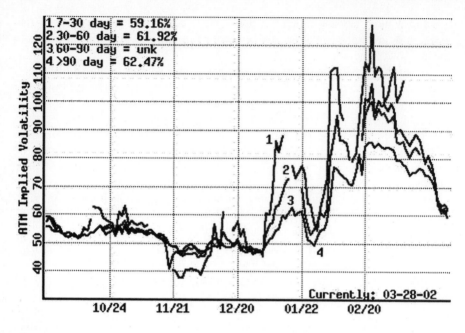

Figure 6.1 Implied Volatility of Sprint PCS (Courtesy of Optionetics.com)

Events That Cause Surges in Implied Volatility

Individual Stocks

- New product announcements, FDA drug approval, industry-specific news.
- Talk that a company might announce better or worse than expected earnings.
- Takeover rumors; news of a management change or a stock split.
- Accounting irregularities and/or corporate fraud.

Market wide

- Aggressive put buying.
- Hedging unusual events such as war, political uncertainty, fear of market crashes (e.g., October 1987), and changes in interest rates.
- Economic events, contagion, comments from economists or Fed officials, and irrational exuberance.

---

strategists estimate what the value of an option is using statistical volatility (or assumptions about volatility other than implied volatility), they are computing what is known as a theoretical value.

Since the implied volatility of an option is always changing, the market price, or the value of the option at any given time, can deviate from this theoretical value. The reason why the theoretical value of an option and market price of that same option will not always coincide is due to differing assumptions regarding volatility. For example, if the theoretical value of an option is computed using the statistical volatility of the stock equal to 10 percent, but the implied volatility of the option is actually 20 percent, the market price of the option will be greater than the theoretical value.

Since we can calculate the statistical volatility of a stock mathematically, it is common practice to compare the theoretical value of an option with the current market price. For example, let's say that the statistical volatility of XYZ is 30 percent. When we place this figure into an option pricing model to determine the theoretical value of an XYZ July call, it shows a price well below the current price for the option. For instance, perhaps our theoretical value of the option is $3 a contract; but when we pull up a quote of the XYZ July call, the current market price is $4 a contract. The difference is due to the fact that the market is expecting volatility to be higher in the future and prices the options accordingly. Thus, the implied volatility of the option is greater than the statistical volatility that was used to compute the theoretical value of the option.

Since implied volatility is a measure of expectations, if IV is higher than statistical volatility, traders expect the future volatility of that stock to be high relative to the stock's past level of volatility. In this case, options are said to be expensive. But if implied volatility is low compared to historical volatility, market players are expecting lower levels of volatility and options are said to be cheap. Therefore, statistical volatility is an important gauge for judging whether current levels of implied volatility are appropriate.

Let us now consider a specific example designed to compare the statistical volatility of a stock with the implied volatility of the stock's option. Again, the purpose is to gauge whether the options are cheap and suitable for purchase, or expensive and better for selling. Later, we will examine what specific strategies can be implemented once it is clear whether the options are cheap or expensive. For now, the purpose is simply to compare statistical and implied volatility and to gauge the relative attractiveness of an option's premium, which involves a comparison of implied volatility over time as well as a comparison of implied and statistical volatility.

STATISTICAL VOLATILITY VERSUS IMPLIED VOLATILITY EXAMPLE

In early March 2002, a rumor surfaced that wireless telephone service provider Leap Wireless International (LWIN) was a possible takeover candidate. At the time, the wireless industry was suffering from intense competition and deteriorating profits. Some analyst justified the takeover speculation by arguing that consolidation in the industry made sense because many of the wireless operators had overlapping phone networks. Thus, merging some of the companies would serve to lower costs and improve efficiency. Subsequently, shares of Leap Wireless, which traded on the Nasdaq Stock Market under the symbol LWIN, were considered a prime target for takeover.

The speculative takeover talk fueled aggressive buying of both the LWIN stock and LWIN call options. Beginning on March 4, the stock jumped nearly 100 percent in three days! Such activity is not completely out of the ordinary on Wall Street. Generally, when a company is taken over, shareholders are rewarded because the takeover price is usually above the stock price in the market. Indeed, identifying potential mergers can be a source of superior profits. Unfortunately, most takeover talk eventually proves false. Nevertheless, when rumors surface, trading activity in the shares and options of the takeover candidate is often brisk. LWIN in early 2002 was no exception.

Unusually strong demand for options often causes implied volatility to jump higher. In the case of a takeover rumor, the call options generally see growing investor interest and, as a result, the implied volatility will rise. Using the Optionetics.com Platinum site, Figure 6.2 was created to illustrate LWIN's implied volatility. The chart shows four lines; each line corresponds to a different expiration date for the options. For example, the top line shows the options contracts that are expiring in 7 to 30 days, and the bottom line shows the longer-term options that expire in 90 days or more. Notice the sharp rise in implied volatility of LWIN options in early 2002 when the rumors surfaced. Early in January, IV was in the 80 percent range (which, incidentally, is a high level). By mid-February, the implied volatility of LWIN had almost doubled and was approaching 160 percent—an extremely high level.

The rise in implied volatility of LWIN options in early 2002 suggests that options were becoming expensive due to the takeover talk surrounding the wireless telecommunication operator. In order to confirm that the options were expensive, the options strategist should compare the implied volatility to the stock's actual volatility. In this case, let us consider the relationship between the IV and statistical volatility of LWIN. Figure 6.3 provides a comparison of the implied volatility of

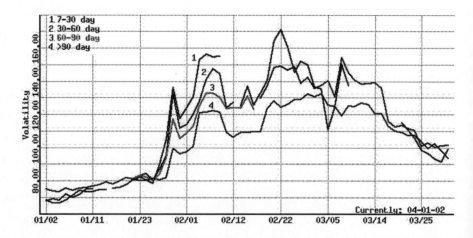

Figure 6.2   Implied Volatility Chart for LWIN (Courtesy of Optionetics.com)

LWIN options and the statistical volatility of shares of Leap Wireless when the rumors surfaced. This particular chart compares the IV on options that expire within 30 days to the 20-day statistical volatility. The chart was created in Optionetics.com Platinum and can be duplicated for any optionable stock or index.

Notice that, when the rumor mill was churning in January 2002, the IV/SV chart was approaching 1.5. That means the implied volatility was one and a half times, or 50 percent greater than, the statistical volatility. Therefore, while the implied volatility chart was gradually edging higher and approaching 160 percent, the implied volatility was rising above the underlying stock's statistical volatility. Comparing the IV to the statistical volatility, then, confirms that LWIN options were expensive in early January 2002.

Figure 6.3 shows that the IV of LWIN options relative to the SV of Leap Wireless shares started moving lower in early February 2002. When the chart reads 1.0, it indicates that implied volatility of the options is equal to the statistical volatility of the stock. When it falls below 1.0 it suggests that the statistical volatility is greater than the IV. Notice from Figure 6.4 that the stock spiked sharply higher in early March. Indeed, shares of LWIN were becoming more volatile, just as (referring to Figure 6.2) implied volatility began moving lower. The result was a downward slope in the IV/SV chart (Figure 6.3), which fell toward 0.6. Therefore, relative to statistical volatility, LWIN options were expensive until mid-February

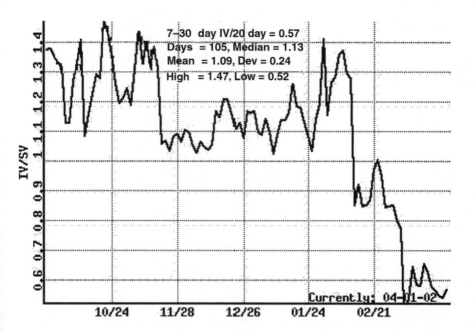

Figure 6.3   Implied Volatility/Statistical Volatility Chart for LWIN (Courtesy of Optionetics.com)

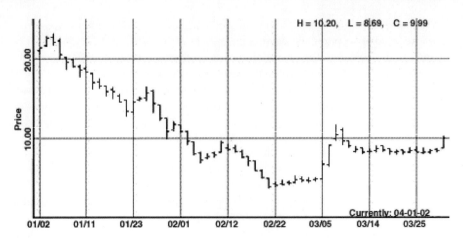

Figure 6.4 LWIN Stock Price Chart (Courtesy of Optionetics.com)

when the IV/SV chart moved toward 1.0. From there, it moved toward 0.6 and was a sign that LWIN options had become cheap relative to statistical volatility.

It is interesting to note in the case of LWIN that the implied volatility moved sharply higher in mid-February and then the actual volatility of the stock spiked higher in early March. In essence, since IV reflects expectations of future volatility, in this case its spike in mid-February accurately forecasted the increase in statistical volatility in March. The options market sometimes has an uncanny ability to foreshadow changes in the volatility of both stocks and the overall market.

BUYING OPTIONS AND THE PROTECTIVE PUT

Now, in order to gain an appreciation for how implied volatility helps a trader in actual trading, let's look at two different strategies that rely on a firm understanding of implied volatility for success: the protective put (long put) and the covered call. Both strategies combine stock with options. To illustrate the importance of implied volatility, let's monitor the impact changes in the implied volatility of LWIN options have on the outcome of these two strategies. Let's start with the protective put.

For the novice options strategist, the protective put can be a great way to get hands-on experience trading options. This strategy is designed to protect a stock holding and/or lock in profits in the event of a decline in the price of that stock. Furthermore, the protective put can be an ideal way for stock market investors to gravitate into the world of options trading and also limit the risk associated with a simple buy-and-hold stock strategy. Basically, the protective put has the same risk profile as simply buying a call. As a result, most advanced options traders avoid the strategy. Nevertheless, in certain circumstances, the protective put is appropriate.

Suppose a trader has been watching Leap Wireless and believes the shares have promise. Yet, it is a volatile stock and the investor in question knows there is serious risk in simply owning shares. Rather than simply buying LWIN shares, the trader decides to establish a hedged position by owning shares of Leap Wireless stock and also buying a put option. For instance, since one LWIN put option contract represents the right to sell 100 Leap Wireless shares, the investor can buy one put contract for every 100 shares owned.

For example, if LWIN is trading for $11 a share, you can create a protective put by purchasing a put with a $10 strike price. This strategy gives the owner of the put the right to sell his or her shares for $10 until the option expires. The maximum risk of owning the LWIN shares then becomes the difference between the price paid for LWIN and the strike price, along with the cost of the option (including commissions). In this case, for every 100 shares, the maximum risk is $11 minus $10 plus the cost of the option. Profits occur if shares of Leap Wireless rise high enough to offset the cost of the put (and commissions); but no matter what, the investor can exercise the put option and unload shares for $10. Note, however, that the right to sell (or put) the stock is valid only until the option expires—the third Friday of the option's expiration month. The position is no longer hedged once expiration occurs.

This trade, known as the protective put, is a simple way to establish a position in a stock and eliminate some of the risk. First, until the put expires, the risk to the downside is limited. Second, there is profit potential should LWIN make a significant move to the upside. The protective put provides insurance on a long stock position just in case the stock takes a dive.

The protective put is a better strategy when implied volatility is low and options are relatively cheap. This generally occurs after a stock has advanced. That is, when prices are falling implied volatility tends to rise; but when stock prices are rising, implied volatility tends to fall. In the case of LWIN, there was an unusual event that caused implied volatility to jump higher. Namely, when takeover rumors surfaced in early 2002, implied volatility rose and the options became expensive.

Suppose the options strategist unknowingly establishes the protective put on Leap Wireless when the implied volatility is high and set to move lower. To be specific, on March 7, 2002, the option strategist purchases 100 shares of LWIN for $10.35 a share and also purchases an LWIN April 10 put at the high price of the day: $2.15. The trade cost is $1,250 ($1,035 for the stock and $215 for the option) plus commissions. Plugging the option price (along with the stock price, the time left until expiration, the strike price of the option, and the prevailing interest rate) into an option pricing model reveals that the IV of the LWIN April 10 put is 133 percent at the time of the purchase.

Roughly one month later, the trader checks price quotes on LWIN and the LWIN April 10 put. On April 2, 2002, the stock is unchanged! It is still trading for $10.35. The April 10 put, however, is currently trading for only 60 cents. Therefore, the value of the position, which cost $1,250 to establish, is now worth only $1,095— that's a one-month loss of 12.4 percent! What happened?

In this example, two factors caused the LWIN options to lose value and the protective put to suffer a loss: time decay and a drop in IV. First, recall that options are wasting assets. As time passes, the value of an options contract will diminish. In this case, time decay alone caused the option to lose $1.15 in value. Later, we will see how to measure the negative impact of time decay on the options. The second reason for the loss is due to the drop in IV. Recall from Figure 6.2 that the implied volatility of LWIN options started falling in March 2002. Consequently, while the option strategist paid IV of more than 130 percent in March 2002, when the LWIN April 10 put was trading for 60 cents implied volatility had fallen to 90 percent. In sum, time decay caused the option to lose roughly $1.15 in value while the drop in IV resulted in another 40-cent loss in premium.

SELLING OPTIONS AND THE COVERED CALL

The covered call or buy/write is one of the most common option strategies used today. The strategy can be implemented in cash, margin, or individual retirement accounts (IRAs). Furthermore, it is less risky than simply owning a stock. Like the protective put, the strategy works best when the stock price moves higher. However, the covered call offers less potential reward than simply owning shares or the protective put. Basically, the strategy works best when the stock moves only modestly higher. This allows the trader to keep the premium received for selling a call against a stock that is already owned.

The covered call strategy employs both stocks and call options. One call is sold for every 100 shares of stock that are held. There are two ways to establish the position:

Protective Put

Strategy = Buy the underlying security and buy an ATM or OTM put option.

Market Opportunity = Seeks to profit from an increase in the value of the underlying asset, but uses the put as protection in case of a decline.

Maximum Risk = Limited to stock price – the strike price + the price paid for the put option premium.

Maximum Profit = Unlimited as the stock moves higher.

Breakeven = Stock price + put option premium.

Margin = 50 percent of the stock and no margin for the long put.

1. Simultaneously purchase the stock and sell a call.

2. Sell call options against a stock that is already held in a portfolio.

In the covered call strategy, the owner of stock is also a seller, or writer, of calls. The writer, in turn, receives cash for selling the calls. The money received is equal to the premiums of the call option, or the call option's price in the market. In exchange for the cash payment, the writer agrees to sell the stock (or have the stock called from him or her) at the option's strike price until the expiration of the call option—the Friday before the third Saturday of the option's expiration month. When a covered call writer is forced to sell his or her stock, it is known as assignment.

This buy/write strategy is generally established using out-of-the-money calls such that the call options that are being sold have strike prices above the current market price of the stock. For instance, assume 100 shares of XYZ are currently being held in a brokerage account. The account holder wants to find a way to generate some income from the portfolio, but does not have much cash in the account for investments such as bonds, CDs, or money market funds. One alternative is to sell a call against the XYZ stock. If the stock is currently trading for $50 a share and the XYZ July 55 call is priced at $2, selling a July 55 call will yield $200 into the account ($2 × 100 shares = $200).

What is the investor's risk? First, if the stock falls, there is virtually unlimited risk to the downside all the way to zero—the same risk that was present on the stock before the call was sold. However, the covered call strategy lowers the breakeven a little. The breakeven for stock (not including commissions) is simply the price of the stock at the initiation of the trade ($50). The breakeven for a covered call is the price of the underlying asset at initiation minus the premium received from the sale of the call. In this example, the breakeven is $48 ($50 – $2).

Now let's see what happens if the stock rises above $55 a share. In this case, the stock could be called away from the investor. If assigned, the investor receives $5,500 ($55 × 100 shares) and keeps the $200 in premium received for selling the call, but no longer owns the stock—a total profit of $700 if the stock was originally purchased at $50. However, while the result of having the stock called is not a financial loss, the investor no longer participates in any further appreciation in the stock price. Therefore, the covered call limits the potential profit of holding a stock at the call's strike price. However, if XYZ stays between $50 and $55 a share, chances are the stock will not be called and the investor will get to keep the stock and the option premium, as well as any dividends paid by XYZ.

Therefore, the covered call is best used when the investor is moderately bullish on a stock—whether the stock is already in an existing portfolio or a new purchase. If the strategist is wildly bullish, though, the covered call is not an ideal strategy. Why? The investor is at risk of being assigned if XYZ rises above the strike price of the option. In other words, in exchange for the premium received from the option, the investor becomes obligated to sell the stock at the strike price. If the stock rises above that strike price, it is likely that the call owner will exercise the right to buy the stock at the strike price. While the covered call is not appropriate if one is wildly bullish on a stock, it certainly is not an ideal strategy if the investor is bearish. Losses begin to occur when the stock price falls below the purchase price of the stock minus the premium received for the call. In the XYZ example, anything below $48 results in a loss. Therefore, the covered call strategy is not a low-risk trade. Basically, by using the strategy, the investor is offsetting with the sale of calls some of the cost of purchasing a stock. As a result, the covered call is only moderately less risky than simply owning the stock, and offers less reward potential.

The best time to establish the covered call is when the implied volatility of options is high. In this case, the option strategist is taking in the maximum possible premium. Let's return to our LWIN example and the strategist seeking to participate in a potential rally in shares of Leap Wireless International. Just as with the protective put buyer, the strategist buys 100 shares of LWIN on March 7 with the stock trading for $10.35 a share. This time, however, rather than buying a put, the strategist sells one April 12.5 call contract. On March 7, the strategist was able to sell the call for $1.50 a contract with an IV of 120 percent. The cost of the trade, then, is $885 ($1,035 for the stock minus $150 for selling the call option) plus commissions. Note: The premium of an option is always listed in point value. To calculate the actual cost, simply multiply the point value by 100.

On April 2, 2002, the strategist checks the price quote of the LWIN stock and options. Again, the stock is unchanged at $10.35. The LWIN April 12.5 call options, however, have fallen in value and are worth only 25 cents. The position is now

---

Covered Call

Strategy = Buy the underlying security and sell an out-of-the-money call option.

Market Opportunity = Look for a bullish to neutral market where a slow rise in the price of the underlying is anticipated with little risk of decline.

Maximum Risk = Virtually unlimited to the downside below the breakeven all the way to zero.

Maximum Profit = Limited to the credit received from the short call option + (short call strike price – price of long underlying asset) times value per point.

Breakeven = Price of the underlying asset at initiation – short call premium received.

Margin = The amount is subject to your broker's discretion.

worth $1,010, which represents, roughly, a one-month 14 percent gain. Each options contract lost $1.10 in value due to time decay. In this case, the options lost another 15 cents due to changes in implied volatility.

In conclusion, strategies that involve buying options will be adversely affected by falling implied volatility, and strategies that involve selling options will benefit from falling IV. The opposite is also true. Rising IV is a boon to the option buyer, but the nemesis of the option seller. Time decay works the same way, and to a greater degree. Thus, in order to understand and trade options successfully, it is imperative to know how to measure and monitor changes in implied volatility.

THE GREEKS

Speaking of measurement tools, the "greeks" deserve commentary at this time. As we know, implied volatility is derived from the price of the option in the open market and an option pricing model, but it is not the only useful piece of information derived from the model. Recall that, given a level of volatility, option pricing models can be used to solve for the option's theoretical price. In addition, whether one is solving for price or implied volatility, the Black-Scholes option pricing model will also yield the so-called greeks—delta, theta, vega, and gamma. Each risk measurement tool provides the option strategist with important information regarding the options contract.

Delta

Delta, perhaps the most important of the greeks, measures how much the price of an option moves for each point change in the underlying stock or index. Delta will range from 0.00 to 1.00 for call options and −1.00 to 0.00 for put options (put options have negative deltas because the option price moves inversely with the price moves of the underlying asset). In a move to simplify the process, however, deltas are usually expressed without the decimal point. Thus, a delta of +.50 is usually assigned a value of +50. This is also how we will express them henceforth. For instance, a delta of +50 means that if the stock moves up $1, the value of the option will increase about $.50. If the stock decreases $1, then the option will decrease by about $.50. Similarly, if the delta of the option is −25, then a $1 increase in the stock price will result in a $.25 decline in the price of the option, and a $1 decrease in the value of the underlying results in a $.25 increase in the value of the option. The delta of an option changes depending on just how far in-the-money (ITM) or out-of-the-money (OTM) the option strike is located. Deep ITM options (calls or puts) will have deltas approaching 100, while deep OTM options (calls or puts) will have deltas approaching zero. An option with a delta close to zero is not extremely sensitive to price changes in the underlying asset. On the other hand, a call with an delta of 1.00 will move dollar

> ***Fixed and variable deltas:*** There are two kinds of deltas: fixed and variable. Fixed deltas do not change regardless of price movement. Stock shares have a fixed delta that is positive for long shares and negative for short shares, with a fixed ratio of 1:1. Thus, buying 100 shares of stock comes with a delta of +100, while selling 100 shares of stock has a delta of –100. The deltas will not change regardless of how the price fluctuates; only increasing the number of shares changes the delta. Options, however, have variable deltas. The delta value of an option changes as the price of the underlying asset moves the option in- and out-of-the-money. For example, let's say XYZ stock is currently selling at $50 and you decide to buy a call with a strike price of $50. Since the option strike price and the current price of the underlying stock are identical, the option is said to be at-the-money (ATM). See Appendix F for a complete chart of variable option delta values.

for dollar with the price changes in the stock or index. The delta of an option also conveys an option's bias for ending up in-the-money by expiration. Thus, an option with a delta of 25 has a 25 percent chance of ending up in-the-money by expiration.

To calculate an option delta, simply divide the change in the premium of the option by the change in the market price of the underlying stock. For example, if the price of an option falls from $3 to $2.50 and the underlying stock falls from $50 to $49, then the option delta is .50 ($3 – $2.50/$50 – $49 = .50). This means the option has a 50 percent chance of ending up in-the-money by expiration. However, the more common way of computing delta uses an option pricing model. Traders rarely compute delta by hand.

Table 6.1 provides the greeks for the LWIN example discussed in the preceding section. Again, the option prices were taken on March 7, 2002, but the options expire in April (the third Friday). Note that the call option has a delta of almost .50, which means that each $1 price move in shares of LWIN results in a 50-cent increase in the April 12.5 call. The put option, on the other hand, has a negative delta. It will gain 35 cents in value for each $1 decline in Leap Wireless shares.

Gamma

Gamma measures the changes in delta for each point change in the underlying stock or index's price. A high gamma means that the delta of your position will change very quickly for a relatively small movement in the underlying asset. It is a measure of the size of your position—the more options you have in a trade, the larger the gamma will be. A high gamma helps make a delta-neutral trade profitable more quickly, as adjustments to your position can be made with smaller (hence more likely) movements of the stock than with a lower gamma.

Table 6.1 shows the gamma for the April 12.5 LWIN call and the April 10 LWIN put. For example, as the stock moves $1 higher, the delta will increase by 0.473.

Table 6.1 Examples of Greeks (LWIN)

Greeks on LWIN April Options on March 7, 2002		
	April 12.5 Call	April 10 Put
Delta	0.473	−0.350
Gamma	0.073	0.060
Theta	−0.016	−0.015
Vega	0.019	0.017

Obviously, the delta cannot continue moving higher at this rate indefinitely as the stock price moves higher because delta never exceeds 1.00. Therefore, the further the stock moves in-the-money, the greater the delta and the smaller the gamma. In fact, gamma is at its highest value when options are at-the-money and diminishes as the stock price moves away from the strike price. Eventually, gamma approaches zero as the option moves deep in- or out-of-the-money. Unlike delta, gamma is always a positive number for puts and calls alike.

Theta

Theta measures the rate of time decay for an option. Theta is always expressed as a negative number because both puts and calls suffer from time decay. The rate of time decay is not linear, however. As an option approaches expiration, the rate of time decay increases. Therefore, options with one month until expiration will have a greater theta than an equivalent option with six months until expiration. Notice from Table 6.1 that both the put and the call are losing about 1.5 cents of value as each day passes.

Vega

For the volatility trader, vega is perhaps the most important greek. Some traders prefer to use the term "tau" to describe this risk measurement because vega is not actually a Greek letter. Nevertheless, vega reflects how much an option price changes for each percentage change in volatility. It is always expressed as a positive number, whether it is a put or a call.

All else being equal, higher-volatility stocks will have higher-priced options than low-volatility stocks. As a result, when the volatility of a stock increases, so will the value of the stock's options—whether puts or calls. But when the volatility of a stock falls, option premiums will decline as well. Vega is simply the mathematical term used to quantify the changes in the value of an option for each change in the volatility of an asset.

Which measure of volatility are we referring to when discussing vega: statistical or implied? Recall that, when plugging option prices into the Black-Scholes model, we are solving for implied volatility. As the implied volatility of an option changes, the price of that option will change as well. Generally speaking, when an option price rises, it is due to an increase in implied volatility. This can occur even when the statistical volatility of the stock remains unchanged. Therefore, vega measures how much the option price changes as the implied volatility fluctuates.

In the case of the LWIN example, vega equals 0.019 for the call and 0.017 for the put. As the implied volatility of the option increases by 1 percent, the call will increase in value by 1.9 cents and the put by 1.7 cents. Therefore, option positions that involve the purchase of puts and calls will increase in value, while trades that involve the sale of options will decrease in value as implied volatility increases. In sum, vega is simply the means of quantifying the volatility phenomenon discussed with respect to LWIN, the protective put, and the covered call.

CONCLUSION

The concepts outlined in this chapter are an essential part of the puzzle. Trading options without a clear understanding of implied volatility, based only on charts and other indicators, can be a big mistake. For example, many new option traders notice how stocks tend to show increases in volatility immediately following their earnings announcements. Therefore, many traders feel placing certain strategies such as a straddle—the simultaneous purchase of a call and put—would be profitable more often than not. However, implied volatility tends to fall sharply after the earnings news is out, so even a fairly large move in the stock can result in a trading loss because of a collapse in implied volatility. Before the earnings announcement, implied volatility shoots higher in anticipation of the stock exhibiting higher volatility from the announcement. Once the news is out, implied volatility drops unless another volatile event for the stock is on the horizon.

The important factor to consider before becoming an option buyer or seller is the current level of implied volatility being reflected in the option's price. As we have seen, no two options have the same levels of implied volatility at any point in time. Even two options with different strike prices or expiration months on the same stock can have different levels of implied volatility. In addition, implied volatility is always in a state of flux. Therefore, for each specific option, the strategist must consider the level of implied volatility at that specific point in time.

Armed with the ability to measure the implied volatility of an option, the strategist is better equipped to determine whether it is cheap or expensive. Of course, this cannot be done in a vacuum. The important factor to consider is the relationship between the current level of implied volatility relative to the stock's historical volatility and the implied volatility of that option over time. By doing so, the strategist will be able to gauge if the options are cheap or expensive and also know which of the specific strategies covered throughout the remainder of this book are most promising.

7

VIX and Other Sentiment Indicators

Since the first option contract was listed for trading on the Chicago Board Options Exchange almost three decades ago, trading of options has grown enormously popular. During the year 2000, almost 800 million contracts traded hands, or 2.9 million a day. Today, five different exchanges list options. What was once an unregulated and inefficient process in the early 1970s has become a vibrant and well-organized marketplace today.

Now that option trading has grown into a major investment arena, it has also become a window into market psychology. Millions of investors trade options today. When the mood toward stocks and the market turns pessimistic, those investors will lean toward caution and buy put options for downside protection. Conversely, when investors turn optimistic or even euphoric regarding stocks and the U.S. market, speculative activity will lead to an increase in call buying.

Looking at the options market to glean information about investor psychology is also known as sentiment analysis. It is especially useful in the contrarian approach to investing. That is, when investors, or the crowd, are predominantly optimistic, chances are the majority is wrong and it pays to bet against them. Conversely, when the crowd is predominantly pessimistic regarding the market, the contrarian will become optimistic. In short, the contrarian is generally betting against the crowd and develops strong conviction when the emotions of greed and fear reach extremes. How do extreme emotions cause mispricing in the stock market? When investors become euphoric, optimistic, and bullish, they can drive prices too high and create overbought conditions. Conversely, when fear, panic, and mayhem overcome the market, stock prices can fall too low and create oversold conditions.

Although the art of sentiment analysis dates back centuries and has given rise to a wide array of tools available for studying market sentiment (see *The Stock Market Course*), the following discussion centers on the options market. To be more precise, this chapter details how to take information from the options market—implied volatility indicators and put/call ratios—to gauge market sentiment. The key to using sentiment analysis successfully lies in identifying extremes. That is, when looking at the trading in the options market, it is important to note that the crowd is not always wrong. Instead, investors are generally on the wrong side of the markets at extremes, or during periods of strong emotion. For that reason, there is an adage on Wall Street that goes, "The crowd is usually right on the trends, but wrong at both ends." Throughout this chapter, we'll explore the study of sentiment analysis in order to help the reader stay on the right side of the trends and avoid being wrong at the ends.

CBOE VOLATILITY INDEX (VIX)

No discussion of volatility would be complete without a close look at the CBOE Volatility Index, or VIX. Created by the Chicago Board Options Exchange in 1986, VIX has become the number one gauge of market volatility available today. It is unique in that it offers up-to-the-minute (real-time) information regarding market volatility because it is computed throughout the trading day. Therefore, current readings from VIX are available at the click of the mouse without cumbersome calculations. Just go to the Optionetics.com home page and enter $VIX in the quote box (see Figure 7.1).

VIX provides up-to-the-minute readings of market volatility. However, VIX is not a gauge of actual volatility, but a measure of implied volatility. As we saw in prior chapters, implied volatility is derived using an option valuation model. In the case of VIX, the options are on the S&P 100. Known mainly by its ticker symbol OEX, the S&P 100, in turn, is an index that reflects 100 of the largest companies with stocks trading on the U.S. exchanges. At one time, OEX options were among the most popular and most actively traded. Indeed, the S&P 100 was the first index to offer listed options back in 1983. Since that time, however, other indexes have

Cboe Volatility Index ($VIX)			
		Delayed Quote as of MAY 10, 2001, 2:20:07 PM (E.T.)	
Last	27.19	Change	↓-0.63
Open	27.020	% Change	↓-2.26%
High	27.570	Volume	N/A
Low	26.710	Exchange	INDEX
52 Week High	41.984	52 Week Low	18.125

Figure 7.1 CBOE Volatility Index (Courtesy of Optionetics.com)

attracted greater investor interest, and OEX is no longer among the most actively traded. Nevertheless, the trading of OEX options continues and they remain a popular vehicle for many large and professional traders. VIX is a measure of the implied volatility of OEX options, and therefore it represents the market consensus view regarding the future volatility of 100 of the largest and most actively traded stocks on the U.S. exchanges.

COMPUTING VIX

Before trying to interpret the fluctuations of VIX, let's take a closer look at how the index is constructed. Created by the Chicago Board Options Exchange, VIX is based on the implied volatilities of eight OEX option contracts weighted in such a way as to reflect the implied volatility of a 30 calendar day (or 20 trading day) at-the-money option. (Calendar days and trading days are never equal because there is no trading on the weekends.) VIX is computed on a real-time basis throughout the day from the price changes in the option contracts and the value of the OEX.

The CBOE uses the Black-Scholes option valuation model to compute the implied volatility on the OEX. Furthermore, unlike the majority of other index options, the S&P 100 settles American style, and the model takes into account the fact that the stocks within the index pay dividends. The prices used to calculate the implied volatilities are the averages of the bids and offers. Finally, as with any option pricing model, other variables (time to expiration, striking price, risk-free interest rate, and anticipated dividends) are plugged into the Black-Scholes model to solve for the OEX implied volatility. Therefore, to compute VIX requires three components:

1. An option valuation model: Black-Scholes.

2. The parameters or variables, except implied volatility (strike price, risk-free rate, time to expiration, and expected dividends).

3. Option prices: (bid + ask)/2.

HISTORY OF VIX

Implied volatility is not a measure of an asset's past price performance, but of market expectations about future volatility. VIX is no exception. During times of uncertainty and market turmoil, VIX will rise to reflect expectations regarding future volatility. This is often due to aggressive buying of OEX put options. Recall that the S&P 100 represents a basket of 100 of the largest, most commonly traded stocks on the U.S. stock exchanges. It was also the first index to have listed options. Therefore, it has become a popular tool for professional investors for hedging portfolios. By buying OEX put options, investors with large portfolios of U.S. stocks can offset some of their losses when the market goes into a freefall. The puts will increase in value when the stock market falls and serve as protection. For that reason, VIX is often referred to as the "fear gauge." When professional investors become nervous, the increase demand for OEX puts causes VIX to rise; during times of relative tranquility in the U.S. stock market, VIX will move lower to reflect investor expectations of continuing low market volatility.

Figure 7.2 shows the full history of VIX dating back to 1986. Notice how the volatility index spent most of the 1990s below 25 percent; with few exceptions, the OEX was making a gradual climb during that period. Since 1998, however, beginning with the global financial crisis and going forward to the earnings recession of 2000–2001, marketwide levels of volatility increased dramatically. During that period, VIX was rarely below 25 percent.

The periodic spikes in the volatility index are another interesting aspect of the chart. Shortly after its debut, during the market crash in October 1987, VIX hit a record high of 173 percent, which has yet to be surpassed. In the mini-crash of 1989 after problems associated with UAL Corporation and its restructuring, VIX spiked again. In 1990, when Iraq invaded Kuwait and the United States became embroiled in a war in the Middle East, the volatility index spiked twice: once when Iraq moved into Kuwait in 1990, and again in 1991 after the United Nations authorized coalition forces to attack Iraq.

More recently, in October 1997, investors were spooked when the Dow Jones Industrial Average tumbled 555 points. VIX jumped to 55.5 percent. In the fall of 1998, as the impact of the global financial crisis was beginning to shake U.S. markets, market anxiety once again increased: The volatility index soared above 65 percent. Since

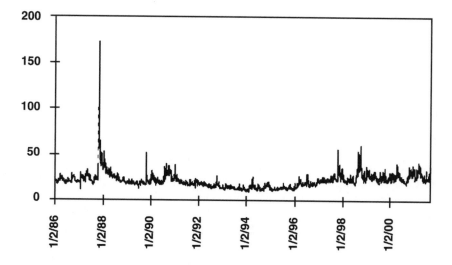

Figure 7.2   Long-Term Chart of VIX

that time, the index has moved above 40 percent on only four occasions: during the April 2000 technology sector sell-off; again in April 2001 at the end of a sharp two-month decline in the OEX; in September 2001, when another spike in VIX occurred after the terrorist attack on the World Trade Center; and finally in July 2002, after WorldCom revealed accounting irregularities and stocks tumbled on the news. The volatility index hit a high of 57.31 on September 21, 2001 (not shown on the chart).

On Friday, July 19, 2002, the stock market—which had already been reeling from a series of corporate scandals and earnings worries—tumbled 390 points. The drop caused a fair amount of investor angst over the weekend, and when the market reopened on Monday, July 22, the Dow fell another 235 points. This decline was followed by another 82-point loss on Tuesday. The steep three-day slide led to a sharp rise in the volatility index, which, on Tuesday, July 23, 2002, closed above the 50 percent mark for the first time since 1987.

NORMAL TRADING RANGE

Outside of its spikes, VIX spends long periods of time within a fairly well defined range. The average closing value of the volatility index since its creation in 1986 is roughly 20.5, and the median is 19.5. Over the recent past, the trend has been for those values to increase somewhat. In 1998, for example, VIX showed its second widest trading range ever. In that year, the index spent most of its time between 18.6 percent and 42.7 percent. In comparison, the range was 17.4 percent to 24.9 percent in 1986.

By historical standards, the implied volatility on OEX options remains relatively high. From 1999 until April 2001, VIX fluctuated between 16.6 percent and 42 percent. The closing high and low values were 18.2 percent and 39.7 percent. Figure 7.3 shows that, over this time period, VIX traded mostly in the mid-20s.

VXN

The creation of the S&P 100 index, or OEX, option contract was a revolutionary event for the options market. As we have already seen, the creation of the first standardized options contract coincided with the founding of the Chicago Board Options Exchange in 1973. In 1983, the exchange once again demonstrated its foresight by listing options on the first index—the OEX. The innovation proved enormously popular, and by the late 1990s options were active not only on the OEX, but also on a host of other indexes.

In fact, by the year 2000 the OEX was no longer the most popular index to trade. Figure 7.4 shows the average daily volume of OEX options by month from May 1998 until December 2000. Notice the drop in total OEX option volume through the years. The S&P 100 fell in popularity as other products were launched. Today the S&P 500 index ($SPX) and the Dow Jones Industrial Average ($DJX) also have listed options that have developed greater appeal. One reason for the increased popularity of the

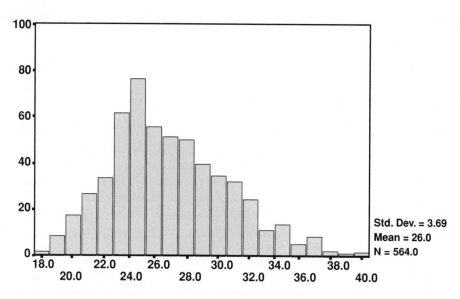

Figure 7.3   VIX Closing Values (January 1999–March 2001)

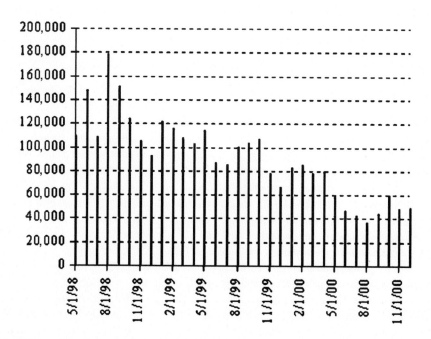

Figure 7.4   OEX Average Daily Option Volume (Monthly)

SPX and the DJX over the OEX stems from how the options settle. The S&P 500 and the Dow Jones Industrial Average options settle European style, which means that exercise can take place only at the option's expiration. There is no risk of early assignment associated with the European-style option, which is an attractive characteristic for option sellers. In contrast, the OEX settles American style, and exercise can take place on any trading day prior to expiration.

The proliferation of other index option contracts has been the most important factor behind the drop in OEX option trading. In Chapter 2, during the discussion of the stock market, readers were introduced to a host of different market and sector indexes. Among the most popular for options traders today is the Nasdaq 100 index. Recall that the Nasdaq 100 represents 100 of the largest nonfinancial stocks listed on the Nasdaq. Therefore, it consists of such familiar names as Cisco Systems (CSCO), Microsoft (MSFT), and Intel (INTC). Indeed, roughly 75 percent of the index is comprised of large, well-known technology stocks.

After the global financial crisis, beginning in the fall of 1998, technology was by far the strongest sector of the stock market. From its low of 1,063 in October 1998, the Nasdaq 100 index increased fourfold over the next 18 months. As the index approached a summit near the 5,000 level in March 2000, investors had fallen in love with technology. Indeed, technology was by far America's favorite sector for investing.

The popularity of technology led many index traders to gravitate from the S&P 100 to options on the NDX and similar indexes. In 1999, the American Stock Exchange started listing options on the Nasdaq 100 Index Trust, or QQQ. Meanwhile, the Chicago Board Options Exchange, which had already listed options on the NDX, created the Mini-Nasdaq 100 (MNX), or Minx, options in August 2000. The MNX is almost exactly the same as the NDX, with one important difference: The Mini-Nasdaq 100 index is equal to one-tenth of the Nasdaq 100. Therefore, the price of the MNX is always below that of the NDX, and as a result the option premiums are lower as well. The lower option premiums, in turn, allow investors to implement trading strategies on the Mini-Nasdaq 100 with less trading capital. In essence, the Mini-Nasdaq 100 was the CBOE's answer to the growing trading activity of the QQQ on the AMEX. At the time, QQQ options were listed only on the AMEX. Today, however, due to changes in rules regarding listing of options, the QQQ is listed on all five option exchanges.

Both the QQQ and the MNX have proven to be enormously popular. Professionals turn to the QQQ and MNX puts to hedge their growing exposure to technology stocks, while speculators trade the QQQ and MNX on the call side. Volumes on the two index products eventually dwarfed that of the OEX options, which continues to be the case today. The trading volumes associated with the QQQ, MNX, SPX, DJX, and a handful of other index products have surpassed that of the OEX.

In response to the growing interest in Nasdaq 100 options, the Chicago Board Options Exchange launched an implied volatility indicator on the NDX in January 2001. Known by its ticker symbol, VXN (sometimes called Vixen), the new implied volatility indicator was created to track the implied volatility of the popular NDX options contract. Like VIX, it is updated continually throughout the trading day. At the same time, although the index was launched only in January 2001, CBOE calculated historical prices going back to January 1995. Figure 7.5 shows the performance of the NDX along with VXN.

Notice the commentary at the top of the chart in Figure 7.5 (borrowed from the CBOE's web site): "Note that there can be a somewhat negative correlation between VXN and NDX; often after stock prices fall, the price for option protection rises." This is the same relationship we saw earlier with VIX! In fact, Figure 7.6 confirms another strong correlation between the VIX and VXN. Historically, VXN has been higher than VIX, which reflects greater volatility within the technology sector. Nevertheless, the two indicators tend to move in similar directions most of the time.

QQV

Sometimes trading starts to feel like a spy game, so stay with me on this one. Responding to the growing popularity of QQQ options trading on the American Stock Exchange, the Chicago Board Options Exchange launched the Mini-Nasdaq 100 index. Simultaneously, the AMEX recognized the need for an implied volatility indicator. In fact, within days of the launch of VXN, the AMEX announced the debut of

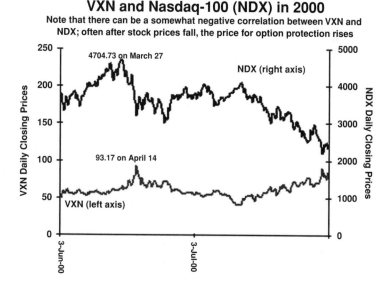

Figure 7.5   Historical View of NDX and VXN (*Source:* Provided as a courtesy by Chicago Board Options Exchange, Inc.)

VXN and VIX Since 1995

(Jan. 3, 1995–March 1, 2001)
VXN is based on the implied volatilities of the Nasdaq-100 (NDX) options,
while the VIX volatility index is based on the implied volatilities of the S&P
100 (OEX) options

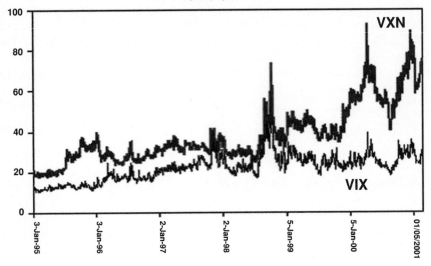

Figure 7.6   VIX and VXN Compared (*Source:* Provided as a courtesy by Chicago
Board Options Exchange, Inc.)

its own proprietary implied volatility indicator: the QQQ volatility index or the
QQV (see Figure 7.7). The QQQ Volatility Index, as you can imagine, is a composite measure of implied volatility on QQQ options. Like VIX, it is computed in real-
time and available throughout the day.

    While the computations of VXN and QQV are basically the same, and both are
measures of the implied volatility of Nasdaq 100 options, they are not always equal
in value. One reason for this is that the QQQ is different from the MNX. The Mini-
Nasdaq 100 equals one-tenth of the NDX, but the QQQ is designed to equal one-
fortieth of the Nasdaq 100. Another key difference between the two is that, while
the CBOE calculates the Nasdaq 100 volatility index (and VIX) using trading days,
the American Stock Exchange uses calendar days when computing the implied
volatility on QQQ options. Without going into the precise math, using trading days
instead of calendar days means that, all else being equal, VXN will be higher than
QQV. Finally, while the NDX and the Mini-Nasdaq 100 (MNX) options settle European style, the QQQ options are American style. Therefore, exercise and assign-

Qqq Volatility Index ($QQV)			
		Delayed Quote as of MAY 11, 2001, 12:19:21 PM (E.T.)	
Last	55.69	Change	↓-1.04
Open	57.930	% Change	↓-1.83%
High	57.930	Volume	N/A
Low	55.480	Exchange	INDEX
52 Week High	74.891	52 Week Low	49.297

Figure 7.7   QQV Quotation (Courtesy of Optionetics.com)

ment can occur at any time prior to expiration with QQQ options, but only at expiration for the NDX and MNX.

However, regardless of whether the trader is watching VIX, VXN, or the QQV, the analysis is the same. During periods of high market volatility, all three implied volatility indicators tend to rise. Basically, option players are aggressively buying index options with the belief that the high levels of market volatility are likely to stay. In other words, traders begin pricing in expectation of high market volatility, and that causes implied volatility on index options to rise. However, VIX, VXN, and QQV tend to fall when investors become complacent toward the outlook for the market and expect volatility to fall.

Therefore, VIX, QQV, and VXN are measures of implied volatility that gauge market sentiment and provide buy and sell signals in the stock market. Thus, when implied volatility is used to time buying and selling in the stock market, it is also being used as a sentiment indicator and a measure of crowd psychology. Ultimately, it is an endeavor in contrary thinking. Specifically, when VIX, QQV, or VXN rise, it suggests that implied volatility on index options is increasing. What does this tell us? It says that there is increasing demand for index options (puts generally), which is driving the option premiums higher. Historically, when traders expect market volatility to rise going forward or during periods of worry, anxiety, or panic:

- Investors will aggressively hedge their bets and portfolios.

- The demand and prices for OEX, NDX, and QQQ puts will spike higher.

Conversely, when implied volatility declines:

- Implied volatility on OEX options is low.

- There is little demand for OEX options.

- Traders are complacent toward the market.

At these times, VIX earns its moniker as the "fear gauge," which makes it an extremely useful tool that provides an excellent measure of real-time market activity.

USING IMPLIED VOLATILITY INDICATORS
AND STATISTICAL VOLATILITY

You sometimes hear option traders use the adage, "When VIX is high, it's time to buy, but when VIX is low, it's time to go." As we have seen, VIX refers to the CBOE Volatility Index, which gauges the market prices of S&P 100 index options. As VIX falls, it suggests that investors are complacent and, from a contrarian perspective, it is a sign that greater levels of market volatility might follow. Why? In a nutshell, because periods of high volatility are often preceded by high levels of bullishness and complacency on the part of investors. In essence, it is when the crowd least expects things to go wrong that they usually do. Therefore, relative optimism often sets the table for market turbulence because unexpected events catch investors vulnerable and unaware; they are then forced to change their viewpoints, and, in the stock market, that means selling.

Therefore, "when VIX is high, it's time to buy, but when VIX is low, it's time to go." The philosophy underlying the adage is that when VIX is high, it is time to turn bullish on stocks and become a buyer. When implied volatility is high, it suggests that investors are relatively pessimistic and expect high levels of volatility going forward. At that time, the contrarian turns bullish on the market and begins to buy stocks. But when VIX is low, it is time to go, or get out of the market. The crowd is complacent and optimistic. From a contrarian approach, it is a poor time to buy stocks and, in fact, "it's time to go." It is vital to recognize that sentiment analysis deals with the search for extremes. When the investment public, or the crowd, begins to display extreme signs of either fear or greed, they push prices too far in one direction or the other. For example, when fear strikes the market, VIX will spike higher. In that case, investors have possibly overreacted, out of fear, and pushed stock prices too far to the downside. Conversely, when VIX is low, it suggests that investors are bullish or complacent. That, in turn, is the type of psychology that occurs near market tops. In short, high VIX means buy stocks (not options); but a low VIX urges caution. This, of course, is a rule of thumb and not a precise timing tool.

The study of market sentiment is the search for extremes—high VIX readings suggest that investors are overreacting and excessive pessimism toward the stock market is not only driving VIX higher, but also pushing stocks too low. However, it is generally not enough for the crowd to be modestly bullish or moderately bearish for the contrarian thinker to bet against them. Recall the Wall Street saying, "The crowd is usually right on the trends, but wrong at both ends." Not exactly poetry, but more often than not it's true. When the crowd begins to display extreme levels of fear and pessimism or greed and optimism, the situation becomes unsustainable. The trick is in knowing how to identify extremes. The VIX can help you, but you have to know exactly what is considered high and low.

Earlier in this chapter, we saw the long-term trend with respect to VIX. It is important to consider the indicator's range in the past. For instance, let's say VIX has been trading mainly between 20 percent and 35 percent. Therefore, when VIX approaches the lower end of its range (20 percent), it is considered indicative of relatively high levels of complacency; when VIX rises toward 35 percent, it is a sign of relatively high levels of pessimism and investor anxiety. The key is to chart each indicator—VIX, VXN, and QQV—to establish what is and what is not "extreme."

Now let's focus on the relationship between actual volatility and the underlying index. For instance, in looking at VIX, is it useful to compare it to the actual volatility of the OEX? As we have seen, implied volatility is a measure derived from the prevailing option prices in the market; it does not necessarily reflect *past* levels of volatility. Since it is derived from option prices, implied volatility is largely based on expectations about future volatility. For instance, when investors expect great market volatility going forward, option premiums will rise. In the case of VIX, it reflects market expectations regarding the future volatility of the S&P 100, or OEX.

As we have seen, there are other measures of volatility besides IV. Historical volatility only considers past prices of the underlying asset, and not the price of the options. Statistical, or actual, volatility is an example. Mathematically, it is computed as the annualized standard deviation of closing prices over a period of days (e.g., 10, 30, 90 days). In this example, the statistical volatility is for the OEX, computed using the closing prices of the S&P 100 over time.

When considering VIX, then, it is important to keep in mind its relationship to the OEX actual volatility. Specifically, rather than simply viewing VIX as high and low in absolute terms, let's consider it relative to the OEX statistical volatility. For instance, as of this writing, VIX is trading below 23 percent. That value, in turn, is the lowest level of OEX implied volatility since July 2001 and a historically low reading. Is it time to go? Well, at that same time, the 20-day statistical volatility of the OEX is 23 percent. Basically, VIX and the statistical volatility are equal. Is this normal? Not at all! In fact, it is unusual to see the statistical or actual volatility of the OEX fall to or below the current value of VIX.

To illustrate, Figure 7.8 compares VIX with OEX 20-day statistical volatility. The heavy black line represents the difference between VIX and statistical volatility. Notice that the black line stays above zero most of the time. Basically, it is rare to see VIX dip below the actual volatility of the OEX. It did so in January 2001, April 2001, and the spring of 2002. All three occasions turned out to be major tops in the market.

PUT/CALL RATIOS

While put/call ratios have little to do with volatility, the subject is discussed here because, when used in combination with implied volatility indicators, the ratios offer meaningful insight into investor sentiment. Most options traders are speculators. That is, they bet on the rise and fall of a stock or market by purchasing puts and calls. While reading this book will give you the skills to implement more complex and sophisticated strategies like spreads and straddles, most option players are simply option buyers. This, in turn, will put you in the top 10 percent of all options

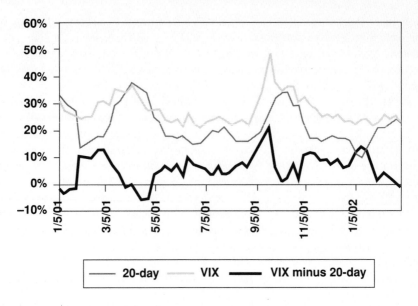

Figure 7.8   VIX with 20-Day Statistical Volatility Comparison

traders because the truth is that most options traders are either hedgers or speculators and their strategies are limited to the straight purchase of puts and calls.

A great deal of the options activity in the market comes in the form of simply
buying options. When market conditions change and investor sentiment alters as
well, the ratio of put buying to call buying will also change. For instance, when turmoil hits the U.S. stock market, panic and fear reign, and investors head for the ex-
its; heavy put buying often accompanies the mayhem. This is true for individual
stocks and the market as a whole (i.e., indexes). Conversely, when stock prices head
higher and investors become euphoric, this greed translates into high levels of call
buying. Investors and option traders are attracted to activity. So when stocks fall,
put buying rises; when stocks leap forward, call activity increases.

One simple way to monitor overall levels of put and call buying is through the
put-to-call ratio. The computation is straightforward. For any given stock, index, or
market, the total number of puts traded is divided by the total number of calls. This
is most often done for each individual trading session.

Put/call ratio = Daily total put volume/Daily total call volume

In a fashion somewhat similar to our discussion of implied volatility indicators, interpreting changes in put/call ratios is also an exercise in contrary thinking. In other words, the analyst is looking for signs of extreme emotion. For
instance, heavy call buying is the sign of excessive optimism on the part of investors, while high levels of put activity are evidence of excessive negative

sentiment. Contrarians look for extremes by focusing on excessive levels of bearish or bullish sentiment and then trade against the crowd. Although the crowd is not always wrong, when emotions—fear and greed—reach extremes, it usually pays to bet against them. Like implied volatility indicators, put-to-call ratios can help identify those extremes.

In order to better understand how to use put-to-call ratios as sentiment indicators, let us consider an example. One of the more widely used put/call ratios is computed as the total volume of puts divided by the total volume of calls on the Chicago Board Options Exchange. The exact statistics are available daily on the exchange's web site—www.cboe.com—and a number of other data vendors. Figure 7.9 shows the CBOE total put-to-call ratio graphically. The chart shows the 10-day average of the ratio to smooth out the data over time (refer back to Chapter 2 for a discussion of averaging techniques). Since there is almost always more call than put activity on the CBOE, the ratio mainly fluctuates between 0.50 and 1.00.

When the CBOE put-to-call ratio rises toward the high end or above 1.00, as it did in the fall of 1998 before the market bottom, it is a sign of:

• Excessive market pessimism.

• Heavy put buying.

The trader should become alert for buying opportunities. On the other hand, when it falls to the lower end of the range, as it did in March 2000 before the market top, it is a sign of:

• Excessive optimism.

• Speculative activity.

• Heavy call buying.

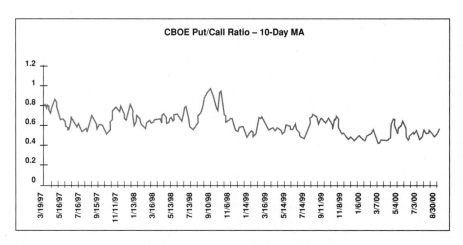

Figure 7.9 Total CBOE Put versus Call Volume (*Source:* CBOE)

That, in turn, will make the trader cautious and on the lookout for downside trading opportunities. Therefore, low readings from the CBOE put-to-call ratio generally coincide with market tops, and high readings with market bottoms. Again, the trader wants to understand the values that the put-to-call ratio has displayed over time and give greater weighting to its extreme values.

Traders use different option contracts to compute put/call ratios. The previous example uses the total volume of all options trading on the Chicago Board Options Exchange. Alternatively, the strategist can look at the trading activity on the American Stock Exchange or Philadelphia Stock Exchange. Some analysts like to consider all the trading across all five of the key option exchanges. It can also be worthwhile to compute the put-to-call ratio for only stock options or, as we will see shortly, only index options.

At Optionetics.com, investors can compute put/call ratios on individual stocks and chart them. For example, Figure 7.10 shows the three-month put/call ratio for AOL Time Warner (AOL). Notice that the chart includes both the current value of the put-to-call ratio and the average over time. One important factor to consider when looking at the chart is the highs and lows that mark extreme readings. Also, the strategist pays special attention to times when the put-to-call ratio deviates significantly from its long-term average. In addition, it's important to understand that each stock, index, or market will have a unique put-to-call ratio, and the readings from IBM, for example,

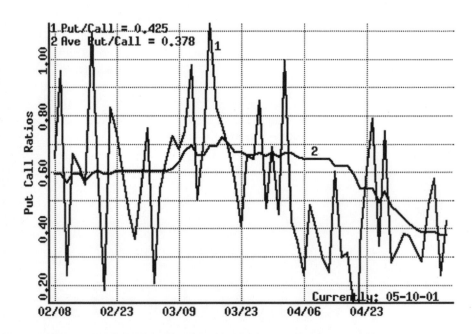

Figure 7.10   AOL Put/Call Ratio (Courtesy of Optionetics.com)

will tell very little about investor sentiment toward General Electric. It is therefore important to consider the extreme values of each put-to-call ratio individually.

For example, in contrast to stock option put/call ratios, index ratios are generally greater than 1.00. The reason is simple: Index options are widely used by large institutions looking to hedge portfolios through the use of put options. Thus, there is, on average, greater put buying than call buying associated with index options. Figure 7.11 offers a look at the OEX put/call ratio. In this chart, a 3-day average is used to smooth out the data. Some traders use 10-, 20-, and even 50-day moving put/call averages.

USING IMPLIED VOLATILITY INDICATORS ALONG WITH PUT/CALL RATIOS

Both implied volatility indicators and put-to-call ratios give unique information regarding investor sentiment toward a stock, index, or market. By using them together, the strategist can get a better sense of whether investors are predominantly bullish or bearish, and whether emotions have reached an extreme. A final piece of the puzzle is volume. For example, if there is an extremely high reading from the OEX put-to-call ratio and VIX spikes higher, it is generally interpreted as a positive signal from a contrarian approach. However, if there isn't any noticeable increase in put activity or volume, the contrarian might treat the readings suspiciously.

In order to better understand how to use put-to-call ratios, implied volatility, and volume statistics together, let's consider an example. The CBOE index put-to-call ratio was mentioned briefly earlier. This contrarian indicator measures the number of index put options traded on the Chicago Board Options Exchange against the number of index call options. On two Fridays, February 22 and March 1, 2002, the

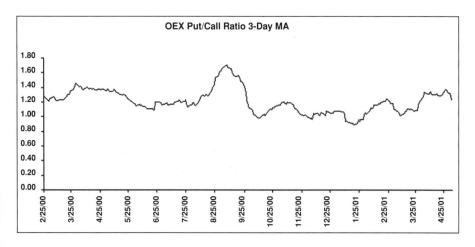

Figure 7.11   OEX Put/Call Ratio Using 3-Day Moving Average (*Source:* CBOE)

CBOE index put-to-call ratio rose to abnormally high levels, and that trend, in turn, suggested a large increase in both index put activity and bearish sentiment. From a contrarian point of view, such high readings are interpreted as excessive pessimism and, therefore, a reason to turn bullish on the stock market. In this case, however, there were a few reasons to treat the high readings with a bit of skepticism.

Since the CBOE index put-to-call ratio equals the number of index puts traded on the Chicago Board Options Exchange divided by the number of index calls, when it rises above 2.00 it tells us that there is more than twice as much put as call activity on the exchange. As noted earlier, because index options are often used as hedging tools for professional investors, there is almost always more index put volume than call volume. Consequently, since the index put-to-call ratio is computed as the number of index puts traded divided by the number of index calls traded, the ratio will almost always be above 1.00 (suggesting more put than call activity).

In early 2002, however, the index put-to-call ratio neared or surpassed 2.00 on two occasions. Seeing such high ratios of put to call buying within days of one another is unusual. Consequently, the high readings were saying that index option traders had turned negative or bearish on the market and started hedging their bets. Again, from a contrarian perspective, the high levels of bearish sentiment are considered a positive for the stock market and a reason to be bullish. Figure 7.12 displays the index put-to-call ratio graphically (smoothed out using a 2-day moving average). Notice that the index put-to-call ratio spiked higher in late 2001 and early 2002.

While the index put-to-call ratio moved gradually higher, it is interesting to note

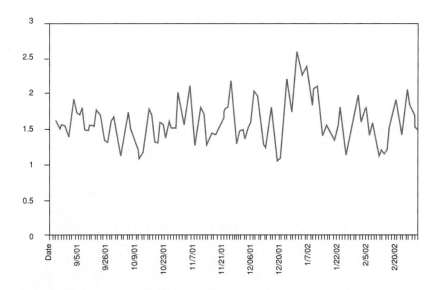

Figure 7.12   CBOE Index Put-to-Call Ratio Using 2-Day Moving Average (Courtesy of Optionetics.com)

that it did not rise to the high of the year. Interestingly, the high occurred on January 4, which also marked an important top in the Dow Jones Industrial Average. Therefore, the index put-to-call ratio actually showed high relative levels of index put activity near a market top. This, of course, is opposite to what the contrarian would expect. Instead, the index put-to-call ratio is generally considered bullish for the market when it records such high readings. Put another way, earlier in the year 2002, the index put-to-call ratio gave an extremely misleading and false signal.

Perhaps one reason the index put-to-call ratio generated a false signal was the unusually low put volume at that time. Take a look at the index put volume shown in Figure 7.13. Notice that during late December and early January volume was extremely low. For example, put volume was fraction of the September 2001 levels, when the market indeed formed a bottom. In short, the light index put volume during early January 2002 distorted the readings from the index put-to-call ratio, which helps to explain why it generated a false signal. Volume remained lackluster after that time.

Another factor to consider when studying the index put-to-call ratio is the level of implied volatility assigned to index options at the time the indicator gives a buy or sell signal. This is relatively easy to do using the CBOE Volatility Index or the Nasdaq 100 Implied Volatility Index. Recall that VIX and VXN offer real-time information regarding implied volatility of index options (specifically, the S&P 100 index and the Nasdaq 100 index options). Generally, when growing levels of pessimism or bearish sentiment in the market occur, and index option traders are aggressively buying put options to hedge portfolios, the implied volatility of index options will rise. For example, notice Figure 7.14. In September 2001, when the

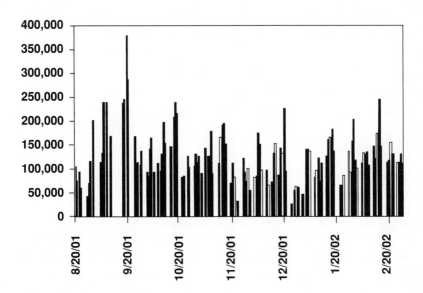

Figure 7.13   Index Put Volume

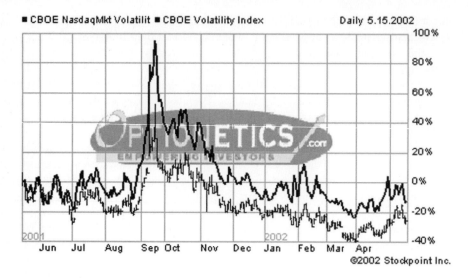

Figure 7.14   The Chart of Both VIX and VXN (Courtesy of Optionetics.com)

market was characterized by fear and pessimism after the terrorist attacks of September 11, VIX and VXN spiked higher. Recall that put volume was also high. Interestingly, however, the index put-to-call ratio was not giving bullish or high readings at that time. Therefore, in September 2001, implied volatility and volume provided evidence of growing levels of fear and pessimism. In early 2002, on the other hand, the index put-to-call ratio spiked higher but there was no confirmation from either implied volatility indicators or volume statistics.

CONCLUSION

Sentiment analysis is the act of thinking contrary to the bias of the investing public. When traders adopt a contrarian view of the market, they are betting against the crowd. The theory is that investors (the masses) are generally wrong during important turning points in the market. Therefore, when the majority of traders are bullish, the contrarian turns bearish. Conversely, when pessimism reigns, the contrarian strategist will become bullish. However, it is important to note that the crowd is not always wrong, but generally wrong before the market makes an important top or a major bottom. The saying goes that "the crowd is right on the trend, but wrong at both ends." There are several indicators that can be used to identify extremes.

The activity in the options market reflects the actual trading decisions of millions of investors. Therefore, it can be a source of valuable information concerning crowd psychology at any given moment. Most of these option traders are betting on the direction of the stock or the market through the purchase of puts and calls. Put-to-call ratios can help quantify the relative levels of put and call activity. The most widely watched such ratio is the CBOE put-to-call ratio. The indicator is a comparison of the puts traded each day compared to call volume on the Chicago Board Options Exchange. During times when traders turn excessively bullish, the number of calls traded will increase relative to the number of puts. Generally, there is more call than put buying when dealing with stock options. For that reason, the total CBOE put/call ratio is often less than 1.00. When excessive levels of optimism exist, the total CBOE put/call ratio will fall below .5. On the other hand, when traders turn bearish, it will spike above 1.00.

Another important tool for gauging investor sentiment is the CBOE Volatility Index, or VIX, often referred to as the market's "fear gauge." VIX is a measure of implied volatility on S&P 100 options. During times of market turbulence, professional investors will turn to OEX put options for protection or to hedge investment portfolios. The aggressive buying of OEX puts, in turn, leads to a surge in implied volatility and a rise in VIX. Therefore, when VIX rises, it is a sign of investor angst. Conversely, when VIX falls to low levels, it suggests investor bullishness or complacency. Therefore, when the volatility index falls to the low end of its recent trading range (18 to 23 percent), traders should turn cautious. On the other hand, when VIX spikes to the upper end of its recent trading range (35 to 40 percent), the strategist can take it as a signal the market fear has become exaggerated and, consequently, assume selling has been overdone. The trader can then expect a move higher in the stock market.

The Nasdaq 100 Volatility Index, or VXN, was developed early in 2001 by the CBOE. It is similar to VIX. However, VXN measures the implied volatility on Nasdaq 100 Index options, instead of the OEX. Again, when studying VXN the trader is looking for relatively low readings (45 to 50 percent) from VXN to presage a market top. Conversely, high readings (75 percent and higher) signal extreme market fear and are a sign that the market is set to rebound.

As the buying and selling takes place in the stock and options markets, sometimes emotions become strong. The trading crowd often takes on characteristics that are quite similar to mob behavior. When these emotions reach extremes of fear and greed, profit opportunities arise for the savvy trader, the contrarian, who is willing to bet against the crowd. Implied volatility indexes and put-to-call ratios are two of the primary tools for gauging investor sentiment. Both come directly from the world of options. As we have seen throughout the chapter, VIX, VXN, and QQV provide real-time and up-to-the-minute readings of index option implied volatility. In order to make sense of those readings, the analyst must first understand what the normal range of each indicator is, and then identify when it has deviated from that normal range and reached an extreme. Put-to-call ratios are used in a similar fashion. Each stock, index, or market will have a unique put-to-call ratio that must be considered over time. In addition, whether utilizing put-to-call ratios or implied volatility, those tools are best used together and in combination with volume statistics. By doing so, the option strategist will have a better handle on what the crowd is doing and feeling, and that can help identify important turning points in the market.

8

Exploiting Low Volatility

When we first set out to write this book, we had two goals in mind. The first was to teach traders the meaning of volatility. After reading the first seven chapters of this book, you should now have a comprehensive understanding of, among other things, how the stock and options markets work, how to use option pricing models, and, most importantly, different ways of viewing and measuring volatility. If you do, the first goal of this book has been accomplished. The second aim of this book is to teach the reader to use volatility to trade the way we do. This goal is a little more complex than the first.

Many traders think timing is everything, or that the key to making profits is to buy low and sell high. However, while timing is perhaps the most important factor for the stock trader, the options trader must consider a number of other equally important factors in order to be successful. For example, how will time decay affect the value of the position? In addition, before initiating an options trade, it is paramount to think about the impact changes in volatility can have on the value of the overall position. What happens if we buy a call and volatility falls? What if you establish a neutral trade, like a straddle, and volatility increases? The remainder of this book outlines specific strategies that will teach the reader how to make profits in any market environment. Armed with an understanding of volatility, you should be able to finish the last four chapters of this book and begin growing the value of your brokerage account trading volatility.

Before explaining how to generate profits trading volatility, however, it is important for the reader to have a solid understanding of options and the risks inherent in trading derivatives. For example, if an option appears expensive (implied volatility is high), does it make sense to sell that option? The answer is obviously yes. However, simply selling an option is not always wise. That is, selling uncovered or naked options comes with an extremely high risk. Therefore, before opening a brokerage account and investing money in options, it is imperative to understand options fully and completely. Hopefully, the first seven chapters have helped you to build a solid foundation in that respect.

In addition to understanding the risks inherent in trading options, it is vital to understand the factors that influence option prices in order to make profits on a consistent basis. As we have learned, implied volatility is an important determinant of an option's premium. Recall that implied volatility measures the amount by which an underlying asset is expected to fluctuate in a given period of time. It provides a gauge of what type of volatility option traders expect a stock to exhibit in the future. Implied volatility also gauges the speed of change relative to a stock or the market. Some prefer to think of it as a measure of market confusion. The more confused a market is, the better chance an option has of ending up in-the-money; a violent market moves very quickly, while a stable market moves slowly. Option prices reflect the confusion or volatility associated with a stock or market. All else being equal, the more violent and rapid the market, the more expensive the options contract. Volatility, confusion, and speed of a stock are important factors in determining the valuation of options' premiums.

As a volatility trader, you are seeking out market extremes. Once found, several options strategies can be used to take advantage of either scenario—whether the stock is showing low or high levels of volatility. This chapter will specifically explore trading strategies that are best positioned to make money when volatility is low.

There are several ways to approach volatility trading, and you may have your own ideas about what is considered low volatility. Maybe your gauge is a ratio that compares implied option volatility to a stock's historical volatility. That is a common way of determining what is high or low. Or maybe you look at percentages. Perhaps you simply look at a volatility chart to determine when options are cheap or expensive. Whatever the case may be, the strategies in this chapter work best in a low-volatility environment.

In order to understand and implement the low-volatility strategies covered in this chapter, it's a good idea to review the discussion in Chapter 4 concerning reversion to the mean. In a nutshell, if the volatility has been unusually low for a period of time, we expect that it will eventually revert to its mean, or average, and begin to move higher. Thus, you expect low implied volatility to move higher over time and vice versa.

So, let's get started with some simple trades that work well in low-volatility situations, and gradually move on to more complex strategies. Some of this will be a review of the information covered in Chapter 6. For example, the first strategy—the long call—is based on the same premise presented earlier in the discussion of the covered call. Similarly, the long put is part of the protective put strategy covered in Chapter 6. Nevertheless, each example is different and paves the way for the straddle—our first complex strategy. From there, the reader will be introduced to debit spreads and ratio backspreads.

> ## What Is Reversion to the Mean?
>
> As briefly discussed in Chapter 4, reversion to the mean is an important concept to understand when trading volatility. Basically, although volatility is always in a state of change, the volatility of stocks or indexes can be assigned a "normal" or average value. It is a value that the volatility of an index tends to center around throughout long periods of time. In statistics, the average is also known as the "mean." When volatility diverges greatly from that normal range, there is a tendency for it to revert back to that average, or mean. Therefore, if the volatility of a stock is low relative to its average over a long period of time, there is a tendency for the volatility to increase and revert to its mean. When the volatility of a stock or index is high relative to its long-term average, chances are great that it will fall back toward the mean.

BUYING CALL OPTIONS
BULLISH ENVIRONMENT/LOW VOLATILITY

The long call is the most basic options strategy and one of the most commonly used. The purpose of this example is to highlight how option prices can change when volatility rises from low levels. Remember that call options give the buyer the right, but not the obligation, to purchase an underlying asset for a predetermined price (strike price), for a predetermined amount of time. Call options are available in various strike prices, which will depend on the current market price of the underlying instrument. Expiration dates also vary: from one month out to more than a year in the case of long-term equity anticipation security (LEAPS) options. Depending on the strategist's outlook for the market, one might choose to buy (go long) or sell (go short) a call option.

By choosing to buy or go long a call option, the strategist is purchasing the right to buy the underlying instrument at a specific strike price until the expiration date. Call buyers have unlimited potential to profit on a rise in the price of an underlying stock; risk is limited to the premium paid for the option. Since the premium of a long call costs money; the purchase results in a deduction from the funds in a brokerage account equal to the cost of the call and shows up as a debit in your trading account. The premium amount, or the cost of the call, represents the maximum risk a long call strategy can incur. Therefore, the risk to call buying is limited to the cost of the call. Since calls can be purchased at a fraction of the price of buying stock, it is an economical way to leverage trading capital in order to participate in a bullish move in a stock or index. Call options are a wasting asset, though, and their value declines as they approach expiration.

The long call is in-the-money when the price of the underlying asset rises above the strike price of the call. For example, if IBM is selling for $85 and you have a call with an $80 strike price, the call is in-the-money. The $80 call gives you the right to buy IBM for $80—a savings of $5 per share. When a call is profitable, the strategist can take profits in two ways: exercising the call or offsetting the trade. By exercising a long call, the strategist becomes the owner of 100 shares per option contract at the call strike price of the underlying stock. The strategist can then turn around and sell the underlying asset at the current market (higher) price to garner a profit on the difference between the two (current price – strike price = profit). To close a long call position by offsetting it, you have to sell a call with the same strike price and identical expiration date.

After buying a call option, most traders simply choose to offset it at a future date. If you anticipate a rise in the price of the underlying asset, you need not exercise the call option to leave yourself open to unlimited profit potential. The call's premium will increase in value depending on how high the underlying instrument rises in price beyond the strike price of the call. As the price of the underlying asset rises, the long call becomes more valuable because it gives the owner of the call the right to buy the underlying stock at the lower strike price of the call. That's why you want to go long a call option when you expect the stock price to rise. Theoretically, the profit potential associated with a long call is unlimited because there is no limit to how high a stock price can rise.

Understanding that call options increase in value as the underlying stock or index moves higher is not enough, however. The savvy options trader also needs to understand how changes in implied volatility can impact the position. Specifically, buying call options during periods of low volatility will offer the best risk/reward. Let's look at the S&P 100 (OEX) during different periods to demonstrate this concept.

Figure 8.1 shows information pertaining to an OEX November 565 call option

---

Moneyness Recap

An important concept to understand when trading options is a concept known as moneyness. (See Chapter 5.) The call option is:

- In-the-money (ITM) when the current market price is more than the strike price.

- Out-of-the-money (OTM) when the current market price is less than the strike price.

- At-the-money (ATM) when the current market price is the same as (or close to) the strike price.

   Generally, options that are out-of-the-money are never exercised. In addition, it is possible to make profits even if the call option remains OTM. For example, a trader buys the XYZ 55 call for $250 a contract with XYZ trading for $45 a share. The next week, XYZ is trading for $50 a share and the XYZ 55 call is worth $500. The trader can close the position (by selling an XYZ call with the same strike price and same expiration) and capture the profits. Making a profit on the trade does not require exercising the option.

S&P 100 Index (OEX) Option Trade

Positon	Num	OptSym	Expire	Strike	Type	Entry	Bid/Ask	Model	IV	Vol	OI	Days
Bought	1	OEBKM	Nov. 01	565	Call	16.7	15.5/16/7	16.2	27.9%	45	303	25

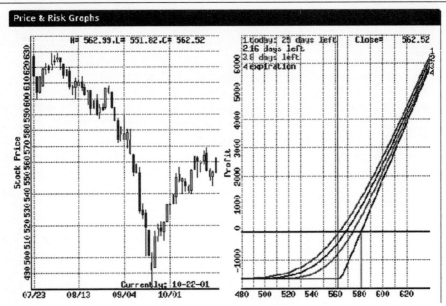

Figure 8.1   OEX November 565 Call Option Data Table and Charts (Courtesy of Optionetics.com)

with 25 days left to expiration. The underlying asset in this example is an index, not a stock. The information was captured on October 22, 2001. Since October is known as a period of historically high volatility for the stock market, options are usually not cheap during this time of year. That was certainly the case in 2001. How do we know? Notice from the table above the price and risk charts (at this point, we are not concerned with the charts themselves) the cost of the at-the-money call option contract was $1,670 ($16.70 × 100 = $1,670) with 25 days left to expiration. At that price, the implied volatility for the option is 27.9 percent. This is not indicative of low volatility, a fact borne out by the volatility graph in Figure 8.2, which shows four months of implied volatility for OEX options. The breakeven for a long call is calculated by adding the call strike price to the premium. In this example, the breakeven is $581.70 ($565 + $16.70), which means the trade won't start making money until OEX climbs to $581.70.

Figure 8.2 shows the implied volatility of the OEX November 565 call option. The chart shows that at the time that the call was purchased—on October 22, 2001—the implied volatility of that particular option was at neither the high end nor

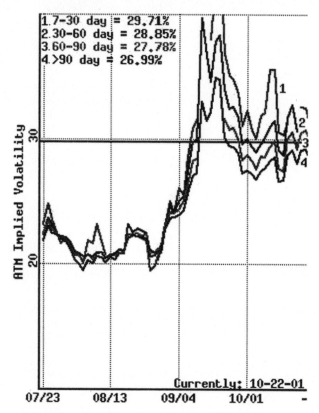

Figure 8.2   OEX IV Chart (Courtesy of Optionetics.com)

the low end of its range. In fact, the reading of 29.7 percent was an average reading for the four months depicted in Figure 8.2, but still somewhat high when compared to the average statistical volatility of the OEX historically.

Now let's look at a trade in the OEX again close to the same price, with the same time to expiration, but with a different volatility. Figure 8.4 shows a long OEX April 570 at-the-money call. The premium for this call is $13.10—much less pricey than the previous example. This option has the same amount of time to expiration (i.e., 25 days) as the November call option discussed before. A quick look at the table confirms that the cost of this call was considerably less than the cost of the one just a few months ago. Why? Look at the implied volatility of 18 percent! That alone will tell you why this position was cheaper.

Figure 8.6 shows the volatility graph and the decline in OEX implied volatility from the time the first call was purchased on October 22, 2001, to the time of the second trade in March 2002. After rising toward 40 percent in September 2001 after the terrorist attacks of 9/11 spooked investors (Figure 8.2), OEX implied volatility

Understanding Japanese Candlesticks

The first chart in Figure 8.1 uses a technique known as Japanese candlesticks. Candlesticks are created from the same data used to create an ordinary price bar on a stock chart. Figure 8.3 shows examples of a price bar that one would find on a normal stock chart and the candlestick equivalent.

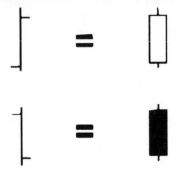

Notice that the open, high, low, and closing prices are incorporated into the creation of the candle itself. The body of the candle is created by the open and close data. The high and low prices help to create the wicks of the candle. When the close is higher than the open, the candle will usually have a white body. This is considered a bullish candle. The black body occurs when the open is higher than the close, indicating a bearish candle. A complete discussion of the significance and predictive ability of candlesticks is beyond the scope of our focus on volatility. Suffice to say that this form of charting is often used because it provides a valuable means of viewing the price behavior of a stock or index.

Figure 8.3   Japanese Candlesticks

S&P 100 Index (OEX) Option Trade

Position	Num	OptSym	Expire	Strike	Type	Entry	Bid/Ask	Model	IV	Vol	OI	Days
Bought	1	OEBDN	Apr 02	570	Call	13.1	12.1/13.1	12.6	18.0%	38	3,399	25

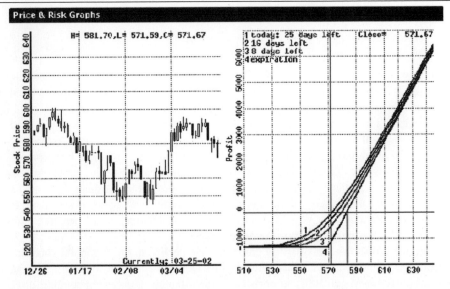

Figure 8.4   OEX April 570 Call Data Table and Charts (Courtesy of Optionetics.com)

Understanding Risk Graphs

Risk graphs are extremely important to the options trader. The graph tells, at a glance, the risk associated with any trade. The profit/loss is plotted on the vertical axis, and the price of the underlying asset is plotted on the horizontal axis. In the case of an OEX call, the graph rises as the price of the OEX increases. It has an upward slope because the profit of a call option increases as the price of the underlying asset rises. Figure 8.5 provides the risk profile for the OEX June 580 call option with the call option trading for $12.90 (12.90 × 100 = $1,290). Each line on the risk graph represents the risk and profit potential of the call based on the value of the OEX at different points in time prior to expiration. Specifically,

- The bottom line (4) represents the profit or loss at expiration.
- Line 3 reflects the P/L with 31 days left until expiration.
- Line 2 reflects the P/L with 62 days left until expiration.
- The top line reflects the P/L with 94 days left until expiration.

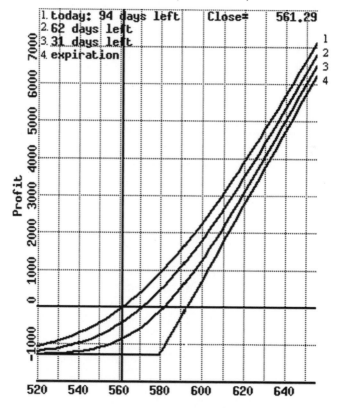

Figure 8.5 OEX June 580 Call Risk Graph (Courtesy of Optionetics.com)

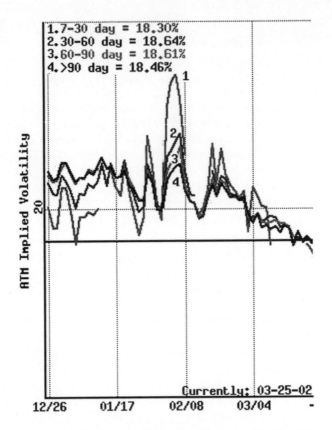

Figure 8.6   Decline in OEX Implied Volatility (Courtesy of Optionetics.com)

began a gradual move lower in late September. As we saw in Chapter 8, the implied volatility of the OEX (measured by VIX) tends to spike higher when investors become nervous or anxious regarding the state of the market.

In late September, some of the fear and uncertainty caused by the 9/11 terrorist attacks started to ease and the stock market started to recover. As Figure 8.7 shows, the OEX made a gradual move higher from September 2001 until March 2002. As that recovery took place, implied volatility moved lower. As we saw from the two examples, from October 22, 2001, until March 25, 2002, implied volatility fell from 27.9 percent to 18.0 percent.

As the OEX recovered, the drop in implied volatility worked against the value of the call options. Why? As time passed, although the OEX made a gradual move higher, the call options did not appreciate as much as one would expect. In fact, we saw that two nearly identical options (the OEX November 565 call on October 22 and the April 570 call on March 25) were priced differently due to the sharp drop in

Figure 8.7   OEX Weekly Chart (Courtesy of Optionetics.com)

volatility. That is, the OEX call options were much cheaper to buy in March 2002 than in October 2001.

The point of this example, then, is to show that the premium of a call option is a function of the implied volatility at the time. This is true of OEX options, as well as options on Microsoft, Coca-Cola, Krispy Kreme Doughnuts, and any other stock or index. The important factor to consider is that implied volatility is always in a state of flux. Buying a call when IV is low increases the odds that the call option will increase in value. When the implied volatility of a call option is high, a greater chance

---

Long Call

Strategy = Buy a call option.

Market Opportunity = Look for a bullish market where a rise above the breakeven is anticipated.

Maximum Risk = Limited to the amount paid for the call.

Maximum Profit = Unlimited as the price of the underlying instrument rises above the breakeven.

Breakeven = Call strike price + call option premium.

Margin = None.

exists that IV will fall, causing the call option to lose value. Again, all of this is based on the concept of reversion to the mean.

BUYING PUT OPTIONS
BEARISH ENVIRONMENT/LOW VOLATILITY

Buying put options is similar to call buying when one considers the impact of implied volatility on the value of the options. Recall that put options give the buyer the right, but not the obligation, to sell an underlying asset at the strike price until market close on the Friday before the third Saturday of the expiration month. Just like call options, put options come in various strike prices depending on the current market price of the underlying instrument. In addition, expiration dates can vary from one month to more than a year (LEAPS options). However, unlike call options, a strategist will go long a put option in anticipation that the stock or index will decline in price.

The put buyer is purchasing the right to sell the underlying instrument at whatever strike price until the expiration. The premium of the long put option will show up as a debit in your trading account. The cost of the premium is the maximum loss you risk by purchasing a put option. Unlike the call that has unlimited profit potential, the maximum profit is limited to the downside because the underlying stock can fall only as low as zero.

Once the underlying stock moves in the anticipated direction—lower—the strategist can capture a profit in one of two ways: exercising the put option or offsetting it to close the position. If the put is exercised, the strategist will become short 100 shares of the underlying stock. If and when the underlying stock falls below the put strike price, the strategist can exercise the put to short the shares at a higher price and then buy the underlying stock at a cheaper price to cover the short and exit the trade (strike price – current price = profit).

The second technique for profiting on a put comes from offsetting it. This is the same concept discussed earlier with respect to the call. If the price of the underlying stock falls, the corresponding put premium increases and the put can then be offset at a profit by selling a put with the same strike and expiration. Theoretically, a long put option will fall in value if the underlying security (index or stock) increases in price.

Put options give the owner the right to sell something at a specific price for a fixed amount of time. A put option is:

- In-the-money (ITM) when the strike price is higher than the market price of the underlying asset.

- Out-of-the-money (OTM) when the strike price is lower than the price of the underlying security.

- At-the-money (ATM) when the price of the underlying is equal (or close) to the strike price.

Just as we learned with call options, buying puts when implied volatility is low gives the trader less overall risk until expiration. When the implied volatility is low, the put options are cheaper than when volatility is high. Again, let's look at an OEX position, this time using puts instead of calls to demonstrate the difference in risks, rewards, and breakevens during various volatilities.

Notice from Figure 8.8 that on October 22, 2001, with the S&P 100 trading for 562.52, the OEX 565 put closed at $19. Figure 8.8 shows the risk graph of owning one of these puts. It is limited to $1,900 ($19 × 100), the cost of one put. To calculate the breakeven, simply subtract the put premium from the put strike price. In this example, the breakeven is $546 ($565 − $19). Furthermore, at that time there were 25 days until expiration and the implied volatility was at 30.7 percent. Figure 8.9 reveals that an IV of 30.7 percent is neither high nor low, but average given the recent range.

Now fast-forward to a similar position on March 25, 2002 (see Figure 8.10). At that time, implied volatility had fallen from its October 22 levels and, in fact, was near its one-year lows. An option with roughly the same characteristics (i.e., at-the-money) and time left until expiration was much cheaper than the at-the-money put in October. Notice the price of the March 02 ATM put: little more than half of the October 22 position.

Why was the put option much cheaper in March 2002 than in October 2001? Well, although the days to expiration are the same, the implied volatility fell from 30.7 percent to 18.9 percent. Figure 8.11 depicts the implied volatility of the OEX falling below 19 percent in March 2002. That's why these options became so cheap!

S&P 100 Index (OEX) Option Trade

Position	Num	OptSym	Expire	Strike	Type	Entry	Bid/Ask	Model	IV	Vol	OI	Days
Bought	1	OEBWN	Nov 01	565	Put	19	17.7/19	18.7	30.7%	45	181	25

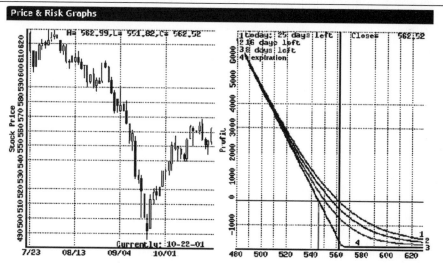

Figure 8.8 Data Table and Charts for OEX November 565 Put on October 22, 2001 (Courtesy of Optionetics.com)

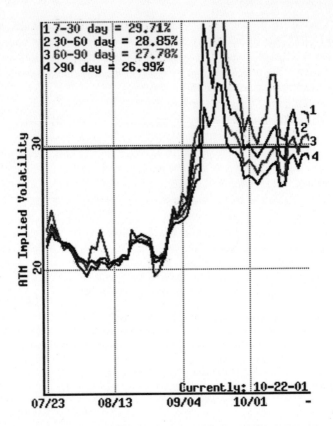

Figure 8.9   Implied Volatility of OEX for Four Months Ending October 22, 2001
(Courtesy of Optionetics.com)

Long Put

Strategy = Buy a put option.

Market Opportunity = Look for a bearish market where you anticipate a fall in the price of the underlying asset below the breakeven.

Maximum Risk = Limited to the price paid for the put option premium.

Maximum Profit = Limited as the stock price falls below the breakeven to zero.

Breakeven = Put strike price – put option premium.

Margin = None.

S&P 100 Index (OEX) Option Trade

Position	Num	OptSym	Expire	Strike	Type	Entry	Bid/Ask	Model	IV	Vol	OI	Days
Bought	1	OEBPN	Apr 02	570	Put	9.9	9.2/9.9	9.6	18.9%	663	3,234	25

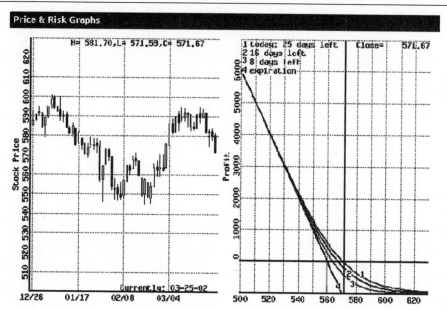

Figure 8.10   Data Table and Charts for OEX April 570 Put (Courtesy of Optionetics.com)

Look at the drop in volatility as these options came down below a level of 20 percent—the lowest level in a year. The option prices reflect the volatility graph. Again, this is the same concept as with the call: Falling IV makes options cheaper.

TRADING LOW VOLATILITY USING A NONDIRECTIONAL STRATEGY

Whether long puts or calls, the best time to buy options is when they're cheap. For example, buying calls during periods of low volatility is a great way to get bullish on a stock for a low premium price, while buying puts on low volatility is also a great way to play a stock that is likely to head south. What about a situation where the strategist expects a big move on a stock, but is not sure of the direction? You might want to go both ways by purchasing what is referred to as a *straddle*.

The straddle is a popular tool for creating a position on a stock where the future direction is uncertain. It consists of the simultaneous purchase of both a call and a put at the same strike price, with the same amount of time to expiration. If the stock

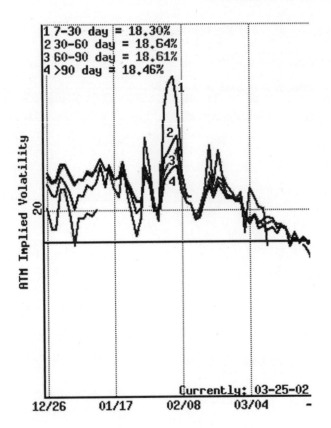

1 7-30 day = 18.30%
2 30-60 day = 18.64%
3 60-90 day = 18.61%
4 >90 day = 18.46%

ATM Implied Volatility

Currently: 03-25-02
12/26   01/17   02/08   03/04   -

Figure 8.11   Implied Volatility of OEX on March 25, 2002 (Courtesy of
Optionetics.com)

makes a big move higher, the call will appreciate and begin to yield profits. If the
stock tanks, the put will increase in value and the strategist will make money on the
put options. An important factor to consider, however, is the volatility of the options
before initiating the trade. Let's look at an example using a stock that was both
cheap in volatility and quiet in stock movement.

Phillip Morris (MO) was among the best-performing components of the Dow
Jones Industrial Average during 2000 and 2001. While the Dow suffered a 12 percent loss during those two years, shares of the consumer products giant more than
doubled. The gains were mostly registered in the year 2000. Indeed, the stock
started moving sideways after the large run-up and then once again started moving
higher. Figure 8.12 shows the price action of MO.

One thing that commonly happens when a stock makes a gradual (not violent)
move higher is the implied volatility begins to edge lower. Figure 8.13 shows the
implied volatility chart for Philip Morris. Notice how as this stock climbed, the

---

What Is a Straddle?

The straddle is the simultaneous purchase of an at-the-money put and an at-the-money call with the same strike price and same expiration, on the same stock or index. The position is established for a debit—a deduction of funds from a trading account—because the investor is buying both a call and a put. The investor's risk is equal to the cost of the options. Profits occur when the stock or index moves above the upside breakeven or below the downside breakeven. Thus, when the underlying security moves down below the breakeven, the put increases in value by a sufficient amount to overcome the cost of the call, or vice versa. For example, if XYZ stock is trading at a price of $50 a share and the October 50 put and October 50 call can be purchased for $2 each, the strategist can buy both the put and the call for a cost (or debit) of $4. The downside breakeven on the trade occurs if the stock price drops to $46 (strike price minus net premium or $50 – $4 = $46). The upside breakeven occurs if XYZ rises above $54 (strike price plus net premium or $50 + $4 = $54). All else being equal, profits begin to be realized when the stock moves below $46 or above $54. The strategist wants the call to increase in value enough to offset the cost of the put or the put to increase enough to cover the cost of the call. Whether the stock or index moves up or down doesn't matter—just as long as it moves enough in one direction or the other.

---

volatility on the options dropped. This opens up an opportunity for buying calls, buying puts, or buying both with a straddle purchase.

If the implied volatility of a stock is low, when does it make sense to purchase a straddle instead of a long put or long call? The straddle is appropriate when the strategist expects the stock to make a large move higher or lower, but is uncertain of the ultimate direction. The data table and charts of the MO straddle are provided in

---

Long Straddle

Strategy = Purchase an ATM call and an ATM put with the same strike price and the same expiration.

Market Opportunity = Look for a market with low implied volatility options where a sharp volatility increase is anticipated.

Maximum Risk = Limited to the net debit paid.

Maximum Profit = Unlimited to the upside and limited to zero on the downside. Profit requires sufficient market movement but does not depend on market direction.

Upside Breakeven = ATM strike price + net debit paid.

Downside Breakeven = ATM strike price – net debit paid.

Margin = None.

Figure 8.12   Stock Price Chart of MO (Courtesy of Optionetics.com)

Figure 8.14. Notice that the risk lies in the center of the graph or if Philip Morris moves sideways for the next 81 days. If, however, Philip Morris were to break out of its range to the upside or the downside, a profit is realized if the trader closes the position outside of the two breakeven lines at $50.90 and $59.10 (the debit of the trade added or subtracted from the strike prices).

The straddle has greater odds of success if purchased when implied volatility is low. Recall that both the long call and the long put benefit from increasing levels of implied volatility. Intuitively, then, it makes sense that the straddle also benefits if IV jumps higher. After all, it involves the simultaneous purchase of a put and a call. For that reason, the best time to purchase a straddle is when implied volatility is low because reversion to the mean tells us it is likely to increase going forward.

LOW-VOLATILITY DEBIT SPREADS

Debit spreads are directional strategies that can also benefit from rising volatility. The most commonly used are the bear put spread and the bull call spread. First, let's

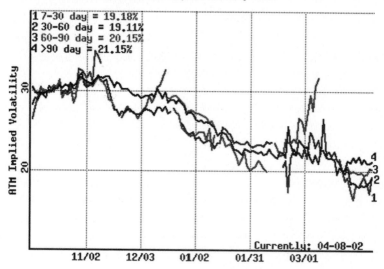

Figure 8.13 Implied Volatility Chart of MO (Courtesy of Optionetics.com)

Philip Morris Companies, Inc. (MO) Straddle

Position	Num	OptSym	Expire	Strike	Type	Entry	Bid/Ask	Model	IV	Vol	OI	Days
Bought	1	MOFK	Jun 02	55	Call	1.35	1.2/1.35	1.2	17.7%	78	2,6691	81
Bought	1	MORK	Jun 02	55	Put	3	2.85/3	2.9	22.3%	48	5,093	81

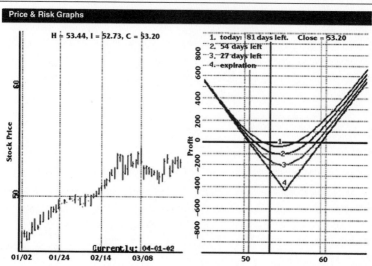

Figure 8.14 Data Table and Charts for MO Straddle (Courtesy of Optionetics.com)

explore the bear put spread using options on the iShares S&P 100 Fund. An example of an exchange-traded fund discussed in Chapter 2, it is designed to equal one-tenth of the S&P 100 index, or OEX. Therefore, in this example, we are not considering a stock, but rather an exchange-traded fund designed to mirror the performance of the OEX. The options for the iShares S&P 100 Fund trade on the Chicago Board Options Exchange under the symbol OEF.

Let's assume that the strategist in this case expects the S&P 100, and thus the OEF, to make a significant move lower between now and mid-October. In early March 2002 the strategist wants to bet on a move lower by purchasing one out-of-the money (OTM) put option. The OEF is trading near $60 at this time, and the strategist is eyeing the May 58, 56, and 54 puts. Although the most conservative choice of the three strikes, the strategist can still make a fairly aggressive bet on a decline in the S&P 100 by purchasing one OEF May 58 put. In this case, the option is out-of-the-money, and therefore the success of the trade hinges on the OEF moving lower. Plugging the relevant variables into the Black-Scholes option pricing model will yield an implied volatility for the option in question.

Here are the details for our trade example:

- Strike price = $58

- Expiration date = May 17, 2002 (the third Friday of the expiration month)

- Underlying asset price (OEF) = $59.43 on March 11

- Interest rate = 5%

- Dividend yield = 1%

- Implied volatility = 20% approximately (using a quote of $1.25 for the OEF October 58 put on March 11)

Table 8.1 shows possible price changes in the May 58 put should the OEF indeed move lower as anticipated. The first column shows hypothetical price changes in the OEF. The second column shows the change in the price of the option given the various price changes in the OEF. In addition, the table shows two possible scenarios.

Directional versus Nondirectional Strategies

Options traders often speak of "nondirectional" strategies. What does this mean? In essence, the strategy makes profits as long as the stock or index makes a significant move higher or lower—like the straddle example we just reviewed. Thus, for nondirectional strategies, directional bias doesn't matter. In contrast, the long call, for instance, is a directional strategy. It profits only when the stock moves in one direction: higher.

Table 8.1 Hypothetical Values of OEF Puts and Bear Put Spread Assuming Different Levels of IV

OEF Hypothetical Price May 1, 2002	Assuming 20 Percent IV			Assuming 25 Percent IV		
	May 58 Put	May 54 Put	Value of Bear Put Spread	May 58 Put	May 54 Put	Value of Bear Put Spread
$62.50	$ 0.05	$0.00	$0.04	$ 0.10	$0.00	$0.10
60.00	0.30	0.00	0.28	0.45	0.02	0.43
57.50	1.20	0.05	1.15	1.42	0.15	1.27
55.00	3.00	0.45	2.55	3.20	0.70	2.47
47.50	10.55	6.55	4.00	10.55	6.55	4.00

Both reflect future projections and the value of the May 58 put on May 1, 2002, or a little more than two weeks prior to expiration. In the first scenario, implied volatility stays the same: 20 percent. In the second, however, the value of the OEF May 58 put option is estimated assuming IV increases from 20 percent to 25 percent.

Notice in Table 8.1 that the value of the put option increases as the OEF moves lower in price. For instance, when it rises to $62.50, the option is worth only 5 cents; but if it falls to $55, it is worth $3. Therefore, as the OEF rises in price, the put option loses value; and as the OEF falls, the put option increases in value. Again, this is a basic characteristic of any put option. At the same time, if the underlying asset remains unchanged (in this case, OEF equals $60 about two weeks prior to expiration), the put option loses value. Why? Time decay. When the underlying asset remains unchanged, both put and call values waste away.

Now, notice the right-hand column of the table. The May 58 put increases more rapidly in value if 25 percent volatility is assumed. In other words, if the implied volatility increases, the value of the put option will also. For that reason, when a stock or an index falls rapidly in value, the put option can see an increase due to the drop in the price of the stock or index and also an increase in implied volatility. For example, if the OEF remains unchanged ($60 a share) and the IV increases to 25 percent, the at-the-money put still loses value, but is worth 45 cents compared to 30 cents when volatility remained the same. A put option that experiences increasing levels of implied volatility will hold greater value, even in the event that the stock or index makes a move in an adverse direction. It is important to note that when the option is deep-in-the-money, the implied volatility will not have a meaningful impact on the option prices. Deep-in-the-money and deep-out-of-the-money options are not highly sensitive to changes in IV.

So far, there is nothing new here. When investors expect implied volatility to increase, they can also expect the value of the option to increase as well. As a general rule, when stocks or indexes are falling rapidly, implied volatility will rise. Other times, implied volatility will spike higher in advance of a major news event, such as a takeover. Anytime there is an unusually strong demand for options—such as when investors are seeking to hedge portfolios with put options amid falling stock prices or speculators are trying to profit from a takeover rumor—option prices and implied volatility will rise.

BEAR PUT DEBIT SPREADS

When implementing more complex strategies, the option strategist must consider the impact of implied volatility on all of the options involved in the trade. For instance, instead of simply buying a put, the strategists in this example might prefer to buy the May 58 put and sell the May 54 put. This strategy is called a bear put spread.

Again, assuming the starting date of the trade is March 11, the OEF is trading for roughly $60 a share, and the May 58 put is quoted for $1.25, the strategist sets out to make a bearish bet on the OEF. In this case, rather than simply buying the May 58 put, the strategist decides to simultaneously sell the May 54 put, which is quoted at a price of 40 cents. The cost of the trade, then, is 85 cents ($1.25 to buy one put minus the premium of 40 cents received for selling the other). The risk associated with the bear put spread is the cost of the trade, in this case 85 cents (or $85). The maximum profit is equal to the difference between the two strike prices minus the cost of the trade. For this example, it equals $315 [($58 − $54) − $.85]. The maximum profit is obtained when OEF falls below the lower strike price. The breakeven is calculated by subtracting the net debit paid from the higher put strike price. In this example, the breakeven is $57.15 ($58 − $.85).

To see the bear put spread in action, take a look at Table 8.1. It shows the value of the spread given the same assumptions discussed earlier. In the fourth and seventh columns, we see the spread increase in value as the OEF moves lower. (This is not the profit or loss, but the value of the spread. To determine the profit or loss, subtract the cost of the trade—85 cents—from the value of the spread at any given time.) Notice that, when the OEF falls below $50, both options are deep-in-the-money and the spread takes on the maximum value of $4 a contract.

What Is a Bear Put Spread?

The bear put spread involves the simultaneous purchase of a put option and sale of a put option, with the same expiration dates, but different strike prices. In general, the strategist will buy an at-the-money or near-the-money put and sell an OTM put. Profits arise as the stock falls. The maximum risk is the difference between the price paid for the ATM put option minus the premium received for the OTM put. The maximum gain is equal to the difference between the two strike prices minus the cost of the trade. The breakeven is calculated by subtracting the net debit paid from the higher put strike price.

Bear Put Spread

Strategy = Buy a higher strike put and sell a lower strike put with the same expiration date.

Market Opportunity = Look for a bearish market where you anticipate a modest decrease in the price of the underlying asset below the strike price of the short put option.

Maximum Risk = Limited to the net debit paid.

Maximum Profit = Limited [(difference in strike prices × 100) – net debit paid].

Breakeven = Higher put strike price – net debit paid.

Margin = Required. The amount is subject to your broker's discretion— should be limited to the net debit on the trade.

In addition, the table shows impact of an increase of volatility on the October 54 put and the bear put spread. Prior to falling deep-in-the-money, the spread will retain more value when volatility increases. That is, the spread retains greater value when the options are at-the-money or near-the-money and implied volatility increases. The position still results in a loss due to time decay, but not as much as if IV would actually fall during that time. Therefore, a rising stock price, time decay, and falling implied volatility can all work against the bear put spread.

BULL CALL DEBIT SPREADS

The bull call spread is similar to the bear put spread, but this time the strategist anticipates a rise in the stock or index. The trade is generally placed by purchasing an

What Is a Bull Call Spread?

The bull call spread involves the simultaneous purchase of a lower strike call and the sale of a higher strike call with the same expiration dates. In practice, the strategist will buy an at-the-money or near-the-money call and sell an OTM call. Profits arise as the stock rises. The maximum risk is the difference between the price paid for the ATM option (plus commissions) minus the premium received for the OTM call. The maximum gain is equal to the difference between the two strike prices minus the cost of the trade. The breakeven is calculated by adding the lower call strike price to the net debit paid.

at-the-money or near-the-money call and simultaneously selling a call with a higher strike price. More aggressive bull call spreads can be initiated using two OTM options. In any case, profits accrue when the stock price moves higher in price, which is directly opposite to the bear put spread. In both cases, however, the trade is done for a debit because the cost of purchasing the at-the-money option is greater than the premium received for selling the out-of-the-money option.

The impact of volatility changes on the bull call spread is similar to the impact on the bear put spread. Namely, if volatility falls it generally has an adverse impact on the overall position. To understand why falling volatility has a negative impact on the debit spread (bull call spread or bear put spread), the strategist must consider how changes in volatility will impact the at-the-money option versus the out-of-the money option. Vega is useful in this respect. Let's consider another example using the OEF.

Once again, let's assume that the OEF is trading for roughly $60 a share on March 11. The strategist believes the index will make a move higher and takes a peek at the OEF options chain (see Figure 8.15). Rather than simply buying a call, the trader decides to buy the OEF May 62 call and sell the OEF May 66 call. The net cost of the trade is $120 ($1.95 to buy the 62 call at the asked price minus 75 cents for the premium received for selling the 66 call) plus commissions. The cost is also the maximum risk. The maximum profit is achieved when the OEF rises above $66 a share, and is equal to $280 ($66 − $62 − $1.20 = $2.80). Since the breakeven is calculated by adding the net debit of the trade to the lower strike price of the long call, the breakeven of this trade is $63.20 ($62 + $1.20). Just as with the bear put spread, in this trade the strategist wants the spread—the difference between the value of the option that is purchased and the value of the option that is sold—to widen.

How will a change in implied volatility impact this position? In order to find out, the trader can take the prices of the options, plug those values into the Black-Scholes option pricing model, and compute the vega for each option. Recall that vega is one of the so-called greeks. It measures the impact of changes in implied volatility on the value of an option. A vega of .25 suggests that the option will increase in value 25 cents for every percentage point increase in implied volatility.

Table 8.2 shows the vegas for the four OEF call options included in Figure 8.15.

Calls

Symbol	Bid	Ask	Strike
OEMET	2.45	2.85	May02-60.000
OEMEB	1.65	1.95	May02-62.000
OEMED	1.15	1.35	May02-64.000
OEMEF	0.75	0.95	May02-66.000

Figure 8.15   OEF Options Chain

> **Options chain:** Options chains are tools traders use to view price quotes across an options series. The chains are viewed as a table, with calls on one half and puts on the other. Each row represents a different contract. These contracts are first sorted by expiration month and then by strike price. Other variables included on the table can vary based on where the options chain is obtained, but generally chains include the last price, the bid, the ask, volume, and open interest. Some options chains also include implied volatility information and the greeks (such as delta, theta, and gamma). A number of different web sites and online brokerage firms provide options chains. Not long ago, they were available mostly to brokerage firms and other professional investors. Today, however, individual investors can go to a number of sites and find options chains. Most online brokerage firms provide them, as do several options-related web sites. For instance, at the Optionetics.com home page, pulling up an options chain for any given stock is simply a matter of entering the ticker symbol in the quote box at the top of the screen and selecting "chain."

The at-the-money and near-the-money calls have vegas equal to .10 and are, therefore, the most sensitive to changes in volatility. The May 66 call is the furthest out-of-the-money and has the lowest vega; it is the least sensitive to changes in implied volatility.

In Table 8.2, notice how the price of each option will differ when we change the volatility assumptions. For example, if implied volatility is only 15 percent, the May 62 call is worth only 95 cents and the May 66 call is worth 15 cents. Therefore, the value of the bull call spread is 80 cents ($.95 – $.15). If we assume IV is equal to 35 percent, the May 62 call is worth $2.95, the May 66 call is worth $1.65, and the bull call spread is worth $1.30. The fact that implied volatility has a greater impact on the at-the-money option than on the out-of-the-money one explains why the bear put spread and the bull call spread do better in a low-volatility scenario.

One final note on low-volatility debit spreads: The bull call spread is more likely to feel a negative impact from falling IV than is the bear put spread. Bull call spreads are successful when the underlying stock or index moves higher. Recall from our discussion of implied volatility in Chapter 6 that as a general rule, when a stock rises, the IV of its options tends to fall. Therefore, establishing a bull call spread in a high-volatility environment depends on (1) the stock moving higher in price and (2) implied volatility remaining relatively high. Thus, if the bull call spread is established when implied volatility is high, there are two main risks: that

Table 8.2 Prices, Implied Volatility, and Vega for OEF Call Options

OEF Call	Option Price	Implied Volatility	Vega	Option Price with IV = 15%	Option Price with IV = 35%
May02-60	$2.85	25.20%	0.100	$1.80	$3.85
May02-62	1.95	25.10	0.100	0.95	2.95
May02-64	1.35	25.80	0.093	0.45	2.25
May02-66	.75	26.00	0.075	0.15	1.65

Bull Call Spread

Strategy = Buy a lower strike call and sell a higher strike call with the same expiration date.

Market Opportunity = Look for a bullish market where you anticipate a modest increase in the price of the underlying above the price of the short call option.

Maximum Risk = Limited to the net debit paid for the spread.

Maximum Profit = Limited [(difference in strike prices × 100) – net debit paid].

Breakeven = Lower call strike price + net debit paid.

Margin = Required. The amount is subject to your broker's discretion—should be limited to the net debit on the trade.

the stock will fail to make a significant move higher and that implied volatility will fall. Bear put spreads, on the other hand, are profitable when the stock or index falls, which generally leads to an increase in IV. Still, whether trading bull call spreads or bear put spreads, the strategist is better off understanding what impact changes in implied volatility will have on the overall position. Vega is useful in that respect.

RATIO BACKSPREADS IN A LOW-VOLATILITY ENVIRONMENT

The call ratio backspread is another type of trade that is best used when implied volatility is low. The strategy involves the simultaneous purchase of OTM call

What Is a Call Ratio Backspread?

A call ratio backspread is constructed by purchasing calls with a higher strike price and selling fewer calls with a lower strike price at no cost or a credit. The ratio of calls purchased to those sold is generally less than 0.67. The most common ratios are 1 to 2 and 2 to 3. This means buying two calls offset by selling one call or buying three calls against selling two. The strategy is usually implemented at no cost, or sometimes for a credit, because the premium received from selling the calls is often equal to, or greater than, the price paid for the long options. The risk in this position is limited and equal to the number of short calls multiplied by the difference in strike prices times 100 minus the net credit (or plus the net debit). The potential reward from the call ratio backspread is unlimited.

options and sale of a smaller number of calls that are at-the-money or near-the-money. The ratio is generally 1 to 2 or 2 to 3. For instance, the trader can sell one at-the-money call and simultaneously buy two out-of-the-money calls. In the case of the call ratio backspread, the strategist is expecting the stock to make a sharp move higher and for the long side of the trade (because there are more long calls than short calls) to yield profits.

Let's look at an example of the call ratio backspread and consider why low implied volatility is important in implementing the trade. Suppose the option strategist is bullish on shares of AOL Time Warner (symbol: AOL) with the stock trading for roughly $21 a share. The strategist expects the stock to make a sizable move higher and looks to see what long-term call options are available on AOL. It is April 2002, and looking over the options chain, the strategist notices the three AOL January 2003 calls with strike prices between $22.50 and $27.50 (see Figure 8.16).

Rather than simply buying a call or setting up a bull call spread, the strategist decides to create a call ratio backspread using the AOL January 2003 22.5 call and the AOL January 2003 27.5 call. In this case, the strategist can buy two calls with the strike price of 27.5 for $1.15 each, or $2.30. The strategist can offset the cost of those two calls by selling one January 2003 22.5 call for $2.30. The risk of the trade is depicted in Figure 8.17 and is limited. In the worst-case scenario, the AOL rises to $27.50 a share at expiration, both long calls expire worthless, and the short call is assigned. Therefore, in this case, the maximum loss is equal to the difference between the two strike prices plus any commissions paid for the trade. The maximum profit, on the other hand, is unlimited. (*Note:* In many cases, the strategist wants to close out the backspread 30 days prior to expiration. You should always close out the short contract by or before expiration if it is in-the-money and your spread has not achieved its objective by moving higher than the long contract strike price—that is, unless you don't mind being assigned. This would mean being prepared to deliver the stock at the strike price of your short contract, even if it is trading higher in the open market.)

A call ratio backspread such as the one on AOL just described will work only when implied volatility is relatively low. In the example, the implied volatility of the January 2003 call options was in the 35 to 38 percent range. If implied volatility was 50 percent, the AOL January 22.5 call would be roughly $3.40 and the January 27.5 call would be worth $1.90. Therefore, a one-for-two call ratio backspread would not be possible. In short, ratio backspreads (whether using puts or calls) are available only when implied volatility is low.

Calls

Symbol	Bid	Ask	Op.Int.	Strike
VANAX	2.3	2.55	2244	Jan03-22.500
VANAE	1.55	1.75	30693	Jan03-25.000
VANAY	0.95	1.15	1816	Jan03-27.500

Figure 8.16   AOL January 2003 LEAPS on April 12, 2002

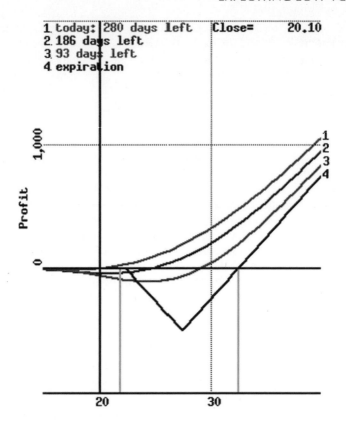

Figure 8.17   AOL Call Ratio Backspread (Courtesy of Optionetics.com)

The advantage of the call ratio backspread over many other strategies is that it is not always necessary for the stock to move higher in order to make money. As we saw in the AOL example, the downside risk to the trade was virtually zero. In fact, shares of AOL Time Warner tanked throughout 2001 and 2002. Therefore, shareholders and call buyers suffered significant losses during that time. However, a call ratio backspread would not result in any meaningful losses. The risk from a sharp downside move in a well-planned call ratio backspread is virtually zero. In fact, in some cases, call ratio backspreads can be established for credits. Therefore, even if the strategist is bullish on a stock—which later tanks like AOL did—the calls expire worthless and the strategist keeps the credit. Ratio backspreads offer option strategists a way of making money regardless of market direction.

PUT RATIO BACKSPREADS

The put ratio backspread is similar to the call ratio backspread. However, as you probably guessed, the put ratio backspread does not use calls. Instead, the trade is

---

Call Ratio Backspread

Strategy = Sell lower strike calls and buy a greater number of higher strike calls (the ratio must be less than 0.67).

Market Opportunity = Look for a market where you anticipate a price rise with increasing volatility. Trade should be placed as a credit trade or at even.

Maximum Risk = Limited [(# short calls × difference in strike prices) × 100 – net credit or + net debit].

Maximum Profit = Unlimited to the upside beyond the breakeven; on the downside, limited to the net credit (if any).

Upside Breakeven = Long call strike price + {[(difference in strike prices × # short calls) – (net debit) *or* + net credit/]/(# long calls – # short calls)}.

Downside Breakeven = If net debit, there is no downside breakeven; if net credit, then downside breakeven = short call strike price + [(net credit)/# short calls].

Margin = Required. The amount is subject to your broker's discretion.

---

constructed selling puts with higher strike prices and buying a greater number of puts with a lower strike price. Just as with the call ratio backspread, the ratio of puts sold to puts purchased is generally 1 to 2 or 2 to 3.

Let us consider an example of a put ratio backspread using International Flavors and Fragrances (symbol: IFF). On April 19, 2002, with IFF trading for $36 a share, the option strategist pulls up an options chain for the stock and sees the November puts included in Figure 8.18. Believing that the stock is due to make a sharp move lower between April and the end of the year, the strategist wants to establish a put

---

What Is a Put Ratio Backspread?

A put ratio backspread is constructed by purchasing puts and selling fewer puts with a higher strike price for no cost or a credit. The ratio of puts purchased to those sold is generally less than 0.67. The most common ratios are 1 to 2 and 2 to 3. This means selling one put offset by buying two puts or selling two against buying three puts. The strategy is usually implemented at no cost, or sometimes for a credit, because the premium received from selling the puts is often equal to, or greater than, the price paid for the long options. The risk in this position is limited and equal to the number of short puts multiplied by the difference in strike prices plus the net credit (or minus the net debit). The potential reward from the put ratio backspread is limited to the stock price going to zero.

Puts

Symbol	Bid	Ask	Op.Int.	
IFFWF	0.65	0.9	0	Nov02-30.000
IFFWG	2.3	2.65	200	Nov02-35.000
IFFWH	5.1	5.5	0	Nov02-40.000

Figure 8.18   Option Chain for IFF on April 19, 2002

ratio backspread. Consequently, a put ratio backspread is created using the IFF November 35 put and two IFF November 30 puts. The put with the higher strike price is sold for $2.30, and the two puts with the lower strike price are purchased for $1.80 (90 cents times two). The trade costs nothing. In fact, the strategist receives a credit equal to the difference between the premium received for selling the put option and the cost of the long put options. In this case, the credit equals 50 cents ($2.30 minus $1.80).

The risk graph for the put ratio backspread is shown in Figure 8.19. Notice that the maximum loss occurs if IFF trades at $30 a share at expiration. Therefore, the maximum risk is equal to the number of short puts times the difference between the two strike prices times 100 minus the credit received (1 × $5 − $50 = $450).

Put Ratio Backspread

Strategy = Sell higher strike puts and buy a greater number of lower strike puts with a ratio less than 2 to 3.

Market Opportunity = Look for a market where you anticipate a price decline with increased volatility. Place as a credit or at even.

Maximum Risk = Limited [(# short puts × difference in strike prices × 100) − net credit *or* + net debit].

Maximum Profit = Unlimited to the downside below the breakeven. Limited on the upside to the net credit, if any.

Upside Breakeven = If net debit, then no upside breakeven; if net credit, then breakeven = short put strike price − (net credit)/# of short puts.

Downside Breakeven = Long put strike price − {[(# short puts × difference in strikes) − (net credit) *or* + (net debit)]/(# long puts − # short puts)}.

Margin = Required. The amount is subject to your broker's discretion.

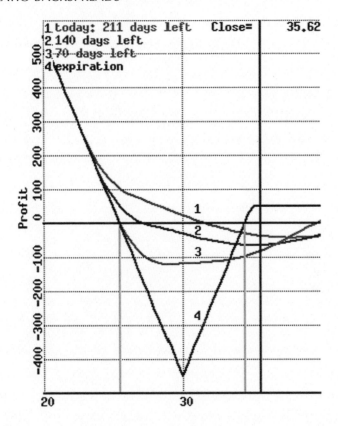

Figure 8.19   Risk Graph for IFF Put Ratio Backspread (Courtesy of Optionetics.com)

The maximum risk occurs with the stock trading at the same level as the lower strike price of the two options at expiration. For that reason, most losing ratio backspreads will be closed 30 days prior to expiration. Profits begin to build when the stock falls below $25 a share and continue to rise as the stock falls. The profit is limited because the stock cannot fall below zero. In addition, notice that if the stock stays above $35 a share the trade is also profitable. Why? Because if the stock remains above the higher of the two strike prices, both puts expire worthless and the trader keeps the credit. For that reason, the put ratio backspread, like the call ratio backspread, can sometimes be constructed at a credit to a create a nondirectional trade (or the type of options trade that makes money whether the stock rises or falls). The key to finding such opportunities is identifying options with low levels of implied volatility and then creating the ratio backspread depending on the outlook for the stock.

CONCLUSION

Trading options is an activity that can provide a lot of personal satisfaction and, at the same time, offer significant financial reward. Many investors start trading options using the most simple and basic trading strategy: the long call. This type of strategy is a directional bet, and its success depends on the stock price moving higher. Most call buyers understand this concept. At the same time, however, changes in implied volatility can also have an effect on the call. Without understanding how IV impacts the call, the trader might be unpleasantly surprised to see the stock price move higher, but the call option move lower in what is known as a "volatility crush."

In addition to understanding the impact of implied volatility on option positions, most successful traders develop a repertoire of different trading strategies. Several have been introduced here. The long call and long put are directional bets that also benefit from rising levels of IV. The straddle is an example of a nondirectional strategy that can make money whether the stock moves higher or lower. It is best to purchase straddles when implied volatility is low. The bull call spread and the bear put spread are examples of debit spreads and are directional bets on the stock. Falling implied volatility generally has a negative impact on the bull call and bear put spreads. The last strategy covered in this chapter is the ratio backspread, which can be established at no cost or a credit. Entry into either a call or put ratio backspread requires low levels of implied volatility.

That concludes our discussion of low implied volatility option strategies. We encourage readers to think them through and look for real-time examples to trade on paper before risking actual cash. Look at the current option prices in the market and screen for stocks with low implied volatility using the Optionetics.com Platinum ranking software. Make sure to use the tools discussed in Chapter 3 such as Bollinger bands, ATR, and statistical volatility to search for stocks that could soon make an explosive move higher or lower. Make predictions concerning what will happen with implied volatility in the future and see if your estimates prove accurate. In addition, a paper trading template for each of these strategies can be found in Appendix G. Through time, certain strategies will seem to fit your trading style more than others. Perhaps none of the low-volatility strategies make sense for you. If so, do not fret. The next chapter explores high-volatility strategies.

9

Exploiting High Volatility

The significance of volatility is often overlooked and underestimated by many traders in the options arena. Low-volatility stocks may often appear too boring to trade options against, while high-volatility stocks seem too risky. Remember that implied volatility is simply a mathematical computation (such as the Black-Scholes model) of the movement of an option based on the activity of the underlying stock or market. When a market makes a rapid move up or down, volatility rises. It's that simple.

Many years of research have shown that markets trading at a very low level of volatility have a high probability of a large move occurring. When volatility is at a very high level, however, a substantial probability exists for the contract to maintain a trading range. If you were to take a coil and compact it together (low volatility), eventually it would spring back to its original shape when released. Conversely, if you were to take the coil spring and stretch it out, once you let go it would pull back to its original shape once again. This is known as reversion to the mean, which was discussed in detail in previous chapters.

Why does reversion to the mean cause changes in volatility? It seems that when a contract is very quiet with low levels of volatility, traders fall asleep and don't expect anything to happen. Of course, this is exactly when everything explodes! Traders are caught by surprise, and when volatility begins to rise, their frantic buying or selling exacerbates the trend. We talked about trading strategies to take advantage of periods of low volatility in Chapter 8.

In contrast, many times when an option contract has been very active and exhibiting high volatility for a period of time, most traders are already in the market and anticipating volatility to remain high. As a result, the option is likely to maintain a wide and volatile range for some time. However, due to reversion to the mean, that pattern won't go on indefinitely. Luckily for the options trader, compared to predicting stock prices, this pattern of high and low volatility is much easier to recognize, understand, and anticipate.

A LOOK BACK AT IMPLIED VOLATILITY

To understand high volatility strategies, let's first take a look back at a graph that I think is the essence of volatility, the CBOE Volatility Index, or VIX. As stated earlier, VIX is the current level of implied volatility for the S&P 100 index options (OEX). This index provides real-time quotes regarding implied volatility in the market. In addition, it can be charted like a stock. Figure 9.1 shows a chart of VIX.

As Figure 9.1 depicts, VIX fluctuates between periods of high and low volatility. It has a clear trading range. Option traders often use the adage, "When VIX is high, it's time to buy, but when VIX is low, it's time to go." As reviewed in Chapter 7, a high VIX is a bullish sign, and a low VIX is a bearish sign. VIX is a sentiment analysis indicator that measures crowd psychology.

Now, let's consider VIX from the vantage point of a volatility trader. When VIX is high, it's time to sell volatility; when VIX is low, it's time to buy volatility. Looking at Figure 9.1, you can see what the September 11, 2001, terrorist attack on the United States did to the volatility of the markets. Within a matter of weeks, volatility in the options market skyrocketed, which created very high options premiums for the U.S. stock market, as well as other markets worldwide. Six months later, volatility fell to yearly lows. Rather than being caught off guard by nationwide and

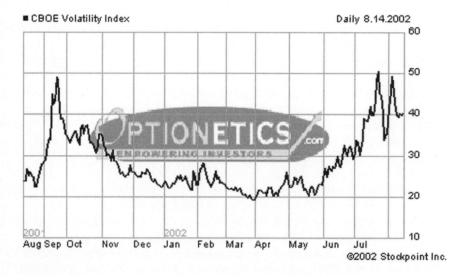

Figure 9.1   Daily Chart of the CBOE Volatility Index, VIX (Courtesy of Optionetics.com)

What Causes Marketwide Spikes in Implied Volatility?

High volatility can result from many different events, including terror, as revealed by the attacks on September 11, 2001. High volatility can also result from natural catastrophes, such as earthquakes and hurricanes; or it can be company related, such as earnings disappointments, company warnings, or accounting irregularities. In 1998, at the peak of the global financial crisis, VIX spiked higher. Similarly, in October 1987 when the market crashed, implied volatility rose to record highs. Extreme spikes in VIX and other implied volatility indicators can be directly attributed to fear, panic, and mayhem in the financial markets.

---

worldwide panics that result from terrorism, weather catastrophes, market crashes, or other disasters, you can apply options strategies that take advantage of imminent changes in volatility levels.

It is one thing to protect yourself from the dangers inherent in investing and quite another to attempt to profit from them. Protection from volatility involves being prepared before the change in volatility actually occurs. As noted in Chapter 1, bear markets and periods of acute volatility are extremely difficult to predict. For that reason, the options strategist is best served by approaches that take into account the fact that stocks can suddenly plummet due to unforeseen reasons. Rule of thumb: Expect volatility to change when you least expect it!

In this chapter, however, the goal is not to outline tools for protecting a portfolio in the event of sudden market volatility. Instead, we are going to look at ways of profiting when periods of high volatility occur, leaving most investors shell-shocked and on the sidelines. Based on the phenomenon of reversion to the mean, periods of high volatility are generally followed by periods of low volatility. When this happens, option premiums decrease. Thus, our objective in high volatility trading is to take advantage of a drop in option prices when the volatility reverts back to a normal pattern.

High volatility traders tend to liken themselves to insurance salespeople selling hurricane insurance at the height of the hurricane season when premiums are highest. The most popular forms of selling premium involve covered calls and naked puts. Let's take a look at each of these.

SELLING OPTIONS PREMIUMS

There are two reasons why a trader might sell a call option. First, the trader might be trying to sell option premium on an underlying stock that he or she already owns. As noted in Chapter 6, a covered call is an option sold against a stock that is already owned. Another reason why a trader might sell a call is because the trader is betting that the stock will either remain flat or go down in price. The trader wants to take in the call option premium in anticipation that it will expire worthless. Both the covered call and the straight sale of a call are strategies that work best in a high volatility environment. Let's review an example of the covered call to see how this works.

COVERED CALL

The covered call is a popular option strategy in which one call is sold to create an open short position against 100 shares of stock already owned by the seller. This strategy is best implemented in a bullish to neutral market where a slow rise in the market price of the underlying stock is anticipated. The covered call technique allows traders to handle moderate price declines because the call premium reduces the position's breakeven. Since the strategist is counting on the time decay of the short option to render the short call worthless, the general rule is not to sell a call more than 45 days out. However, since the profit on a covered call is limited to the premium received, the premium needs to be high enough to balance out the trade's risk.

Covered Call Example

Although already covered in Chapter 6, let's consider another covered call example using a slightly different type of risk graph to demonstrate how the trade works. Suppose the investor owns 100 shares of IBM and wants to write a call option against it. The IBM 30-day call options (the ones with expiration in 30 days) with a strike of 100 are trading at 5 points (a premium of $5). Figure 9.2 shows the risk graph of the trade.

Figure 9.2 tells us that the investor can collect $500 for selling the call, reducing the risk and cost of the IBM stock by 5 points. If IBM were to rise, the most the investor could make on this trade would be the amount profited in IBM plus the premium received from the call option. If the stock falls, money can be lost just as it would be if someone simply owned the stock. However, the trade has made money in the amount received for writing the call option, which is 5 points in the IBM example. The breakeven is calculated by subtracting the short call premium from the price of the underlying asset at initiation.

The trade looks appealing when it involves stocks with high option volatility because the premium received for selling a call is greater when volatility is high. Like stock ownership, this strategy comes with the substantial downside risk involved with owning the stock. But, if you already own the stock, this could be a way to take in extra premium if you feel the stock is going to move sideways.

The following six rules should help you to achieve above-average returns using covered calls:

1. Strive for a balance between acceptable return and downside protection.

2. Look for stocks that you expect will trade in a range over the duration of your covered call option.

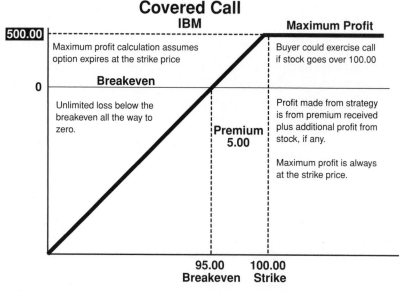

Figure 9.2 Risk Graph of IBM Covered Call (Courtesy of Optionetics.com)

3. Look for call options that have a high implied volatility. This will make the call more attractive to sell and increase your rate of return.

4. Sell call options that have 30 to 45 days to expiration, as these options decay the fastest in time value.

5. Monitor the covered call occasionally to determine whether you need to adjust it due to the movement of the stock.

6. Be prepared to have the stock called away if the price of the underlying stock rises above the call's strike price.

NAKED PUT OPTIONS

In the late 1990s, selling naked put options became the craze of options traders. As technology stocks were flying high, premium sellers came in from everywhere selling put options against these stocks and generating high dollars without sitting on the positions for much time. A naked put option is simply the sale of a put option where the writer of the contract does not hold the underlying short position to cover the contract. When stocks are rising, the put options are not likely to be exercised.

Covered Call

Strategy = Buy the underlying security and sell an OTM call option.

Market Opportunity = Look for a bullish to neutral market where a slow rise in the price of the underlying is anticipated with little risk of decline.

Maximum Risk = Virtually unlimited to the downside below the breakeven all the way to zero.

Maximum Profit = Limited to the credit received from the short call option + (short call strike price − price of long underlying asset) × 100.

Breakeven = Price of the underlying asset at initiation − short call premium received.

Frequently used instead of the covered call, selling puts is a bullish or neutral strategy where profits are earned by receiving premium for the put option.

Let's look at IBM again (see Figure 9.3). If the strategist is bullish on this stock, there are several trading strategies possible. In this case, the trader decides to sell a naked put with a strike price of $100 for 5 points. IBM is currently at $100, and the

---

Let's Get Naked

In options trading, being caught naked is perhaps not as embarrassing as it might sound; but it can still be an unpleasant experience. Basically, selling options naked is an aggressive strategy that comes with limited rewards and unlimited risks. It involves selling options without a hedge or a position in the underlying asset to protect the sale in the event of assignment. In the case of call selling, profits result if the stock falls and the option falls in value or expires worthless. Losses arise if the stock moves higher and the seller is faced with assignment. The naked put seller loses if the stock falls, but gains if the stock moves higher and the put expires worthless. Whether selling puts or calls naked, the maximum profit is equal to the premium received from the sale of the option. The maximum risk associated with naked put selling is the strike price minus zero (because the stock cannot fall below zero) minus the premium received. Theoretically, the maximum risk to uncovered call selling is infinite because there is no limit to how high a stock price can go. Either way, selling naked options has large potential risks. You must be aware of the risks and willing to accept them in order to employ naked options strategies.

Not everyone can sell naked options. Traders who want to sell naked options are required by most brokers to have substantial options experience, as well as a certain amount of cash or equities in their accounts. That amount can vary from broker to broker.

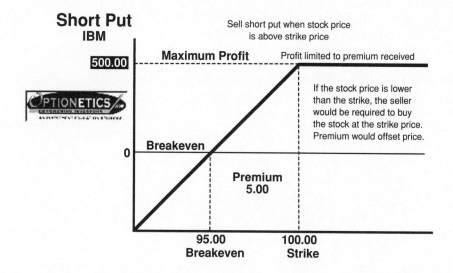

Figure 9.3   Risk Graph of IBM Short Put (Courtesy of Optionetics.com)

IBM 100 put is trading for 5. The breakeven on a short or naked put is calculated by subtracting the put premium from the put strike price. In this case, the breakeven is $95, which means the trader makes a profit on the trade as long as IBM stays above $95. If the trader thinks that the stock would go above $100, he or she could sell a put with a higher strike price (a strike price greater than $100). If the stock price rises above the strike price of the put, the option will expire worthless and the trader will keep the credit. For that reason, the naked put is a bullish strategy; its success depends on the stock price moving higher. It is best applied when implied volatility is high because the premium received for selling the put will be greater.

What happens if the price of the stock drops after the position is opened? First, if the put has not been exercised and if the seller of the put has not closed out the position on expiration day, the stock will be assigned or "put" to the put seller. That means the trader has to buy the stock at the strike price from the assigned option buyer. For example, if the IBM 100 put is sold and the price of the stock falls to $50, the cost to buy the stock is still $100. Therefore, the stock must be bought for $100 a share, but can only be sold in the market for $50—an immediate 50 percent loss. This loss would be offset by the premium initially received for selling the naked put. If the put has been assigned, the strategist could choose to buy the put back just before expiration so that the stock is not put to him or her.

It is vital to understand that selling puts comes with high risk—mostly directional price risk—of the underlying stock falling. For example, it is possible to sell a put and have the stock price fall to zero. The liability in that case would be the entire strike price. In the IBM example, that would equal $100, or $10,000 per naked put contract controlling 100 shares. So when choosing the stocks on which to sell puts, use the same care that you would if you were buying call options.

While I am not a big fan of naked puts, here are six rules to follow to allow for maximum profit potential. These are similar to the covered call rules, in that they both achieve the same reward potential.

1. Strive for a balance between acceptable return and downside protection.

2. Look for stocks that you expect will trade in a range over the duration of your naked put option.

3. Look for put options that have a high implied volatility. This will make the put more attractive to sell and increase your rate of return.

4. Sell put options that have around 30 days to expiration, as these options decay the fastest in time value.

5. Monitor the position carefully to avoid assignment.

6. Be prepared to have the stock delivered to you at the put strike price.

A NOTE ON UNCOVERED OPTION SALES

In the previous example, we considered selling naked puts. But you may wonder why anyone would choose to sell naked options when doing so comes with unlimited risk. This strategy is appealing because time decay eats away at the value of any options contract. In fact, it is an undeniable truth that most options expire

---

Short Put

Strategy = Sell a put option.

Market Opportunity = Look for a bullish or stable market where a rise above the breakeven is anticipated.

Maximum Risk = Limited as the stock price falls below the breakeven until reaching a price of zero.

Maximum Profit = Limited to the credit received from the put option premium.

Breakeven = Put strike price − put option premium.

Margin = Required. The amount is subject to your broker's discretion.

worthless. If so, why bother buying options? Wouldn't it make more sense to sell options and see them waste away while you keep the option premium? That is the thinking of many option strategists and why selling naked options is an often-used strategy.

So what happens when an uncovered position goes against the trader? Well, the risks can be substantial. Remember when Beanie Babies first came out? They instantly became the must-have toy of the moment; within a year some were going for as much as $5,000. It absolutely boggled my mind why anyone would pay that much for a stuffed toy, but I obviously was out of the loop of that trading arena. It seemed everywhere you went, there were swap meets where people could trade their Beanie Babies for cash or other toys. Then, of course, the craze dissipated, leaving a lot of people with a bunch of worthless stuff.

Interestingly enough, the Beanie Baby hysteria was a lot like the Internet craze that ended shortly before the year 2001. The insanity lasted only three short years, but what a ride investors took. Volatility started out low in the 1990s, went to a parabolic high just as the new millennium hit, and then dropped. Some of these high-flying dot-com stocks plummeted from three-digit prices to single digits in a matter of months.

The market volatility resulting from the Internet craze caused a lot of margin calls in the months that followed the peaks in 2000. In fact, most margin calls were the result of two things: too much leverage in high-tech, high-volatility stocks, and naked options positions. Luckily, there is a better way to take in expensive time premiums without sacrificing your entire account simply by hedging your bets for the times that your compass is off and you are wrong about the markets.

As another example, consider how the insurance companies for the World Trade Center were able to stay in business despite millions of dollars that had to be paid in claims after September 11. These companies managed to stay open because they hedged their bets and were liable only to an extent. The large insurance companies basically reinsured themselves through other carriers so that they could handle any catastrophe no matter how large. They simply spread the excess risk that they couldn't handle to create what is known as a credit spread. They sold insurance to the occupants or building owners and bought insurance to protect themselves against claims too deep to handle. If nothing happened, they simply collected premiums from the building owners, and paid a smaller premium to the company they

---

Margin: A deposit made by a trader with a clearinghouse to ensure that he/she will fulfill any financial obligations resulting from trades. This amount will change as the price of the investment changes.

Margin call: A broker's demand that a customer deposit additional funds to cover the price change of the underlying instrument in a trade. The deposit must be made immediately or the broker will be forced to exit the trade, often at a loss to the trader.

were reinsured by, thereby keeping the credit between the two policies. They did not simply sell naked insurance polices. The same thing can be done in the stock market with options contracts. Let's see how.

CREDIT SPREADS

A credit spread is a way of taking in a credit (premium) on a trade without a lot of risk. The objective of a credit spread is the same as that of the option strategies detailed earlier in this chapter: to keep the credit received. That's what insurance companies want to do. The question when selecting credit spreads is whether you want to tilt yourself to a bullish, bearish, or neutral market outlook.

All options strategies that bring in credit require a margin deposit. Depending on the strategy, the margin is usually equivalent to the maximum loss. In the case of naked options (i.e., selling options without hedging them against a long contract), margin requirements will be even higher (often as much as $50,000—or more). Each brokerage is different, and you will need to determine the house rules that govern your account. In this case, however, we are beyond the discussion of naked options, but moving on to a more sophisticated strategy known as the vertical credit spread, of which there are two types: the bull put spread and the bear call spread.

BULL PUT CREDIT SPREADS

The credit spread that works in bullish markets involves put options. A bull put spread involves selling the strike price that is closest to the market value of the underlying asset (stock) and buying a lower put to hedge against risk. The hedge, or lower put, serves as protection in the event that the stock makes a sudden and dramatic move to the downside. The trade is done for a credit because the premium

---

What Is a Bull Put Credit Spread?

The bull put spread is a strategy that can profit if the stock stays the same or moves higher. The trade involves the purchase of a put with a lower strike price (generally, out-of-the-money put) and a sale of a put with a higher strike price (an at-the-money or near-the-money put). Since the put sold will have a higher strike price and a higher premium, the trade is done for a credit. The maximum profit arises when both options expire worthless and the strategist keeps the credit. Losses arise if the stock falls and the short call increases in value more rapidly than the long call. The maximum loss is equal to the difference between the two strike prices minus the credit received. The breakeven is determined by subtracting the net credit received from the trade from the higher put strike price.

received for selling the put with the higher strike price will be greater than the price paid for buying the lower strike put.

Let's look at an example using Cisco Systems (symbol: CSCO). Say the stock is currently quoted at $20 per share. To execute a bull put spread, the strategist could buy the 10 put at 4 and sell the 20 put at 6. Since the net credit is equal to the short premium minus the long premium, the net credit in this example is 2 or $200 per contract [(6 – 4) × 100]. The maximum loss is limited to the difference between the strike prices times 100 shares minus the net credit. In this example, the maximum loss is $800 {[(20 –10) × 100] – 200}. The risk graph for this position would look like Figure 9.4 at expiration.

Although the result of this spread is a lower premium received than if the strategist had simply sold a naked put, the additional risk to zero is hedged off in the event that the stock were to move against the position. The put with the lower strike price serves as protection in the event that the stock falls and the short put is assigned. Conversely, if the stock makes a significant move higher, both puts expire worthless and the trader keeps the credit.

There are a few things to remember when selling put spreads. For example, when selling high-probability at-the-money or out-of-the-money put spreads, the strategist wants to keep the days to expiration short. High probability in this case refers to the fact that the stock would not have to move meaningfully higher for the trade to work. In setting up the bull put spread with in-the-money options, the stock

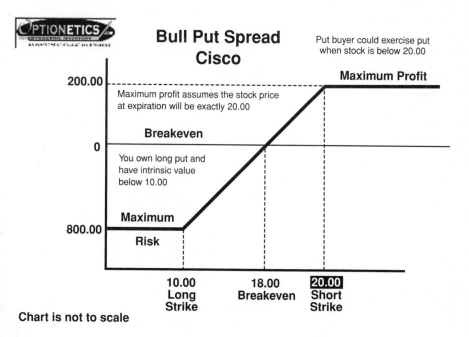

Figure 9.4 Bull Put Spread on Cisco Systems (Courtesy of Optionetics.com)

would have to move above the higher of the two strike prices and the probability of earning the maximum profit is less. In the case of a high-probability credit spread, the strategist wants the options to expire as quickly as possible so that there is less time for the trade to turn against him/her; the less time to expiration, the lower the chances of the stock moving against you.

Selling in-the-money puts and buying at-the-money puts for protection gives the trader a higher credit. It is possible to get some incredible reward-over-risk positions implementing bull put spreads with in-the-money options, but the strategist wants to ensure that there is time value in the put options that are sold. There is a risk that a deep in-the-money option with no time value remaining will be assigned right away before the trade can generate a profit. If there is sufficient time value, the chance of assignment will be slim. Obviously, in-the-money option spreads require a more directional bias, as the stock needs to move higher to profit fully from the credit spread.

BEAR CALL CREDIT SPREADS

The most common bearish credit strategy is a bear call spread. This strategy involves selling the strike price that is closest to the market value of the underlying asset (stock) and buying a higher call to hedge against unlimited risk associated with naked call buying. In contrast to the bull put spread, the strategist wants the stock to fall so that both calls expire worthless, and he or she gets to keep the credit received.

Using Cisco trading for $20, the strategist simultaneously sells the 20 call at 4

Bull Put Spread

Strategy = Buy a lower strike put and sell a higher strike put with the same expiration date.

Market Opportunity = Look for a bullish market where you anticipate an increase in the price of the underlying asset above the strike price of the short put option.

Maximum Risk = Limited [(difference in strike prices × 100) – net credit].

Maximum Profit = Limited to the net credit received when the market closes above the short put option.

Breakeven = Higher put strike price – net credit received.

Margin = Required. The amount is subject to your broker's discretion.

What Is a Bear Call Credit Spread?

A bear call spread is created by purchasing a call with a higher strike price and selling a call with a lower strike price. This strategy is generally established by selling an at-the-money or near-the-money call and selling an out-of-the-money call. The trade is established for a credit because the premium received from selling the call with the lower strike price will be greater than the price paid for the call with the higher strike price. The maximum profit is equal to the credit and will occur when either (1) the stock falls precipitously and the options become deep-out-of-the-money or (2) both options expire worthless. The maximum risk is equal to the difference between the two strike prices minus the credit.

and buys the 30 call at 2. The maximum reward is the net credit received from the combination of the short and long calls. In this example, the maximum reward is $200 [(4 − 2) × 100]. Since the maximum loss is calculated the same way as for the bull put spread, once again the maximum risk is $800 {[(30 − 20) x 100] − 200}. Figure 9.5 shows the risk graph of the bear call spread.

Although the credit spread is less risky than trading naked options, the options strategist wants to be careful when holding the position at expiration. For example, the seller of a bear call spread runs the same risk that any option seller faces when

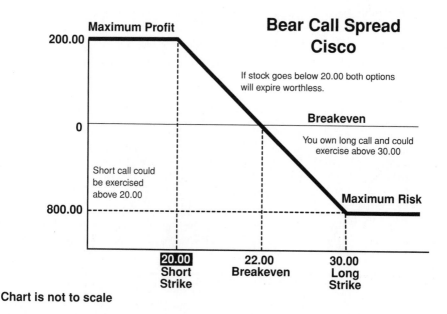

Figure 9.5 Risk Graph for Bear Call Spread on CSCO (Courtesy of Optionetics.com)

the underlying asset trades very close to the strike price of the naked option at expiration. Specifically, the trader will not know whether he/she has been assigned the stock until the Monday following the date of expiration. If the stock, which was trading close to the sold strike on the previous Friday ($20 in our example), suddenly has a large adverse move to the upside, the option seller has to go into the market, buy the stock at market price, and deliver it at the agreed strike price. In the meantime, the long option that was hedging the risk against such moves has expired worthless.

Using credit spreads during high volatility will bring in more premium than a credit spread placed during average volatility. Higher levels of implied volatility either give the credit spread trader more premium using the same strikes or increase the odds of success by being able to create a wider spread with farther out-of-the-money options for higher premiums. Sometimes anticipation of earnings reports in a stock can create high volatility as the earnings release date approaches. The time until expiration is also an important factor to consider. The front month options will almost always have the highest implied volatility just before an earnings report is released.

As an example, consider Figure 9.6, which shows the implied volatility of AOL Time Warner. The chart was created a few days before AOL was set to report

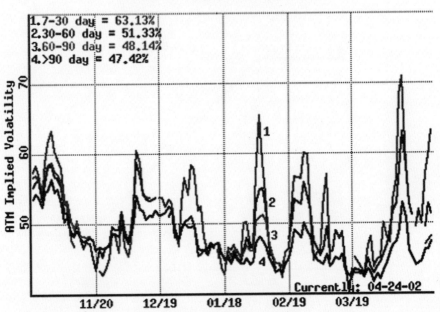

Figure 9.6   Implied Volatility of AOL Time Warner Ahead of Earnings Report
(Courtesy of Optionetics.com)

Volatility skew: Skews in option prices occur when the volatility is higher in some months than others, or in the higher (or lower) strike prices of the same underlying stock. Volatility skews measure and account for the limitations found in most option pricing models and can be used to give traders an edge in estimating an option's worth.

Forward volatility skew: In these markets, the higher strike options (the ones you want to sell) have higher implied volatility and can be overpriced. The lower strike options (the ones you want to buy) enjoy lower implied volatility and are often underpriced.

Reverse volatility skew: In these markets, the lower strike options (the ones you want to sell) have higher implied volatility and can be overpriced. The higher strike options (the ones you want to buy) enjoy lower implied volatility and are often underpriced.

---

earnings. The volatility readings confirm the statements in the previous paragraph. Notice that the 7 to 30 day options (depicted on the top line and representing the front month implied volatility graph) are the most expensive and also the most volatile on the graph. These front month options have had wide swings from top to bottom. Most of the highs occur at or around earnings reports. Thus, to get the most out of a credit spread, it can be lucrative to scan for volatility skews between higher and lower options such that the options you buy have high IV and the options you want to sell have lower IV. By trading volatility skews, you can capture the implied volatility differential between the short and long options and more often than not create a net credit between the options comprising the spread.

Bear Call Spread

Strategy = Buy a higher strike call and sell a lower strike call with the same expiration date.

Market Opportunity = Look for a bearish market where you anticipate a decrease in the price of the underlying asset below the strike price of the short call option.

Maximum Risk = Limited [(difference in strike prices × 100) – net credit].

Maximum Profit = Limited to the net credit received.

Breakeven = Lower call strike price + net credit received.

Margin = Required. The amount is subject to your broker's discretion.

THE BUTTERFLY SPREAD

Now let's say for a moment that the option strategist is looking at the AOL volatility chart and is unsure whether to be a bull or a bear, but believes that there may be some short-term volatility to capture. Why not go both ways with a butterfly spread?

One of the greatest benefits of trading options versus equities is that the opportunity exists to make money when the market is trading in a narrow range. Many stocks have extended periods of consolidation that last for months or even a year or more. These consolidation periods create a unique opportunity that does not exist with conventional investments like stocks and mutual funds. However, there is an options strategy that takes full advantage of the opportunity: the butterfly spread.

RANGE TRADING

Range trading takes advantage of stocks that have been trading within a range for an extended period of time. While other strategies take advantage of stock movement in one direction or another, range trading focuses on stocks that remain rather dormant within a trading range and allow you to take advantage of high volatility, theta decay, and time premiums.

For the remainder of this chapter, we will present a couple of strategies that take advantage of range-trading conditions. These strategies include three or more different option contracts or legs, which means higher commission costs. There are five criteria for using long range-trading strategies.

1. Look for stocks that have been trading within a trading range for a minimum of three months.

2. Identify the support and resistance levels of the range bound market or stock.

3. Once a stock has been identified, look for options with 60 days or more until expiration.

4. If the position is placed in multiples of two or more, adjustments (except for calendar spreads) can be made to increase profits once the trade is placed.

5. Determine your exit strategy prior to placing the trade. Look for preset profit targets or get out before a 50 percent loss.

The butterfly spread is one of the most popular strategies employed by options traders. This is probably due to its widespread reference in many options trading books. Although butterfly spreads can have a bullish or bearish bias, it is preferable to use butterfly spreads as a neutral strategy. There are two basic long butterfly trade scenarios. One uses all calls and the other uses all puts. Both consist of three different strike prices:

What Is a Butterfly Spread?

A long butterfly is a neutral spread that has the following characteristics:

- **Limited Risk:** The most that can be lost on the trade is the premiums paid.
- **Limited Reward:** Difference between highest strike and the short strike minus the net debit. Maximum profit is realized when the stock price equals the short strike.
- **Upside Breakeven:** Highest strike price – net debit paid.
- **Downside Breakeven:** Lowest strike price + net debit paid.
- **Margin Requirements:** The butterfly spread is essentially a combination of two options strategies. It is both a bull spread and a bear spread. Therefore, the collateral requirement is the total required for *both* the bull spread and the bear spread. Despite the fact that the investor's net debit here is smaller than the total margin required, there will be a reduction in the additional buying ability in the margin account. The net collateral investment equals the distance between the strikes plus the net debit. Ultimately, the margin amount is subject to your broker's discretion.

- *The body* (middle strike—usually ATM): Contains options at the equilibrium strike price in between the support and resistance levels.

- *The two wings* (outer strikes—one ITM and one OTM): Composed of options with the strike prices at both ends of the trading range—the support and resistance levels.

So, the structure of most butterfly spreads is a position most often involving three different strike price calls:

- One call is bought at the lowest strike price—usually the support point.

- Two calls are sold at the middle strike price.

- One call is bought at the highest strike price—usually the resistance point.

LONG IRON BUTTERFLY SPREAD EXAMPLE

The butterfly is a market neutral spread trade that can use all calls or all puts. If a combination of both calls and puts is created, it is called an iron butterfly. It contains four option strikes, in contrast to the regular butterfly spread, which contains only three. The format of a long iron butterfly is similar to combining two strategies we have already reviewed: a bear call spread (short lower ATM call and long OTM higher call) and a bull put spread (long lower OTM put and short ATM higher put). An iron butterfly offers the options strategist limited risk and limited reward. The profit range occurs within the trade's downside and upside breakeven points.

What Is a Long Iron Butterfly?

A long iron butterfly is a range-trading strategy with the following characteristics:

- **Limited Risk:** The difference in strikes minus the net credit received for placing the position. This is usually a small value and is the reason why this trade is attractive. Realize that commissions are not calculated in this example and can really eat into the profits.
- **Limited Reward:** Net credit received on placing the position.
- **Upside Breakeven:** Middle short call strike price + net credit received.
- **Downside Breakeven:** Middle short put strike price − net credit received.
- **Margin:** Required. The amount is subject to your broker's discretion.

A long iron butterfly is composed of the following legs:

- Buy one OTM call—usually the resistance point (wing).
- Sell one ATM call—usually the midpoint of the trading range (body).
- Sell one ATM (or slightly OTM) put—usually the midpoint of the trading range (body).
- Buy one OTM put—usually the support point (wing).

Our first example is an iron butterfly created with both puts and calls. Let's look at AOL the day before its earnings announcements to see what kind of a credit can be brought in using the 30-day options. Since the stock closed at $19.30, we'll want to sell at-the-money options and hedge each position through out-of-the-money calls and puts.

Table 9.1 shows various option prices with AOL trading for $19.30. To create the iron butterfly, the strategist wants to sell the at-the-money options (the AOL May 20 call and the AOL May 20 put) and buy the out-of-the-money options (the AOL May 25 call and the AOL May 15 put) for protection. Notice that all of the options have the same expiration date, but there are three different strike prices. This position comes with a limited credit of $230 per spread position [(1.6 + 0.9) − (0.1 + 0.1) = 2.3]. The premiums received for selling the May 20 put and the May 20 call total

Table 9.1 Option Quotes for AOL

Position	Number	Option Symbol	Expire	Strike	Type	Entry
Sold	1	AOLED	May 02	20	Call	0.9
Sold	1	AOLQD	May 02	20	Put	1.6
Bought	1	AOLEE	May 02	25	Call	0.1
Bought	1	AOLQC	May 02	15	Put	0.1

$2.50; this is offset slightly by the cost of purchasing the out-of-the money options for a total of 20 cents. The upside breakeven is calculated by adding the net credit (2.3) to the strike price of the middle short call (20), or 22.30. The downside breakeven is determined by subtracting the net credit (2.3) from the strike price of the middle short put (20), or 17.70. Thus, AOL has to stay between $17.70 and $22.30 for the trade to garner a profit.

The risk graph for the AOL iron butterfly shown in Figure 9.7 tells us a few things. First, there is protection in case AOL falls below $15 a share (the May 15 puts are bought for downside protection) and above $25 a share (the May 25 calls are bought for upside protection). We also see that the breakeven is 2.3 points above and below the strikes of the two options that were sold (i.e., the specific calls and puts with strike prices equal to 20). The maximum profit is achieved if, at expiration, AOL is trading for $20 a share.

Now the chance of AOL being exactly at $20 a share on the third Friday of the

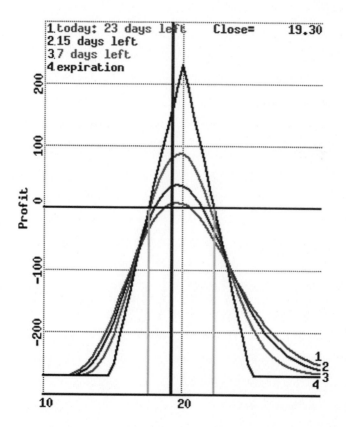

Figure 9.7 Risk Graph for Iron Butterfly Using AOL Puts and Calls (Courtesy of Optionetics.com)

month of May is slim. But if AOL were to stay in a tight trading range over the course of the month, the trade is likely to make some money. How does the volatility trader make money with this position? Let's look at another graph of this trade.

Figure 9.8 is the volatility graph of the position along with a second chart. It looks a bit complicated at first glance, but after looking at each chart the various parts of the puzzle will fit together. First, it is important to note that this trade makes money as volatility falls. If the volatility of AOL falls back to its lows, then the premium should fall into our favor since we sold it (i.e., sold more option premium than received) in the first place. The fact that we sold more premium than we received means that the trade was done for a credit. If we establish a trade for a credit, we benefit from falling levels of implied volatility that cause the premiums to drop. It is similar to when a short seller wants to sell a stock, see it fall in value, and then buy it back at a cheaper price. As sellers or writers of options, we want the premiums to decline due to falling levels of IV (or time decay, or a favorable move in the underlying stock/index). The graph to the left represents the implied options volatility in AOL. It is similar to the chart in Figure 9.6. The graph on the right-hand side shows the trade as the volatility rises or falls. We can see from the second chart that a drop in volatility will make this trade profitable. That is, as volatility falls, the lines shift to the right suggesting increasing profitability.

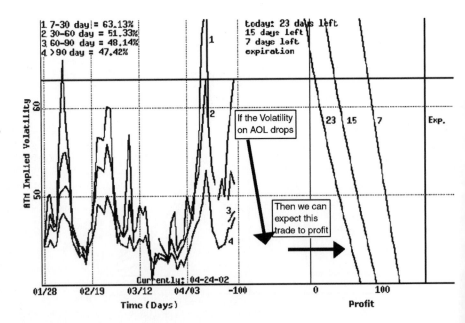

Figure 9.8 Expected Impact of Implied Volatility Changes on AOL Iron Butterfly (Courtesy of Optionetics.com)

Long Iron Butterfly

Strategy = Buy a higher strike call, sell a lower strike call, sell a lower strike put, and buy an even lower strike put.

Market Opportunity = Look for a range bound market that you anticipate to stay between the breakeven points.

Maximum Risk = Limited [(difference between long and short strikes × 100) – net credit received].

Maximum Profit = Limited to the net credit received. Profit exists between breakevens.

Upside Breakeven = Strike price of middle short call + net credit.

Downside Breakeven = Strike price of middle short put – net credit.

Margin = Required. The amount is subject to your broker's discretion.

LONG BUTTERFLY SPREAD

The butterfly can also be constructed with just puts *or* calls. The so-called long butterfly is comprised of two "wings" and a "body," hence the name. The strategist wants to buy the wings and short, or sell, the body. Say the strategist thinks that the stock will continue to stay within its range through the spring and decides to place a butterfly spread. The object is to sell twice as many calls or puts in the body as you buy in each wing, keeping the total number of options bought and sold equal.

Call Butterfly Spread Example

In a call butterfly spread, two calls are bought and two calls are sold. Remember, with options, the quotes must be multiplied by a factor of 100 because each contract represents the control of 100 shares of stock. The total risk, regardless of market direction, is the net debit. Your maximum potential profit is calculated by taking the difference in strike prices of the middle and lower strikes, times 100, minus the debit. Though this is created as a debit spread it will still have the same impact as the iron butterfly with puts and calls discussed in the preceding section. The outcome is the same, expecting that the market drops in volatility.

Let's look at applying a call butterfly to AOL using the data from Table 9.2 to see the risk, reward, and breakeven for this trade. To establish the position, the strategist is buying both the May 15 calls and the May 25 calls, and hedging them by selling the May 20 calls. Notice that this is done at a debit of $270 [(4.4 + 0.1) – (2 × 0.9) × 100]. The net debit is also the maximum risk of the trade. The maximum profit potential

Table 9.2   Option Quotes for AOL Call (Long) Butterfly

Position	Number	Option Symbol	Expire	Strike	Type	Entry
Bought	1	AOLEC	May 02	15	Call	4.4
Sold	2	AOLED	May 02	20	Call	0.9
Bought	1	AOLEE	May 02	25	Call	0.1

is derived by subtracting the net debit from the distance between strikes, or $230 $\{[(25 - 20) - 2.7] \times 100\}$. Notice that this trade has no more risk or reward than the previous iron butterfly example. In Figure 9.9, you can see that the risk and volatility are exactly the same as in the iron butterfly.

To calculate the upside breakeven for the call butterfly, subtract the net debit from the highest strike price; to calculate the downside breakeven, add the net debit to the lowest strike price. In the AOL example, the upside breakeven is $22.30 (25 – 2.7) and the downside breakeven is $17.70 (15 + 2.7). If the stock stays within this

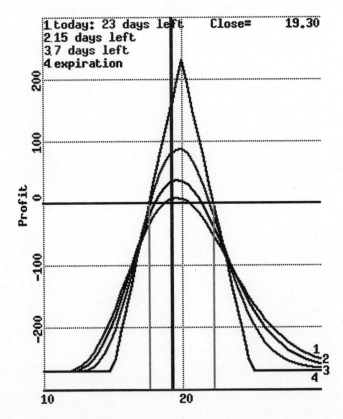

Figure 9.9   Risk Graph of the AOL Call Butterfly (Courtesy of Optionetics.com)

range, the strategist makes a profit by keeping the credit. Losses begin to rise when the stock makes a significant move in either direction and goes beyond either of the breakeven points.

Figure 9.10 shows the impact of changes in volatility on the AOL call butterfly. The graphs are similar to the previous iron butterfly example. When the trade is established, implied volatility on AOL options is rising higher ahead of the earnings report. The spike is depicted on the left-hand chart. If time passes and implied volatility on the options begins to fall, the trade will become more profitable. The chart on the right-hand side of the risk graph represents the potential changes in the profit/loss from changes in volatility. As does the chart on the left, each line represents a different time left until expiration. For example, the line farthest to the right shows what happens with 23 days left until expiration. In this case, the graph is downward sloping and to the right. It tells us that as implied volatility falls, the position generates more profits because the trade benefits from falling levels of IV.

Put Butterfly Spread Example

Put butterfly spreads are created the same way as call butterflies. The only thing that changes with the put butterfly is the use of all puts instead of all calls. The trade will also be done for a net debit. Profits arise if the underlying falls within the spread at

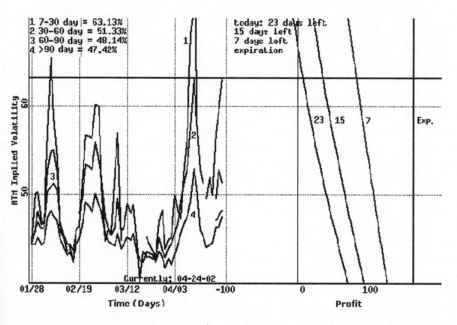

Figure 9.10 Volatility and Vega Graph of the AOL Call Butterfly Example (Courtesy of Optionetics.com)

expiration or if there is a decrease in volatility. For the sake of argument, let's consider put butterflies on AOL and see if there is any difference in the debit, risk, or reward of the position associated with this trade (see Table 9.3).

Is the put butterfly any different from the other two butterflies we have examined? Yes. Although the methods of calculating risk, reward, and breakevens are the same, there is a difference in premium values, which changes the outcome of the calculations. In this trade, the net debit is $260 [(0.1 + 5.7) − (2 × 1.6) × 100]. Thus, since the difference between strikes is 5, the maximum reward on the trade is $240 [(5 − 2.6) × 100]. Therefore, the put butterfly has a $10 better risk/reward potential compared to the first two butterflies. That is, in this case the strategist is risking $260 to make $240 instead of paying a debit of $270 to make $230. While $10 may not seem like a great deal of money, in options trading every increment counts, especially when each spread contains multiple legs, each requiring a commission to process.

Figure 9.11 details the risk graph for the AOL put butterfly trade. Although it shows a slightly different profile than the other two butterflies (in that the risk/reward has a $10 difference), the shape of the risk graph is nearly identical. Therefore, the outcome of the strategy still depends on the stock staying in a fairly narrow range before expiration. A large move in either direction will result in a loss.

Finally, the impact of changes in implied volatility is the same with all butterflies, including the AOL put butterfly. Figure 9.12 shows the volatility graph of the AOL put butterfly. Notice that, as volatility falls (left-hand chart), the profit from the trade increases (right-hand chart). Again, the graph is identical to the iron butterfly as well as the call butterfly. Therefore, when considering butterflies, the strategist must have an idea of what current levels of implied volatility are and also expect that those levels of volatility will decline going forward.

Since the butterfly is designed to take advantage of time premium decay, it is best used on options with less than 30 to 45 days until expiration. Keep in mind that with these rapidly decaying options the strategist might not get enough premium on the options sold (the body) to make the trade worthwhile. It may be necessary to use options with one additional expiration month. Traders should calculate both to see which trade offers the best profit potential given the net amount of money at risk. It is possible to change the risks and rewards of butterflies by changing the strike prices, or even the distances between strikes, but this will also affect the risks and rewards.

Table 9.3 Option Quotes for AOL Put Butterfly

Position	Number	Option Symbol	Expire	Strike	Type	Entry
Bought	1	AOLQC	May 02	15	Put	0.1
Sold	2	AOLQD	May 02	20	Put	1.6
Bought	1	AOLQE	May 02	25	Put	5.7

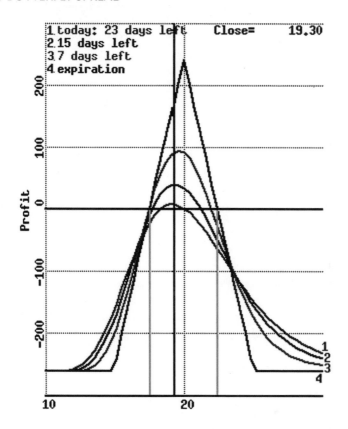

Figure 9.11   Risk Graph of AOL Put Butterfly Spread (Courtesy of Optionetics.com)

Long Butterfly

Strategy = Buy a lower strike option, sell two higher strike options, and buy an even higher strike option (all calls or all puts).

Market Opportunity = Look for a range bound market that is expected to stay between the breakeven points.

Maximum Risk = Limited to the net debit paid.

Maximum Profit = Limited [(difference in strikes × 100) − net debit paid]. Profit exists between breakevens.

Upside Breakeven = Highest strike price − net debit paid.

Downside Breakeven = Lowest strike price + net debit paid.

Margin = Required. The amount is subject to your broker's discretion.

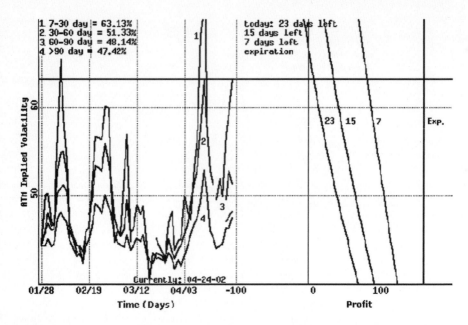

Figure 9.12   Volatility and Vega Graph of the AOL Put Butterfly Spread (Courtesy of Optionetics.com)

CONCLUSION

A friend of mine is an avid fisherman. When he goes fishing, he has so many differ-ent flies and lures and so much tackle, that I don't understand how he makes sense of it all. One time I asked him, "Do you really need all that stuff?" And he told me, "No! Not all the time. But each fly or lure has its own time and place." Like that fisherman setting out to explore new and unknown waters, the option strategist must have an arsenal of trading ideas to use in uncertain and unexpected circumstances. Chapter 8 explored strategies that can profit when implied volatility is low and set to rise. In this chapter, the reader became acquainted with strategies that can deliver profits when implied volatility is high and set to fall. Covered calls, credit spreads, and butterflies are some examples that work well in high volatility situations.

As we have seen, there are several strategies that can make money with a drop in volatility. Some, such as short calls and puts, have higher risks than do others such as credit spreads and butterflies. While there isn't one strategy that will work for every situation all the time, these are popular strategies and relatively easy to understand. The important factor to consider is that when you apply these strategies to high op-tion volatility markets, you can expect to get more reward and have less risk. As in-dicated near the beginning of the chapter, it is better to be an insurance salesperson when everyone needs insurance the most than when no one needs insurance; the pre-miums are higher, and the ability to keep some or all of the premiums is greater, too.

10

Volatility Skews

Are you ready for some really serious stuff? In earlier parts of this book, we learned how volatility can affect a variety of assets such as stocks and indexes. We learned that there are several indicators that can help to chart volatility. We learned about historical volatility and how to use it in actual trading and about implied volatility including an easy way to calculate it, and how options are priced using this information. We learned that there are actual instruments charted on implied volatility such as the CBOE Volatility Index (VIX) and Nasdaq 100 Volatility Index (VXN). Now let's put it all together and learn about something that some of the most sophisticated professional traders use in their trading: volatility skewing.

A volatility skew is created when two or more options on the same underlying stock or index have a sizable difference in terms of implied volatility. This means when comparing various quotes of options and looking at each option contract's implied volatility the strategist detects a big difference between one option and another. If one option has a much higher implied volatility than another on the same stock, there could be a trading opportunity consisting of purchasing the option with the lower volatility and simultaneously selling the option with the higher volatility. In that respect, there are two types of volatility skews to look for:

1. Volatility price skews between differing strikes with the same expiration.

2. Volatility time skews between different months of the same strike.

In this chapter, the reader learns how to evaluate each of these volatility skews, how to identify them, and, of course, how to implement trading strategies that take advantage of volatility skews.

VOLATILITY PRICE SKEWS

Logically, when a trader looks at a group of strike prices in a certain options chain, there is an expectation that the market will keep the option prices in line. That is, every price will maintain the same relationship and the implied volatility of an options contract on a day-to-day basis will remain in a certain range. This makes sense given our earlier discussion of volatility. To be specific, the implied volatility of an options contract does not exist in a vacuum. It is also a function of the historical volatility, as well as market expectations regarding the future volatility, of the underlying asset. Therefore, the implied volatility of the XYZ June option should not be materially different from that of the XYZ January option. And the volatility of the XYZ 50 call should not deviate much from the IV of the XYZ 40 put.

Now, while implied volatility will be the same for different strike prices and different option expiration months for some stocks, it is certainly not carved in stone. For example, the demand for certain options, in certain strike prices, can cause the option premiums and the implied volatilities of those premiums to rise and fall faster then their sister strikes. In a perfect world, if the stock volatility of XYZ were at 50 percent, then it would be easy to assume that all the options for XYZ would also be trading at an implied volatility of 50 percent; but as we have already seen in earlier chapters, that just doesn't happen.

Therefore, the strike prices for a set of options can have different levels of implied volatility. For example, if a large trader came in and bought 1,500 call options with a particular strike, the offer (or market price) on that option would go up faster than the option strikes around it. After the spike, it might be a few hours before that particular option came back down to a premium that reflected a normal price when compared to the options around it.

Table 10.1 shows an example of a hypothetical set of options on XYZ with three different, but similar, levels of implied volatility. Now imagine for a moment that a big trader walks in to buy 1,500 January 50 call options, and as these contracts are traded, the price of the January 50 calls goes up in value. Table 10.2 shows the jump in option prices that occurs while the large order is being filled and implied volatility on the XYZ 50 calls jumps higher.

Note the change in both the premium of the January 50 call and the implied volatility of that same call option. In this case, simply by looking at the difference in implied volatility across the set of options we can see that there is a much heavier buying demand for these call options. This disparity between prices is known as a

Table 10.1   Hypothetical Set of XYZ Calls

Strike	Bid	Offer	IV
50	6.50	6.75	65%
55	3.25	3.50	63%
60	1.50	1.60	60%

Table 10.2 Hypothetical Set of XYZ Calls Assuming Jump in Volatility

Strike	Bid	Offer	IV
50	7.00	7.25	86%
55	3.25	3.50	63%
60	1.50	1.60	60%

volatility skew. Volatility skews like this exist all the time, but not in all stocks; some stocks have a bigger skewing between strikes than do others. Skews that exist in one set of options will not stay in the same issue indefinitely. They come and go, just like highs and lows in the market. Let's look at a few volatility skews on some real data.

DELL COMPUTER

Dell Computer (DELL) was a hot issue in the late 1990s and even into the year 2000. Many investors thought Dell, after making a huge run higher from 1996 to 1999, was simply in a retracement, or giving back a small percentage of its big gains, and would soon begin to set new highs. In January 2000, then, investors were still bullish on the stock, and DELL call options were heavily traded. Let's look at the February calls in early January. At the time, the stock was trading in the mid-40s.

Table 10.3 shows a list of February 2000 DELL call options in early January 2000. First, look at the option bids and offers. Notice how fast the premiums drop as we go further down the strike chain. This is typical of prices. However, look at the

Table 10.3 DELL February 2000 Call Options in Early January 2000

Option Symbol	Strike	Type	Bid	Ask	IV
DLQBE	25.00	Call	21.625	23.125	130.155%
DLQBF	30.00	Call	17.000	17.125	79.653
DLQBZ	32.50	Call	14.854	14.875	82.237
DLQBG	35.00	Call	12.375	12.375	68.522
DLQBU	37.50	Call	10.125	10.250	65.023
DLQBH	40.00	Call	8.125	8.250	62.885
DLQBV	42.50	Call	6.375	6.375	60.775
DLQBI	45.00	Call	4.750	4.875	59.123
DLQBW	47.50	Call	3.375	3.625	57.549
DLQBJ	50.00	Call	2.500	2.562	57.424
DLQBK	55.00	Call	1.250	1.312	58.057
DLQBL	60.00	Call	0.625	0.688	59.782

IV column, which reflects the implied volatility for each strike price. In a perfect world, these would all be close to each other. Not in this case. Clearly, the options with the lower strike prices had much greater levels of implied volatility. Therefore, the table shows that the in-the-money options were clearly in more demand than those that were out-of-the-money. In fact, the DELL 45 to 60 calls had IVs of under 60 percent—less than half the level of the 25 call. The disparity between the implied volatility of the DELL options with different strike prices is what is referred to as a volatility skew.

Let's move forward two years and look at another set of calls on Dell Computer. The data is roughly the same, but instead of looking at the February 2000 calls, Table 10.4 considers the February 2002 calls in the month of January 2002. The calls have roughly the same time to expiration as the February call options in 2000 from the previous example.

It's important to realize that in 2002 Dell Computer was not trading in the mid-40s anymore; the stock was trading in the 20s, or nearly half the price of two years earlier. The implied volatilities for DELL options were lower in 2002, as shown in Table 10.4. The other thing to note is that the implied volatility across each strike price was roughly the same. Notice that there is a skew; the implied volatility drops as the strikes go higher (but not at the rate it did back in January 2000), and the IV rises again above the 35 strike. This should help to illustrate that skewing can come and go with every stock. The situation in Table 10.4 is much more common and what the option strategist can expect in terms of volatility skews across different strike prices. Put differently, the extreme skew on DELL call options in early 2000 was indeed unusual.

As we can see, demand can cause option volatilities to rise in different increments across different strikes. In the case of DELL options, it was strong demand in anticipation of the stock continuing to rise to new highs. What else can cause volatility skewing? What about catastrophes such as the attacks on New York and Washington, D.C., on September 11? Well, just the day before, UAL Corporation (symbol: UAL), the parent company of United Airlines, had options trading with implied volatilities between 35 percent and 40 percent with very little difference in implied volatility across strike prices. Let's look at the market just after the September 11 catastrophe and see if there was a volatility skewing in the airline stocks when the markets resumed trading.

Table 10.4   DELL February 2002 Calls in January 2002

Option Symbol	Strike	Type	Bid	Ask	IV
DLQBE	25.00	Call	5.00	5.20	49.654%
DLQBY	27.50	Call	3.10	3.30	48.193
DLQBF	30.00	Call	1.70	1.85	46.904
DLQBZ	32.50	Call	.75	.90	44.872
DLQBG	35.00	Call	.20	.35	41.239
DLQBU	37.50	Call	.05	.20	43.597
DLQBH	40.00	Call	0	.10	44.622

Table 10.5 shows various put options on UAL on September 17, 2001—the first official day of trading after the terrorist attacks that virtually shut down trading activity on Wall Street. First, notice how the rise in implied volatility occurred across the board. The numbers were two to three times greater than the values recorded prior to the terrorist attack. Second, there is volatility skewing in the puts, as the implied volatility ranges from 80 percent to 106 percent.

Companies can also cause volatility skewing. Tyco (symbol: TYC), for example, had volatilities that were rising shortly after the announcement of its plans to split up into four separate companies as well as rumors of accounting problems. On September 21, 2001, Tyco closed at $40 a share—down 30 percent in just two weeks. Table 10.6 shows the TYC October call options and their volatilities. See how much higher the volatilities are for the in-the-money calls than the out-of-the-money calls. The 25 calls, for instance, have almost double the volatility of the 50 calls.

So now that we have looked at a few tables of options prices, let's see what this data looks like on a graph. Figure 10.1 shows that the 50 calls and puts, as well as the other October puts and calls (from Table 10.6), had implied volatilities in the low 50 percent range. On the left-hand side, the volatility skew graph reflects the implied volatility of TYC call options. With the stock trading at $40 a share, the

Table 10.5   Implied Volatility on UAL September 17, 2001

Option Symbol	Strike	Type	Bid	Ask	IV
UALVC	15.00	Put	35	1.05	88.275%
UALVW	17.50	Put	1.25	2.00	80.908
UALVD	20.00	Put	2.75	3.90	85.309
UALVX	22.50	Put	5.10	6.00	99.517
UALVE	25.00	Put	7.30	8.30	106.368

Table 10.6   Call Options and Volatility Skew on Tyco on September 21, 2001

Option Symbol	Strike	Type	Bid	Ask	IV
TYCJE	25.00	Call	15.80	16.30	102.015%
TYCJY	27.50	Call	13.30	13.90	89.189
TYCJF	30.00	Call	10.90	11.50	79.712
TYCJZ	32.50	Call	8.70	9.20	75.612
TYCJG	35.00	Call	6.60	7.00	69.878
TYCJU	37.50	Call	4.70	5.10	66.005
TYCJH	40.00	Call	3.00	3.40	60.438
TYCJV	42.50	Call	1.85	2.10	58.162
TYCJI	45.00	Call	.95	1.20	55.159
TYCJW	47.50	Call	.50	.60	53.727
TYCJJ	50.00	Call	.15	.35	52.182

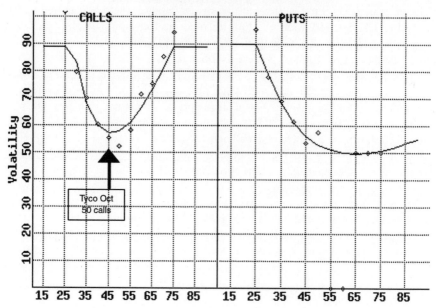

Figure 10.1   Graph of TYC Volatility Skew for October 2001 Options (Courtesy of Optionetics.com)

near-the-money options had the least amount of implied volatility. The deep-in-the-money and the deep-out-of-the-money options had the highest levels of volatility. The right-hand side of Figure 10.1 shows the implied volatility of TYC put options. Again, the near-the-money puts had the lowest levels of volatility. The in-the-money options had slightly higher levels. The deep-out-of-the-money options carried extremely high implied volatility.

What causes this volatility skew to occur? Demand! During the skyrocketing Internet era of the late 1990s, most people focused on the tremendous changes in stock prices. But as an options trader, I looked at the price changes in calls and puts; the strike prices seemed to run forever upward, not to mention the premiums of those strikes. One thing I noticed was the number of web sites that cropped up picking buys and sells for subscribers to take on these options. Another was that clearly technology stocks were getting much better press coverage on TV than regular blue chips, retailers, energy stocks, and so on. This convinced me that many people had been buying stocks based on the amount of "advertising" that was being done in the financial arena.

Although being an options trader was the craze back then, those traders did merely the few strategies that their brokers could actually allow. For example, most brokerage firms allowed covered calls to be traded, even in individual retirement accounts. It was considered a low-risk options trading approach. While that particular strategy accounted for some of the buildup in options trading, the majority of new options traders simply bought outright call options. Buying an outright call option was a way of taking a bullish position in the market using leverage. When Dell Computer was exploding to the upside before the year 2000, the number of call options traded on this stock climbed almost as fast as the stock price itself. It seemed that everyone wanted to make as much money as they could by leveraging capital into call options.

Something I noticed during the period of seemingly insatiable demand for DELL options was the amount of out-of-the-money calls and puts that were active. This actually pushed the offers higher than normal. Now what was causing all the demand in DELL options? Many public traders probably bought DELL options due to the hype the media was giving them, especially from the Internet.

The net result of the rising prices of DELL options was the development of several skewing opportunities. These skews were not very noticeable to the novice; but to the professional, the skews provided a volatility edge. By identifying skew, a trader not only knew which options were in high demand, but also how to create trading strategies that took advantage of the skewing. John Q. Public helped create a large skew in DELL by actively speculating on DELL with out-of-the-money calls. Meanwhile, the institutional traders were buying the out-of-the-money put options as a way of hedging their stock positions, which caused these options to rise. The prices reflected the implied volatilities of each strike price. As a result, some of these strikes actually came out of line.

SMILES, FROWNS, AND SLOPES

Since volatility is mean reverting, it tends to come back to an average over time. By expiration, all volatilities in the same month meet, as time value decays. So knowing how to use volatility skews can give you an edge in deciding which strategy to use and when. How can you take advantage of this information? Simply by knowing how to interpret what options are over- or underpriced compared to others, you can put together volatility-hedged strategies that give you an extra edge in both risk and reward. Let's look at a few graphs and see how to apply them to your trading approach.

A volatility smile represents options with high volatility above and below the ATM and near-ATM strike price, demonstrating that there are discrepancies in both the in-the-money and out-of-the-money options. Figure 10.2 provides an example of the volatility smile. In this example, the option with the lowest implied volatility has a strike price of 50. The strikes with the highest implied volatilities are the 25s and below and the 75s and above. Therefore, if the options strategist is bullish on this stock, creating a bull call spread (discussed in Chapter 8) buying the 50 calls and selling the 75

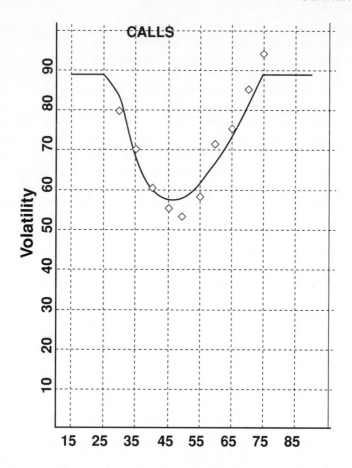

Figure 10.2   Volatility Smile (Courtesy of Optionetics.com)

calls may be a viable strategy. Conversely, if the option strategist is bearish, a credit spread (discussed in Chapter 9) using the 50 calls to sell and hedging them with the 25 calls would be a possible strategy. The important thing to remember here is to buy low (low implied volatility) and sell high (high implied volatility). In Figure 10.2, the optimal buy would be the 50 strike, and everything else (i.e., all of the other options with higher levels of volatility) could be used as a possible hedge.

The volatility smile is the most popular skew graph because it appears most often and can typically be found during periods of high volatility; the higher the volatility, the steeper the skew is likely to be. Back in the dot-com era, these things were so steep even a Hummer wouldn't be able to climb them! I find the steepest slopes to generally be on the call side for stock options. This means they are best suited for bullish trades, such as bull call spreads.

As you might have guessed, the volatility frown is the reverse of the smile. It represents low volatility options above and below the ATM and near-ATM strike price, demonstrating that there are discrepancies in both the in-the-money and out-of-the-money options. In Figure 10.3, the option with a strike price of 40 has the highest implied volatility. The strikes with the lowest implied volatility are the 55s. Therefore, if the strategist is bullish on this stock, simply buying out-of-the-money calls may be a great strategy. Conversely, if the trader is bearish, a credit spread using the 40 calls to sell and hedging them with the 55 calls would be a possible strategy. Once again, just like the volatility smile, the important factor to consider is to buy low (volatility) and sell high (volatility). The option with the 50 strike is the best suited for sale and everything else would be a possible buy to hedge.

The volatility frown is not a chart that traders encounter often. Figure 10.3 was

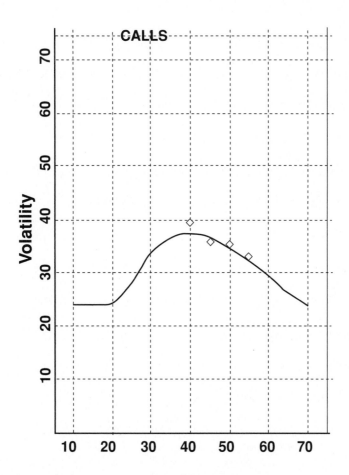

Figure 10.3 Volatility Frown (Courtesy of Optionetics.com)

Volatility smile: Higher volatility options occur above and below the lower volatility ATM and near-ATM options.

Volatility frown: Lower volatility options occur above and below the higher volatility ATM and near-ATM options.

Volatility slope: Higher volatility options slope down to lower volatility as strike prices increase, or slope up from lower to higher volatility as strike prices increase.

---

created using options on Philip Morris, which is often considered a defensive stock (i.e., it generally performs well when most stocks head lower). Frowns are found in stocks such as this because demand is usually at-the-money since those are the only options that typically have significant trading volume. If the option strategist is going to trade the skew on stocks such as this, it is important that the options have sufficient trading activity, or liquidity.

Volatility skews that look like the one in Figure 10.4 are what I refer to as a volatility slope. This particular chart is taken from the OEX or S&P 100 options. There is definitely a skew here, but it's going in one direction. This is almost always indicative of an index market. Since index options are used quite a bit by the

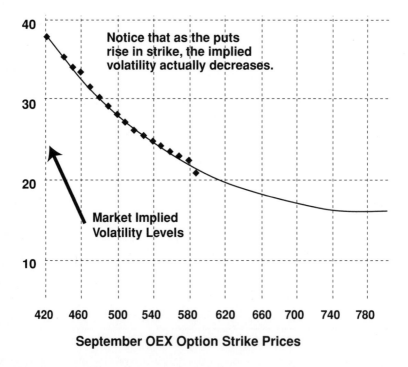

Figure 10.4 Volatility Slope (Courtesy of Optionetics.com)

professionals as a hedging instrument for portfolios, this creates pressure on put options, especially out-of-the-money puts. The 600 puts shown in Figure 10.4 are the cheapest in terms of implied volatility, at just above 20 percent. Going down to the 420 puts, however, we see volatilities at over 35 percent.

The volatility skew on the OEX puts in Figure 10.4 looks similar to the OEX calls, which tells me one thing. Index options, for purposes of volatility, are best used with spreads that are bearish; if bullish, it's best to buy outright calls. Look at the chart again for a moment. If strategists are bullish, they definitely don't want to buy something at a higher volatility than the one that is sold. It's best to go slightly out-of-the-money and buy the outright option. If the strategist is bearish, however, it is better to look to buy the higher strike put and sell the lower strike put—a bear put spread. In this example, the optimum trade involves buying lower volatility and selling higher volatility.

Volatility skews across different strike prices can take on other forms. We have covered the most common three: smiles, frowns, and slopes. Perhaps the most important thing to hammer down here is how to spot them. Once they are identified, and you have an assumption or expectation regarding the future direction of the underlying asset, you will be in a better position to successfully trade them. Basically, you will have additional choices of how to put together a strategy based on what the skew chart may be telling you. Remember, the best way to take advantage of the skew is to remember the simple rule: buy low (implied volatility) and sell high (implied volatility).

SKEW BY EXPIRATION MONTH (SERIES)

In the last few pages, you learned how to take advantage of volatility skews within the same month of a chain by looking at implied volatility across different strike prices. Now let's look horizontally and see whether skews exist across different months of options. The basic idea is the same—to identify disparities among different option contracts on the same underlying stock or index. In this case, rather than looking at different strike prices, the strategist wants to consider the implied volatility of options across different expiration cycles.

Before looking at specific examples of skews across expiration months, let's consider why they exist in the first place. I remember working on the floor of an options exchange and when a big news announcement came in regarding a company, the stock price of the company in question would sometimes start to change violently. My natural instinct was to look at the price changes in the options. It was funny how traders would be worried about the options that were coming off the board (expiring) first and paid virtually no attention to the back months.

When there is a disproportional interest in the front month options, volatility skews often result. I refer to the phenomenon as procrastination. The result is that the options in the front month spike higher and faster than those in the back months. When I saw this happening on the exchange, I knew it had to affect the implied volatility of the options. The front months were moving up in volatility faster than the back months. Then, time went by, and the options seemed to almost always come back together in terms of volatility, as if it was all for nothing.

The same things that made volatility skews appear in different strike prices were causing the months to differ from each other. Rumors, press releases, accounting irregularities and fraud, earnings warnings and reports, analyst upgrades and downgrades, and various other outcries cause this ballooning effect to happen nearly every day for some stocks. I saw this on the exchange and learned to trade it. Now I refer to the phenomenon as volatility skew between months.

Volatility skews between months happen when the options with the same strike price but different expiration months have different levels of implied volatility. It can happen to the dullest of companies as fast as it can happen to the most volatile of them. I remember one day seeing the front month options of Dial Corporation (symbol: DL) spike higher to the point where they were nearly as expensive as the options that expired five months later. What was the important issue regarding Dial? It turns out that the soap company had a major announcement that it was releasing later that day. Wow, was it going to announce a big increase or decrease in earnings? Was the CEO getting ousted? Was this company guilty of accounting irregularities?

Well, despite all the rumors circulating around the floors of exchanges, it turned out that Dial, which already had soap that killed 98 percent of bacteria on contact, announced its soap would now kill 99 percent of bacteria on contact. Talk about a press release! The somewhat disappointing news release caused the gas to come out of the options, and the implied volatility dropped right back to its normal levels. It was actually quite funny, but I'm sure there were plenty of options traders that day who were not laughing.

Now let's look at some tables and charts of volatility skews by months to see what to look for when options are seemingly mispriced from month to month.

Table 10.7 shows various call options for UAL in mid-September 2001. Take a look at the top option; it has the least amount of time to expiration (one month) and an implied volatility of nearly 98 percent. The long-term options, or LEAPS, options at the bottom have volatility in the 40s. Therefore, the long-term options have implied volatility equal to less than half as much as the front month options. We

Table 10.7 UAL Call Options and Implied Volatility on September 17, 2001

Option Symbol	Strike	Type	Bid	Ask	IV
UALJW	17.50	Call	2.00	2.10	97.896%
UALKW	17.50	Call	2.05	2.05	69.517
UALAW	17.50	Call	2.50	3.30	68.939
UALBW	17.50	Call	2.35	2.60	51.816
VUAAC	15.00	Call	4.50	5.70	42.712
AUAAD	20.00	Call	2.95	4.10	49.870

know that at expiration the time value will be gone from the front month options. We also know that the longer-term options will not decay as quickly because they have plenty of time until expiration. In fact, the first two options are priced practically the same. However, the second option doesn't expire for 60 days. Isn't it amazing that the floor traders were so busy driving up the prices (and implied volatility) of the short-term options that they didn't even look at the back month contract? Any trader smart enough to identify the skews in the marketplace would have taken advantage of this and created a potentially risk-free trade.

Figure 10.5 shows the sharp spike in the implied volatility of UAL options in mid-September 2001. Looking at the extreme right shows you how high the volatility rose after September 11. Now look closer at the individual lines; not all spiked higher to the same degree. The 30 to 60 day options rose to a much higher implied volatility (89.26 percent) than the options that had more than 90 days to expiration, which had implied volatility of 63.49 percent. This is quite a volatility skew and can be found more often than most traders might think.

Figure 10.6 shows another example of a volatility skew across expiration months. The top chart shows the price chart of Ciena Corporation (symbol: CIEN) on January 4, 2000. The bottom chart is an implied volatility chart for CIEN options. It shows how volatility skews between months can widen as the stock climbs up just

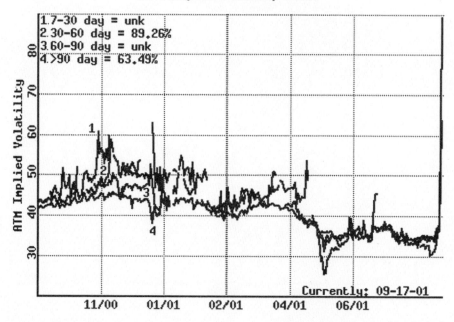

Figure 10.5   Graphical Look at Volatility Skew of UAL (Courtesy of Optionetics.com)

Ciena Corporation

6 Month Stock Price Chart

H= 54.94, L= 52.25, C= 53.19

Currently: 01-04-00

08/05   09/02   10/01   10/29   11/29

6 Month ATM Implied Volatility Chart

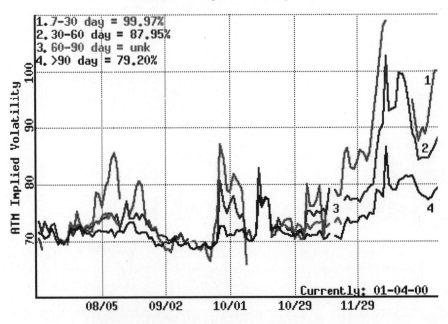

1. 7-30 day = 99.97%
2. 30-60 day = 87.95%
3. 60-90 day = unk
4. >90 day = 79.20%

Currently: 01-04-00

08/05   09/02   10/01   10/29   11/29

Figure 10.6 Price Chart of CIEN and Implied Volatility Graph of CIEN Options
(January 4, 2000) (Courtesy of Optionetics.com)

as fast as skews can widen to the downside. Notice how the more volatile the stock gets, the wider the implied volatilities between months are. For example, the top line on the implied volatility chart reflects options expiring in 7 to 30 days. The implied volatility on those options is almost 100 percent. The bottom line shows the implied volatility of the long-term options, which is equal to 80 percent and much less than the front month options. Let's look at how you can take advantage of skews across expiration months.

DIAGONAL SPREADS

How does the strategist trade skews by expiration months? Welcome to the world of diagonal and horizontal spreads, which work by trying to take out time premium from the front month. A horizontal spread involves the purchase of a longer-term call and the selling of a shorter-term call with the same strike price. This type of strategy is also known as the calendar spread. Diagonal spreads, in contrast, involve different strike prices. Again, the idea is to buy the longer-term option and sell the shorter-term option that has witnessed a spike in implied volatility.

How does the strategist decide between calendar and diagonal spreads? A lot depends on the assumption regarding the direction of the stock over the next 30 days or so. If the strategist has a directional bias on the stock, then perhaps a diagonal spread is more appropriate. For example, buying a longer-term option and selling a shorter-term out-of-the-money option will do the job. The longer-term option should have some intrinsic or real value to help compensate for the overall rise in volatility, while the option sold should have only about 30 days or so to expiration, and consist of nothing but time value. The object is, obviously, to be right on the price; but if you are wrong, the short option will decay in value faster than the long option will, thereby offering some protection.

What Is a Calendar Spread?

A calendar spread is an advanced strategy that takes advantage of volatility skews and theta (time) decay. The low-risk profile makes this strategy inviting. It consists of both the sale and the purchase of an equal number of call (or put) options with the same underlying security, the same strike price, and different expiration dates. A calendar spread is created by shorting the front month option and hedging it by going long an option that expires at a later month. These combined positions offer traders a limited risk position that profits as the short front month options decay faster than the long back month options. The maximum risk of a calendar spread is equal to the net debit of the options. A software package (like the Optionetics Platinum site) is required to determine necessary points of reference such as maximum reward and breakevens.

What Is a Diagonal Spread?

A diagonal spread is a low-risk strategy that consists of both the sale and the purchase of an equal number of call (or put) options with the same underlying security, different strike prices, and different expiration dates. A diagonal spread is created by shorting the front month option and hedging it by going long an option that expires at a later month. The anticipated directional bias of the market is a strong factor in determining which strike prices to use. The maximum risk of a diagonal spread is equal to the net debit of the options. A software package (like the Optionetics Platinum site) is required to determine necessary points of reference such as maximum reward and breakevens.

Placing Calendar and Diagonal Spreads

To place a calendar spread, look to buy cheap options and sell expensive options—a volatility skew in which the premiums on the current month options are inflated, but the outer months are still inexpensive. Once calendar or diagonal spread opportunities have been identified, they are best placed using limit orders. Doing so guarantees that each trade will take advantage of its respective volatility skew. In the best of all possible scenarios, the short option will expire worthless so that you can keep the credit and the stock climbs or falls enough for the long option to be profitable. The only obstacle to this plan comes from volatility. A dramatic move by the underlying stock in either direction could unbalance the spread, causing it to widen.

Table 10.8 shows a volatility skew that might be attractive to the diagonal spread strategist with a bullish view on the stock. The options are on shares of Dynegy (symbol: DYN) in late April 2002. The stock experienced high volatility during the few days prior to April 26 after the company issued a grim earnings forecast. Consequently, the implied volatility of the front month options (May 2002) soared to nearly 150 percent. Compared to the implied volatility of the January 2004 LEAPS (60.80 percent), the short-term options became quite expensive.

Given the disparity between the DYN front month and LEAPS options, one possible bullish trading strategy is a diagonal spread using the short-term out-of-the-money call options and the long-term in-the-money call options. With the stock trading for $14.50 a share, the strategist would buy the January 2004 LEAPS with a strike price of 10 and sell the May 2002 15 call. The short call is out-of-the-money and consists of only time value. In contrast, the long call is deep-in-the-money and has intrinsic value.

Figure 10.7 shows the risk graph of the bullish diagonal spread on DYN. The trade is done for a debit because the long option costs $7.50, which is more than the premium received for selling the short-term call ($1.90). The debit of $560

Table 10.8   Dynegy Option Quotes and Implied Volatility (April 26, 2002)

Position	Number	Option Symbol	Expire	Strike	Type	Entry	Bid/Ask	Model	IV
Bought	1	KYKAB	Jan 04	10	Call	7.5	7/7.5	7.1	60.80%
Sold	1	DYNEC	May 02	15	Call	1.9	1.9/2.2	2	146.10%

represents the maximum risk for this trade. In the event that the stock rises before expiration and the short call is assigned at $15 a share, the long call can be exercised for only $10 a share. The breakeven, which requires some kind of trading software to calculate, is equal to $13.10. This is due to the fact that the short option offers some downside protection equal to the amount of the premium received. The maximum gain is $150 a contract and occurs if the stock trades at the higher of the two strike prices—$15 a share—at expiration. Therefore, the trade is moderately bullish. In

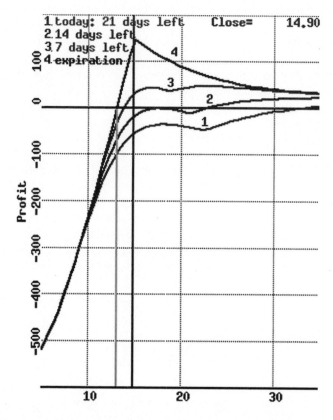

Figure 10.7   Risk Graph for Bullish Diagonal Spread on DYN (April 26, 2002) (Courtesy of Optionetics.com)

that case, the long call retains most of its value, but the short-term option expires worthless. At that point, the position should be closed.

Once the strategist identifies a volatility skew across expiration months for a set of options, a wide array of possibilities exist for the use of diagonal spreads. For instance, the strategist can sell a further out-of-the-money option to make the strategy more aggressive. In the previous example, instead of selling the DYN 15 call, the strategist can go deeper out-of-the-money and sell the DYN 17.5 call (see Table 10.9). The implied volatility of the 17.5 was also high (nearly 128 percent) at that time.

Buying the January 2004 10 LEAPS and selling the May 2002 17.5 call is depicted on the risk graph in Figure 10.8. Notice that the shape of the risk graph is similar to the one in Figure 10.7. However, the potential losses are greater. In addition, the breakeven is equal to $14.50, compared to $13.10. Basically, the 17.50 call has less time value premium than the 15 call and the downside protection from selling the option is also less. Although the potential losses are greater and the breakeven is at a higher price, the more aggressive diagonal spread has greater potential rewards as the stock price moves higher. In this case, the maximum reward is $260 a contract, compared to $150 for our first diagonal spread example. Once again, the maximum profit arises if the stock moves higher at expiration: in this case, to $17.50—the strike at which the short-term option expires worthless.

Diagonal spreads using calls can also be created if there is a volatility skew between the short-term and long-term options and the strategist is bearish on the stock. Table 10.10 gives the data and Figure 10.9 shows the risk graph associated with selling the June 2002 DYN 12.5 call and buying the January 2004 20 call. Notice that in this case the risk graph takes on a completely different slope. In addition, the trade is done for a credit because the short-term option is worth more than the long-term option. Profits increase when the stock price falls because the short-term option is in-the-money. The success of the trade requires that the stock falls and the short-term option loses value faster than the long option. If the stock price falls below the lower strike price at expiration, the trader gets to keep the credit. For that reason, the maximum profit occurs at the strike price of the short option ($12.50) at expiration—the point where the short option expires worthless and the long option retains most of its value. The risk associated with this spread comes into play if the stock price moves higher.

Obviously, there are a multitude of ways to structure diagonal spreads to profit

Table 10.9   Data Table for Aggressive Diagonal Spread

Position	Number	Option Symbol	Expire	Strike	Type	Entry	Bid/Ask	Model	IV
Bought	1	KYKAB	Jan 04	10	Call	7.5	7/7.5	7.1	60.50%
Sold	1	DYNEW	May 02	17.50	Call	.85	.85/ 1.05	1.0	127.80%

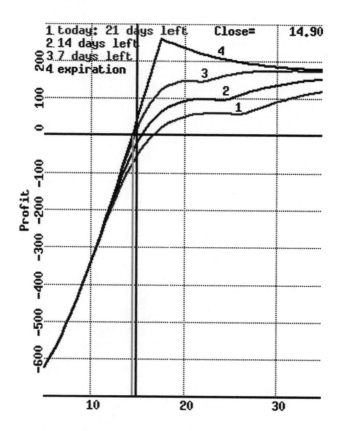

Figure 10.8 Aggressive Diagonal Spread on DYN (April 26, 2002) (Courtesy of Optionetics.com)

Table 10.10 Data Table for Bearish Diagonal Spread Using Calls

Position	Number	Option Symbol	Expire	Strike	Type	Entry	Bid/Ask	Model	IV
Bought	1	KYKAD	Jan 04	20	Call	3.3	2.95/3.3	3.2	54.10%
Sold	1	DYNFV	Jun 02	12.5	Call	3.9	3.9/4.1	4	121.20%

from a volatility skew between months. Each trade selection depends on the strategist's outlook for the stock—bullish, bearish, or neutral. Second, although not covered here, diagonal spreads with put options are viable when there are skews between options with differing expiration months. Again, as with call options, put diagonal spreads can be created to take advantage of volatility skews and can be structured based on the strategist's directional outlook for the stock.

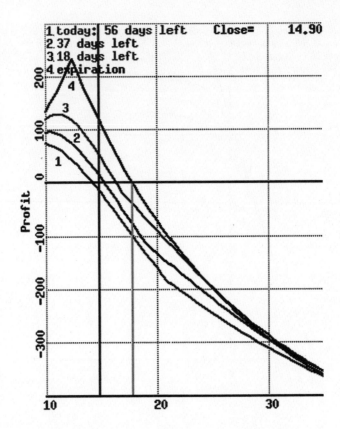

Figure 10.9 Bearish Diagonal Spread Using DYN Calls (Courtesy of Optionetics.com)

There are two keys to success when structuring diagonal spreads. First, the diagonal trader should carefully look at the risk graph and feel comfortable with the risk/reward trade-off. Notice that many of the trades offer limited rewards that are much less than the potential risks. In most cases, the strategist will want to exit the position when the first option has expired and the high levels of implied volatility on the short option have dissipated. In addition, when the options are in-the-money, there is always the possibility of assignment, and the strategist wants to be cognizant of that fact. Second, the key to success is identifying and understanding the volatility skew. Obviously, the strategy will have limited chances of success if the strategist is buying an option with high volatility and selling another one with low volatility. In that case, reversion to the mean works against the trade.

HORIZONTAL OR CALENDAR SPREADS

Calendar spreads are another way to take advantage of volatility skews. This strategy is quite similar to diagonal spreads, but with one important difference. Basically, the strategist creating a calendar spread is using options with the same strike price but different expiration dates. Like the diagonal spread, the longer-term option is purchased and the shorter-term option is sold simultaneously. Calendar spreads can be created with a bullish, bearish, or neutral bias. The trade is usually done for a debit because the long-term option will have a higher premium than the option that is sold. The maximum risk is equal to the net debit.

Like the diagonal spread discussed earlier, the primary objective of the calendar spread is to have time eat away at the short option while the long option retains its value. The difference in implied volatility across expiration months is the volatility skew that the strategist is trying to exploit. The key to success in this strategy is finding options with unusually high implied volatility in the front months and low to normal implied volatility in the back months.

Table 10.11 shows two call options on Gilead Sciences (symbol: GILD). This biotechnology stock faced intense selling pressure in late September, right before the information in the table was captured. A skew resulted between the near-term and longer-term call options. The May 2002 GILD 30 call had implied volatility of 76.50 percent, while the November 2002 30 call had implied volatility of only 56.20 percent.

While the volatility skew present in GILD options in April 2002 was not extreme, it provided enough of a price difference for a bullish calendar spread. In this case, however, the expectation would be that the stock price was indeed going to move higher before the May 2002 call expired. So, as in our diagonal spread, the strategist buys the long-term (November 2002) call and sells the short-term call. The trade is done for a debit equaling the difference between the price paid for the long-term option and the premium received for the short-term option. That is also the maximum risk of the trade: a total of $335 per contract for the GILD calendar spread. As Figure 10.10 shows, losses are assured if the stock falls in price. Furthermore, the maximum profit for the trade occurs if the stock price is equal to the strike price ($30 a share) when the short-term option expires. At that point, the strategist can either close the position or sell another short-term option if implied volatility in the front month is still high.

Table 10.11   Gilead Sciences Call Options (April 26, 2002)

Position	Number	Option Symbol	Expire	Strike	Type	Entry	Bid/Ask	Model	IV
Bought	1	GDQKF	Nov 02	30	Call	5	4.6/5	4.8	56.20%
Sold	1	GDQEF	May 02	30	Call	1.65	1.65/1.85	1.8	76.50%

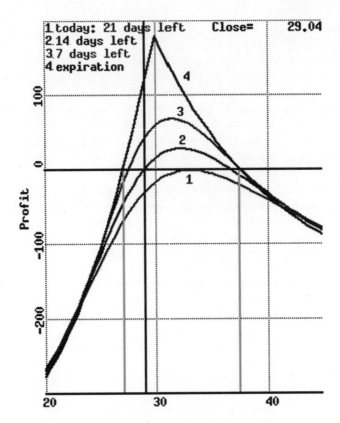

Figure 10.10   Risk Graph for Bullish Calendar Spread on GILD (Courtesy of Optionetics.com)

In addition, Figure 10.10 shows that the calendar spread on GILD will also begin to lose money if the stock price moves too high before the short call expires. Ideally, the strategist wants the stock to trade between $28 and $37 before expiration because those are the breakeven points. Therefore, while the calendar spread has a bullish bias, it is also profitable if the stock remains within a range. For that reason, it is suitable whether the trader is bullish or neutral on the underlying asset. Establishing calendar spreads with out-of-the-money options will give the trade more of a bullish tilt; but it will also have lower odds of success. Again, the primary concern to the volatility trader is that the skew between the front month and long-term options be sufficient enough to warrant the placement of a calendar spread.

While the bullish calendar spread is suitable if the strategist thinks the stock will stay range bound or edge higher, the put calendar spread is more appealing if expectations are that the stock will fall. The primary consideration is that there is a reasonable skew between the front month put and the longer-term put. In Table 10.12, two GILD puts with different levels of implied volatility provide an example. The

Table 10.12 GILD Put Options (April 26, 2002)

Position	Number	Option Symbol	Expire	Strike	Type	Entry	Bid/Ask	Model	IV
Bought	1	GDQWE	Nov 02	25	Put	3.4	3.1/3.4	3.3	67.40%
Sold	1	GDQQE	May 02	25	Put	.65	.65/.85	0.7	86.70%

first is a longer-term put (November 2002) with the stock trading for $29 a share. The second is a short-term put (May 2002). Notice the difference in implied volatility between the two options.

If the strategist believes GILD is likely to fall, one potential trade is the bearish calendar spread using the two put options from Table 10.12. In this case, the strategist sells the short-term put and buys the long-term put. The trade is done for a debit and, in this case, costs the strategist $275. The debit is the maximum risk of the trade. As Figure 10.11 shows, the trade makes a profit when the stock price moves

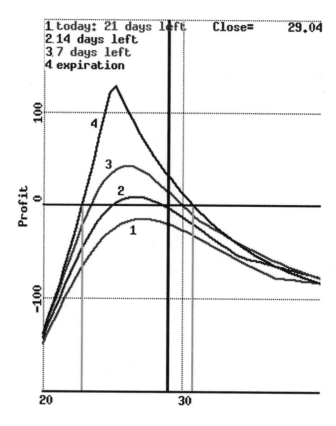

Figure 10.11 Risk Graph of Calendar Spread Using GILD Put Options (Courtesy of Optionetics.com)

gradually lower or remains range bound. The maximum profit occurs if the stock price is equal to the strike price ($25 a share) at expiration.

Calendar spreads are an ideal strategy to take advantage of volatility skews between expiration months. The examples just given only scratch the surface of the possibilities. In addition, sometimes the front month options become so expensive that these trades can be done for a credit! The two keys again are:

1. *Map out each trade in terms of risk/reward potential and plot them on a risk graph.* Calendar spreads can be bullish, bearish, or neutral. It is essential to understand the position's bias before establishing the calendar spread. If it doesn't feel right, don't do it!

2. *Identify attractive volatility skews that are essential to the trade's success.* The greater the disparity between the front month and back month options, the better the odds that the calendar spread will achieve success.

CONCLUSION

This chapter covers some of the most sophisticated topics volatility traders will ever face. In fact, an understanding of the principles outlined in the first 10 chapters of this book will place you in the top 10 percent of all options traders. Throughout the book, the reader has been introduced to a number of important concepts and resources such as indicators that can help to chart volatility, the two key measures of volatility (historical and implied), stocks, indexes, options, sentiment analysis, reversion to the mean, and specific strategies to use in different market environments. All work together to give the reader the foundation for becoming a strategic volatility trader.

In this chapter, the attention turns to a concept known as volatility skews. Used mostly by professional traders to identify trading opportunities, volatility skews occur when two or more options on the same underlying stock or index have a sizable difference in implied volatility. To identify skews, the strategist looks at various quotes across a series of options to identify each option contract's implied volatility. Some brokerage firms and data services offer option chains with implied volatility information. This provides an easy way to see implied volatility across a group of options. When there is a significant difference in IV between one option and another, a skew exists. If so, trading opportunities are often possible by purchasing the option with the lower volatility and simultaneously selling the option with the higher volatility.

There are two types of volatility skews: price skews and time skews. Price skews exist when the implied volatility differs across strike prices of options, on the same stock and the same expiration months. Time skews are identified by different levels of implied volatility on stock options with the same strike prices, but different expiration months. In this chapter, the reader learns how to identify each of these volatility skews, how to evaluate them, and, of course, how to implement trading strategies using volatility skews.

How does the strategist take advantage of time skews? Although a number of ways exist, two strategies were discussed in this chapter: calendar and diagonal spreads. A calendar spread involves the purchase of a longer-term call and the sale of a shorter-term call with the same strike price. Diagonal spreads, on the other hand, involve different strike prices. Again, the idea is to buy the longer-term option and sell the shorter-term option that has witnessed a spike in implied volatility.

Deciding which spread to use—diagonal or calendar—depends on the trader's expectations regarding the direction of the stock. If the strategist believes that the stock is likely to make a significant move higher or lower over the next 30 days, the diagonal spread is probably more appropriate. Buying a longer-term option while selling a shorter-term out-of-the-money option is an example of a diagonal spread. The object is, obviously, to be right on the future direction of the stock and benefit from an increase in value of the longer-term option; but if wrong, the short option will decay in value faster than the long option and offer some protection.

If the strategist is moderately bullish, somewhat bearish, or neutral on a stock, the calendar spread is an attractive strategy. In creating this type of spread, the strategist is using options with the same strike price but different expiration dates. As with the diagonal spread, the longer-term option is purchased and the shorter-term option is sold simultaneously. Calendar spreads can be created with a bullish (calls), bearish (puts), or neutral (puts or calls) bias. Like the diagonal spreads, the primary objective of the calendar spread is to have time eat away at the short option while the long option retains its value. The strategist is trying to exploit the difference in implied volatility across expiration months, or the so-called time skew. Additional short-term options can be sold each month; this is referred to as rolling forward.

In conclusion, both time skews and price skews can offer attractive trading opportunities to the savvy strategist. The first step is to identify the skew by looking at options chains or using graphing capabilities available on some options software programs like Optionetics Platinum. Next, the strategist will want to develop a trading strategy to capture profits from the skew. This will generally involve either diagonal and calendar spreads, which will, in turn, depend on whether the strategist is bullish, bearish, or neutral on the underlying asset.

Throughout the past 10 chapters, we have tried to explain various ways of using volatility to find profitable trades and why our approach can deliver more consistent results than the traditional buy-and-hold approach to investing. If you have made it this far, chances are that you are well on your way to understanding and developing investment strategies that can work whether volatility is high or low.

At the same time, while most of the critical elements that underlie our trading success have been covered, there has not been quite enough room on these pages for everything we wanted to say. For instance, there are certain rules and caveats for strategies such as straddles that are important to implement and understand.

In addition, many brokers will not allow investors to implement all of the investment strategies described here without sufficient collateral requirements—an important part of options trading not fully covered within this text. Several other advanced strategies have been omitted altogether.

Despite its drawbacks, however, this book should provide you with all the information you need to start trading volatility by arming you with an arsenal of innovative tools to use in any market condition. In addition, we are always available to answer questions on our message boards at Optionetics.com. On that site, you will also find a host of different trading resources, articles, and trading ideas from other options strategists to supplement the discussions from this text. Please come and visit. In the meantime, best of luck in the markets and remember that trading implied volatility is a lot like trading stocks—buy it low and sell it high.

11
Final Summary

In setting out to write a book about volatility, we had two goals in mind. The first was to describe volatility and the second was to explain how to trade volatility. What is volatility? Often, people associate the word "volatility" with falling stock prices. For example, you may have heard a television commentator on the evening news say, "The Dow Jones Industrial Average fell 215 points today in a volatile trading session." Yet, while volatility is often associated with chaos and panic in the financial markets, stocks can also exhibit high levels of volatility when moving higher. For instance, takeover rumors can sometimes cause a stock to surge 20 or 30 percent in one trading session. Therefore, an important factor to consider when looking at volatility is to understand that it goes both ways and is not always associated with falling stock prices. During the technology run in the late 1990s, Internet stocks were surging in both price and volatility.

Another important consideration when looking at volatility is that it runs along a spectrum; periods occur when volatility is high, and there are other times when it is low. The options strategist wants to understand whether the volatility of a stock or market at any given time is high or low and increasing or decreasing. There is an important concept when dealing with the stock market known as "reversion to the mean." In the context of this book, reversion to the mean deals primarily with volatility. That is, stocks tend to have an average level of volatility over time. When a stock begins trading wildly and volatility is reaching unusual highs, the path of least resistance is for volatility to fall. Conversely, volatility often increases following periods of low volatility or quiet trading. In any event, it is important to understand that volatility is always changing and in a state of flux. Each stock and index has a fairly normal or average range of volatility and when there are extreme deviations from that average, the option strategist is specifically on the lookout for reversion to the mean.

Obviously, in order to gauge levels of volatility for a stock or market, it is important to have an objective measure for gauging it. Sometimes the chart pattern of a stock like IBM or an index like the Dow Jones Industrial Average can be revealing. We saw in the early chapters how to use stock charts to get a look at the past price action of a stock, which is a quick and useful way to get an idea of a stock's volatility. In addition, indicators such as moving averages, Bollinger bands, and Average True Range are all charting tools that offer information regarding a stock or index's level of past volatility.

One of the most widely used methods for measuring volatility is known as statistical volatility. Sometimes called historical or actual volatility, it is computed using the past prices of a stock or index. Mathematically, statistical volatility is computed as the annualized standard deviation of stock prices over a fixed number of days (e.g., 20, 30, or 50 days) and is expressed as a percentage. When a stock trades wildly and the closing prices vary considerably from one day to the next, statistical volatility will rise. When a stock trades within a narrow range and closing prices change little from one day to the next, statistical volatility will fall. Therefore, looking at statistical volatility over time can give the trader a sense of whether a stock or index has a tendency to trade chaotically or quietly. Charts of statistical volatility for most stocks and options can be found at www.optionetics.com.

In Chapter 6, the reader was introduced to one of the most challenging concepts that novice option traders face: implied volatility. Unlike statistical volatility, which measures a stock's price changes in the past, implied volatility is derived from the price of a stock's options in the marketplace. In order to compute implied volatility, the trader needs several pieces of information that relate to the stock option: When does the option expire? What is the strike price of the option? What is the market price of the option? What is the price of the stock? What is the current interest rate? Does the stock pay any dividends? Equipped with the answers to those questions, the option strategist can compute IV using an option pricing model like the one developed by Fischer Black and Myron Scholes (the Black-Scholes option pricing model). An easier way to find implied volatility is simply to go to the Optionetics.com Platinum site, where it can be found for almost any stock or index with the click of a mouse.

Like any other measure of volatility, IV is always in a state of flux. Sometimes aggressive demand for a stock option will cause premiums to climb. This can occur when a takeover rumor surfaces, or when a company rattles Wall Street with a disappointing earnings report, or concerns over a company's corporate accounting begin to weigh on a stock. Basically, any time options traders expect a stock to exhibit high levels of volatility going forward, demand for the stock's options will increase and the premiums will rise. When all of the other variables—such as the stock price, time left until expiration, and the strike price of the option—remain the same, the increase in the option premium is due solely to the increase in IV. Therefore, when implied volatility is on the rise, option prices are becoming more expensive. Conversely, when IV is low or falling, premiums are becoming cheaper. Once again, there is usually an average range for a given stock option's implied volatility, which is useful to consider over time. When premiums become quite high, there is a chance that IV will revert to the mean—that is, fall. On the other hand, when option premiums (implied volatility) are low relative to a stock's past levels of implied volatility, chances are it will rise.

In addition to comparing implied volatility over time, it is also useful to compare it to a stock's statistical volatility. Both implied and statistical volatility are computed as percentages and are therefore easy to compare. If a stock has an implied volatility much higher than its actual (statistical) volatility, this suggests that options traders and market makers expect the stock to exhibit greater volatility going forward than it did in the past. Why? Because statistical volatility is derived from the stock price over time, but implied volatility is derived from the option prices in the market. Therefore, if implied volatility is high relative to statistical volatility, it suggests the market is pricing in expectations for greater volatility going forward. When IV deviates substantially from statistical volatility, it is perhaps a sign that options are overvalued. This relationship (between actual and implied volatility) was discussed in detail in Chapter 7.

Once the strategist knows how to evaluate a stock in terms of volatility, the first objective of this book has been accomplished. The most common tool for measuring a stock's historical volatility is statistical volatility, but chart patterns, Bollinger bands, and ATR are also useful in that respect. Furthermore, an understanding of implied volatility, which tells whether options are cheap or expensive, is critical to successful options trading. All of these tools can be used together to determine the appropriateness of option prices in the market at any given time.

The second objective of this book is to arm the reader with an arsenal of strategies that can be deployed during any market condition. The volatility trader has to be able to: (1) understand and quantify relative levels of volatility, and (2) let that information dictate his or her trading approach. In addition, knowing whether options are cheap or expensive will dictate the option strategist's modus operandi. There are certain strategies that work well in a low volatility environment (covered in detail in Chapter 8). Option buyers are best served going long puts and calls in a low volatility environment because that is when options are cheapest. For that reason, straddles (which involve the simultaneous purchase of puts and calls) are most appropriate when implied volatility is low and the strategist expects a reversion to the mean. Other low volatility strategies include the protective put, debit spreads, and ratio backspreads.

Chapter 9 explained tactics that work best in a high volatility environment, including the most basic strategy, the covered call. In fact, high levels of implied volatility are beneficial anytime the option strategist is a net seller of option premium. For that reason, in addition to the covered call, Chapter 9 covered the short put, credit spreads, and various butterfly spreads.

Volatility skews can also create trading opportunities by capturing price disparities between different options on the same stocks. There are two types: price skews and time skews. Whether the strategist identifies a price skew or a time skew, there are potential trading opportunities to be exploited by selling the expensive options and buying cheaper options. Calendar and diagonal spreads are among the best ways to capture profits when different levels of implied volatility exist on options of the same underlying stock. Strategies for trading volatility skews were discussed at length in Chapter 10.

Hopefully, the tools and strategies outlined in this book will give the reader a sense of confidence and assurance that it is possible to navigate in even the most turbulent waters. Over the past couple of years, many investors have had to swallow a hefty dose of market volatility, and, in many cases, that has meant lost wealth. Not only were there the collapse of the Internet bubble, the economic and earnings recession, and the terrorist attacks of September 11, 2001, but also a wave of corporate scandals and bankruptcies rattled investor confidence in 2002. Investors began to wonder who could be trusted? As a result, by the middle of the year 2002, many investors decided it was wiser to move to the sidelines and take their money out of the stock market.

Yet, while disengaging from the market might provide a greater sense of safety as well as immunity from the dark side of corporate America, it also assures a zero return on one's investment dollars. An alternative is to take a more active approach to the market. For example, trading volatility provides opportunities in any market condition—not just when stocks are rising. In addition, a variety of different risk/reward scenarios can be created, and none of them depend on a chief executive officer, financial statements, or recommendations from a Wall Street analyst. In short, options empower investors to remain immune from corporate corruption and take complete control of their financial situation. Armed with an understanding of volatility and the appropriate strategies for exploiting periods of time when options are either cheap or expensive, the strategist can make money in almost any market environment. The traditional buy-and-hold approach to investing ultimately requires the stock market to move higher in order to garner any profits. In the long run, it generally does. But, as we saw in the first chapter of this book, there are also prolonged periods of time when stocks fall, and those episodes can leave the majority of investors dismayed. Therefore, trading volatility requires the investor to adopt an entirely different train of thought: that falling stocks doesn't mean lost wealth. In fact, bear markets provide an equal number of trading opportunities to the volatility trader. The key is to understand that volatility is always in a state of flux and to adapt the trading approach based on the current market environment. We hope that this book has both helped you to understand how volatility works in the marketplace and given you a means to learn how to use volatility to trade the markets successfully.

Good luck and great trading.

Appendix **A**

Studying the Market

BULL AND BEAR MARKETS

The stock market can move in one direction through prolonged periods of time that can last years or decades. Traders often talk of "bull" and "bear" markets when describing these trends. Bull markets are prolonged periods when stocks move higher. The reason they are named after the beast is because bulls buck up with their horns. Bear markets are long-term downward movements and are labeled as such because bears swat down with their claws.

Corrections

Within bull and bear markets, there are inevitably countermoves. These so-called "corrections" can last a few days or several months. During a bull market, a correction will take stocks lower before the upward trend resumes. In a bear market, a correction is actually a rally that takes stocks higher before the bear market resumes its course. Pullbacks are simply minor countermoves during bull or bear markets and corrections. The barometer for judging whether stocks are in a bull market or a bear market is generally one of the market averages—the Dow Jones Industrial Average, the S&P 500, the Nasdaq Composite index, and others.

Definitions

- *Bull market:* A sustained move higher in the stock market of 20 percent or more from a previous low.

- **Bear market:** A sustained move lower in the stock market of 20 percent or more from a previous high.

- **Correction:** A countermove during either a bull or a bear market that takes stocks between 5 percent and 20 percent counter to the current trend.

- **Pullback:** A move of 5 percent or less counter to the current trend. For example, if stocks fall 5 percent or less either during a bull market or during a bear market correction (rally), it is considered a pullback.

- **Bull trap:** A sharp pullback during a bull market that causes investors to sell and bet against the market. However, the market then recovers and the bull market resumes.

- **Bear trap:** A sharp move higher during a bear market that encourages investors to buy stocks and get in the market. The rally turns out to be a false move, however, and the bear returns thereafter.

THREE WAYS TO STUDY THE MARKET

There are three schools of thought underlying each method of studying stocks or the market: fundamental, technical, and sentiment analysis. Many investors use a combination of all three approaches when making investment decisions, but naturally come to give greater weight to one form over the others. We are technical traders and rely more heavily on chart patterns, indicators, and volume-based studies. Others prefer to look at the market using a fundamental approach, which considers stock-specific information such as earnings and book values, and the overall economy. A third, less common tool is sentiment analysis, which examines the psychology and human nature within financial markets. Even the trader who specializes in one of the three approaches to the market should understand the premises underlying the other two.

Fundamental Analysis

There are two ways to look at the market using the fundamental approach: bottom-up and top-down.

Bottom-Up Approach

The fundamental analyst using the bottom-up approach considers each stock individually. For example, a value investor is concerned primarily with a company's balance sheet, cash flow, book value, and other financial data. Most of this information can be found on the company's financial statements. Growth stock investors also take a bottom-up fundamental approach to investing, but look for companies that will exhibit high rates of future earnings growth. Unlike value investors, who look at balance sheets, book values, and other measures of value, growth stock investors are concerned about the company's ability to reinvest current earnings and generate growth.

- *Price-to-earnings (P/E) ratio:* One common fundamental tool that growth stock investors use is the price-to-earnings ratio. In general, stocks that deliver high earnings growth rates will command higher price-to-earnings ratios. Stocks with slow earnings growth rates will generally trade at lower P/E ratios. Why is this so? Well, consider two companies, both earning $1 per share a year. Now, suppose one company grows earnings by 20 percent over the next five years and the other by only 1 percent. In five years, the fast growing company will have earnings of $2.50 while the slow-growth company will have earnings of only $1.10. In short, investors will pay higher prices per earnings (P/E ratios) for those stocks expected to grow earnings the fastest, because their earnings will be worth more in the future.

- *Price-to-earnings growth rate (PEG) ratio:* If P/E ratios are generally a function of growth rates, some investors prefer to look at the price-to-earnings growth rate (PEG) ratio when looking at stocks. The ratio is computed as a company's P/E divided by its earnings growth rate. Stocks that trade at P/E ratios well below their earnings growth rates (PEG < 1) are considered undervalued, and stocks with P/E ratios well above their expected growth rates (PEG > 1) are considered overvalued.

- *Earnings surprises:* Look for companies that consistently beat Wall Street expectations and the "whisper number." Avoid companies that consistently disappoint with poor earnings results. Net profit margins should be increasing, or at least remaining constant from one year to the next.

- *Management:* Management effectiveness ratios help to determine how efficiently the company has used its assets and how successful the company is in executing its business strategy.

  - *Return on equity (ROE):* This is calculated by dividing a company's net income by stockholders' equity. One company's ROE can be compared to another's within the same sector or industry group to indicate a company's dominance within its industry.

  - *Return on assets (ROA):* This is calculated by dividing net income by total assets. A high ROA indicates less waste and more productivity. Locating an efficient company is a promising situation.

  - *Debt:* Look at the company's overall debt level when considering ROE; borrowed money can help generate larger ROE but more risk is involved. More debt indicates more cash is spent to service the debt (principal and interest). Comparisons between companies using ROA must also consider overall debt levels. How much leverage did it take to achieve their respective ROA? More debt indicates a less stable financial condition, which makes the company more vulnerable when economic slowdowns occur. Corporate wrongdoing often comes in the form of hiding debt.

- *Other tools:* Growth stock investors rely heavily on analyst earnings esti-mates, past earnings growth rates, a company's management, sales, products, and any stock-specific information that relates to the company's ability to im-prove revenues and income.

Top-Down Approach

Macroeconomic analysis is key for the top-down analyst. The top-down analyst is primarily concerned with the impact of economic events on stocks as a whole. For example, as we saw in Chapter 1, there is an important relationship between interest rates and the stock market. Historically, higher interest rates have caused stock prices to fall and volatility to increase.

Market Relationships—Volatility and Interest Rates

Interest Rates	Bonds	Stocks	Volatility
Rising	Falling	Falling	Rising
Falling	Rising	Rising	Falling
Stable	Stable	Rising/stable	Stable

In addition to interest rates, the top-down analyst is looking at other economic factors such as energy prices, Federal Reserve policy, money supply, and other as-pects that can cause changes in stock prices collectively. After developing a clear picture of expectations regarding the future direction of the economy, the top-down analyst will make an assessment concerning different industry groups—oil, semi-conductor, banking, and so on. Then, based on the outlook for the economy and the specific sectors, the top-down analyst will make individual stock selections.

Technical Analysis

Chart readers are often disparaged on Wall Street. After all, there is no formal schooling that teaches the art of reading charts, or technical analysis. So acquiring these skills requires a great deal of self-study and personal experience. Yet, despite the fact that no major university is offering an MBA in technical analysis, most in-vestors use technical analysis in one form or another. In fact, simply looking at the trading volume for a particular market or a stock falls into the realm of technical analysis. Basically, technical analysis is the study of supply and demand for stocks. It is not at all concerned with earnings, interest rates, or other fundamental information. Instead, the technical analyst considers the buying and selling pres-sure associated with a stock. The idea is the same one that applies to commodities or any other option-style market. Namely, increasing demand relative to supply causes prices to rise. Conversely, too much supply compared to demand will lead to falling prices.

Technical Tools

In an effort to monitor the forces of supply and demand for a market or a stock, the technical analyst has several tools at his or her disposal. The stock chart is the primary tool, but there are others. When looking at the market as a whole, the technical analyst may consider any of the following technical tools:

- The advance/decline line.

- Up volume and down volume.

- The number of stocks setting new 52-week highs compared to stocks setting new 52-week lows.

Charting

The main things to be aware of when looking at a chart are: trend lines, support, resistance, and breakouts.

- *Trend line:* A line drawn that connects a series of either highs or lows in a trend. The trend line can represent either support as in an uptrend line or resistance as in a downtrend line.

- *Support:* The price level at which a stock or index will receive considerable buying pressure. Technical analysts believe demand at the support level will keep a stock's price from falling lower.

- *Resistance:* The price level at which a stock or index will receive considerable selling pressure. An increasing supply of stock at resistance levels will prevent the stock or index from rising further.

- *Breakout:* When a stock breaks through the resistance level, it's called a "breakout"—a key component for a major up move. Traders look for this move as a signal to buy, because those with long positions are now making money.

Chart Patterns

Patterns, including the following examples, also provide the technical analyst with information regarding the price pattern of a stock or market.

- *Cup and handle:* A cup and handle pattern indicates price accumulation and is often observed on bar charts. This pattern usually lasts from at least two months to as long as a year. The cup is in the shape of a "U" and the handle is usually more than one or two weeks in duration. The handle is a slight downward drift with low trading volume from the right-hand side of the formation. (See Figure A.1.)

- *Double bottom or top:* The double bottom is a price pattern or market average that has declined two times to the same approximate level, indicating the existence of a support level and a possibility that the downward trend has ended.

Figure A.1   Cup and Handle Pattern

Conversely, a double top describes a pattern that has advanced two times to reach the same resistance level. The first top must be followed by a break-through of the support level before climbing back up to the top again. After the second peak, the stock most likely falls back to the support level before continuing to trend or reversing. (See Figure A.2.)

- *Head and shoulders:* A head and shoulders is a bearish price pattern that has three peaks, resembling a head and two shoulders. The stock price moves up to its first peak (the left shoulder), drops back, then moves to a higher peak (the head), drops again but recovers to another, lower peak (the right shoulder). Technical analysts generally consider a head and shoulders formation to be a very bearish indication. An inverted head and shoulders indicates a market advance. (See Figure A.3.)

Charting indicators

(See Appendix B for greater detail.)

- *Moving averages:* The moving average (MA) helps to confirm a trend by averaging past prices and calculating their average. As a new unit of time passes, the MA drops the previous unit, so that the MA is continually updated. Simple moving averages work well as a lagging indicator, but critics point out that all days receive equal weighting in the calculation. Exponential moving averages give increased weighting to the most recent day, thereby making the average react slightly faster than a simple mathematical moving average.

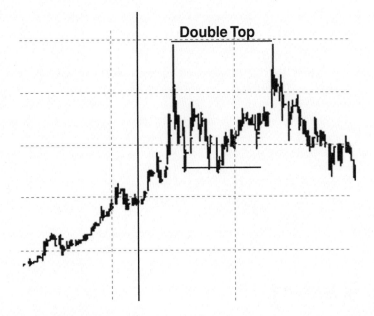

Figure A.2 Double Top Pattern

Figure A.3 Head and Shoulders Pattern

- *Oscillators:* These are technical indicators used to identify overbought and oversold price regions using a fixed scale (0 to 100). Oscillators help measure whether the market is overbought or oversold and are anticipatory in nature.

- *Bollinger bands:* Bollinger bands plot trading bands above and below a simple moving average. The standard deviation of closing prices for a period equal to the moving average employed is used to determine the bandwidth. This causes the bands to tighten in quiet markets and loosen in volatile markets. The bands can be used to determine overbought and oversold levels, locate reversal areas, project targets for market moves, and determine appropriate stop levels. The bands are often used in conjunction with indicators such as Relative Strength Index (RSI), moving average convergence/divergence (MACD) histogram, Commodity Channel Index (CCI), and rate of change. Divergences between Bollinger bands and other indicators show potential action points. As a general guideline, look for buying opportunities when prices are in the lower band, and selling opportunities when the price activity is in the upper band.

Sentiment Analysis

Options traders often use sentiment analysis when studying the market. It is such an important part of options trading that an entire chapter (Chapter 7) was dedicated to the topic. In a nutshell, sentiment analysis is the art of studying crowd psychology. Almost invariably, at major turning points in a stock or market the crowd will be almost unanimous in market outlook. For example, market tops are generally accompanied by euphoria, optimism, and bullishness because prolonged periods of rising prices (a bull market) generates large amounts of wealth and a general sense of well being. Unfortunately, market tops usually occur when everyone has already put money in the market and there are very few buyers left. On the other hand, market bottoms are generally characterized by a mass feeling of negativity, bearishness, and despair. At that point even die-hard bulls have thrown in the towel, and the subsequent absence of sellers sets the table for a move higher in the stock market. Sentiment analysis, then, requires traders to develop the art of contrary thinking. Humphrey B. Neill made the following observations in his book *The Art of Contrary Thinking* (Caldwell, ID: Caxton Printers, 10th ed., 1992)

> Because a crowd does not think, but acts on impulses, public opinions are frequently wrong. By the same token, because a crowd is carried away by feeling, or sentiment, you will find the public participating enthusiastically in various manias after the mania has got well under momentum. This is illustrated in the stock market. The crowd—the public—will remain indifferent when prices are low and fluctuating but little. The public is attracted by activity and by the movement of prices. It is especially attracted to rising prices.

Extreme Behavior

One recent example of mob behavior in the stock market occurred in the fall of 1998. The sell-off in one stock market in Asia eventually led to a drop in another Asian country, and then another in Europe, and then in South America, until the panic selling hit U.S. shores. Investors reacted collectively, and stock markets around the globe went into a free fall. The so-called "contagion" was an example of extreme crowd behavior. As stock markets fell, the headlines in the financial newspapers turned dire, and just when things appeared the worst, the stock market in the United States made a significant move higher that continued from October 1998 until March 2000.

Contrary Thinking

As a tool for gauging the prevailing market psychology, sentiment analysis is an endeavor in contrary thinking. One of the assumptions underlying the study of sentiment data is that, in the long run, it pays to bet against the crowd. But it is important to note that the crowd is not always wrong. There is an expression among contrarian thinkers that says, "The crowd is usually right on the trends, but wrong at both ends." In a rising, or bull, market, investors are buying stocks, and in a declining, or bear, market the crowd is selling. Basically, during significant market trends, it is more profitable to go in the direction of the market rather than contrary to it. The important turning points, however, often catch the crowd unaware. For that reason, it is when the market begins to show extreme levels of fear or greed that the situation is ripe for a reversal. Sentiment analysis is really a tool for identifying the extreme crowd behavior, or "the ends."

Sentiment Analysis Tools

There are several tools available that can be used to study market sentiment. Some are straightforward and easy to understand, like scheduled and breaking news that influences public sentiment. Other tools are more complex and require a bit of study (see Appendix D).

Optimism Measurements

- Excessive call option buying: low put/call ratio.
- Volatility Index (VIX) at the low end of its range.
- The retail investor becoming very active.
- Net purchases of mutual funds versus redemptions.
- Low liquidity (cash) on sidelines.
- Advance/decline ratio very strong, near historical highs.
- Closed-end funds trading at a premium to their net asset values (NAVs).
- Technical indicators signaling overbought conditions.

Pessimism Measurements

- Excessive put option buying: high put/call ratio.

- Volatility Index (VIX) at the high end of its range.

- Retail investors leaving the market.

- Net redemptions of mutual funds versus purchases.

- Advance/decline line weak, near historical lows.

- Closed-end funds trading at a discount to their NAVs.

- Technical indicators signaling oversold condition.

POPULAR INDEXES

A list of 72 of the top indexes appears in Table A.1.

Table A.1   Popular Indexes

Symbol	Index	Symbol	Index
$XAL	Airline Index	$NYA	NYSE Composite Index
$ISSA	AMEX Advance/Decline Issues	$TRIN	NYSE Short-Term Trade Index
$XAX	AMEX Composite Index	$XOI	Oil Index
$XMI	AMEX Major Market Index	$DRG	Pharmaceutical Index
$XOI	AMEX Oil & Gas Index	$BKX	PHLX Bank Sector Index
$AVOL	AMEX Volume	$BMX	PHLX Computer Box Maker Sector
$BTK	Biotechnology Index	$FOP	PHLX Fiber Optics Index
$MNX	CBOE Mini-NDX Index	$FPP	PHLX Forest & Paper Sector Index
$DDX	Disk Drive Index	$XAU	PHLX Gold and Silver Index
$COMP	Dow Jones Composite Index	$OSX	PHLX Oil Service Sector Index
$INDU	Dow Jones Industrial Average	$SOX	PHLX Semiconductor Sector Index
$DJX	Dow Jones Industrial Index	$DOT	PHLX TheStreet.com Internet Index
$TRAN	Dow Jones Transportation Index	$YLS	PHLX Wireless Index
$UTIL	Dow Jones Utilities Index	$PSE	PSE High Technology Index
$FCHI	France Cac-40 Index	$RUI	Russell 1000 Index
$FTSE	FTSE 100 Index	$RUT	Russell 2000 Index
$GDAX	Germany Dax Index	$RUA	Russell 3000 Index
$GSO	GSTI Software Index	$OEX	S&P 100 Index
$JPN	Japan Index	$SPX	S&P 500 Index
$VIX	Market Volatility Index	$SGX	S&P Barra Growth Index
$MEX	Mexico Index	$SVX	S&P Barra Value Index
$MVB	Morgan Stanley Biotech Index	$MID	S&P MidCap 400 Index
$CMR	Morgan Stanley Consumer Index	$SRX	S&P Super Composite Index
$CYC	Morgan Stanley Cyclical Index	$TRX	S&P Transport Index
$MSH	Morgan Stanley High Tech Index	$XBD	Securities Broker Dealer Index
$MGO	Morgan Stanley Oil Service Index	$SOX	Semiconductor Index
$MVR	Morgan Stanley Retail Index	$ICX	TheStreet.com e-Commerce Index
$ISSQ	Nasdaq Advance/Decline Issues	$TSE-TC	Toronto 35 Index
$COMPQ	Nasdaq Composite Index	$TOP-TC	TSE 100 Index
$IXCO	Nasdaq High Tech Index	$UTY	Utility Sector Index
$NDX	Nasdaq 100 Index	$XVG	Value Line Index (Geometric)
$VXN	Nasdaq 100 Volatility Index	$WSX	Wilshire Composite Index
$QQV	Nasdaq QQQ Volatility Index	$FVX	5-Year T-Note Index
$QVOL	Nasdaq Volume	$TNX	10-Year T-Note Index
$XNG	Natural Gas Index	$IRX	13-Week T-Bill Index
$ISSU	NYSE Advance/Decline Issues	$TYX	30-Year T-Bond Index

Appendix B

Stock Charts and Technical Tools

OHLC CHARTS

There are many different types of charts available to the technical trader today. The open, high, low, close (OHLC) chart is the one we use most often, and it is a common way of viewing the performance of a stock. Also known as the range bar chart, the graph provides the technical analyst with a wealth of information concerning the price changes in a stock.

Figure B.1 provides an example of an OHLC chart for International Business Machines (IBM). In this example, we have created a range bar chart, which means that each bar (vertical line) represents one day of trading data. On the left side of each bar appears a small horizontal line. It represents the open or the price of the first trade of the day. The length of the bar from highest point to lowest point reflects the high and low prices of the stock each day. When the bars are long, it suggests that the stock traded in a wide range; when the vertical bar is short, the stock traded in a narrow range. Finally, a small horizontal line on the right side of each bar indicates the close, which is the last trade of the day. Therefore, it takes four pieces of data to construct a daily range bar or OHLC chart—the opening, high and low, and closing prices of the day. OHLC charts can also be created using weekly and monthly data.

Each OHLC bar gives an idea of whether bulls or bears are in control of a stock or market. In a healthy advance, the bulls are firmly in control and driving prices higher. As evidence, the technical analyst wants to see the stock closing near the highs of the day. This is easy to see in an OHLC chart. Recall that the

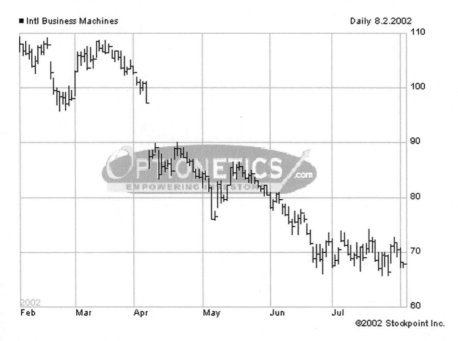

Figure B.1   OHLC Chart of International Business Machines (Courtesy of
Optionetics.com)

right horizontal on each OHLC bar represents the closing price. When these closing lines appear near the top of each vertical bar on the chart, it suggests that the
bulls have the stock in control. In contrast, when the bears seize a stock, the
chartist is looking to confirm that the stock is closing near the low price of the
day. For example, on the IBM chart (Figure B.1), during the decline in mid-
March before the sharp sell-off in early April 2002, the stock was finishing most
trading sessions near the lows of the day. This was a sign that bears were firmly in
control of IBM during that time.

TREND LINES

In studying stock charts, the technical analyst will consider several factors. The
first and most obvious is the direction of the prevailing trend. During an uptrend
in a stock, lines can be drawn along the lows of the OHLC price chart. Conversely, in a downtrend, chartists draw a trend line going across the highs. Notice
the examples on the daily chart of IBM in Figure B.2. Three lines have been
drawn to illustrate three different trends.

Figure B.2   Price Chart of International Business Machines with Trend Lines (Courtesy of Optionetics.com)

Trend lines can be used to identify changes in the direction of a stock. Well established trend lines often serve as support or resistance for a stock. That is, stocks sometimes have difficulty moving above a downward sloping trend line or below an upward sloping one. Therefore, when a stock does penetrate a trend line, it is considered to be an important technical signal. In the IBM example, the upward sloping trend line was broken in February 2001 and signaled a potential trend reversal. As a rule, longer-term trend lines hold the most significance. Therefore, when a long-term trend line on a monthly chart is penetrated, it is more meaningful than when a short-term trend line is violated on a daily chart. Finally, trend lines are generally drawn along congestion areas of the chart and omit unusual spikes. For example, during the first downward sloping trend line there is a spike higher in November 2000 that rises above the trend line. It is disregarded because it is not consistent with the longer-term trend.

CHARTS AND VOLATILITY

The OHLC chart also provides information regarding a stock's volatility, and for that reason, it is extremely important to option traders. Since the length of each bar is determined by the high and low prices of the day, short bars suggest that the stock is exhibiting low volatility. In that case, the trading ranges between the daily high and low prices are small. But when the bars are longer, it means there is a bigger difference between the highs and lows of the day. Therefore, longer bars suggest greater volatility. As an example, notice the bars within the rectangles on the Terayon Communications (symbol: TERN) chart in Figure B.3. In those instances, the bars are tall and suggest high volatility. Within the circle, however, the bars become short and volatility in TERN is relatively low.

CHART PATTERNS, CONSOLIDATION, AND VOLATILITY

Consolidation is a period of time in which a stock moves mostly sideways. It can last a few days or a few weeks and generally occurs after a stock has made a sizable move in one direction or another. During a time of consolidation, investors take the time to evaluate the situation and make an assessment of which way the stock will go. There is often a sense of uncertainty, which tends to build as the consolidation continues. Finally, the stock makes its move and investors get a better sense of what to do: buy or sell. There are often limit orders just outside the consolidation area

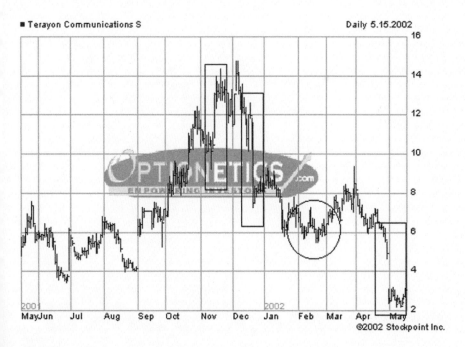

Figure B.3   TERN Chart with Periods of High and Low Volatility (Courtesy of Optionetics. com)

that exacerbate the trend. In the end, volatility jumps higher. For that reason consolidation patterns are important for the options trader to understand.

Like a climber moving up a mountain, stocks sometimes need a rest. It's just not possible to make long-term advances without pausing a time or two. The mountain climber might stop to take a breath, drink some water, or find a more suitable path. Similarly, a rapidly ascending stock will sometimes stop before a major news report like an earnings announcement or a conference call, during quiet holiday trading, or, quite often, because of profit taking. Likewise, during declines stocks rarely fall for long periods of time without pauses. Instead, there is often a series of consolidation periods during and at the end of the decline.

On charts, a period of consolidation appears as a congestion area or a period of sideways trading. Sometimes, two parallel lines can be drawn across the highs and lows that define the congestion area. Other times, the consolidation phase takes the form of triangles or wedges. Each pattern type has different implications.

For example, the one-year chart of E*Trade (symbol: ET) demonstrates a number of different patterns (see Figure B.4). The chart itself is interesting because it shows

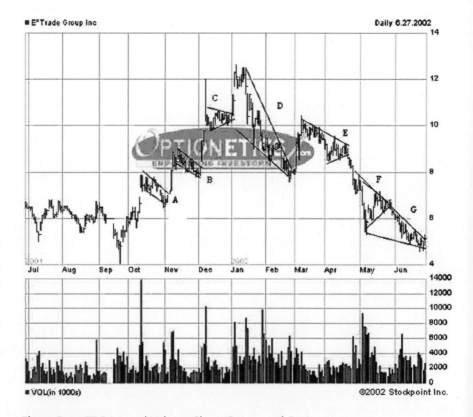

Figure B.4   ET Price and Volume Chart (Courtesy of Optionetics.com)

how ET made a round trip. That is, the stock was trading for $5 a share in July 2001. Then a rally took the stock above $12 or 140 percent higher, before it collapsed and fell back to its current level—roughly $5 a share. When a stock makes a large advance, reverses lower, and eventually gives back all of its gains, technical analysts say the stock has made a round trip. That was the case with ET, and throughout the process a number of different chart and volume patterns also developed.

When a stock makes a round trip, it has experienced two clear trends. During the initial move, the stock develops a bullish trend that takes prices higher over the course of several months or even years. In Figure B.4 of E*Trade, the first move developed from September 2001 and lasted until January 2002. The second trend is, obviously, the move lower that takes prices back to the point of origin. On ET, the downtrend develops from January 2002 until present. Within the two trends on the chart, there are a number of different patterns that are labeled A, B, C, D, E, F, and G.

The first three patterns (A, B, C) on the chart are examples of continuation patterns. That is, they occur during a trend and can be taken to suggest that the upward price movement in the stock is likely to continue. As an analogy, consider a mountain climber making an ascent toward a mountain peak. After climbing 100 yards, the climber might opt to take a rest for a few moments or simply slow down for a spell. Similarly, after a rapid advance, a stock will take a pause and/or move sideways. During these periods of sideways movement, chart patterns often develop that resemble flags or pennants. These types of formations are normal and often indicative of a healthy trend. Figures A and B consist of two parallel lines and are known as flags. The letter C highlights an example of the pennant. Some traders call this pattern a triangle because it nearly comes to a point. In any event, during healthy moves higher in a stock, flags and pennants often develop and are followed by another jump in the stock.

The next pattern is neither a flag nor a pennant. D shows the formation of a downward-sloping wedge. The wedge is a pattern that consists of two trend lines with the same slope (rising or falling) but at slightly different angles. Listless and uneventful trading generally follows the falling wedge. Notice on the chart of ET: After jumping higher after the formation of the wedge, the stock made little movement for a period of weeks. The rising wedge, on the other hand, is often followed by rising volume and volatility. Wedges generally take more time to develop than either flags or pennants. Pattern G shows the recent formation of another wedge. Therefore, it wouldn't be surprising to see ET come out of this pattern and move sideways for a period of weeks. Finally, E and F show continuation patterns during the stock's downtrend.

Another interesting element of the ET chart is the volume pattern during the two trends. Volume appears at the bottom of the chart. Notice that during the advance of the stock there are several tall bars that accompany each successive flag or pennant. This is important because during a healthy advance, volume will rise and accompany the up days. When a stock is experiencing a strong downtrend, volume will increase during the moves lower. That's why technical analysts say that volume goes with the trend.

Regardless of the type of technical chart formation (rectangle, triangle, wedge, etc.) that characterizes the consolidation phase, there is a tendency for volatility to fall as it happens. Since consolidation often occurs after a dramatic advance or decline, the period of sideways trading reflects a change of trend. Consequently, not only does the actual volatility (as measured by statistical volatility) of the stock fall, but the option premiums (implied volatility) will also. The best way to illustrate this concept is through an example.

Figure B.5 shows the action of the Dow Jones Transportation Average ($DTX) from August until December 2001. After the attacks of September 11, 2001, airline stocks and the Transportation Average suffered large losses. The sharp drop is clear on the chart. The average stopped falling in late September and then made an ascent followed by a period of sideways trading. The period from the end of September until mid-November, which saw the Transportation Average move only modestly higher, was a period of consolidation after a sharp sell-off. Trading became narrower and narrower until the index finally broke out of the congestion area (an ascending right triangle in this case) and began a five-month 25 percent advance.

During the consolidation period that followed the sharp drop in the Transportation Average, the volatility of the index fell sharply. Figure B.6 shows the statistical volatility (SV) at that time. Recall that SV is a measure of volatility that is derived from past stock or index prices. It is computed as the annualized standard deviation of closing prices over a period of days. Therefore, Figure B.6 shows the

Figure B.5   DTX, August to December 2001 (Courtesy of Optionetics.com)

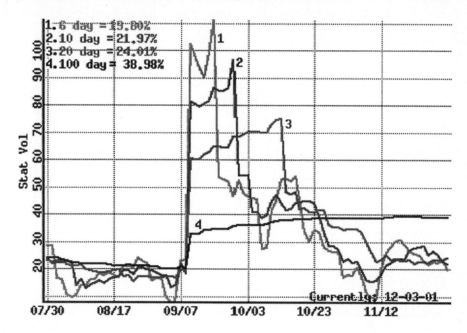

Figure B.6   Statistical Volatility, DTX, August to December 2001 (Courtesy of Optionetics.com)

6-day, 10-day, 20-day, and 100-day statistical volatility of the Transportation Average from August until December 2001. Notice how it declines while the stock is consolidating.

Importantly, there is a tendency not only for SV to fall when a stock enters a consolidation period, but for implied volatility (IV) to fall as well. Recall that implied volatility is a measure of a stock or index's volatility that is derived from option prices and an option pricing model. While statistical volatility measures past prices, implied volatility offers a sense of what the market expects regarding volatility going forward. When market participants (options traders, market makers, and hedgers) expect a stock or index to exhibit high volatility, IV will rise; when the market expects low volatility, IV will fall. Figure B.7 shows the IV of DTX options during the four months ended December 2001. Like SV, the implied volatility of options on the Transportation Average also fell.

Given that consolidation can impact volatility, these periods of sideways trading can be helpful to the options buyer. As we have seen, falling IV often follows consolidation. Furthermore, implied volatility is one of the most important factors in determining option prices. As IV falls, so do option premiums. Therefore, option prices often fall when a stock moves into a period of consolidation. In addition, the longer it lasts, the more likely that IV will fall. If so, the options become cheaper and offer better entry points for positions that involve long options.

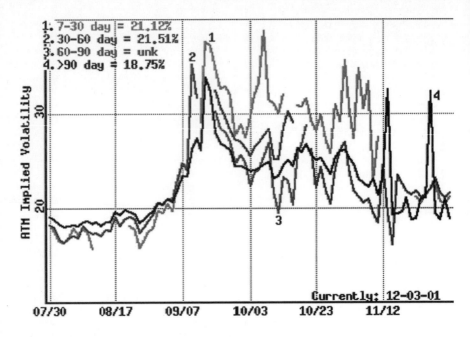

Figure B.7   Implied Volatility, DTX, August to December 2001 (Courtesy of Optionetics.com).

VOLUME

Trading volume is perhaps the single most important indicator used in technical analysis. When a stock is rising and volume increases, this suggests that buyers are actively bidding the price higher and short sellers are running for cover. Strong volume during an advance is considered a bullish sign. Conversely, when volume swells during a decline, bears are driving prices lower, bulls are in pain, and the action of the stock is considered poor. Therefore, studying volume gives the analyst a better sense of whether the bulls or bears are in control of the stock and to what degree.

Volume is the total number of shares associated with a specific stock or market. Also known as turnover, it reflects the number of shares bought or sold relative to a specific security. For instance, if you purchase 100 shares of Microsoft, the volume of that trade is equal to 100. Volume is considered during daily time periods. For instance, on Wednesday, May 8, 2002, total volume on the Nasdaq Stock Market equaled 2,300,910,515. Daily volume is generally defined as the number of shares traded in one day and can be considered for one individual stock or an entire market. On a chart, volume is plotted as a histogram such as in Figure B.8. Tall bars suggest heavy volume while short bars indicate periods of low trading volume.

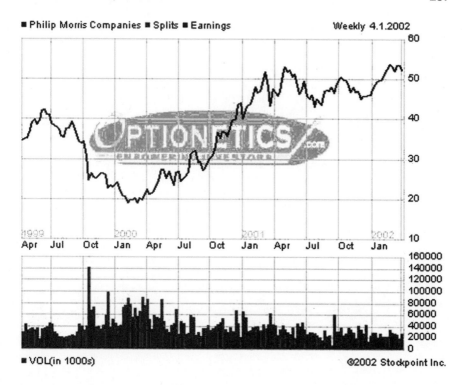

■ Philip Morris Companies ■ Splits ■ Earnings   Weekly 4.1.2002

Figure B.8   Price Chart of MO with Volume (Courtesy of Optionetics.com)

ON-BALANCE VOLUME

One technical indicator that gives a sense of the volume underlying a stock's advance or decline is known as On-Balance Volume (OBV) on most charting software. Developed by Joseph Granville, On-Balance Volume attempts to measure the buying and selling pressure by considering daily volume during a stock's advance verses volume during a stock's decline. OBV is a running total. When a stock finishes the day higher, the volume is added to the running total; if a stock finishes the day lower, the day's volume is subtracted. The same can be done for weekly and monthly periods, but daily is the most common.

On-Balance Volume (OBV) is rarely computed by hand and is viewed graphically using charting software instead. OBV is plotted as a line below the price chart. An example is provided in the chart of Alcoa Inc. (AA) (see Figure B.9). Since the technical analyst wants to see increasing volume when the stock price is rising, a rising OBV line is a bullish sign (i.e., there is more volume on the up days than down days and On-Balance Volume is confirming the trend). Conversely, when On-Balance Volume is downward sloping, it suggests more volume on days

Figure B.9 Alcoa Chart with On-Balance Volume Indicator (Courtesy of Optionetics.com)

when the stock is falling, and that is interpreted as a negative sign: The sellers are dominating trading.

In addition to looking at the slope of OBV, the indicator gives trading signals in two other ways. First, when OBV develops a clear slope or direction and then suddenly shifts direction (as in October), it hints at a trend reversal. In other words, the momentum has shifted and the stock price is likely to follow On-Balance Volume in reversing course. Second, if a stock rises to new highs, but OBV falls or fails to set a new high, that suggests that the trend is running out of steam and a potential reversal is at hand. Notice on the chart above, in November–December, Alcoa's On Balance Volume stopped setting new highs well before the stock hit its peak. Also, notice the action in January–February 2002, OBV started moving higher before the stock. This was a sign of hidden strength and increased buying volume.

MOVING AVERAGES

A moving average is simply the average price of a stock over a number of days. The average is computed using closing prices—the price of the last trade of the day. Suppose for the past six trading days a stock has closed at $40, $44, $50, $48, $50, and $52. The four-day moving average at the end of the fifth day is $48 [($44 + $50 + $48 + $50)/4 = $48]. As each new day is added, the earliest price is removed to create a "moving" average. So, in the previous example, the four-day moving average at the end of the sixth day equals ($50 + $48 + $50 + $52)/4, or $50. Moving averages are most often used over periods of 9, 20, 50, or 200 days. Moving averages are plotted along with stock prices on charts.

Before using a moving average as a tool, an important factor to consider is the number of days to be used in computing the average. A 50-day MA, for example, will behave differently from a 200-day moving average. The shorter the time frame, the more sensitive the moving average will be to price changes in the stock. Consider Figure B.10, which shows the stock price action of International Business Machines (IBM) along with both the 50-day MA (gray line) and the 200-day (black line). Notice that the 50-day moving average fluctuates more than the 200-day. It captures a shorter time frame. Some traders will use very short-term moving averages like a 9-day MA. The general rule is to use a moving average that corresponds with the timeframe of your trading strategy. For instance, in looking at a stock for a

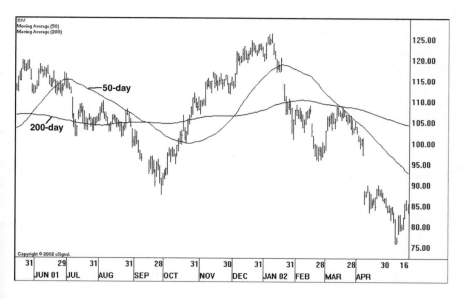

Figure B.10   OHLC Chart of IBM with 50-Day and 200-Day Moving Averages (*Source:* eSignal)

potential bull call spread using a long-term strategy, a 9-day moving average will be too short.

The first way to use a moving average is to consider its slope. For instance, if a moving average is upward sloping, it suggests that the trend is healthy. It is a bullish sign for the stock. A downward sloping moving average indicates weakness and is considered bearish. Notice on the chart of IBM (see Figure B.10) that the 50-day moving average changes direction much faster than the longer-term (200-day) moving average. In November 2001, it began an upward slope and did not change direction until January 2002. When it eventually developed a downward slope, it was followed by a sharp decline in the stock.

A second way to study moving averages is to look for buy and sell signals by considering when the stock price crosses over the moving average. For instance, when the stock price of IBM rose above the 50-day moving average in mid-October 2001, it triggered a buy signal. Conversely, when the stock price fell below the 50-day moving average in January 2002, the indicator gave a sell reading. Again, the fewer the number of days used to compute the moving averages, the greater the number of buy and sell signals. A break of a long-term (e.g., 200-day) moving average holds more technical importance than a break of a shorter-term MA (i.e., 50-day).

Moving averages can also serve as support and resistance zones. For instance, on the chart of IBM, in March 2002, the 200-day moving average served as a resistance area for the stock price. Technical analysts watch the 200-day moving average closely in this respect. Interestingly, at that same time, the 50-day MA also served as a resistance area for the stock. Look at IBM move lower alongside the 200-day moving average in spring 2002. This is not uncommon. The reverse also holds true. That is, stocks frequently ride along the top of moving averages.

The final way of using moving averages is to look at the crossovers between two moving averages. When the short-term moving average crosses over the longer MA, it triggers a buy signal. It occurred on the IBM chart in early December 2001 and the stock surged. Conversely, when the 50-day moving average drops below the 200-day, a sell signal is triggered. On the IBM chart, it occurred in March 2002 and shortly before the stock tumbled.

MOVING AVERAGE CONVERGENCE/DIVERGENCE

The moving average convergence/divergence (MACD) indicator can be among the most useful tools to the technical analyst. It can effectively provide trading signals on long-term or short-term charts—daily, weekly, and monthly graphs. MACD is considered a trend-following indicator. Therefore, it can help to determine whether a trend in a stock is healthy and likely to continue or set for a reversal instead. MACD is viewed on a stock chart either as lines or as a histogram.

MACD can be plotted using two lines: a fast line and a slow line. The fast line is computed as the difference between two moving averages with different time periods. One moving average will be the average over a relatively short period of time—for example, 12 days. The second moving average is the average price change in a stock over a longer period of time (e.g., 26 days). After the 12-day and 26-day MAs are computed, the 26-day MA is subtracted from the 12-day MA to create the fast line. The slow line (or sometimes called the signal line) is simply the 9-day MA.

Moving average convergence/divergence is a trend-following indicator and not a reliable indicator for sideways-moving markets. During periods when a stock or index is rising, the fast line will rise more rapidly than the slow line. Furthermore, when one line changes faster than the other, the difference between the two lines will increase. This is known as the divergence. In a downward-trending market, the fast line will drop below the slow line. The fast line reacts faster to the most recent price changes and moves quicker than the slow line.

Technical analysts look for crossovers between the two lines to generate trading signals. For example, if the fast line is above the slow line, then moves lower and crosses the slow line, a sell signal is triggered. Conversely, when the fast line is below the slow line and then rises above it, a buy signal is triggered. The daily chart in Figure B.11 shows some examples using Celera Genomics Group—Applera Corp. (symbol: CRA). On the far left-hand side of the chart, the fast line is below the slow line. Then, in late September 2001, it rises above the slow line and gives the first buy signal. It gives another in early November 2001. A sell signal is recorded when the fast line falls below the slow line in early December 2001. Another buy signal occurs in early February 2002.

MACD is often plotted as a histogram. In Figure B.11, the MACD histogram is-

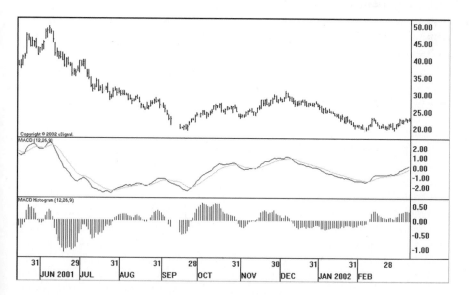

Figure B.11   CRA with MACD Indicator (*Source:* eSignal)

depicted graphically on the bottom of a stock or index chart along a zero line. When the fast line is above the slow line, the MACD histogram will be positive and sit above the zero line. If the fast line is below the slow line, the histogram will be below the zero line and negative. The MACD histogram shows the difference between the long-term and short-term moving averages, and is either positive or negative.

The MACD histogram is generally used as a confirmation tool. For instance, when the fast line is moving up at a faster pace than the slow line, the MACD histogram rises into positive territory and confirms the move higher in the stock or index. If the stock or index is rallying and MACD histogram is not moving higher, the rally is not confirmed and is likely to prove short-lived. The same analysis is used during market declines. Therefore, the MACD histogram is primarily used to gauge the health of the trend in a stock or index, if it is moving in the same direction, the stock's trend is considered healthy.

The most powerful trading signals from the MACD histogram occur when the histogram fails to confirm the rise or fall in the stock. For example, on the CRA chart, in early December the stock rose to new highs, but the MACD histogram did not. That, in turn, signaled what is known as a "bearish divergence" or "bearish nonconfirmation," which was a sign that the rally in CRA was running out of gas. In early February, however, shares fell to new lows, while the MACD histogram set a higher low or "bullish divergence." That, in turn, suggested that CRA was set to reverse and move higher.

MACD can also be applied to weekly and monthly charts. In the case of a weekly chart, the moving averages would be, using the previous example, 12 weeks, 26 weeks, and 9 weeks. On a monthly chart, the moving averages would represent not days or weeks, but months. In general, the most important trading signals occur on the longer-term chart. As a rule, when MACD gives conflicting signals on the daily, weekly, and monthly charts, the analyst defers to the longer-term (monthly) chart's trading signal.

STOCHASTICS

Stochastics is one of the most widely used computer program indicators today. Based on the work of George Lane, the indicator was popularized in an article, "Lane's Stochastics," in *Technical Analysis of Stocks & Commodities* magazine (May/June 1984). Today, stochastics is a popular indicator that comes with almost any charting software package. It is considered an oscillator, or overbought/oversold indicator, and there are a number of different ways it can be used.

Stochastics gives an indication of the relationship between a stock's current price and its recent trading range. In a bullish market, when a stock is moving higher, the stock has a tendency to close near the high points of the day. When the rise is running out of steam, however, the stock will have a tendency to close away from the highs of the day. The bulls, which were previously driving the stock higher, have exhausted their buying power. At that point, investors are hesitant to continue driving the stock higher, and they begin taking profits. As the buyers run out of gas, the stock price starts to close below the highs of the day. In contrast, during a bearish market a stock will close near the lows of the day. Near the end of the downtrend, however, sellers have exhausted their supply and the stock begins closing off the day's lows.

Stochastics attempts to measure whether stocks are closing near their highs or lows of the day. In the book *Trading for a Living* (John Wiley & Sons, 1993), Dr. Alexander Elder puts it this way:

> Stochastics measures the capacity of bulls or bears to close the market near the upper or lower end of the recent range. When prices rally, markets tend to close near the high. If bulls can lift prices up during the day but cannot close them near the top, stochastics turns down. It shows that bulls are weaker than they seem and gives a sell signal.

There are a number of different ways to use stochastics as a trading tool. In general, the indicator is best used for stocks that are moving within a trading range rather than trending dramatically higher or lower. For example, the weekly chart in Figure B.12 shows the stock price action of eBay Inc. (symbol: EBAY) over the

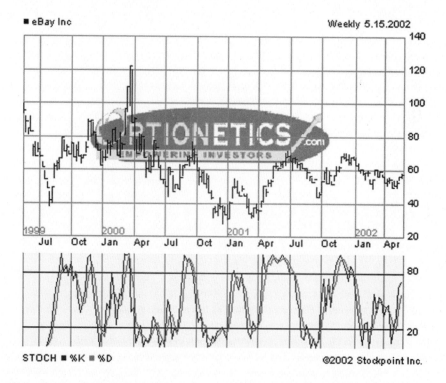

Figure B.12   Chart of EBAY with Stochastics (Courtesy of Optionetics.com)

course of three years along with stochastics. Notice that the indicator consists of two lines—a fast line and a slow line. On the far right-hand side of the chart, the fast line dips below the slow line.

The first way to use stochastics is to look at the crossover between the fast and slow lines. For instance, in the fall of 2001 after EBAY has experienced a steep decline, the fast line rises above the slow line and triggers a buy signal. In contrast, in early 2002 the fast line falls below the slow line and sends a sell signal. Many traders do not like using stochastics in this manner, however. Why? The lines cross over often and generate too many trading signals.

A more common way to use stochastics is to measure overbought/oversold conditions. If a stock is overbought, it has risen very rapidly and is likely to make a move lower. An oversold stock, on the other hand, has fallen dramatically and is due for a short-term rally. Using stochastics, when both the fast and slow lines rise above 80 percent (top horizontal line), the stock is considered overbought. Conversely, when the indicator falls below 20 percent (lower horizontal line), the stock is oversold. Notice on the EBAY chart that the stock became dramatically overbought in late 2001, but oversold three times near the end of the chart.

According to the indicator's developer, George Lane, the most powerful signals occur when stochastics diverge from the stock price. For instance, if a stock price rises to a new high, but stochastics makes a lower high, the indicator triggers a sell signal. When stochastics (or any other indicator) fails to confirm new highs in a stock, it is known as a bearish divergence. Conversely, if a stock price sets a new low but stochastics begins a move higher, it is considered a bullish divergence and a buy signal. An example of a bullish divergence occurred with shares of EBAY in mid-2000. As one can see from the chart, the stock set a new low, but stochastics was moving higher.

RELATIVE STRENGTH INDEX

The Relative Strength Index (RSI) is another type of oscillator. Developed by J. Welles Wilder Jr., RSI is common on almost any computer trading software program available today and, therefore, does not require manual computation. Instead, the Relative Strength Index is generally viewed on a stock chart underneath the price chart. For instance, the chart in Figure B.9 includes the recent price action of TheStreet.com Internet Index ($DOT), along with RSI.

There are basically three ways to use the Relative Strength Index. The first is to identify overbought and oversold conditions. RSI will fluctuate between 0 and 100. In Figure B.13, RSI on TheStreet.com Internet Index has mainly been between, roughly, 20 percent and 80 percent, which is the normal range. But when the indicator dropped below 20 percent in late September 2001, it was a sign of deeply oversold conditions and hinted at a snapback. And snap back the index did.

The second way to use oscillators is as a confirmation tool. When looking at trends, RSI should be setting new highs or new lows along with the index. For instance, when TheStreet.com Internet Index set a new high in early 2002, RSI did not. In fact, the

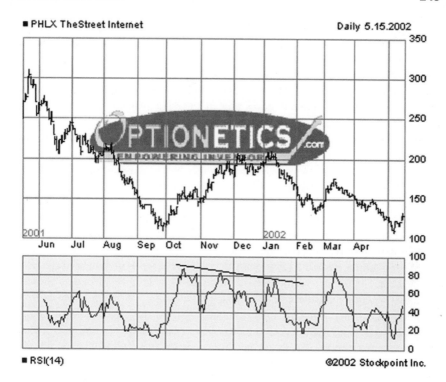

Figure B.13   Chart of TheStreet.com Internet Index with RSI Indicator (Courtesy of Optionetics.com)

indicator had taken on a downward slope. That delivered a sell signal, known as a bearish divergence or nonconfirmation. It hinted that a reversal might be on the way.

Finally, when looking at the Relative Strength Index, the chart analyst wants to consider the slope of the indicator. An upward-sloping RSI is the sign of a healthy advance, and a downward-sloping RSI is evidence of a strong decline. Most oscillators are used in the same fashion as RSI, but each is unique in its own way and must be considered individually.

BOLLINGER BANDS

John Bollinger is credited with the creation of Bollinger bands. The indicator is computed as the standard deviation of the moving average. Standard deviation is a statistical term that means the variability of the distribution. For the less mathematically inclined, a stock with wildly swinging price movements will have a greater standard deviation than a stock with a relatively stable price. Importantly, according to statistical probabilities, regardless of whether a stock has a high or low standard deviation, its price tends to remain within two standard deviations of its moving average 95 percent of the time. Bollinger bands consists of two bands (an upper and lower band). One sits two standard deviations above the moving average and the other two standard deviations below the moving average. Therefore, stocks should stay within the ranges defined by Bollinger bands 95 percent of the time.

Bollinger bands can be used in two ways. The first is as an overbought or oversold indicator. Using Bollinger bands in this manner is based on the assumption that once a stock price diverges meaningfully from its average value, it has a tendency to move back towards its moving average. This kind of movement is the phenomenon known as reversion to the mean. In the case of Bollinger bands, if a stock moves above two standard deviations of its normal range, it will rise above the upper Bollinger band and is likely to fall back towards its moving average. On the other hand, if a stock falls below the lower band, it is likely to respond by moving higher. Therefore, stock is considered overbought when it rises above the top Bollinger band (or more than 2 standard deviations above its moving average) and over sold below the lower Bollinger band (or more than 2 standard deviations below its moving average).

Figure B.14 provides some specific examples of a stock penetrating a Bollinger band and signaling overbought or oversold conditions. The chart looks at Oracle Corporation (symbol: ORCL). In November 2001, the chart breaks above its upper Bollinger band (highlighted with the downward-pointing arrow) and then makes a significant move lower. It was overbought. In December 2001, however, the stock falls below its lower band and signals oversold conditions. Notice the sharp rally

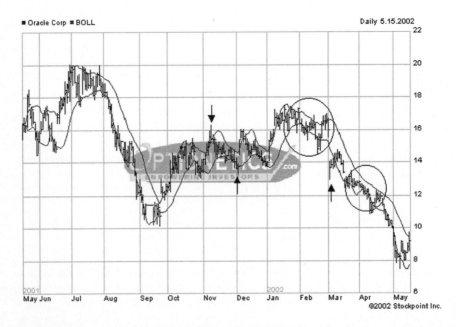

Figure B.14   Oracle Chart with Bollinger Bands (Courtesy of Optionetics.com)

the next day. Used in this manner, Bollinger bands can be applied to daily, weekly, or monthly charts; the longer the time frame on the chart, the more important the overbought and oversold readings.

The second way to use Bollinger bands is as a tool for measuring the volatility of a stock. Stocks with high standard deviations tend to swing more wildly and move a greater distance from their moving averages. In that case, the bands are wide and reflect the higher standard deviation and greater volatility. In contrast, stocks that trade in a narrow range have lower standard deviations around the mean. In that case, the bands will contract and become narrow. On the ORCL chart, two separate periods of quiet trading are highlighted with circles. The bands become narrow. However, notice that each period is followed by an increase in volatility. Again, reversion to the mean affects both stock prices and volatility.

AVERAGE TRUE RANGE

Average True Range (ATR) is derived from past prices and is another tool for measuring historical volatility. Developed by J. Welles Wilder Jr., ATR is used to gauge an asset's daily price swings. Most other measures of historical volatility, such as statistical volatility, consider only closing prices for a stock or index and do not consider the open, high, and low prices of the day. ATR, however, considers the close, high, and low prices. The Average True Range is the average of the true

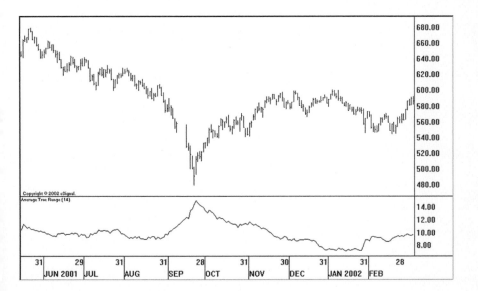

Figure B.15   S&P 100 Chart with Average True Range Indicator (*Source:* eSignal)

ranges (TRs) over a period of days—generally 14 days. As each day of new data is added, the earliest is dropped. The true range is computed as the greatest of:

- The distance between the day's high and low.

- The distance from the previous day's high to the low.

- The distance from the previous day's high to the high.

Like most indicators, ATR is generally viewed graphically rather than numerically. Figure B.15 shows the Average True Range for the S&P 100 index. ATR is generally not used to predict the future price movements in a stock or index. Instead, ATR gauges the price swings or activity level of a stock or index. Low levels occur during periods of narrow and quiet trading. High levels occur during sharp moves and violent swings. Either case—extremely high or low levels of volatility—is usually short-lived and not likely to be sustained for long periods of time. Notice on the chart of the OEX that the ATR spiked higher after the post-9/11 attack sell-off, but then began a move lower. Again, it is reversion to the mean at work.

Appendix C

Statistical and Implied Volatility

STATISTICAL VOLATILITY

Statistical volatility is computed as the annualized standard deviation of past prices over a period of time (10, 30, 90 days). It is considered a measure of historical volatility, because it looks at past prices. It is discussed in term of percentages. Statistical volatility can be computed over different time frames, and the number of days under consideration will vary depending on the options trader's trading time frame. For instance, is the trade long-term or short-term in nature? If it is short-term, the strategist is best served looking at a 20- or 30-day statistical volatility. In contrast, longer-term trades will give greater weight to the 100-day volatility. Here is the formula for computing statistical volatility:

$$v = \sqrt{\frac{\sum_{n=1}^{n}(X_i - X)^2}{n-1}}$$

Where:
X_i = lognormal $(\ln)(P_i/P_i - 1)$
X = average of X_i over a period of n days
n = number of days

Historical Volatility

Definition

Historical volatility is the volatility shown by the underlying security *in the past.* The most common way of computing historical volatility is by using a measure known as statistical volatility, which is the annualized standard deviation over a specified period of days (10, 20, 90 days).

Applications

Determine whether a stock is experiencing high or low volatility.

• **High volatility:** Stocks experiencing high volatility tend to be overpriced.

• **Low volatility:** Stocks experiencing low volatility tend to be underpriced.

Graph

The chart in Figure C.1 shows the statistical volatility of the Nasdaq 100 QQQ. Each line on the chart represents a different statistical volatility. For instance, the top line (or the one that rises the most on the right-hand side of the chart) shows the 6-day statistical volatility. The nearly horizontal line moving across the chart shows the 100-day statistical volatility. Notice that, at the end of the chart, statistical volatility jumps higher. This was the result of a 10 percent surge in the Nasdaq 100 QQQ on May 8, 2002.

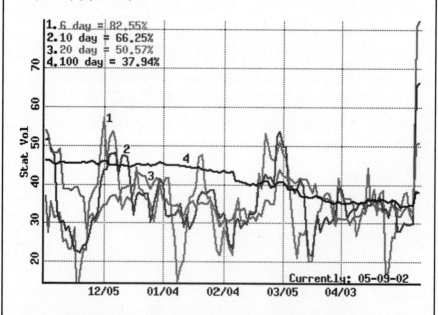

Figure C.1   Statistical Volatility of the Nasdaq 100 QQQ (Courtesy of Optionetics.com)

IMPLIED VOLATILITY

Another important measure of volatility comes from not past prices, but rather the current prices of options in the market. This so-called "implied volatility" is derived using an option's price, the strike price, and the time to expiration, along with the price of the underlying asset (accounting for dividends), and the prevailing risk-free interest rate (T-bill). Those variables are then plugged into an option pricing model (such as Black-Scholes) to arrive at a level of volatility implied by the option. Options on each individual stock or index will have a unique level of implied volatility. In addition, implied volatility is constantly changing and can vary dramatically from one day, week, or month to the next.

Implied Volatility

Definition

Implied volatility is computed by using an option pricing model. The most common option pricing model for computing implied volatility is the Black-Scholes model; it requires the following inputs: the option price, the strike price of the option, the stock price, the time left until expiration, the prevailing interest rates, and any dividends paid by the underlying stock. Since implied volatility is determined using the current option prices in the marketplace (and not the past closing prices of the stock like historical volatility, which does not use option prices at all), implied volatility is forward looking. In other words, it reflects what traders and market makers believe the volatility will be *in the future*. Therefore, when traders say premiums are high or low for a particular option, in essence they are talking about changes in implied volatility.

Applications

Determine whether options are experiencing volatility skew:

• Between different strikes.

• Between different months.

Graph

The chart in Figure C.2 is an implied volatility graph for the Nasdaq 100 QQQ options from the fall of 2001 until the spring of 2002. As one can see, implied volatility fell until April 2002. At that point, however, the graph makes a sharp move higher, which suggests that implied volatility (and the option premiums for the Nasdaq 100 QQQ) is increasing.

(Continued)

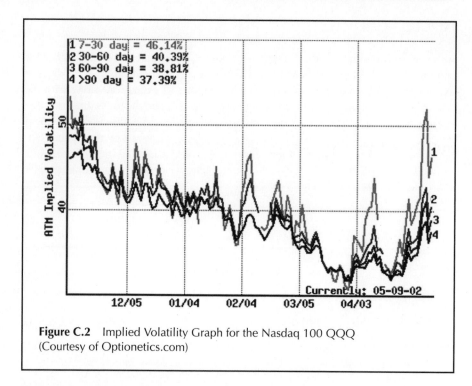

Figure C.2 Implied Volatility Graph for the Nasdaq 100 QQQ
(Courtesy of Optionetics.com)

Since implied volatility is derived from the market prices of options, it is also a reflection of market expectations regarding a stock or index's future level of volatility. When market participants (traders, hedgers, market makers) expect a stock or index to exhibit high levels of volatility, the option premiums of those options will rise. For example, it is not unusual to see the implied volatility of a stock option increase ahead of an earnings report because the options market begins to price in expectations of greater volatility. In addition, all else being equal, the implied volatility of a high flying stock will be greater than that of a stock that has been trading quietly and in a narrow range. The most common gauge of marketwide levels of implied volatility is the CBOE Volatility Index or VIX (see Appendix D).

Appendix D

Sentiment Indicators

VIX

The Chicago Board Options Exchange (CBOE) developed the Volatility Index (VIX) in 1993 as a way to measure market volatility. At the time, the S&P 100 index (OEX) options were among the most actively traded and closely followed options contracts. The volatility index measures the premiums or the amount of volatility implied in the OEX options. During times when option traders expect high market volatility, the premiums on OEX options will become more expensive. When VIX was created, the idea of implied volatility was not novel (in fact, the concept was developed by Fischer Black and Myron Scholes in the early 1970s). What made the CBOE Volatility Index useful was that it offered option traders real-time information regarding the implied volatility of OEX options. It was the first implied volatility indicator of its kind.

In addition to being used as a tool for gauging option premiums (implied volatility) in the market, VIX is also used as a sentiment indicator. Sentiment analysis, in turn, is the act of contrary thinking (see Appendix A). That is, when the majority of investors, or the crowd, is bullish, the contrarian will turn bearish. Conversely, when the crowd is mostly bullish, the contrarian will turn bearish. VIX is used as a measure of overall levels of market bullishness or bearishness.

Since the volatility index is a measure of implied volatility, and implied volatility tends to rise when options market participants (traders, hedgers, market makers, etc.) expect the market to experience greater volatility going forward, VIX moves higher when fear and panic hit the market. Notice from Figure D.1 how VIX spiked higher after the September 11, 2001, terrorist attacks. That was a period of extreme market anxiety that also happened to represent a major bottom in the stock market. In contrast, low VIX readings suggest that the market is expecting quiet trading and

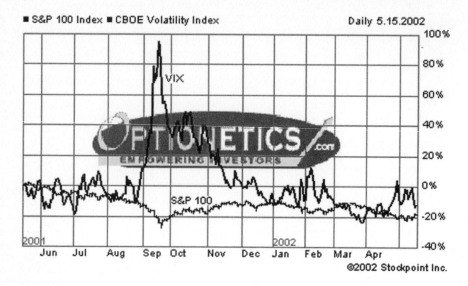

Figure D.1 Chart of S&P 100 and CBOE Volatility Index (Courtesy of Optionetics.com)

low volatility going forward. Extremely low VIX readings often occur when the crowd is predominantly bullish or euphoric and, therefore, near market tops. There is a saying among options traders relative to the CBOE Volatility Index, "When VIX is high, it's time to buy, but when VIX is low, it's time to go."

VXN AND QQV

The CBOE also launched an implied volatility indicator based on Nasdaq 100 options. The Nasdaq 100 Volatility Index was created in the year 2000 and is a measure of the implied volatility being afforded to Nasdaq 100 index options. The Nasdaq 100, in turn, is an index of mostly technology-related companies. Like VIX, the Nasdaq 100 Volatility Index is a real-time index that offers traders an immediate reading of the implied volatility being assigned to Nasdaq 100 index options. It can be viewed anytime throughout the day by using the symbol VXN. When it is high, it suggests that the market is expecting the Nasdaq 100 to exhibit high levels of volatility. When VXN is low, it tells us that the market expects the Nasdaq 100 to show low levels of volatility.

Under the ticker symbol QQV, the QQQ Volatility Index was launched on January 23, 2001. The index is designed to measure the implied volatility of the popular Nasdaq 100 QQQ options. It is similar to VXN, but has a different underlying asset. While VXN is based on the Nasdaq 100 index options, the QQV is based on the

Nasdaq 100 QQQ options, or Qs. The Nasdaq 100 QQQ, in turn, is an exchange-traded fund with shares listed on the American Stock Exchange. Unlike the Nasdaq 100 index, which cannot be bought or sold, the Qs trade like stocks. Each share is designed to equal approximately one-fortieth the value of the Nasdaq 100.

Both VXN and QQV are used in the same manner as the CBOE Volatility Index. The difference is that while VIX measures the implied volatility of S&P 100 index options, VXN and QQV gauge the implied volatility of the Nasdaq 100 Index and the Qs. Therefore, since the QQQ is equal to 1/40th of the Nasdaq 100, both the VXN and QQV will give similar readings and both reflect the happenings within the technology sector. That is, since the Nasdaq 100 Index consists mostly of technology-related stocks, VXN and QQV measure the implied volatility within the technology sector. Figure D.2 shows the similar performance between the two indicators. Again, high readings in the indexes often occur at market bottoms, and low readings sometimes coincide with market tops.

PUT-TO-CALL RATIOS

One of the most important tools in the study of market sentiment is the put/call ratio. The ratio can be computed for an entire market, an index, or an individual stock. One of the earliest put/call ratios was based on S&P 100 index options. As with any put/call ratio, the OEX put/call ratio measures relative levels of put and call buying.

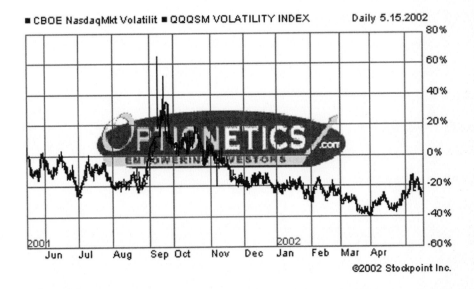

Figure D.2 Chart of Nasdaq 100 Volatility Index and QQQ Volatility Index (Courtesy of Optionetics.com)

It is calculated by dividing the daily number of OEX puts by the number of OEX calls traded. For example, on October 15, 1998, 103,255 OEX puts and 51,449 calls traded hands. Therefore, there was about twice as much put volume as call volume; thus, the OEX put-to-call ratio on that day was 2.01.

Put-to-call ratios increase during periods of rising put relative to call buying. Remember that puts make money when stocks or indexes fall and, therefore, generally reflect bearish bets by options traders. History has shown that a high level of index put buying (relative to calls) often reflects excessive amounts of pessimism or fear. That is, from a contrarian perspective, sentiment has become extremely bearish and most investors are probably wrong. If so, it is time to turn bullish. Therefore, market bottoms often coincide with high OEX put/call ratios. For instance, as noted, on October 15, 1998, the ratio was 2.01. How does this compare to past readings? Look at Figure D.3. On the far right-hand side, the ratio spikes higher. The high reading reflects October 15, 1998 (2.01), which was almost a significant bottom for the OEX. Notice the low value in late August; the reading of only 0.66 coincided with a market top. As a guide, an OEX put/call ratio below 1.00 is bearish, between 1.00 and 1.50 neutral, and above 1.50 bullish (although this ratio has lost some of its usefulness through the years because OEX options no longer receive as much interest from options traders).

Some traders prefer to use the CBOE total put/call ratio—which measures the total number of puts versus the number of calls traded on the Chicago Board Options Exchange (the numbers can be found for each trading at the CBOE web site, www.cboe.com). There is almost always more call than put activity on the CBOE on any given trading day. Therefore, the CBOE put/call ratio is usually below 1.00.

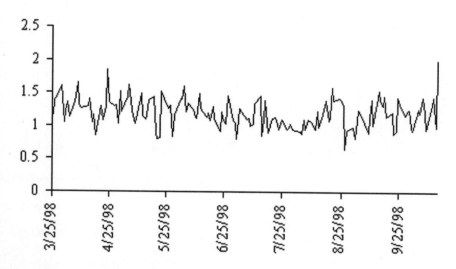

Figure D.3   OEX Put-to-Call Ratio

A CBOE put/call ratio below 0.50 is bearish, between 0.50 and 0.85 neutral, and above 0.85 is bullish.

In addition to the OEX and the total CBOE put/call ratios, put-to-call ratios can be computed for almost any stock or index with actively traded options. The fastest way to do this is by using the charting capabilities on the Optionetics.com Platinum site. Notice the put/call ratio for Intel Corporation (symbol: INTC) depicted in Figure D.4 and the large spike in late February 2002. The sharp jump reflects a large amount of put (relative to call) buying and occurred prior to a three-week 20 percent advance in Intel shares. As a note, the more options activity associated with the stock or index, the more useful the ratio. Additionally, each stock, index, or market will have a unique put/call ratio and a unique trading range. It is important to consider each individually. Only when the ratio moves outside its normal range and to an extreme will it offer evidence of excessive fear or greed.

MEDIA

Simply looking at the covers of major magazines and newspapers can help you determine whether the financial press is optimistic or pessimistic. For example, the major magazines are known to print elaborate cover stories regarding a bear market just as the bear market is reaching an end. Obviously, news events—both scheduled and

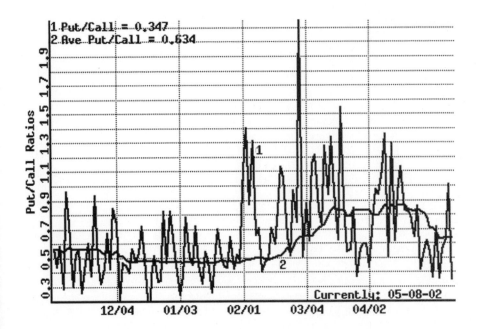

Figure D.4 INTC Put-to-Call Ratio (Courtesy of Optionetics.com)

breaking news—can have a colossal effect on the market. The resulting transitory price swings can and do present beautiful opportunities to buy at a discount or sell into an artificially inflated market. Keep in mind that small investors are generally easily swayed by media coverage of a stock. They tend to jump in without reviewing all the facts and often end up on the losing side of a trend. This is another reason to use sentiment as a contrarian indicator! Although media coverage is a vital element of a stock's advance or decline, do not be fooled by the current unprecedented variety of media coverage.

Years of trading will make you realize that to become successful in this business, you have to develop an approach to life that includes a trading filter. This filter is responsible for accepting all visual and audio information and distilling it into important trading information while throwing away all the useless stuff. If you don't open yourself up to receive information from the perspective of a trader, you run the risk of letting important information slip through your fingers. There are clues everywhere. Developing an information filter is an essential part of learning to be a successful trader.

Newspapers used to be a trader's primary source for market information. But in recent times, we have seen an explosion in the number of media sources. From cable television to the Internet, each medium offers traders a wellspring of trading information. Let's take a look at a few important media sources that influence market sentiment.

Television

Television is not just a source of daily news, it is the center of the entertainment industry. It's very important to keep your eyes open for investment opportunities while watching television. As an exceptional medium for distributing information, television offers traders plenty of useful information for spotting profitable investment opportunities. Specifically, you should watch commercials with a discerning eye. Keep a list of products that you see again and again. Which products or services have been newly introduced? What companies have the most compelling advertising campaigns? These are all clues to the psychology of the consumer-driven markets.

News programs also provide important tidbits of market information. There are a few specific shows that can give you an additional edge including "Trader's First Choice" on CNBC (Cable Business News). This is a show watched by traders and investors throughout the trading day. CNBC was born from the Financial News Network (FNN), which was watched widely by the investment community. Before, during, and after trading hours, CNBC broadcasts market information on many issues including stocks and futures. The channel has expert commentators and guests giving their market summaries and opinions all day long. As with any news organization, they report on stories they believe to be interesting to their target audience—the investment community. They talk about what is hot and what is not. They focus on the most market-moving information they can find because that's the business they are in. You can find great investment ideas by listening to their programming. Before the market opens, you will see a recap of stocks on the screen. These are the closing prices of the day before. You will also see futures prices mixed in every few minutes. At 8:30 A.M., after a government or economic report, bond prices will be shown in the lower right-hand corner for about 10 minutes or so.

Beginning at 9:30 A.M. and up until 9:45 A.M. eastern time, you will see the market averages running real-time across your screen. The top line usually represents the NYSE stocks, and from time to time futures will appear. The bottom line represents the Nasdaq-AMEX and over-the-counter stocks, as well as real-time market averages that appear approximately every minute. From 9:45 A.M. until 4:15 P.M., stock prices will be quoted on the screen throughout the day. These are displayed as the ticker symbol, followed by shares traded, followed by the last trade and the change in price since yesterday's close (on some stations). For example, $IBM_{10,000.00}^{98.50}$ translates as saying that IBM last traded 10,000 shares at $98.50. If you see the symbol and the price, then that was the last quoted price of the stock. Averages that are quoted include the Dow Jones Industrial Average (DJIA), the Standard & Poor's 500 Cash Index, and others. This information is followed by the daily change of the index. This information is useful to anyone who has the time to watch the markets on a daily basis.

Local television programming is certainly not as concise as that on CNBC; however, you can pick up information on local companies that may be useful. Of course, if nothing else, the local reporter will eventually mention the Dow Jones Industrial Average, which can at least tip you off to the general mood of the market.

There are several national television shows that have segments on investing and trading, including CNN, nightly business news reports, and a few others. Unfortunately, most of them lack a great deal of specialized information. Either they do not focus on the investment community or they intersperse business news with general news stories. Bottom line: if a company is headlined in the national news, that will most likely have an effect on the stock's price.

Print Media

To become a successful trader, it is essential to be able to read a newspaper efficiently and intelligently. *The Wall Street Journal* and *Investor's Business Daily* are the most comprehensive suppliers of crucial information about the financial markets. A successful investor can scan these newspapers in about five minutes to spot potential opportunities. In order to accomplish this, you must train yourself to disregard all the fluff and get to the meat of the information.

It is also important to keep tabs on what is happening in your area by scanning the local papers that highlight regional companies more regularly. They often offer insights that the national newspapers miss and give you an opportunity to get a better understanding of local potential investments.

There are also several magazines that offer excellent information on a multitude of trading-related subjects. Here are some valuable resources for sentiment information:

- *Barron's:* This outstanding magazine offers breaking and scheduled financial news and commentary from *The Wall Street Journal* Interactive Edition, plus exclusive weekday coverage from industry giant and pioneer *Barron's*.

- *Business 2.0:* This insightful business magazine offers readers a host of market information and data from the cyber world's cutting edge.

- *Business Week:* This popular magazine has been around for a long time offering a great selection of business news and commentary.

- *Fortune:* This well-written magazine offers lists of top company performers, industry medians, and of course the famous Fortune 500. Top analysts give an inclusive analysis of the unique Fortune 500 macro view of financial events.

- *Investor's Business Daily—Option Guide:* An exceptional biweekly publication to spot stocks with options that can make big moves. This periodical reviews every stock that has options, complete with pertinent charts of stocks that are entering trends or experiencing events. It also hosts a detailed education area, including options and graphs. It is worth its weight in gold many times over once you understand the risks and rewards associated with options strategies and techniques used to maximize gain and minimize risk.

- *Technical Analysis of Stocks & Commodities:* Good cross section of stock and commodity information. More technical analysis oriented than other periodicals, but a very good source of interesting trading ideas designed to foster trader success by offering information on technical trading strategies, charting patterns, indicators, and computerized trading methods through well-researched feature articles.

- *Wired:* Well-known for its cutting-edge style and lively commentary, *Wired* magazine provides plenty of interesting news, articles, commentary, and market analysis with an inclination for high-technology subjects and dot-com companies.

- *Worth:* This magazine offers a variety of investment articles, feature stories, and archived stories from previous editions. There is also an online link to the complete Peter Lynch archives, a section for investor resources, and Investing 101 for beginners.

Internet

As the vanguard of the media front, the Internet has radically changed the way we do business, communicate, advertise, work, and live our daily lives. In addition, the introduction of online trading has revolutionized the investment industry and changed the nature of the way we seek market information. A vast amount of market information can be accessed from the Internet—so much so that there is an entire book on this subject by George Fontanills, entitled *Trade Options Online* (John Wiley & Sons, 1999). The following sites represent the cream of the crop:

- *BigCharts* (http//bigcharts.marketwatch.com): BigCharts is sure to become one of your favorite free sites. It features easily customized intraday charts, historical quotes, and snapshot quotes and profiles on more than 34,000 stocks, mutual funds, and indexes. With excellent design and very user-friendly, BigCharts also offers information on the big movers and losers in the main markets, momentum charts, and other goodies. You'll find links to this site from all over the Internet.

- *CBS MarketWatch* (http//cbs.marketwatch.com): CBS MarketWatch is sure to be on everyone's bookmark list, with comprehensive coverage of news, headlines, and market data. Plenty of web sites link to CBS MarketWatch to access the latest breaking and scheduled news. The discussion page has forums to discuss stocks, mutual funds, futures and options, and global investing.

- *ClearStation* (http//clearstation.etrade.com): This site focuses on technical information, including customized charts, graphs, and company profiles. Enjoy custom portfolios, quotes, charts, message boards, and daily e-mail alerts plus recommendations that are actually worthwhile. Check out the "Tag and Bag" features.

- *EDGAR-Online* (www.edgar-online.com): This first-rate site is a classic financial resource. It allows you to access EDGAR filings using an electronic data-gathering analysis retrieval tool (now, that's impressive!) to locate the SEC filings that interest you. Check out the exclusive drill-down tools, "IPO Express" feature, and insider trading updates. Program an alert to let you know when a company you are watching files a new document. Although this is a subscription-based site, it does offer a few free services including custom portfolios.

- *eSignal* (www.esignal.com): eSignal is a major dynamic quote provider and excellent research and analysis site. In addition to real-time, delayed, and end-of-day prices, you get a multitude of additional services, including news, movers and shakers, charts, customized portfolios, and alerts for a fee. The comprehensive site also offers delayed snapshot quotes and lots of valuable information, news, and commentary. eSignal is compatible with many trading software programs.

- *InfoBeat* (www.infobeat.com): InfoBeat is a one-stop shopping site for information delivered right to your computer. Just click on "Finance" to set up portfolios of stocks and receive daily e-mail messages containing closing prices and pertinent news. Click on "Select" and then "Business and Finance" to browse the extensive selection of e-mail newsletters and columnists from leading publishers that you can receive free.

- *The Motley Fool* (www.fool.com): One of the most popular sites on the Internet! The Motley Fool site seeks to educate, amuse, and continually enrich the investment process for the hundreds of thousands of eager investors that use the Motley Fool books and this site to maximize their trading profits. This extremely entertaining site has a vast amount of current and educational investment information, including quotes, charts, financials, portfolios, news and ideas, and some of the most heavily trafficked bulletin boards of the Internet. It also offers a newsletter service, "Motley Fool Stock Advisor," with refreshing articles and commentary on everything from market movement to specific companies for a small subscription fee. Don't be fooled by the "foolish" bravado—this site has plenty of investor clout.

- *Optionetics Platinum* (www.platinum.optionetics.com): Once you start looking at the volatility of options and stocks, this site is a must-have bookmark. This options analysis site is dedicated to providing an immense amount of information, including free stock options rankings and strategy searches. Detail such as call and put prices, implied volatility (IV), skew charts, and the greeks (delta, vega, gamma, and theta) as well as open interest, is also available to help you find everything you need to succeed as a volatility trader.

- *Lycos Finance* (http//finance.lycos.com): This site offers a ton of useful information, including delayed and real-time quotes, charts, earnings estimates and reports, top business stories, NYSE most active gainers and losers, and a market guide with in-depth information on individual companies. You can also subscribe to LiveCharts for a real-time, dynamic quote service.

- *The Red Herring Online* (www.herring.com): One of the most popular financial "webzines," this site offers a multitude of insider news, analysis, and commentary by highly respected journalists. You'll also find some of the best stories on high-tech stocks on the Net. Check out the search tools and the featured links to other great investment articles.

- *TheStreet.com* (www.thestreet.com): Hosted by controversial analyst Jim Cramer, this extremely popular site offers insightful articles on stocks, options, funds, taxes, and the international finance scene. Register for a free 30-day trial of the premium subscription service and you'll find yourself in the loop encountering the clever commentary of a cadre of bantering journalists three times a day delivered right to your desktop. TheStreet.com's engaging articles and perceptive market analyses no doubt help to shape the mass psychology of the marketplace.

- *Zacks Investment Research* (http//my.zacks.com): Zacks Investment Research is a very popular financial site that offers a variety of free and subscription services. It provides access to research produced by more than 3,000 analysts and approximately 240 brokerage firms. It also features a vast array of brokerage and equity research, screening, and advisory tools.

INVESTOR AND ADVISER SENTIMENT

Another way to track market sentiment is to survey the opinions of professional advisers. Several financial publications such as *Investors Intelligence* and *Market Vane* conduct weekly polls to gauge relative levels of bullishness and bearishness among investors. Although this information is relatively straightforward, this percentage of bullish investment advisers in comparison to the number of bearish investment advisers can be interpreted to be contrarian in nature since a vast number of advisers are wrong a lot of the time. Therefore, more bulls than bears may indicate that the market is topping out, getting ready for a fall.

The easiest way to locate adviser information is to check either *Investor's Business Daily*'s "Bulls vs. Bears" graph or the *Investors Intelligence* newsletter (call 914-632-0422). The latter has been surveying advisory services since 1963; its study confirms that the majority of advice from investment advisers is wrong. Therefore, if there are more bearish investors than bullish, the contrarian approach would be bullish.

ADDITIONAL SENTIMENT TOOLS

- *Rampart Time Index:* This indicator (a regular feature in *Barron's*), is indicated two ways: the Composite Call Index and the Composite Put Index. Both measure the time premium on six-month near-the-money option contracts for 1,836 stocks and show at a glance, on a broad scale, the premiums options traders are willing to pay for a call or put.

- *Volume:* Volume precedes price and is a potent indicator of shifting sentiment. When important news concerning a company is disseminated, there will sometimes be abnormally large trading volume in that company's stock. Sometimes volume spikes will tip you off when sentiment in a stock is shifting. Go online or check the newspapers for "Most Active" lists to find stocks with unusual volume activity.

- *Odd-lot short sellers:* This is the total number of shares sold short in odd lots during a month—in other words, the number of shares sold short in quantities of less than 100 shares. Since investors trading in odd lots are considered less sophisticated, a large number of odd-lot short sellers is interpreted as a bullish sign, while a low number is a bearish sign for the market.

- *Implied volatility:* Demand (or lack thereof) causes implied volatility (IV) to fluctuate in value. Start by comparing IV to its historical volatility. A high IV indicates high premium is in the option pricing due to high demand, greed or fear is growing, and IV is not sustainable. A low IV indicates low demand and indifference. A below-average or above-average IV will eventually correct itself; the emotional aspects of its price will return to a more balanced level. Remember: buy low IV; sell high IV!

- *Advance/decline ratio:* The A/D ratio shows the number of advancing (gaining in value) stocks versus the number of declining issues. A strong (positive) number is a good indicator the rally underway is solid. A weak number in an advancing market means the advance is limited in its breadth, and the rally is therefore suspect. A declining market with a lopsided A/D line (more negatives than positive) means there is a widespread retracement in prices occurring, and signals overall weakness in the market. However, a relatively even A/D reading in a down market indicates the bears have control, but only by a narrow margin.

- *Short interest ratio:* Short interest ratio is a popular indicator that helps to gauge negative investment sentiment. The short interest ratio indicates the number of trading days required to repurchase all of the shares that have been sold short. A short interest ratio of 2 would tell us that based on the current volume of trading it would take two days' volume to cover all shorts. A high short interest ratio is usually a sign of a bullish market, while a low short interest ratio is generally a sign of a bearish market.

Appendix **E**

Using Risk Graphs

The risk graph offers a way of seeing the potential for profit or loss from an option trade graphically. The chart plots the profit from the option on the vertical axis along with the price of the stock along the horizontal axis. The graph in Figure E.1 is an example and considers the risk graph for one December QQQ 30 call that was purchased (hypothetically) in early May for $4.80. The potential profit from the call is plotted along the vertical axis and the QQQ price on the horizontal axis. The chart was created using Optionetics.com Platinum. Line number 4, the lowest of the four lines on the graph, reflects the profit or loss potential for the QQQ call at expiration. Notice that if the QQQ finishes at expiration for $30 a share or less the trade loses $480, which is equal to the cost of the trade (or one QQQ December 30 call). Why? At $30 or less, the option expires worthless. Also notice that the chart does not fall below –$480. Therefore, that represents the maximum risk of holding the option until expiration. As the QQQ moves higher in price, however, the call begins to increase in value. At expiration, the trade will be profitable if QQQ rises above $34.80. That level is highlighted on the chart in the lower right-hand quadrant by a vertical gray line. The other three risk curves (lines 1, 2, and 3) offer a view of the potential risk or reward of owning the QQQ December call option with time left until expiration. For example, the top risk curve (number 1) shows the profit and loss with 226 days until expiration, and line number 3 shows the risk graph for the trade with 75 days left until expiration.

Just as risk graphs can be plotted for call options, the same process can be done for put options. Figure E.2 shows the profit/loss potential for buying one QQQ December 25 put in May. Again, the profit and loss is reflected on the vertical axis and the price of the QQQ on the horizontal axis. In contrast to the call, however, the put generates profits if the stock moves lower. The cost of the trade is $120, and that represents the maximum lost. The breakeven at expiration (bottom line)

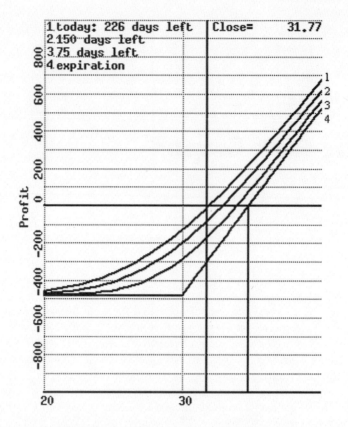

Figure E.1   Risk Graph of QQQ Call (Courtesy of Optionetics.com)

is $23.80. It is highlighted with a gray vertical line in the lower left-hand part of the graph.

Risk graphs give the option strategist a bird's-eye view of the profit and loss potential, not just at expiration, but also as the option loses time value. They are simple, convenient, and can be created quickly using Optionetics.com Platinum or other options trading software. In addition, creating risk graphs is not limited to simple calls and puts, but can also be created for more complex strategies such as spreads and straddles. Each strategy will have a different risk graph that should be considered individually. By doing so, the option strategist will get a quick visual presentation of the profit and loss potential of any option strategy, which can save a substantial amount of time when searching for that next potentially winning trade.

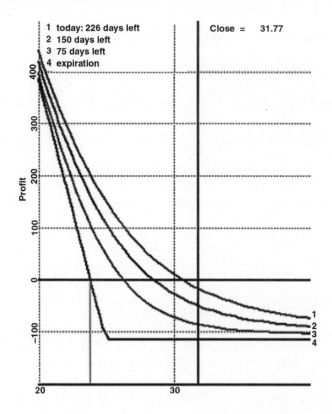

Figure E.2   Risk Graph of QQQ Put (Courtesy of Optionetics.com)

Appendix F

Option Reviews

OPTION EXPIRATION MONTH CODES

Every option has a specific symbol that represents it. Each symbol includes information regarding the strike price and expiration date. Table F.1 reveals each month's corresponding letter.

Table F.1 Option Expiration Month Codes

	Jan.	Feb.	Mar.	Apr.	May	Jun.
Calls	A	B	C	D	E	F
Puts	M	N	O	P	Q	R

	Jul.	Aug.	Sep.	Oct.	Nov.	Dec.
Calls	G	H	I	J	K	L
Puts	S	T	U	V	W	X

STRIKE PRICE CODES

Option symbols contain information that corresponds to the strike price of a specific option. Table F.2 reveals the particular letter that corresponds to specific strike prices.

Table F.2   Strike Price Codes

A	B	C	D	E	F	G	H	I
5	10	15	20	25	30	35	40	45
105	110	115	120	125	130	135	140	145
205	210	215	220	225	230	235	240	245
305	310	315	320	325	330	335	340	345
405	410	415	420	425	430	435	440	445
505	510	515	520	525	530	535	540	545
605	610	615	620	625	630	635	640	645
705	710	715	720	725	730	735	740	745

J	K	L	M	N	O	P	Q	R
50	55	60	65	70	75	80	85	90
150	155	160	165	170	175	180	185	190
250	255	260	265	270	275	280	285	290
350	355	360	365	370	375	380	385	390
450	455	460	465	470	475	480	485	490
550	555	560	565	570	575	580	585	590
650	655	660	665	670	675	680	685	690
750	755	760	765	770	775	780	785	790

S	T	U	V	W	X	Y	Z
95	100	7.5	12.5	17.5	22.5	27.5	32.5
195	200	37.5	42.5	47.5	52.5	57.5	62.5
295	300	67.5	72.5	77.5	82.5	87.5	92.5
395	400	97.5	102.5	107.5	112.5	117.5	122.5
495	500	127.5	132.5	137.5	142.5	147.5	152.5
595	600	157.5	162.5	167.5	172.5	177.5	182.5
695	700	187.5	192.5	197.5	202.5	207.5	212.5
795	800	217.5	222.5	227.5	232.5	237.5	242.5

VARIABLE OPTIONS DELTAS

All options are provided a delta relative to the 100 deltas of the underlying security. If 100 shares of stock are equal to 100 deltas, then the corresponding options must have delta values of less than 100. You can estimate an option's delta using Table F.3 depending on the movement of the underlying stock.

Table F.3   Variable Options Deltas

OPTION STRIKES	CALLS		PUTS	
	Long	Short	Long	Short
ATM	+50	−50	−50	+50
ITM				
1 Strike	+60 to +65	−60 to −65	−60 to −65	+60 to +65
2 Strikes	+70 to +75	−70 to −75	−70 to −75	+70 to +75
3 Strikes	+80 to +85	−80 to −85	−80 to −85	+80 to +85
OTM				
1 Strike	+35 to +40	−35 to −40	−35 to −40	+35 to +40
2 Strikes	+25 to +30	−25 to −30	−25 to −30	+25 to +30
3 Strikes	+15 to +20	−15 to −20	−15 to −20	+15 to +20

GOVERNMENT REPORTS

There are a number of government reports that enable investors to keep tabs on the nuts and bolts of our economy. (See Table F.4.) Keeping abreast of these reports is a big priority for investors who use them to anticipate economic trends and assess their impact on the marketplace.

Table F.4   Government Reports Matrix

Component	Release Date	Advancing Number	Declining Number
Employment Report	First Friday of the month.	A rise in unemployment rate is a positive sign for the bond market.	A decrease in unemployment numbers is a positive sign for the stock market.

Table F.4 Government Reports Matrix

Component	Release Date	Advancing Number	Declining Number
Nonfarm Jobs Growth	First week of the month.	Job creation is a good thing. It is a sign that companies are expanding and prospects are good for future growth. However, job creation must be looked at in conjunction with unemployment and productivity figures—if the number of new jobs is growing significantly faster than the jobs can be absorbed by the workforce, then the elements are in place for inflationary wage pressures.	Declining jobs indicates a contraction of the economy and portends real problems for the stock market in general.
Wholesale Trade Inventories (Very accurate indicator, even though the lag is two months.)	Second week each month.	If inventories rise, consumption is slowing. Rising inventory-to-sales ratio reflects a slowdown in the economy.	If inventories are falling, consumption is on the rise. If inventory-to-sales ratio begins to fall, consumer spending has increased—more consumer confidence.
Import and Export Prices	Around mid-month.	Imports constitute 15% of U.S. consumption. They also directly affect the profitability of U.S. companies. Higher prices from imports translate to higher prices of domestic goods. This is good news for business; bad for the consumer.	If import prices fall, U.S. companies must lower prices to compete—bad for businesses, good for consumers.
Employment Situation (The single most closely watched economic statistic offers timeliness and accuracy and is an important indicator of economic activity.)	First week of the month.	This gives a good indication of emerging wage pressures in average hourly earnings component. This is a good proxy for GDP growth; rising numbers mean economy is expanding. May or may not be greeted as good news by the market.	Declining numbers would indicate that wages and jobs are on the decline. May be interpreted either way by the market, depending on desired interest rate change.

(Continued)

Table F.4   *(Continued)*

Component	Release Date	Advancing Number	Declining Number
Employment Cost Index (ECI)	Once a quarter, toward the end of month, for preceding quarter.	ECI analyzes wages and fringe benefits. Rising wages alone have less meaning, but are used in conjunction with other reports, like housing starts.	Lower wages mean a slowing economy, and are used in conjunction with other economic measure-ments to gauge the economy's strength.
Consumer Price Index (CPI)	Data released around the 15th of each month, 8:30 A.M. eastern time.	Since the CPI describes price changes of a basket of consumer goods, a rising numbers mean inflationary pressures at work. This is bad for the stock market because inflation is held in check by raising interest rates.	A drop in prices is generally considered a good sign for consumers and good for the market.
Producer Price Index (PPI)	Previous month's data are released during the second full week of the current month.	Increases may or may not be good news: If interest rates are declining, then a rising number means the economy is reacting to the rate cuts. If rates are increasing, this is bad because further rate hikes may be required.	Decreases mean the economy is slowing. It is best to look at trends. Prolonged slowing may lead to recession. However, if rates have been increasing, decreasing numbers would mean no further hikes are necessary. This is usually good news for the market.
National Association of Purchasing Management Index (NAPM)	First of month.	Accelerates the economy.	Slows the economy.
Retail Sales	Mid-month.	People are spending more and confidence is high; it's a good sign for the market.	People spend less and confidence shrinks; it's a bad sign for the market, especially retail stocks.

Table F.4   *(Continued)*

Component	Release Date	Advancing Number	Declining Number
Gross Domestic Product (GDP)	Released one month after end of quarter.	GDP takes into account consumer demand, trade balance, and so on. Economy expanding is good news, but not too fast—the Fed raises rates when that happens.	Decrease means economy slowing. If it continues Fed will possibly lower rates which would be good for market.
Housing Starts and Sales of New and Existing Homes	Released third week of month.	Increasing starts indicate confidence—a good sign for the market.	Decrease means economy slowing— red flag for Fed to be on lookout for downturn in economy. Market reaction is anybody's guess.
Construction Spending	First of month.	This is a lagging indicator— reports come in only after buildings are finished. An increase in numbers is a good sign.	Since it's a lagging indicator, it may serve to confirm that the economy is slowing and rates need to be lowered, which would be good for the market.
Industrial Production Index	Mid-month, 9:15 A.M. eastern time.	This would indicate the slack is being taken out of the economy; we're maxing out.	Factories slowing down might be considered bad for the market and is considered bad for the economy.
Personal Income and Consumption Expenditures	Third or 4th week after the month it reports on.	Increase is positive, but does not have much impact as it reports after other key data (employment and retail sales).	Prolonged decrease in consumer demand is definitely bad for consumer stocks.
Factory Orders— Durable Goods and Nondurable Goods	Four weeks from end of reporting month (8:30 A.M. ET). However, everyone keys off of the advance release one week earlier.	This is a leading indicator of industrial demand. Numbers going up is generally a positive for the markets.	Slowing demand means a slowing economy, if it stays in a declining mode for several months. This might adversely affect markets, but if it prompts interest rate reductions it could be good for the stock market.

OPTIONS STRATEGY QUICK REFERENCE GUIDE

Table F.5 is designed as a quick reference guide to the strategies covered in this book. The "Guide Codes" at the bottom of the table spell out the abbreviations used in the table. For a more in-depth look, strategy reviews can be found in the pages following this guide that detail the calculations for maximum risk and reward as well as breakevens.

Table F.5   Options Strategy Quick Reference Guide

Strategy	Risk Profile	Trade	Market Outlook	Reward Potential	Risk Potential	Time Decay Effects	Volatility Outlook
Long Call		B1-C	Bullish	Unlimited	Limited	Detrimental	Low
Long Put		B1-P	Bearish	Limited	Limited	Detrimental	Low
Covered Call		B100-U S1-C	Lightly bullish to neutral	Limited	Unlimited	Helpful	High
Bull Call Spread		B1-LC S1-HC	Bullish	Limited	Limited	Mixed	Low
Bear Put Spread		S1-LP B1-HP	Bearish	Limited	Limited	Mixed	Low
Bull Put Spread		B1-LP SI-HP	Moderately bullish	Limited	Limited	Mixed	High
Bear Call Spread		S1-LC BI-HC	Moderately bearish	Limited	Limited	Mixed	High
Call Ratio Backspread		S1-LC B2-HC	Very bullish	Limited	Limited	Mixed	Low
Put Ratio Backspread		S1-HP B2-LP	Very bearish	Limited	Limited	Mixed	Low
Long Straddle		B1-ATM-C B1-ATM-P	Volatile	Unlimited	Limited	Detrimental	High
Long Butterfly Spread		B1-LC/P S2-HC/P B1-HP/P	Stable	Limited	Limited	Helpful	High
Long Iron Butterfly Spread		S1-ATM-C B1-OTM-C S1-ATM-P B1-OTM-P	Stable	Limited	Limited	Helpful	High
Diagonal Spread		B1 LT C/P S1 ST C/P Different strikes	Stable	Unlimited	Limited	Helpful	Skews
Calendar Spread		B1 LT C/P S1 ST C/P Same strikes	Stable	Unlimited	Limited	Helpful	Skews

Guide Codes		
B = Buy	HC = Higher strike call	ATM = At-the-money
S = Sell	LC = Lower strike call	OTM = Out-of-the-money
1 = 1 contract	HP = Higher strike put	ITM = In-the-money
2 = 2 contracts	LP = Lower strike put	LT = Long-term
U = Underlying stock	C/P = Call or put	ST = Short-term

STRATEGY SUMMARIES

Long Stock

Strategy = Buy shares of stock.

Market Opportunity = Look for a bullish market where a rise in the price of the stock is anticipated.

Maximum Risk = Limited to the full price of the stock shares as they fall to zero.

Maximum Profit = Unlimited as the stock price rises above the initial entry price.

Breakeven = Price of the stock at initiation.

Margin = Required. Usually 50 percent of the total cost of the shares.

Short Stock

Strategy = Sell shares of stock.

Market Opportunity = Look for a bearish market where a fall in the price of the stock is anticipated.

Maximum Risk = Unlimited as the stock price rises.

Maximum Profit = Limited to the full price of the stock shares as they fall to zero.

Breakeven = Price of the stock at initiation.

Margin = Required. Usually 150 percent of the total cost of the shares.

Long Call

Strategy = Buy a call option.

Market Opportunity = Look for a bullish market where a rise above the breakeven is anticipated.

Maximum Risk = Limited to the amount paid for the call.

Maximum Profit = Unlimited as the price of the underlying instrument rises above the breakeven.

Breakeven = Call strike price + call option premium.

Margin = None.

Short Call

Strategy = Sell a call option.

Market Opportunity = Look for a bearish or stable market where you anticipate a fall in the price of the underlying below the breakeven.

Maximum Risk = Unlimited as the stock price rises above the breakeven.

Maximum Profit = Limited to the credit received from the call option premium.

Breakeven = Call strike price + call option premium.

Margin = Required. Amount subject to broker's discretion.

Long Put

Strategy = Buy a put option.

Market Opportunity = Look for a bearish market where you anticipate a fall in the price of the underlying below the breakeven.

Maximum Risk = Limited to the price paid for the put option premium.

Maximum Profit = Limited as the stock price falls to zero below the breakeven.

Breakeven = Put strike price – put option premium.

Margin = None.

Short Put

Strategy = Sell a put option.

Market Opportunity = Look for a bullish or stable market where a rise above the breakeven is anticipated.

Maximum Risk = Unlimited as the stock price falls below the breakeven.

Maximum Profit = Limited to the credit received from the put option premium.

Breakeven = Put strike price – put option premium.

Margin = Required. Amount subject to broker's discretion.

Protective Put

Strategy = Buy the underlying stock and purchase an ATM put option.

Market Opportunity = Look for a bullish market where you anticipate a rise in the price of the underlying stock, but want to protect the downside.

Maximum Risk = Limited to the cost of the stock – put strike price + put premium.

Maximum Profit = Unlimited to the upside as the stock price moves higher. Limited to the downside as the stock price falls below the breakeven.

Breakeven = Stock price + put premium.

Margin = None for the option and 50 percent of the stock price.

Covered Call

Strategy = Buy the underlying security and sell an OTM call option.

Market Opportunity = Look for a bullish to neutral market where a slow rise in the price of the underlying is anticipated with little risk of decline.

Maximum Risk = Virtually unlimited to the downside below the breakeven all the way to zero.

Maximum Profit = Limited to the credit received from the short call option + (short call strike price – price of long underlying asset) × 100.

Breakeven = Price of the underlying asset at initiation – short call premium received.

Margin = Amount subject to broker's discretion.

Bull Call Spread

Strategy = Buy a lower strike call and sell a higher strike call with the same expiration date.

Market Opportunity = Look for a bullish market where you anticipate a modest increase in the price of the underlying above the price of the short call option.

Maximum Risk = Limited to the net debit paid for the spread.

Maximum Profit = Limited [(difference in strike prices × 100) – net debit paid].

Breakeven = Lower call strike price + net debit paid.

Margin = Required. Amount subject to broker's discretion—should be limited to the net debit on the trade.

Bear Put Spread

Strategy = Buy a higher strike put and sell a lower strike put with the same expiration date.

Market Opportunity = Look for a bearish market where you anticipate a modest decrease in the price of the underlying asset below the strike price of the short put option.

Maximum Risk = Limited to the net debit paid.

Maximum Profit = Limited [(difference in strike prices × 100) – net debit paid].

Breakeven = Higher put strike price – net debit paid.

Margin = Required. Amount subject to broker's discretion.

Bull Put Spread

Strategy = Buy a lower strike put and sell a higher strike put with the same expiration date.

Market Opportunity = Look for a bullish market where you anticipate an increase in the price of the underlying asset above the strike price of the short put option.

Maximum Risk = Limited [(difference in strike prices × 100) – net credit].

Maximum Profit = Limited to the net credit received when the market closes above the short put option.

Breakeven = Higher put strike price – net credit received.

Margin = Required. Amount subject to broker's discretion.

Bear Call Spread

Strategy = Buy a higher strike call and sell a lower strike call with the same expiration date.

Market Opportunity = Look for a bearish market where you anticipate a decrease in the price of the underlying asset below the strike price of the short call option.

Maximum Risk = Limited [(difference in strike prices × 100) – net credit].

Maximum Profit = Limited to the net credit received.

Breakeven = Lower call strike price + net credit received.

Margin = Required. Amount subject to broker's discretion.

278

Call Ratio Backspread

Strategy = Sell lower strike calls and buy a greater number of higher strike calls (the ratio must be less than .67).

Market Opportunity = Look for a market where you anticipate a price rise with increasing volatility; place as a credit or at even.

Maximum Risk = Limited [(# short calls × difference in strike prices) × 100 – net credit or + net debit].

Maximum Profit = Unlimited to the upside beyond the breakeven; on the downside, limited to the net credit (if any).

Upside Breakeven = Higher strike call + [(difference in strike prices × # short calls)/(# long calls – # short calls)] – net credit or + net debit.

Downside Breakeven = Strike price of the short call + net credit (or – net debit).

Margin = Required. Amount subject to broker's discretion.

Put Ratio Backspread

Strategy = Sell higher strike puts and buy a greater number of lower strike puts with a ratio less than 0.67.

Market Opportunity = Look for a market where you anticipate a price decline with increased volatility; place as a credit or at even.

Maximum Risk = Limited [(# short puts × difference in strike prices × 100) – net credit or + net debit].

Maximum Profit = Limited to the downside below the breakeven as the stock falls to zero. Limited on the upside to the net credit, if any.

Upside Breakeven = Higher strike put – net credit (or + net debit).

Downside Breakeven = Lower strike price – [(# short puts × difference in strikes)/(# long puts – # short puts)] + net credit (or – net debit).

Margin = Required. Amount subject to broker's discretion.

Long Straddle

Strategy = Purchase an ATM call and an ATM put with the same strike price and the same expiration.

Market Opportunity = Look for a market with low implied volatility options where a sharp volatility increase is anticipated.

Maximum Risk = Limited to the net debit paid.

Maximum Profit = Unlimited to the upside and downside beyond the breakevens. Profit requires sufficient market movement but does not depend on market direction.

Upside Breakeven = ATM strike price + net debit paid.

Downside Breakeven = ATM strike price – net debit paid.

Margin = None.

Long Butterfly

Strategy = Buy a lower strike option, sell two higher strike options, and buy a higher strike option (all calls or all puts).

Market Opportunity = Look for a range bound market that is expected to stay between the breakeven points.

Maximum Risk = Limited to the net debit paid.

Maximum Profit = Limited [(difference in strikes × 100) – net debit paid]. Profit exists between breakevens.

Upside Breakeven = Highest strike price – net debit paid.

Downside Breakeven = Lowest strike price + net debit paid.

Margin = Amount subject to broker's discretion.

Long Iron Butterfly

Strategy = Buy a higher strike call, sell a lower strike call, sell a lower strike put, and buy an even lower strike put.

Market Opportunity = Look for a range bound market that you anticipate to stay between the breakeven points.

Maximum Risk = Limited [(difference between long and short strikes × 100) – net credit received].

Maximum Profit = Limited to the net credit received. Profit exists between breakevens.

Upside Breakeven = Strike price of middle short call + net credit.

Downside Breakeven = Strike price of middle short put – net credit.

Margin = Amount subject to broker's discretion.

Calendar Spread

Strategy = Sell a short-term option and buy a long-term option using at-the-money options with as small a net debit as possible (use all calls or all puts). Calls can be used for a more bullish bias and puts can be used for a more bearish bias.

Market Opportunity = Look for a range bound market that is expected to stay between the breakeven points for an extended period of time.

Maximum Risk = Limited to the net debit paid.

Maximum Profit = Limited. Use software for accurate calculation.

Upside Breakeven = Use software for accurate calculation.

Downside Breakeven = Use software for accurate calculation.

Margin = Amount subject to broker's discretion.

Diagonal Spread

Strategy = Sell a short-term option and buy a long-term option with different strikes and as small a net debit as possible (use all calls or all puts).

- A bullish diagonal spread employs a long call with a distant expiration date and a lower strike price along with a short call with a closer expiration date and a higher strike price.

- A bearish diagonal spread combines a long put with a distant expiration date and a higher strike price along with a short put with a closer expiration date and a lower strike price.

Market Opportunity = Look for a range bound market that is expected to stay between the breakeven points for an extended period of time.

Maximum Risk = Limited to the net debit paid.

Maximum Profit = Limited. Use software for accurate calculation.

Upside Breakeven = Use software for accurate calculation.

Downside Breakeven = Use software for accurate calculation.

Margin = Amount subject to broker's discretion.

STRATEGY REVIEWS

Covered Call Review

A covered call (Figure F.1) is a conservative income strategy designed to provide limited protection against decreases in the price of a long underlying stock position. In order to place a covered call, the following 13 rules should be observed:

1. Look for a range bound market or a bullish market where you anticipate a steady increase in the price of the underlying stock.

2. Check to see if the stock has liquid options available.

3. Review call option premiums and strike prices no more than 45 days out.

4. Investigate implied volatility values to see whether the options are over-priced or undervalued. Look for expensive options to get the most out of selling the call.

5. Explore past price trends and liquidity by reviewing price and volume charts over the past year.

6. Choose a higher strike call no more than two months out to sell against long shares of the underlying stock and then calculate the maximum profit, which is limited to the credit received from the sale of the short call plus the profit

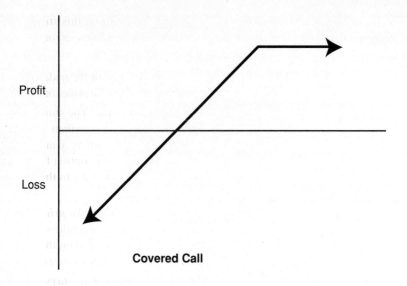

Profit

Loss

Covered Call

Figure F.1   Covered Call

made from the difference between the stock's price at initiation and the call strike price.

7. Determine which spread to place. To do this, look at:

   • **Unlimited Risk:** Unlimited to the downside as the stock falls below the breakeven to zero.

   • **Limited Reward:** Limited to the credit received from the short call plus the strike price minus the initial stock price.

   • **Breakeven:** Calculated by subtracting the short call premium from the price of the underlying stock at initiation.

8. Create a risk profile of the most promising option combination and graphically determine the trade's feasibility. Note the unlimited risk beyond the breakeven.

9. Write down the trade in your trader's journal before placing the trade with your broker to minimize mistakes made in placing the order and to keep a record of the trade.

10. Make an exit plan before you place the trade. You must be willing to sell the long stock at the short call's strike price in case the call is assigned and exercised.

11. Contact your broker to buy and sell the chosen options. Place the trade as a limit order so that you limit the net debit of the trade.

12. Watch the market closely as it fluctuates. The profit on this strategy is un-limited—a loss occurs if the underlying stock closes at or below the breakeven point.

13. Choose an exit strategy depending on the movement of the underlying stock and the effects of changes in the implied volatility on the prices of the options.

   - *The price of the stock rises above the short strike.* The short call is as-signed and exercised by the option holder. You can then use the 100 shares from the original long stock position to satisfy your obligation to deliver 100 shares of the underlying stock to the option holder at the short call strike price. This scenario allows you to take in the maximum profit.

   - *The price of the stock falls below the short call strike price, but stays above the initial stock price.* The short call expires worthless and you get to keep the premium received. No losses have occurred on the long stock position and you are ready to sell another call to offset your risk.

   - *The stock falls below the initial stock price but stays above the breakeven.* The long stock position starts to lose money, but this loss is offset by the credit received from the short call. As long as the stock stays above the breakeven, the position will break even or make a small profit.

   - *The stock falls below the breakeven.* Let the short option expire worth-less and use the credit received to partially hedge the loss on the long stock position.

Bull Call Spread Review

In order to place a bull call spread (Figure F.2), the following 13 rules should be observed:

1. Look for a low volatility, bullish market where you anticipate a modest in-crease in the price of the underlying stock.

2. Check to see whether this stock has liquid options available.

3. Review call options premiums for different expiration dates and strike prices. Bull call spreads are best placed on stocks that have at least 90 days until expiration. The utilization of LEAP option is a good idea for this strat-egy. LEAPS give you the opportunity to have time work for you.

4. Investigate implied volatility values to see whether the options are over-priced or undervalued.

5. Explore past price trends and liquidity by reviewing price and volume charts over the past year.

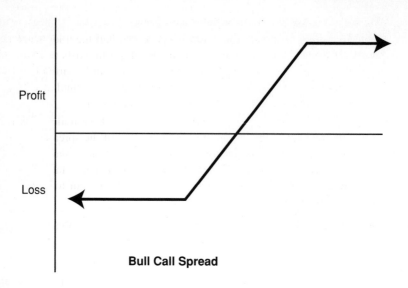

Profit

Loss

Bull Call Spread

Figure F.2 Bull Call Spread

6. Choose a lower strike call to buy and a higher strike call to sell. Both options must have the same expiration date. The higher the price and volatility, the wider the strikes can be. In general, a good combination is relatively low "buy" strikes combined with higher "sell" strikes. Get the breakeven low enough that you can sleep at night. The lower "buy" strikes lower the breakeven point. Give yourself plenty of room to profit if the stock runs; this is accomplished by choosing higher "sell" strikes.

7. Determine which spread to place. To do this, look at:
   - **Limited Risk:** The most that can be lost is the net debit of the two options.
   - **Limited Reward:** Calculated by multiplying the difference in strike prices by 100 and then subtracting the net debit paid.
   - **Breakeven:** Calculated by adding the lower strike price to the net debit.
   - **Return on Investment:** Reward/risk ratio.

8. Create a risk profile for the trade to graphically determine the trade's feasibility. The risk profile for a bull call spread visually reveals the strategy's limited risk and profit parameters. Notice how the maximum profit occurs at the short call strike price.

9. Write down the trade in your trader's journal before placing the trade with your broker to minimize mistakes made in placing the order and to keep a record of the trade.

10. Create an exit strategy before you place the trade.

- Consider doing two contracts at once. Try to exit half the trade when the value of the trade has doubled or when enough profit exists to cover the cost of the double contracts. Then the other trade will be virtually a free trade and you can take more of a risk, allowing it to accumulate a bigger profit. Close out the entire trade at 30 days to expiration.

- If you have only one contract, exit the remainder of the trade when it is worth 80 percent of the maximum possible value of the spread. The reason for this rule is that it usually takes a very long time to see the last 20 percent of value in a profitable vertical spread. It's better to take the trade off and look for new trades where the money can be put to better use. Close out the trade at 30 days to expiration.

11. Contact your broker to buy and sell the chosen call options. Place the trade as a limit order so that you limit the net debit of the trade.

12. Watch the market closely as it fluctuates. The profit on this strategy is limited—a loss occurs if the underlying stock closes at or below the breakeven point.

13. Choose an exit strategy based on the price movement of the underlying stock and the effects of changes in the implied volatility of the prices of the options.

- *The underlying stock rises above the short strike.* The short call is assigned and if it is exercised by the option holder you are obligated to deliver 100 shares (per call) to the option holder at the short strike price. Exercise the long call to buy the underlying stock at the lower strike and deliver these shares to the option holder. The resulting profit is the maximum profit available.

- *The underlying stock rises above the breakeven, but not as high as the short strike.* Sell a call with the long call strike and buy a call with the short strike. There should be a small profit remaining.

- *The underlying stock remains below the breakeven, but above the long strike.* Sell a call with the long strike and buy a call with the short strike, which will partially offset the initial debit or allow you to pocket a small profit; or sell the long call to offset the trade's net debit and let the short option expire worthless.

- *The underlying stock falls below the long option.* Close out the entire trade at 30 days to expiration.

Bear Put Spread Review

In order to place a bear put spread (Figure F.3), the following 13 rules should be observed:

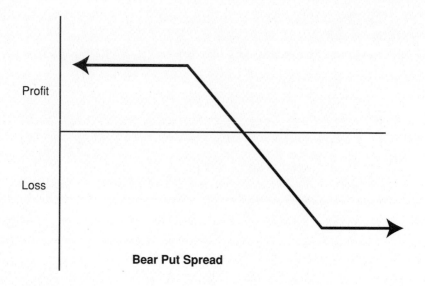

Figure F.3   Bear Put Spread

1. Look for a bearish market where you anticipate a modest decrease in the price of the underlying stock.

2. Check to see whether this stock has liquid options available.

3. Review put options premiums for different expiration dates and strike prices. Buy options with at least 90 days until expiration.

4. Investigate implied volatility values to see if the options are overpriced or undervalued. These spreads are best placed when volatility is low.

5. Explore past price trends and liquidity by reviewing price and volume charts over the past year. Look for chart patterns over the past one to three years to determine where you believe the stock should be by the date of expiration of the LEAPS spread.

6. Choose a higher strike put to buy and a lower strike put to sell. Both options must have the same expiration date.

7. Determine which spread to place. Remember, the higher the price and volatility, the wider the strikes can be. To do this, look at:

   • **Limited Risk:** The most that can be lost on the trade is the net debit of the two option premiums.

   • **Limited Reward:** Calculated by multiplying the difference in strike prices by 100 and then subtracting the net debit paid.

- **Breakeven:** Calculated by subtracting the net debit from the long strike price.
- **Return on Investment:** Reward/risk ratio.

8. Create a risk profile for the trade to graphically determine the trade's feasibility. If the underlying stock increases or exceeds the price of the short put, the trade reaches its maximum risk (loss) potential. Conversely, if the price of the underlying stock decreases or falls below the strike price of the long put, the maximum reward is attained.

9. Write down the trade in your trader's journal before placing the trade with your broker to minimize mistakes made in placing the order and to keep a record of the trade.

10. Make an exit plan before you place the trade.
    - Consider doing two contracts at once. Try to exit half the trade if the value of the trade doubles or when enough profit exists to cover the cost of the double contracts. Then the other trade will be virtually a free trade and you can take more of a risk, allowing it to accumulate a bigger profit. Close out the entire trade at 30 days to expiration.
    - If you have only one contract, exit the remainder of the trade when it is worth 80 percent of its maximum value. Close out the trade at 30 days to expiration.

11. Contact your broker to buy and sell the chosen put options. Place the trade as a limit order so that you limit the net debit of the trade.

12. Watch the market closely as it fluctuates. The profit on this strategy is limited—a loss occurs if the underlying stock rises to or above breakeven point.

13. Choose an exit strategy based on the price movement of the underlying stock and the effects of the changes in implied volatility on the prices of the options.
    - *The underlying stock falls below the short strike.* The short put is assigned and if exercised by the option holder, you are obligated to purchase 100 shares (per option) of the underlying stock from the option holder at the short put strike price. By exercising the long put, you can turn around and sell the shares received from the assigned option holder at the higher long put strike and pocket the difference—the maximum profit available.
    - *The underlying stock falls below the breakeven, but not as low as the short strike.* Sell a put with the long put strike and buy a put with the short strike. There should be a small profit remaining.
    - *The underlying stock remains above the breakeven, but below the long strike.* Sell a put with the long strike and buy a put with the short strike, which will partially offset the initial debit or allow you to pocket a small

profit; or wait until expiration and sell the long put to offset the trade's net debit and let the short option expire worthless.

- *The underlying stock rises above the long option.* Close out the entire trade at 30 days to expiration.

Bull Put Spread Review

In order to place a bull put spread (Figure F.4), the following 14 rules should be observed:

1. Look for a bullish market where you anticipate a modest increase in the price of the underlying stock.

2. Check to see whether this stock has liquid options available.

3. Review put options premiums for different expiration dates and strike prices. Look for combinations that produce high net credits. The Optionetics.com Platinum site allows for searches that will quickly qualify candidates for you. Since the maximum profit is limited to the net credit initially received, keep the net credit as high as possible to make the trade worthwhile.

4. Investigate implied volatility values to see whether the options are over-priced or undervalued. Look for options with forward volatility skews—

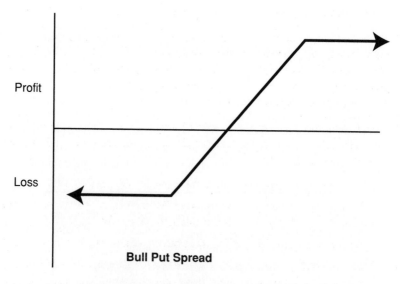

Bull Put Spread

Figure F.4   Bull Put Spread

where the higher strike option you are selling has higher IV than the lower strike option you are purchasing.

5. Explore past price trends and liquidity by reviewing price and volume charts over the past year.

6. Choose a lower strike put to buy and a higher strike put to sell. Both options must have the same expiration date. Keep the short strike at-the-money. Try to avoid selling an in-the-money put because it is already in danger of assignment and subsequent exercise.

7. Place bull put spreads using options with 45 days or less until expiration. Since the profit on this strategy depends on the options expiring worthless by expiration, it is best to use options with 45 days or less until expiration to give the underlying stock less time to move into a position where the short put will be assigned and the maximum loss occur.

8. Determine which spread to place. To do this, look at:
   - **Limited Risk:** The most you can lose is the difference between strikes times 100 minus the net credit received.
   - **Limited Reward:** The net credit received from placing the combination position.
   - **Breakeven:** Calculated by subtracting the net credit from the short put strike price. Make sure the breakeven is within the underlying stock's trading range.
   - **Return on Investment:** Reward/risk ratio.

9. Create a risk profile for the trade to graphically determine the trade's feasibility. It will show a limited profit above the upside breakeven and a limited loss below the downside breakeven, as in Figure F.4. In the best scenario, the underlying stock moves above the higher strike price by expiration and the short option expires worthless.

10. Write down the trade in your trader's journal before placing the trade with your broker to minimize mistakes made in placing the order and to keep a record of the trade.

11. Make an exit plan before you place the trade.
    - If the stock price keeps the short put OTM, then carry the trade until expiration, letting both options expire and gaining the full return.
    - If the short put is ITM or ATM, then buy it back at expiration, selling the long put as well (if it has any value in it).

12. Contact your broker to buy and sell the chosen put options. Place the trade as a limit order so that you maximize the net credit of the trade.

13. Watch the market closely as it fluctuates. The profit on this strategy is limited—a loss occurs if the underlying stock falls to or below the breakeven point.

14. Choose an exit strategy based on the price movement of the underlying stock and the effects of changes in the implied volatility on the prices of the options.

   • *The underlying stock rises above the short strike.* Options expire worthless and you keep the initial credit received (maximum profit).

   • *The underlying stock rises above the breakeven, but not as high as the short strike.* Buy back the short put to avoid assignment and exercise. If the short put is assigned and exercised by the option holder, you are then obligated to purchase 100 shares of the underlying stock at the short strike price. You can either keep the shares in hopes of a reversal or sell them at the current price for a small loss, which is balanced out by the initial credit received. To bring in additional money, sell the long put.

   • *The underlying stock remains below the breakeven, but above the long strike.* Buy back the short put to avoid assignment and exercise. If the short put is assigned and exercised by the option holder, you are then obligated to purchase 100 shares of the underlying stock at the short strike price. You can either keep the shares in hopes of a reversal or sell them at the current price for a small loss, which is not completely balanced out by the initial credit received. To mitigate this loss, sell the long put.

   • *The underlying stock falls below the long option.* Buy back the short put to avoid assignment and exercise. If the short put is assigned and exercised by the option holder, you are then obligated to purchase 100 shares of the underlying stock at the short strike price. By exercising the long put, you can sell these shares at the long strike price. This loss is partially mitigated by the initial credit received and results in the trade's maximum loss.

Bear Call Spread Review

In order to place a bear call spread (Figure F.5), the following 14 rules should be observed:

1. Look for a moderately bearish market where you anticipate a modest decrease in the price of the underlying stock—not a large move.

2. Check to see if this stock has liquid options available.

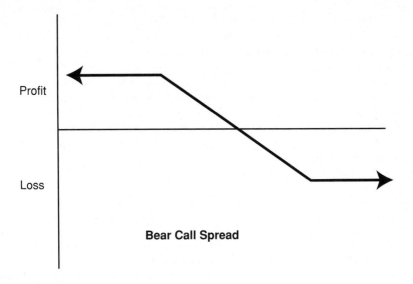

Figure F.5 Bear Call Spread

3. Review call options premiums for different expiration dates and strike prices. Look for combinations that produce high net credits. The Optionetics.com Platinum site allows for searches that will quickly qualify promising candidates for you. Since the maximum profit is limited to the net credit initially received, keep the net credit as high as possible to make the trade worthwhile.

4. Investigate implied volatility values to see whether the options are overpriced or undervalued. Look for options with a reverse volatility skew— lower strike options have higher implied volatility and higher strike options have lower implied volatility.

5. Explore past price trends and liquidity by reviewing price and volume charts over the past year.

6. Choose a higher strike call to buy and a lower strike call to sell. Both options must have the same expiration date.

7. Place bear call spreads using options with 45 days or less until expiration.

8. Determine which spread to place. To do this, look at:
   - **Limited Risk:** The most you can lose is the difference in strike prices minus the net credit.

- **Limited Reward:** The maximum reward is the net credit received from placing the combination position.
- **Breakeven:** Lowest strike price plus net credit received.
- **Return on Investment:** Reward/risk ratio.

9. Create a risk profile for the trade to graphically determine the trade's feasibility. The risk graph of a bear call spread slants downward from left to right, displaying its bearish bias. If the underlying stock falls to or past the price of the short call, the trade reaches its maximum profit potential. Conversely, if the price of the underlying stock rises to or exceeds the strike price of the long call, the maximum limited loss occurs.

10. Write down the trade in your trader's journal before placing the trade with your broker to minimize mistakes made in placing the order and to keep a record of the trade.

11. Make an exit plan before you place the trade.
    - If the stock price keeps the short call OTM, then carry the trade until expiration, letting both options expire and gaining the full return.
    - If the short call is ITM or ATM, then buy it back at expiration, selling the long put as well (if it has any value in it).

12. Contact your broker to buy and sell the chosen call options. Place the trade as a limit order so that you maximize the net credit of the trade.

13. Watch the market closely as it fluctuates. The profit on this strategy is limited—a loss occurs if the underlying stock rises to or above the breakeven point.

14. Choose an exit strategy based on the price movement of the underlying stock and the effects of changes in the implied volatility on the price of the options.
    - *The underlying stock falls below the short strike.* Let the options expire worthless to make the maximum profit (the initial credit received).
    - *The underlying stock falls below the breakeven, but not as low as the short strike.* Buy back the short call to avoid assignment and exercise. If the short call is assigned and exercised by the option holder, you are then obligated to deliver 100 shares of the underlying stock to the option holder at the short strike by purchasing these shares at the current price. The loss is offset by the initial credit received. By selling the long call, you can bring in an additional small profit.
    - *The underlying stock remains above the breakeven, but below the long strike.* Buy back the short call to avoid assignment and exercise. If the short call is assigned and exercised by the option holder, you are then obligated to deliver 100 shares of the underlying stock to the option holder

at the short strike price by purchasing these shares at the current price. This loss is mitigated by the initial credit received. Sell the long call for additional money to mitigate the loss.

- ***The underlying stock rises above the long option.*** Buy back the short call to avoid assignment and exercise. If the short call is assigned and exercised by the option holder, you are then obligated to deliver 100 shares of the underlying stock to the option holder at the short strike. By exercising the long call, you can turn around and buy those shares at the long call strike price regardless of how high the underlying stock has risen. This limits your loss to the maximum of the trade. The loss is partially mitigated by the initial credit received on the trade.

Call Ratio Backspread Review

In order to place a call ratio backspread (Figure F.6), the following 14 rules should be observed:

1. Look for a bullish market where you anticipate a large increase in the price of the underlying stock. Choose a stock that is a leader in its field, has an increasing stream of earnings, and exhibits quarter-over-quarter growth.

2. Check to see whether this stock has liquid options available.

3. Review options premiums for different expiration dates and strike prices. Place the position as a credit or as close to at-even as you can. Use options

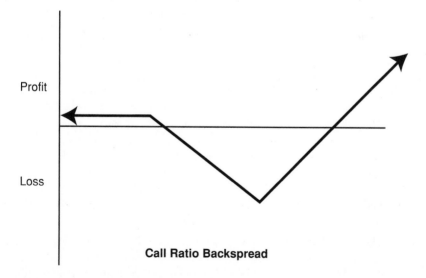

Call Ratio Backspread

Figure F.6   Call Ratio Backspread

with greater than 90 days until expiration. LEAPS options are a good choice since they provide an opportunity for time to work in your favor.

4. Investigate implied volatility values to see whether the options are overpriced or undervalued. This strategy is best placed in markets with a reverse volatility skew. In this environment, the lower strike options (the ones you want to sell) have higher implied volatility and can be overpriced. The higher strike options (the ones you want to buy) enjoy lower implied volatility and are often underpriced. By trading the reverse volatility skew, you can capture the implied volatility differential between the short and long options.

5. Explore past price trends and liquidity by reviewing price and volume charts over the past year.

6. A call ratio backspread is composed of selling the lower strike call (ITM or ATM) and buying a greater number of higher strike calls (OTM). It is not usually recommended to place positions with ratios greater than 0.67—use ratios that are a multiple of 1 to 2 (the most common) or 2 to 3. All options must have the same expiration date.

7. Look at options with at least 60 to 90 days until expiration to give the trade enough time to move into the money.

8. Determine which spread to place. To do this, look at:
   - **Limited Risk:** The number of short calls times the difference in strike price minus the net credit (or plus the net debit).
   - **Unlimited Reward:** Unlimited beyond the upside breakeven.
   - **Upside Breakeven:**
     Step 1: Difference in strike price times the number of short calls, divided by the number of long calls minus the number of short calls.
     Step 2: Take this value and add it to the higher strike price; then subtract the net credit.
   - **Downside Breakeven:** Lower strike price plus net credit.

9. Create a risk profile of the most promising option combination and graphically determine the trade's feasibility.

10. Write down the trade in your trader's journal before placing the trade with your broker to minimize mistakes made in placing the order and to keep a record of the trade.

11. Make an exit plan before you place the trade. How much money is the maximum amount you are willing to lose? How much profit do you want to make on the trade? For example, exit the trade when you have a 50 percent

profit at least 30 days prior to expiration of the options. Exit with a reasonable 50 percent gain. If not, then you should exit before the major amount of time decay occurs during the option's last 30 days.

12. Contact your broker to buy and sell the chosen options. Place the trade as a limit order.

13. You do not have to watch the market too closely on this type of trade. The profit on this strategy is unlimited.

14. Choose an exit strategy based on the price movement of the underlying stock and the effects of the changes in implied volatility on the prices of the options.

   • *The underlying stock falls below the downside breakeven.* Once you have made a reasonable profit (50 percent +), you should close out one short and one of the long positions. Since the other long option is now working with free money, you can afford to hold onto it for additional profit. It is recommended that you close out the position before 30 days until expiration unless you feel strongly that the stock will continue to decrease.

   • *The underlying stock rises between the upside and downside breakevens.* You should exit the entire position and take the loss.

   • *The underlying stock exceeds the upside breakeven.* Let the options expire worthless, or sell the long call at expiration to mitigate the loss.

Put Ratio Backspread Review

In order to place a put ratio backspread (Figure F.7), the following 14 rules should be observed:

1. Look for a bearish, low implied volatility market where you anticipate a sharp decline in the price of the underlying stock with increased volatility. Choose a stock that is a leader in its fields, has an increasing stream of earnings, and exhibits quarter-over-quarter growth.

2. Check to see whether this stock has liquid options available.

3. Review options premiums for different expiration dates and strike prices. Ideally use options with at least 90 days until expiration. LEAP options are also a good alternative for put ratio backspreads.

4. Investigate implied volatility values to see if the options are overpriced or undervalued. This strategy is best placed in markets with a forward volatility skew. In this environment, the higher strike options (the ones

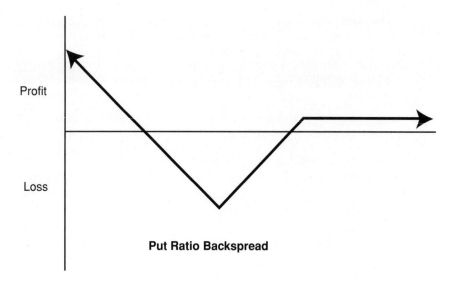

Figure F.7   Put Ratio Backspread

you want to sell) have higher implied volatility and can be overpriced. The lower strike options (the ones you want to buy) enjoy lower implied volatility and are often underpriced. By trading the forward volatility skew, you can capture the implied volatility differential between the short and long options.

5. Explore past price trends and liquidity by reviewing price and volume charts over the past year.

6. A put ratio backspread is created by selling a higher strike put (ITM or ATM) and buying a greater number of lower strike puts (OTM). It is not recommended to place position with ratios greater than 0.67. Use ratios that are a multiple of 1 to 2 (the most common) or 2 to 3. All options must have the same expiration date.

7. Look at options with at least 90 days or greater until expiration to give the trade enough time to move into the money.

8. Determine which spread to place. To do this, look at:
   - **Limited Risk:** The number of short puts times the difference in strike price minus the net credit (or plus the net debit).
   - **Limited Reward:** Limited beyond the downside breakeven until the stock reaches zero.
   - **Upside Breakeven:** Higher strike price minus net credit.

- **Downside Breakeven:**
  Step 1: Difference in strike price times the number of short puts, divided by the number of long puts minus the number of short puts.
  Step 2: Take this value, subtract it from lower strike price, and then add the net credit or subtract the net debit.

9. Create a risk profile of the most promising option combination and graphically determine the trade's feasibility.

10. Write down the trade in your trader's journal before placing the trade with your broker to minimize mistakes made in placing the order and to keep a record of the trade.

11. Make an exit plan before you place the trade. How much money is the maximum amount you are willing to lose? How much profit do you want to make on the trade?

12. Contact your broker to buy and sell the chosen options. Place the trade as a limit order.

13. You do not have to watch the market too closely on this type of trade. The profit on this strategy is limited as the stock falls to zero.

14. Choose an exit strategy based on the price movement of the underlying stock and the effects of changes in the implied volatility on the prices of the options.

    - *The underlying stock falls below the lower break even.* Once you have made a reasonable profit (50 percent +), you should close out the short put and one of the long positions. Since the other long option is now working with free money, you can afford to hold onto it for additional profit. It is recommended that you close out the position before 30 days until expiration unless you feel strongly that the stock will continue to decrease.

    - *The underlying stock rises between the lower and higher breakevens.* You should exit the entire position and take the loss if there is one.

    - *The underlying stock exceeds the higher breakeven.* Let the options expire worthless, or sell the long put at expiration to mitigate the loss.

Long Straddle Review

In order to place a long straddle (Figure F.8), the following 14 rules should be observed:

1. Look for a market with low volatility about to experience a sharp increase in volatility that moves the stock price in either direction beyond the upside or downside breakeven. The best long straddle opportunities are in

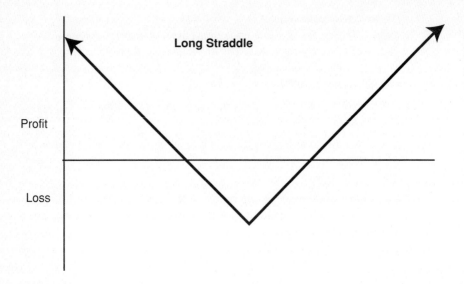

Figure F.8   Long Straddle

markets that are experiencing price consolidation, as they are often followed by a breakout. To find these consolidating markets, look through
your charts for familiar ascending, descending, or symmetric triangles. As
the stock price approaches the apex (point) of these triangles, they build
up energy, much like a coiled spring. At some point this energy needs to
be released, and that results in the price moving quickly. You don't care in
which direction because you are straddling.

2. Check to see whether this stock has liquid options available.

3. Review options premiums for different expiration dates and strike prices.

4. Investigate implied volatility values to see whether the options are overpriced or undervalued. Look for cheap options—those options that are at the
   low end of their implied volatility ranges, priced at less than the historical
   volatility of the underlying stock.

5. Explore past price trends and liquidity by reviewing price and volume
   charts over the past year.

6. A long straddle is composed of the simultaneous purchase of an ATM call
   and an ATM put with the same expiration month.

7. Place straddles with at least 60 to 90 days until expiration. You can also use
   LEAPS, except the premiums are often very high and would be profitable
   only with a very large movement in the underlying stock.

8. Determine which spread to place. To do this, look at:

   - **Limited Risk:** The most that can be lost on the trade is the double premiums paid.

   - **Unlimited Reward:** In both directions beyond the upside or downside breakevens (until the stock reaches zero).

   - **Upside Breakeven:** Calculated by adding the call strike price to the net debit paid.

   - **Downside Breakeven:** Calculated by subtracting the net debit from the put strike price.

9. Create a risk profile of the most promising option combination and graphically determine the trade's feasibility. A long straddle will have a V-shaped risk profile at expiration showing unlimited reward above and below the breakevens.

10. Write down the trade in your trader's journal before placing the trade with your broker to minimize mistakes made in placing the order and to keep a record of the trade.

11. Make an exit plan before you place the trade. For example, exit the trade when you have a 50 percent profit at least 30 days prior to expiration of the options. If you have a winner, you do not want to see it become a loser. In this case, exit with a reasonable 50 percent gain. If not, then you should exit before the major amount of time decay occurs, which is during the option's last 30 days. If you have multiple contracts, you can also adjust the position back to delta neutral to increase profit potential.

12. Contact your broker to buy and sell the chosen options. Place the trade as a limit order so that you limit the net debit of the trade.

13. Watch the market closely as it fluctuates. The profit on this strategy is unlimited—a loss occurs if the underlying stock closes between the breakeven points.

14. Choose an exit strategy based on the price movement of the underlying stock and the effects of changes in implied volatility on the prices of the options for the long straddle:

   - *XYZ falls below the downside breakeven.* You can close the put position for a profit. You can hold the call for a possible stock reversal.

   - *XYZ falls within the downside and upside breakevens.* This is the range of risk and will cause you to close out the position at a loss. The maximum risk is equal to the double premiums paid.

   - *XYZ rises above the upside breakeven.* You are in your profit zone again and can close the call position for a profit. You can hold the worthless put for a possible stock reversal.

Long Butterfly Spread Review

In order to place a long butterfly spread (Figure F.9), the following 14 rules should be observed:

1. Look for a sideways-moving market that is expected to remain within the breakeven points.

2. Check to see whether this stock has liquid options available.

3. Review options premiums for different expiration dates and strike prices. Make sure you have enough option premium to make the trade worthwhile, especially considering the commission fees of a multicontract spread.

4. Investigate implied volatility values to see if the options are overpriced or undervalued.

5. Explore past price trends and liquidity by reviewing price and volume charts over the past year.

6. A long butterfly is composed of all calls or all puts with the same expiration. Buy a lower strike option (at the support level), sell two higher strike options (at the equilibrium point), and buy one even higher option (at the resistance level).

7. Look at options with less than 45 days until expiration.

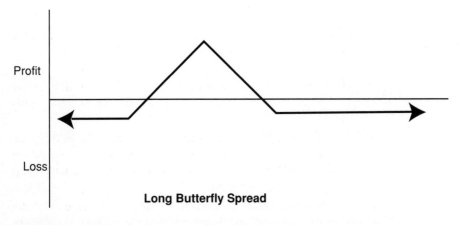

Long Butterfly Spread

Figure F.9   Long Butterfly Spread

8. Determine which spread to place. To do this, look at:
   - **Limited Risk:** Limited to the net debit paid or the options.
   - **Limited Reward:** Difference between highest strike and the short strike minus the net debit. Maximum profit is realized when the stock price equals the short strike.
   - **Upside Breakeven:** Highest strike price minus net debit paid.
   - **Downside Breakeven:** Lowest strike price plus net debit paid.
   - **Return on Investment:** Reward/risk ratio.

9. Create a risk profile of the most promising option combination and graphically determine the trade's feasibility. The risk curve of a long butterfly is shown in Figure F.9. The risk graph shows a limited risk outside of the breakevens and limited reward inside the breakevens.

10. Write down the trade in your trader's journal before placing the trade with your broker to minimize mistakes made in placing the order and to keep a record of the trade.

11. Make an exit plan before you place the trade. For example, exit the trade when you have a 50 percent profit or 30 days prior to expiration of the options. Exit with a reasonable 50 percent gain. If not, then you should exit before the major amount of time decay occurs during the option's last 30 days.

12. Contact your broker to buy and sell the chosen options. Place the trade as a limit order so that you limit the net debit of the trade.

13. Watch the market closely as it fluctuates. The profit on this strategy is limited—a loss occurs if the underlying stock closes outside the breakeven points.

14. Choose an exit strategy based on the price movement of the underlying stock and the effects of changes in the implied volatility on the prices of the options.
   - *XYZ falls below the downside breakeven.* Let your position expire worthless. The cost for this trade will be the net premium paid (plus commissions).
   - *XYZ falls within the downside and upside breakevens.* This is the range of profitability. Ideally you want to sell the long options and let the short options expire worthless. The maximum profit is when the underlying stock is equal to the short strike price.
   - *XYZ rises above the upside breakeven.* Either exit the trade or, if the short options are assigned and exercised, exercise your long options to counter.

Long Iron Butterfly Spread Review

In order to place a long iron butterfly spread (Figure F.10), the following 14 rules should be observed:

1. Look for a sideways-moving market that is expected to remain within the breakeven points.

2. Check to see whether this stock has liquid options available.

3. Review options premiums for different expiration dates and strike prices. Make sure you have enough option premium to make the trade worthwhile, especially considering the commission fees of a multicontract spread.

4. Investigate implied volatility values to see whether the options are over-priced or undervalued.

5. Explore past price trends and liquidity by reviewing price and volume charts over the past year.

6. A long iron butterfly is composed of four options with the same expiration. Buy one higher strike OTM call (at the resistance level), sell one ATM lower strike call, sell one slightly OTM lower strike put, and buy one even lower strike put (at the support level).

7. Look at options with at least 45 days until expiration.

8. Determine which spread to place. To do this, look at:
   - **Limited Risk:** The difference in strikes minus the net credit received for placing the position. This is usually a small value and is the reason why

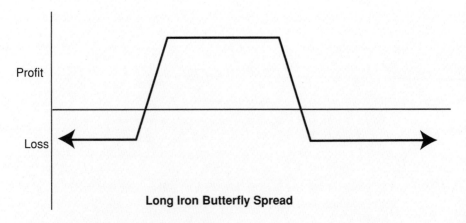

Long Iron Butterfly Spread

Figure F.10   Long Iron Butterfly Spread

this trade is attractive. Realize that commissions are not calculated in this example and can really eat into the profits.

- **Limited Reward:** Net credit received on placing the position.

- **Upside Breakeven:** Middle short call strike price plus net credit received.

- **Downside Breakeven:** Middle short put strike price minus net credit received.

- **Return on Investment:** Reward/risk ratio.

9. Create a risk profile of the most promising option combination and graphically determine the trade's feasibility. A risk graph for a long iron butterfly is very similar to the risk curve of a long butterfly, once again showing a limited risk outside of the breakevens and a limited reward between the breakevens.

10. Write down the trade in your trader's journal before placing the trade with your broker to minimize mistakes made in placing the order and to keep a record of the trade.

11. Make an exit plan before you place the trade. For example, exit the trade when you have a 50 percent profit or 30 days prior to expiration of the options. Exit with a reasonable 50 percent gain. If not, then you should exit before the major amount of time decay occurs during the option's last 30 days.

12. Contact your broker to buy and sell the chosen options. Place the trade as a limit order so that you limit the net debit of the trade.

13. Watch the market closely as it fluctuates. The profit on this strategy is limited—a loss occurs if the underlying stock closes outside the breakeven points.

14. Choose an exit strategy based on the price movement of the underlying stock and the effects of changes in implied volatility on the price of the options.

- *XYZ falls below the downside breakeven.* You should exit the trade to make sure you are not assigned the put side of your position. The calls can expire worthless. You're in the maximum risk range.

- *XYZ falls within the downside and upside breakevens.* This is the profit range, and ideally the position expires near the short strike price.

- *XYZ rises above the upside breakeven.* Similarly to the downside breakeven, you should exit the trade to make sure you are not assigned the call side of your position. The put options can expire worthless.

Calendar Spread Review

In order to place a calendar spread (Figure F.11), the following 14 rules should be observed:

1. Look for a market that has been range bound for at least three months and is expected to remain within a range for an extended period of time. A dramatic move by the underlying stock in either direction could unbalance the spread, causing it to widen.

2. Check to see whether this stock has liquid options available.

3. Review options premiums for different expiration dates and strike prices. We recommend using at-the-money options with as small a debit as possible.

4. Investigate implied volatility to look for volatility skew where short-term options have higher volatility to sell (causing you to receive higher premiums) than the longer-term options (the ones you will purchase).

5. Explore past price trends and liquidity by reviewing price and volume charts over the past year.

6. A calendar spread can be bullish or bearish in bias.
   - A bullish calendar spread employs an ATM long call with a distant expiration and an ATM short call with a closer expiration date.
   - A bearish calendar spread combines an ATM long put with a distant expiration date and an ATM short put with a closer expiration date.

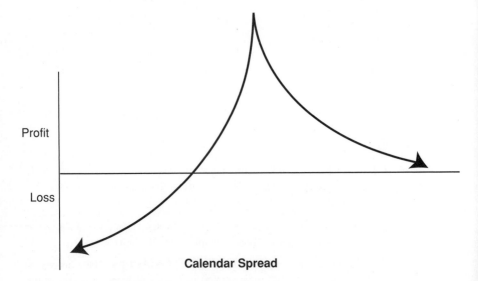

Figure F.11   Calendar Spread

7. Look at a variety of options with at least 90 days until expiration for the long option and less than 45 days for the short option.

8. Determine which spread to place. To do this, look at:

   - **Limited Risk:** Limited to the net debit when the position is placed. If you replay the long leg then your limited risk continues to decrease because you take in additional credit for replaying this strategy.

   - **Limited Reward:** Use software for calculation. The reward is limited but the exact maximum potential varies based on several factors including volatility, expiration months, and stock price.

   - **Breakevens and Return on Investment:** Since this is a more complex trade you should have a software package available to calculate your maximum risk, breakevens, and return on investment. The Platinum site at Optionetics.com provides this service.

9. Create a risk profile of the most promising option combination and graphically determine the trade's feasibility. A calendar spread (see the risk graph in Figure F.11) has limited risk and limited reward. It is a more complicated strategy, so a computerized risk graph is required for determining the needed variables of maximum profit and breakevens.

10. Write the trade in your trader's journal before placing the trade with your broker to minimize mistakes made in placing the order and to keep a record of the trade.

11. Make an exit plan before you place the trade. If the stock keeps the short option OTM, hold until expiration to keep the full credit. If the stock moves the short option ITM, you can either exit the trade for a loss, or buy back the short option prior to expiration and roll out the short option to the next month.

12. Contact your broker to buy and sell the chosen options. Place the trade as a limit order.

13. Watch the market closely as it fluctuates. The profit on this strategy is limited—a loss occurs if the underlying stock closes outside the breakeven points.

14. Choose an exit strategy based on the price movement of the underlying stock.

   For a bearish calendar spread:

   - *XYZ falls below the downside breakeven.* Both puts would increase in value one for one so they would offset each other, so the most you would lose is the premium paid.

   - *XYZ falls within the downside and upside breakevens.* If the stock falls within this range, you will make a profit. The largest profit potential occurs if the short-term option expires worthless and the long-term option retains time value. That is, the short-term option has lost value at a faster rate than the long-term option. At that point, close the trade or sell another short-term option. Once you have made a profit selling short-term puts, you can hold the long-term option for potential profits, close the position, roll out the short option to the next month, or use it as part of another strategy: for example, a bear put spread.

- *XYZ rises above the upside breakeven.* The short put would expire worthless and the long put may still have value.

For a bullish calendar spread:

- *XYZ falls below the breakeven.* You are in the maximum risk range. Exit the position for the loss.

- *XYZ falls within the downside and upside breakevens.* If the stock moves into this range, you will make a profit. The largest profit potential occurs if the short-term option expires worthless and the long-term option retains time value. That is, the short-term option has lost value at a faster rate than the long-term option. At that point, close the trade or sell another short-term option. Once you have made a profit selling short-term calls, you can hold the long-term call for potential profits, close the position, roll out the short option to the next month, or use it as part of another strategy: for example, bull call spread.

- *XYZ rises above the breakeven.* You are in the profit zone and can ideally let the short-term option expire and repeat the position by rolling forward the next month option.

Diagonal Spread Review

In order to place a diagonal time spread (Figure F.12), the following 14 rules should be observed:

1. Look for a market that has been range bound for at least three months and is expected to remain within a range or move modestly higher or lower over an extended period of time. A dramatic move by the underlying stock in either direction could unbalance the spread, causing it to widen.

2. Check to see whether this stock has liquid options available.

3. Review the option premiums for different expiration dates and strike prices.

4. Investigate implied volatility to look for volatility skew where short-term options have a higher volatility (causing you to receive higher premiums) than the longer-term options (the ones you will purchase). Unlike the calendar spread, look for different strike prices between the long-term and the short-term options.

5. Explore past price trends and liquidity by reviewing price and volume charts over the past year.

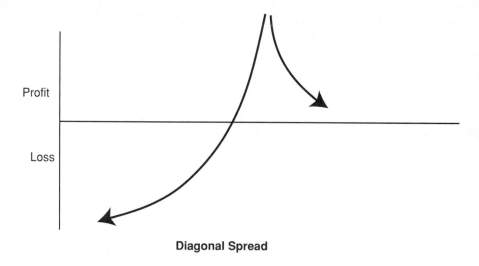

Diagonal Spread

Figure F.12   Diagonal Spread

6. A diagonal spread can be bullish or bearish in bias.
   - A bullish diagonal spread employs a long call with a distant expiration and a lower strike price along with a short call with a closer expiration date and a higher strike price.
   - A bearish diagonal spread combines a long put with a distant expiration date and a higher strike price along with a short put with a closer expiration date and a lower strike price.

7. Look at a variety of options with at least 90 days until expiration for the long option and less than 45 days for the short option.

8. Determine which spread to place. To do this, look at:
   - **Limited Risk:** Limited to the net debit when the position is placed. If you sell more than one short option then your limited risk continues to decrease because you take in additional credit for replaying this strategy.
   - **Limited Reward:** Use software for calculation. The reward is limited but the exact maximum potential varies based on several factors including volatility, expiration months, and stock price.
   - **Breakevens and Return on Investment:** Since this is a more complex trade you should have a software package available to calculate your maximum risk, breakevens, and return on investment. The Platinum site at Optionetics.com provides this service.

9. Create a risk profile of the most promising option combination and graphically determine the trade's feasibility. A diagonal spread (see Figure F.12)

has limited risk and limited reward. It is a more complicated strategy, so a computerized risk graph is required for determining the needed variables of maximum profit and breakevens.

10. Write the trade in your trader's journal before placing the trade with your broker to minimize mistakes made in placing the order and to keep a record of the trade.

11. Make an exit plan before you place the trade. If the stock keeps the short option OTM, hold until expiration to keep the full credit. If the stock moves the short option ITM, you can either exit the trade for a loss, or buy back the short option prior to expiration and roll out the short option to the next month.

12. Contact your broker to buy and sell the chosen options. Place the trade as a limit order.

13. Watch the market closely as it fluctuates. The profit on this strategy is limited—a loss occurs if the underlying stock moves too far in one direction or the other.

14. Choose an exit strategy based on the price movement of the underlying stock and the effects of changes in implied volatility on the prices of the options.

For a bearish diagonal spread:

- *XYZ falls below the downside breakeven*. Both puts will increase in value and offset each other. The most you would lose is the premium.

- *XYZ falls within the downside and upside breakevens.* If the stock falls within this range, you will make a profit. The largest profit occurs if the stock falls to the lower strike price (but not below) and the short put expires worthless. At that point, the long put will still have intrinsic and time value. Close the position, or sell another short-term put. Check the implied volatility first.

- *XYZ rises above the upside breakeven.* Both puts could expire worthless and you would lose the premium paid.

For a bullish diagonal spread:

- *XYZ falls below the breakeven.* You are in the maximum risk range. Exit the position for the loss.

- *XYZ falls within the downside and upside breakeven*. If the stock trades at the higher of the two strike prices at expiration, then the maximum profit is attained. In that case, the long call retains most of its value, but the short-term option expires worthless. At that point, the position should be closed or another call can be sold.

- *XYZ rises above the breakeven.* You are in your profit zone and can ideally let the short-term option expire worthless and repeat the position with the next month option.

Appendix **G**

Paper Trading Your Way to Success

Perhaps the best way to get the hang of trading options is to practice employing managed-risk options strategies through paper trading. The art of paper trading involves using real-time quotes and markets in hypothetical trades to test your knowledge and market savvy. The following pages are designed to help you apply the various options strategies reviewed in this manual to real-world trading. The spread templates in this section provide an organized format for making calculations of a specific trade using an options strategy described in this book as well as a way to track the progress of the trade. Feel free to photocopy the paper trading templates contained in this guide as needed for additional practice. You should continue paper trading until you gain enough confidence in the use of each strategy that you feel ready to spot an opportunity and use real money to place the trade.

For most investors, your paper trading prices will be based on those found on the Internet, or in *The Wall Street Journal* or *Investor's Business Daily*. We highly recommend using Optionetics.com to get your quotes since we can attest to their accuracy. Once you have determined where to get the price quotes, you need to decide which stocks to use for each trade. Go back over the material in each chapter to determine what kind of market conditions need to appear in order to prompt the use of the right strategy. When you find a stock that looks appropriate, look up the list of available options and try out various combinations of strikes and months until you find the best trade you can using the calculations for maximum risk, maximum reward, and breakevens. Make sure that you keep detailed notes as to why you chose that stock and any events that occur while you are waiting for the trade to become profitable on paper.

Once you decide on a trade, you can use the paper trading forms to track the progress of the trade as the prices fluctuate each day. You can also track it simultaneously using the Portfolio service at Optionetics.com. Before you place the trade, make sure to decide on an exit price if the trade loses money, and stick to it. Deciding ahead of time exactly how much money you can afford to lose is essential to becoming a successful options trader. Now, since you are simply paper trading, you may want to highlight your exit point and then continue to track the trade to see how it fares after this point. Although there will be times when your trade will turn around and head back into the profit zone, more often than not you'll get to witness it fall even further. But paper trading is about learning from your mistakes as much as it is learning from your successes, so get ready for an interesting journey.

Do not expect the first few trades that you place to make you a millionaire. Trading is a cumulative process that requires knowledge, experience, insight, and perseverance to master. Paper trading is a practical method of gaining experience without putting money on the line. Nonetheless, you must take this process seriously in order to learn from it. If you are diligent in your tracking process, you will gain a deeper understanding of each strategy that will serve you well when you enter the real-world marketplace.

Low Volatility Strategies	*High Volatility Strategies*	*Volatility Skew Strategies*
Long Straddle	Bull Put Spread	Calendar Spread
Bull Call Spread	Bear Call Spread	Diagonal Spread
Bear Put Spread	Long Butterfly Spread	
Call Ratio Backspread	Long Iron Butterfly Spread	
Put Ratio Backspread		

Table G.1   Covered Call

COVERED CALL

Strategy: Sell a higher strike call with less than 60 days to expiration against 100 long shares of the underlying stock.

Entry Date:	**Underlying Stock:**
Option Expiration Month:	**Stock Price:**
Short Strike Price to Sell:	**Higher Call Premium:**
Maximum Reward: Unlimited beyond downside breakeven	**Maximum Risk:** (Strike price – initial stock price) + short call credit
Breakeven: Initial stock price – call premium	**Exit Strategy:**
Reasons for Taking Trade:	**Technical Analysis:**

COVERED CALL TRADE:

		LONG STOCK			SHORT CALL			TRADE
DATE	STOCK PRICE	NO. OF SHARES	PROFIT/ LOSS	PREMIUM	IV	PROFIT/ LOSS		NET PROFIT/LOSS

Events That Influenced Stock Movement

Table G.2   Bull Call Spread

BULL CALL SPREAD	
Strategy: Buy a lower strike call and sell a higher strike call with the same expiration.	
Entry Date:	**Underlying Stock:**
Option Expiration Month:	**Stock Price:**
Long Lower Strike Price to Buy:	**Long Lower Call Premium:**
Short Higher Strike Price to Sell:	**Short Higher Call Premium:**
Maximum Risk: Long premium – short premium = net debit	**Maximum Reward:** (Difference in strikes × 100) – net debit
Breakeven: Lower strike price + net debit	**Exit Strategy:**
Reasons for Taking Trade:	**Technical Analysis:**

BULL CALL SPREAD TRADE:

DATE	STOCK PRICE	LONG STOCK			SHORT CALL			TRADE NET PROFIT/LOSS
		PREMIUM	IV	PROFIT/ LOSS	PREMIUM	IV	PROFIT/ LOSS	

Events That Influenced Stock Movement

Table G.3 Bear Put Spread

BEAR PUT SPREAD	
Strategy: Buy a higher strike put and sell a lower strike put with the same expiration.	
Entry Date:	**Underlying Stock:**
Option Expiration Month:	**Stock Price:**
Long Higher Strike Price to Buy:	**Long Higher Put Premium:**
Short Lower Strike Price to Sell:	**Short Lower Put Premium:**
Maximum Risk: Long premium – short premium = net debit	**Maximum Reward:** (Difference in strikes × 100) – net debit
Breakeven: Higher strike price – net debit	**Exit Strategy:**
Reasons for Taking Trade:	**Technical Analysis:**

BEAR PUT SPREAD TRADE:

		LONG PUT			SHORT PUT			TRADE
DATE	STOCK PRICE	PREMIUM	IV	PROFIT/ LOSS	PREMIUM	IV	PROFIT/ LOSS	NET PROFIT/LOSS

Events That Influenced Stock Movement

Table G.4   Bull Put Spread

BULL PUT SPREAD

Strategy: Buy a lower strike put and sell a higher strike put with the same expiration.

Entry Date:	**Underlying Stock:**
Option Expiration Month:	**Stock Price:**
Long Lower Strike Price to Buy:	**Long Lower Put Premium:**
Short Higher Strike Price to Sell:	**Short Higher Put Premium:**
Maximum Risk: (Difference in strikes × 100) – net credit	**Maximum Reward:** Short premium – long premium = net credit
Breakeven: Higher strike price – net credit	**Exit Strategy:**
Reasons for Taking Trade:	**Technical Analysis:**

BULL PUT SPREAD TRADE:

		LONG PUT			SHORT PUT			TRADE
DATE	STOCK PRICE	PREMIUM	IV	PROFIT/ LOSS	PREMIUM	IV	PROFIT/ LOSS	NET PROFIT/LOSS

Events That Influenced Stock Movement

Table G.5 Bear Call Spread

BEAR CALL SPREAD

Strategy: Buy a higher strike call and sell a lower strike call with the same expiration.

Entry Date:	**Underlying Stock:**
Option Expiration Month:	**Stock Price:**
Long Higher Strike Price to Buy:	**Long Higher Call Premium:**
Short Lower Strike Price to Sell:	**Short Lower Call Premium:**
Maximum Risk: (Difference in strikes × 100) – net credit	**Maximum Reward:** Short premium – long premium = net credit
Breakeven: Lower strike price + net credit	**Exit Strategy:**
Reasons for Taking Trade:	**Technical Analysis:**

BEAR CALL SPREAD TRADE:

		LONG CALL			SHORT CALL			TRADE
DATE	STOCK PRICE	PREMIUM	IV	PROFIT/ LOSS	PREMIUM	IV	PROFIT/ LOSS	NET PROFIT/LOSS

Events That Influenced Stock Movement

315

Table G.6 Call Ratio Backspread

CALL RATIO BACKSPREAD

Strategy: Sell lower strike calls and buy a greater number of higher strike calls with the same expiration (the ratio must be less than .67).

Entry Date:	**Underlying Stock:**
Option Expiration Month:	**Stock Price:**
Higher Strike Price to Buy:	**# × Long Call Premium:**
Lower Strike Price to Sell:	**# × Short Call Premium:**
Maximum Risk: [(# short calls × difference in strikes) × 100] − net credit (or + net debit)	**Maximum Reward:** Unlimited to the upside beyond the breakeven.
Upside Breakeven: Higher strike + [(difference in strikes × # of short calls) divided by (# of long calls − # of short calls)] − net credit (or + net debit)	**Downside Breakeven:** Short strike price + net credit (or − net debit)
Reasons for Taking Trade:	**Exit Strategy:**

CALL RATIO BACKSPREAD TRADE:

		LONG CALLS				SHORT CALLS				TRADE NET
DATE	STOCK PRICE	NO. OF CONTRACTS	PREMIUM	IV	PROFIT/ LOSS	NO. OF CONTRACTS	PREMIUM	IV	PROFIT/ LOSS	PROFIT/ LOSS

Events That Influenced Stock Movement

Table G.7 Put Ratio Backspread

PUT RATIO BACKSPREAD

Strategy: Sell higher strike puts and buy a greater number of lower strike puts with the same expiration (the ratio must be less than .67).

Entry Date:	*Underlying Stock:*
Option Expiration Month:	*Stock Price:*
Lower Strike Price to Buy:	*# × Long Call Premium:*
Higher Strike Price to Sell:	*# × Short Call Premium:*
Maximum Risk: [(# short puts × difference in strikes) × 100] – net credit (or + net debit)	*Maximum Reward:* Unlimited to the downside beyond the breakeven.
Upside Breakeven: Short strike price – net credit (or + net debit)	*Downside Breakeven:* Lower strike – [(difference in strikes × # of short puts) divided by (# of long puts – # of short puts)] + net credit (or – net debit)
Reasons for Taking Trade:	*Exit Strategy:*

PUT RATIO BACKSPREAD TRADE:

DATE	STOCK PRICE	LONG PUTS				SHORT PUTS				TRADE NET
		NO. OF CONTRACTS	PREMIUM	IV	PROFIT/ LOSS	NO. OF CONTRACTS	PREMIUM	IV	PROFIT/ LOSS	PROFIT/ LOSS

Events That Influenced Stock Movement

Table G.8 Long Straddle

LONG STRADDLE

Strategy: Buy an equal number of puts and calls with the same at-the-money strike price and expiration month.

Entry Date:	**Underlying Stock:**
Expiration and Strike:	**Stock Price:**
ATM Call Premium to Buy:	**ATM Put Premium to Buy:**
Maximum Risk: (Call premium + put premium) × 100 = net debit	**Maximum Reward:** Unlimited beyond breakevens
Upside Breakeven: Strike price + net debit	**Downside Breakeven:** Strike price − net debit
Reasons for Taking Trade:	**Technical Analysis:**

LONG STRADDLE TRADE:

		LONG CALLS			LONG PUTS			TRADE
DATE	STOCK PRICE	PREMIUM	IV	PROFIT/ LOSS	PREMIUM	IV	PROFIT/ LOSS	NET PROFIT/LOSS

Events That Influenced Stock Movement

Table G.9   Long Butterfly Spread

LONG BUTTERFLY SPREAD

Strategy: Use all calls or all puts. Buy a higher strike at resistance, sell two higher strikes at equilibrium, and buy a lower strike at support.

Entry Date:	**Underlying Stock:**
Option Expiration Month:	**Stock Price:**
Highest Strike Option:	**Premium to Buy:**
Middle Strike Option:	**2 Premiums to Sell:**
Lowest Strike Option:	**Premium to Buy:**
Maximum Risk: (Long – short premiums) × 100 = net debit	**Maximum Reward:** [(Higher strike – short strike) × 100] – net debit
Upside Breakeven: Highest strike price – net debit	**Downside Breakeven:** Lowest strike price + net debit
Reasons for Taking Trade:	**Exit Strategy:**

LONG BUTTERFLY SPREAD TRADE:

		HIGHER LONG OPTION			MIDDLE SHORT OPTIONS			LOWER LONG OPTION			TRADE
DATE	STOCK PRICE	PREMIUM	IV	PROFIT/ LOSS	PREMIUM	IV	PROFIT/ LOSS	PREMIUM	IV	PROFIT/ LOSS	NET PROFIT/ LOSS

Events That Influenced Stock Movement

Table G.10 Long Iron Butterfly

LONG IRON BUTTERFLY

Strategy: Buy a higher strike call at resistance, sell an ATM strike call, sell a lower strike put, and buy an even lower strike put at support.

Entry Date:	**Underlying Stock:**
Option Expiration Month:	**Stock Price:**
Highest Strike Call:	**Premium to Buy:**
Middle Strike Call:	**Premium to Sell:**
Middle Strike Put:	**Premium to Sell:**
Lowest Strike Put:	**Premium to Buy:**
Maximum Risk: Difference in strikes minus the net credit	**Maximum Reward:** (Short − long premiums) × 100 = net credit
Upside Breakeven: Middle short call strike price + net credit	**Downside Breakeven:** Middle short put strike price − net credit
Reasons for Taking Trade:	**Exit Strategy:**

LONG IRON BUTTERFLY TRADE:

		HIGHER LONG CALL			MIDDLE SHORT CALL			MIDDLE SHORT PUT			LOWER LONG PUT			TRADE
DATE	STOCK PRICE	PREMIUM	IV	PROFIT/ LOSS	PREMIUM	IV	PROFIT/ LOSS	PREMIUM	IV	PROFIT/ LOSS	PREMIUM	IV	PROFIT/ LOSS	NET PROFIT/ LOSS

Events That Influenced Stock Movement

Table G.11   Calendar Spread

CALENDAR SPREAD

Strategy: Sell a short-term option and buy a long-term option using at-the-money options with as small a net debit as possible (use all calls or all puts). Calls can be used for a more bullish bias and puts can be used for a more bearish bias. This spread profits as the short front month options decay faster than the long back month options.

Entry Date:	**Underlying Stock:**
Option Strike Price:	**Stock Price:**
Long-Term Option Premium to Buy:	**Expiration Month:**
Short-Term Option Premium to Sell:	**Expiration Month:**
Maximum Risk: (Long premium − short premium) × 100 = net debit	**Maximum Reward:** Use software to compute.
Upside Breakeven: Use software to compute.	**Downside Breakeven:** Use software to compute.
Reasons for Taking Trade:	**Exit Strategy:**

CALENDAR SPREAD TRADE:

		LONG-TERM OPTION TO BUY			SHORT-TERM OPTION TO SELL			TRADE
DATE	STOCK PRICE	PREMIUM	IV	PROFIT/ LOSS	PREMIUM	IV	PROFIT/ LOSS	NET PROFIT/LOSS

Events That Influenced Stock Movement

Table G.12 Diagonal Spread

DIAGONAL SPREAD

Strategy: Sell a short-term option and buy a long-term option using different strikes with as small a net debit as possible (use all calls or all puts). This spread profits as the short front month options decay faster than the long back month options. For a bullish diagonal spread, buy a call with a distant expiration date and a lower strike price and sell a call with a closer expiration date and a higher strike price. For a bearish diagonal spread, buy a put with a distant expiration date and a higher strike price and sell a put with a closer expiration date and a lower strike price.

Entry Date:	**Underlying Stock:**
Option Strike Price:	**Stock Price:**
Long-Term Option Premium to Buy:	**Expiration Month:**
Short-Term Option Premium to Sell:	**Expiration Month:**
Maximum Risk: (Long – short premiums) × 100 = net debit	**Maximum Reward:** Use software to compute.
Upside Breakeven: Use software to compute.	**Downside Breakeven:** Use software to compute.
Reasons for Taking Trade:	**Exit Strategy:**

DIAGONAL SPREAD TRADE:

DATE	STOCK PRICE	LONG-TERM OPTION TO BUY			SHORT-TERM OPTION TO SELL			TRADE NET PROFIT/LOSS
		PREMIUM	IV	PROFIT/ LOSS	PREMIUM	IV	PROFIT/ LOSS	

Events That Influenced Stock Movement

Index

AAA rating, 77
Accounting fraud, 96
Actual volatility, *see* Historical volatility
Adelphia, 18
Advance/decline line, 221, 264
Adviser sentiment, 263
Aggressive diagonal spread, 204–205
Aggressive investors, 37, 166
Alcoa Inc. (AA), 237–238
American Stock Exchange (AMEX):
  Airline Index ($XAL), 31, 88
  Biotechnology Index ($BTK), 31, 61, 88
  Natural Gas Index ($XNG), 88
  performance of, 24, 26, 77, 85–86, 89, 116, 124
  QQV (QQQ volatility index), 117–119
American-style options, 74, 88–89, 116, 118
America Online (AOL), 43–44, 46–47, 53, 61, 71. *See also* AOL Time Warner (AOL)
Analysis paralysis, 59
Analyst upgrades/downgrades, 198
Announcements, impact of, 3, 37, 93, 96, 108, 197, 232, 257–258
AOL Time Warner (AOL), 45, 78, 124, 155–156, 174–175, 178–185
Art of Contrary Thinking, The (Neill), 224
Arthur Andersen, 18
Asian currency crisis, 17
Ask price, 27, 33, 85
Assignment, stock options, 74, 116
AT&T (T), 25
At-the-money (ATM) options:
  bear call credit spread, 173
  bear put debit spread, 150–151
  bull call debit spread, 151–152
  butterfly spread, 177–178
  characteristics of, 74, 79, 84, 133
  credit spreads, 170–173
  greeks, 106–107
  implied volatility and, 95, 106–107, 135
  long iron butterfly spread, 178
  low-volatility environment, 135
  puts, 140–141, 170–172
  volatility skews, 196

Average True Range (ATR):
  historical volatility and, 39, 45, 47, 51, 53, 69
  implications of, 247–248
  standard deviation *vs.*, 67–68
  using, 64–66
Avon Products, 15

Baker, James, 16
Balance sheets, 218
Barron's, 260, 263
Bay of Pigs, 14
Beanie Babies, 169
Bear call credit spreads, 172–175, 195
Bear call spreads:
  characteristics of, 175, 194
  strategy, *see* Bear call spread strategy
Bear call spread strategy:
  review of, 290–293
  stock analysis template, 314
  summary of, 278
Bearish diagonal spread, 205–206
Bearish divergence, 242, 244
Bearish environment, 140–143
Bearish investors, 120, 128
Bearish market, 236, 243, 264, 286, 290, 295
Bearish nonconfirmation, 242
Bearish sentiment, 123, 126–127
Bear market, *see* Bearish market
  average duration, 20
  causes of, 10–16
  characteristics of, 10
  defined, 20, 218
  Great Depression, 9, 12–14
  historical perspective, 10–17
  selling in, 54
  wealth preservation and, 21–22
Bear put debit spreads, 150–151
Bear put spread:
  characteristics of, 147
  review of, 285–288
  stock analysis template, 312
  summary of, 278
Bear trap, defined, 218
Beta, historical volatility and, 39, 50–51, 53
Bid price, 27, 33, 85

BigCharts, 261
Black, Fischer, 36, 81, 92, 214
Black-Scholes option pricing model, 36, 38,
    80–81, 92, 105, 108, 112, 148, 214
Black Tuesday, 9–10
Blitzer, David, 10
Bloody Monday, 53
Bollinger, John, 47, 58, 245
Bollinger bands:
    charting, 224
    convergence and divergence of, 59, 68
    historical volatility and, 38–40, 47–48, 50–51,
        53
    implications of, 245–247
    standard deviations and, 67
    trading with, 58–60, 90
Bond investments, 13, 220
Book value, 218
Book-to-bill ratio, 30–31
Bottoms, Bollinger bands, 59
Breakeven, *see specific types of options strategies*
Breakout, charting, 221
Breakout moves, 60
Bristol-Myers, 18
Brokerage firm:
    index options, 88
    margin account requirements, 170
    in options trading, generally, 90
    stock options, 74, 86–87
Brokers, role in options trading, 86–87
Bull call debit spread, 151–154
Bull call spread:
    characteristics of, 146, 148, 151–154, 193–194
    strategy, *see* Bull call spread strategy
Bull call spread strategy:
    review of, 283–285
    stock analysis template, 311
    summary of, 277
Bullish diagonal spread, 203
Bullish divergence, 242, 244
Bullish environment, call options, 132–140
Bullish investors, 103, 110, 120, 128–129
Bullish market, 73, 236, 242, 288, 293
Bullish sentiment, 123, 126, 128
Bullish trends, 233
Bull market, *see* Bullish market
    characteristics of, 10
    defined, 217
    historical perspective, 20
Bull put credit spreads, characteristics of,
    170–172
Bull put spread strategy:
    review of, 288–290
    stock analysis template, 313
    summary of, 278

Bull trap, defined, 218
Business 2.0, 260
Business Week, 260
Butterfly spreads:
    call, example of, 181–183
    characteristics of, 176–177
    long, 181–186
    long iron, example of, 177–181
    put, example of, 183–186
    range trading and, 176–177
Buy-and-hold philosophy, 6, 19–21, 100,
    211
Buy low/sell high theory, 3
Buy signals, 57–58, 67–68, 127
Buy/write strategy, 103

Calendar spread:
    bearish, 209–210, 305
    bullish, 208–209, 304
    characteristics of, generally, 207–210
    defined, 201
    placing, 202
    stock analysis template, 320
    strategy, *see* Calendar spread strategy
Calendar spread strategy:
    review of, 304–306
    summary of, 280
Call butterfly spread, 181–183
Call options:
    buying, 122–123, 132–140
    characteristics of, 72–73, 75–76, 78–79, 83,
        87, 89, 94
    covered, 102–103, 164–165
    risk management, 100
Call ratio backspread strategy:
    characteristics of, 157
    review of, 293–295
    stock analysis template, 315
    summary of, 279
Call writer, 72
Carter, Jimmy, 15
Cash flow, 218
CBOE Internet Index ($INX), 31, 88
CBOE Volatility Index (VIX):
    characteristics of, 111–112, 118–119, 129,
        162–163
    computing, 112
    defined, 95, 111
    as "fear gauge," 113, 119–120, 129
    high, implications of, 120–121, 127–128
    history of, 112–114
    low, implications of, 120–121, 127–128
    normal trading range, 114
CBS MarketWatch, 261
CBS MarketWatch 75 ($MWX), 89

Celera Genomics Corp.-Applera Corp. (CRA), 241
Chaos, 7
Charting:
 breakout, 221
 characteristics of, 40, 43–51, 95, 121
 chart patterns, 221–222
 historical volatility, 250
 indicators, 222, 224
 resistance, 221
 support, 221
 trend lines, 221
Chicago Board Options Exchange (CBOE):
 performance, 21, 72, 76, 80–81, 85–86, 88–89, 110, 129
 put-to-call ratios, 123–126, 129
Ciena Corporation (CIEN), 61–63, 65, 199–200
Cisco Systems (CSCO), 84, 116, 171–173
ClearStation, 261
Closing price:
 implied volatility and, 121
 moving averages and, 58
 significance of, 40–41, 44
Closing transactions, 78
CNBC, 258–259
CNN, 259
Coca-Cola (KO), 73, 139
Cold War, 14
Colgate-Palmolive (CL), 45–46
Collateral, 212
Commissions, options trading, 87
Commodity Channel Index (CCI), 224
Commodity prices, 64–65
Common Stocks as Long-Term Investments (Smith), 9
Computer software programs, moving averages, 58
Consolidation patterns, 231–235
Construction Spending report, 273
Consumer Price Index (CPI), 272
Contagion, 17, 225
Contrarian investors, 120, 123, 125–128, 225
Corporate misconduct, 17–19
Corrections:
 defined, 20, 217
 implications of, 55, 217
Correlation, implications of, 67–68
Covered calls:
 characteristics of, 83, 102–105
 risk management, 102–105
 strategy, *see* Covered call strategy
Covered call strategy:
 review of, 281–283
 stock analysis template, 310
 summary of, 277

Covered call writing, 87
Credit spreads:
 bear call, 172–175, 195
 bull put, 170–172
 characteristics of, generally, 169–172
Crises/chaos, impact of:
 bear markets, 10–17, 21–22
 buy-and-hold philosophy, 19–21
 corporate misconduct, 17–19
 Global Financial Crisis, 17, 113–114, 116
Crowd psychology, 110, 119, 123, 128–129
Cup and handle pattern, 221–222

Debit spreads:
 bear put, 150–151
 bull call, 151–154
 low-volatility, 146–150
Debt ratios, 219
Deep-in-the-money options, 75, 105, 107, 149
Deep-out-of-the-money options, 79–80, 105, 107, 149
Defense stocks, 89
Dell Computer (DELL), 86, 189–193
Delta(s), 76, 105–106
Delta neutral strategies, 76
Delta-neutral trade portfolio, 106
Derivatives, 91
Diagonal spread(s):
 bearish, 307
 bullish, 307
 calendar spreads *vs.*, 202
 characteristics of, 201–206
 defined, 202
 strategy, *see* Diagonal spread strategy
Diagonal spread strategy:
 review of, 306–308
 stock analysis template, 321
 summary of, 281
Dial Corporation (DL), 198–199
Directional price risk, 167–168
Directional strategies, defined, 148
Dividend(s), generally:
 bear put spread, 148
 covered calls and, 103
 impact of, 112
 option prices and, 79, 93–94
 payout ratio, 94
Dogs of the Dow Index ($MUT), 89
Dot-com stocks, 169, 194
Double bottom/double top, 221–222
Double contracts, 285, 292
Dow, Charles, 9, 29–30
Dow Jones Industrial Average, 8–10, 20, 22–23, 27–30, 34–35, 39, 53, 87–89, 113–114, 116, 127, 214, 259

Dow Jones Newswire, 84
Dow Jones Rail Average, 27
Dow Jones Transportation Average ($DTX),
   234–236
Downtrends, 241, 243
Dynegy (DYN), 202–206

Earnings announcements, impact of, 37, 81, 96,
   108, 163
Earnings reports:
   implied volatility and, 174–175
   volatility skews, 198
Earnings surprises, 219
Eastman Kodak (EK), 15, 55–56
eBay Inc. (EBAY), 243–244
Economic conditions, impact on stock market, 14,
   113–114
EDGAR-Online, 261
18-day moving average, 58
Elder, Dr. Alexander, 243
Employment Cost Index (ECI), 272
Employment report, 270
Employment Situation report, 271
Enron, 18
Entry points, 57
eSignal, 261
E*Trade (ET), 232–233
European-style options, 74, 88–89, 116
Exchange-traded funds (ETFs), 31–33
Ex-dividends, 94
Exercising an option:
   calls, 132–133
   index, 88
   put options, 140–143
   QQQ options, 118–119
   stock, 74–75, 77–78, 88
Exit points, 57
Exit strategy, 282, 285, 287, 289, 292, 294–295,
   297, 299, 301, 303, 305, 308
Expiration date, *see specific types of options
   strategies*
   bear put spread, 148
   call options, 132–133
   significance of, 60, 72–73, 77–78, 92, 101,
      107, 112
Expiration month (series), 197–201
Exponential moving average, 222
Extreme volatility, 63

Factory Orders—Durable Goods and Nondurable
   Goods report, 273
Fair value, 61
Fastow, Andrew, 18
Fear, market sentiment, 110, 119, 123, 129, 163
Federal Open Market Committee (FOMC), 13

Federal Reserve, 12–15, 17
Federal Reserve Act (1913), 13
Federal Reserve Board, 11
50-day moving average (MA), 48, 55, 58,
   239–240
50-day time frames, 61
Financial magazines, as information resource,
   257–258, 260
Financial markets:
   changing nature of, 16–17
   unpredictability of, 7
First Index Investment Trust, 20
Fixed deltas, 106
Flags, 233
Fortune, 260
Forward volatility skew, 175
Frown, 194–196
Fundamental analysis:
   bottom-up approach, 218–220
   market relationships, 220
   top-down approach, 220
Future earnings, 218
Futures options, 88

Gamma, 106–107
Gap down/gap up, 65
Gaps, volatility measurement, 64–65
General Electric, 9, 125
General Motors (GM), 44–45
Get-rich-quick schemes, 90
Gilead Sciences (GILD), 207–210
Global Crossing, 18
Global Financial Crisis, 17, 113–114, 116
Going long, 132
Going short, 132
Government Reports matrix, 270–273
Granville, Joseph, 237
Great Depression, 9, 12–14
Greed, market sentiment and, 119, 123, 129
Greeks:
   delta, 105–106
   gamma, 106–107
   theta, 107, 201
   vega, 107–108, 152–153, 183, 186
Gross Domestic Product (GDP), 273
Growth stock investors, 218
GSTI Computer Software Index ($GSO), 88
Gustafson, Gordon, 67–68

Halliburton Co. (HAL), 55–57, 61
Head and shoulders, 222–223
Hedging, 2, 90, 93, 96, 119, 122, 126, 178,
   197
Hewlett Packard, 15
High-beta stock, 50

High volatility:
  defined, 250
  example of, 33–34
  implications of, 21–22, 36, 54
  investment strategies, *see* High volatility
    strategies
  moving averages and, 58
  option prices and, 94
  on stock charts, 45, 47
High volatility strategies:
  butterfly spreads, 176–186
  covered calls, 164–165
  credit spreads, 170–176
  implied volatility and, 162–163
  long straddles, 318
  naked put options, 165–168
  overview, 310
  range trading, 176–177
  selling options premium, 163–164
  uncovered option sales, 168–170
High-yield stocks, 94
Histograms, 224, 236, 242
Historical volatility:
  applications, 250
  defined, 36, 39, 51, 95, 250
  implications of, generally, 71
  implied volatility distinguished from, 38–39
  measurement of, 40
  trading, 53–54
Holding Company Depository Receipts
    (HOLDRs), 31–34
Horizontal spreads, 207–210
Housing Starts and Sales of New and Existing
    Homes report, 273

IBM, 65–66, 69, 72–73, 82, 92, 124, 132,
    164–165, 166–168, 214, 228–230, 239–240
Illiquid markets, 84
ImClone, 19
Implied volatility (IV):
  analysis of, 92
  applications, 251
  bear put spread, 148–149
  bull call spread, 152–153
  buying options, 100–102, 133–139
  calculation of, 112
  call options, generally, 133–139
  call ratio backspread, 155
  covered call, 102–105
  credit spreads, 174
  defined, 39, 91–93, 251
  fluctuation of, 92–94
  gauging, 93–95
  graph, 251–252
  greeks, 108, 152

historical volatility distinguished from, 38–39,
    109
  implications of, generally, 5, 36, 38–39,
    108–109, 162–163, 214–215, 235–236
  influential factors, 96
  iron butterfly, 180
  marketwide spikes, causes of, 163
  OEX options, 114, 119, 133–144
  option prices and, 108
  protective put, 100–102
  put options, 141–143
  selling options, 102–105
  in sentiment analysis, 264
  statistical volatility *vs.*, example of, 97–100
  stock options and, 70
  vega, 107–108
  VIX, 120–121, 125–129
Import and Export Prices report, 271
Indexes:
  characteristics of, 27–34. *See also specific*
    indexes
  popular, 226–227
Index options, 23, 87–89
Indicators:
  Average True Range (ATR), 64–66, 69
  Bollinger bands, 58–60, 68–69
  moving averages, 54–58, 68
Individual retirement accounts (IRAs), 102, 193
Industrial Production Index, 273
Inflation, 14–16
InfoBeat, 261–262
Information resources:
  financial magazines, 257–258, 260, 263
  financial newspapers, 19, 25, 29, 259, 309
  Optionetics, 40–41, 43, 45, 63, 69, 76, 80, 84,
    95, 124, 153, 160, 212, 262, 266, 291, 307,
    310
  television programs, 258–259
  web sites, 260–263
Initial public offering (IPO), 24–25
Intel (INTC), 25–27, 30, 32, 116
Interest rate(s):
  bear put spread and, 148
  falling, 13, 15–16
  market relationships, 220
  option prices and, 79–80, 84, 94
  rising, 12–15, 28
International Flavor and Fragrances (IFF), 157–158
International Securities Exchange (ISE), 77,
    84–86
Internet stocks, 191
In-the-money (ITM) options:
  butterfly spreads, 177
  characteristics of, generally, 74–77
  deltas, 105–106

In-the-money (ITM) options *(Continued)*
  diagonal spreads, 204
  high-volatility environment, 172
  liquidity and, 84
  low-volatility environment, 131–133, 140
  option prices, 79–80
Intraday stock prices, 26, 33
Intrinsic value, 75–76, 78–80
Investment Company Institute, 20
Investor confidence, 19
Investor psychology, 54
Investor sentiment, 125, 263
Investor's Business Daily, 259–260, 263, 309
Investors Intelligence, 263
iShares S&P 100 Fund, 148

Japanese candlesticks, 136
Japanese stock market, 17
J.P. Morgan Chase, 48–49

Krispy Kreme Doughnuts, 139

Lane, George, 244
Latin American crises, 17
Leap Wireless International (LWIN):
  covered calls, 104–105
  gamma, 106–107
  implied *vs.* statistical volatility, 97–100
  protective put, 100–102
Life of the option, 78
Line charts, 44–45
Liquidity:
  index options, 89
  significance of, 13, 196
  stock options, 84
Liquidmetal Technologies, 25
Long butterfly spread:
  characteristics of, 181–186
  strategy, *see* Long butterfly strategy
Long butterfly strategy:
  review of, 300–302
  stock analysis template, 318
  summary of, 280
Long call:
  characteristics of, 60, 131–140, 146
  strategy, *see* Long call strategy
Long call strategy, summary of, 275
Long iron butterfly:
  characteristics of, 177–181
  strategy, *see* Long iron butterfly strategy
  stock analysis template, 319
Long iron butterfly strategy:
  review of, 302–303
  stock analysis template, 319
  summary of, 280

Long put, *see* Protective put strategy
  characteristics of, 60, 131, 142, 146
  strategy, *see* Long put strategy
Long put strategy, summary of, 276
Long stock strategy, summary of, 275
Long straddle:
  characteristics of, 144–146
  strategy, *see* Long straddle strategy
Long straddle strategy:
  review of, 297–299
  stock analysis template, 317
  summary of, 279
Long-term average, 63
Long Term Capital Management, 17
Long-term equity anticipation security (LEAPS),
    73, 132, 140, 198, 202, 204, 283, 286, 294,
    298
Long-term investments, 6, 21
Long-term trends, 55, 69
Low volatility:
  defined, 250
  example of, 33–34, 36
  investment strategies, *see* Low volatility
    strategies
  option prices and, 79–81, 94, 107
Low volatility strategies:
  call options, buying, 132–140, 160, 215
  debit spreads, 146–154, 160
  long straddles, 297–299
  overview, 310
  put options, 140–143, 215
  ratio backspreads, 154–160
  trading with nondirectional strategy, 143–146
Low-yield stocks, 94
LSI Logic, 30
Lycos Finance, 262

Macroeconomics, 220
Malkiel, Burton, 16
Management changes, impact of, 96
Management effectiveness ratios, 219
Margin, *see specific types of options strategies*
  covered calls, 104
  defined, 169
  protective put, 102
Margin accounts, 3, 10–11
Margin call, 11, 169
Margin debt, 11–12
Market conditions, 6, 122
Market makers, 94, 235
Market psychology, 110
Market recovery, 19
Market relationships, 220
Market sentiment, 111, 119–120, 122
Market Vane, 263

Media, sentiment indicator:
  characteristics of, 257–258
  Internet, 260–263
  print, 259–260
  television, 258–259
Merger tax, 16
Merrill Lynch, 25, 32
Mexican peso crisis, 17
Micro Strategy (MSTR), 3
Microsoft (MSFT), 25, 32, 69, 82–83, 92, 116, 139, 236
Mini-Nasdaq 100 (MNX)/Minx, 89, 116–119
Mob psychology, 54, 225
Monetary policy, 13
Moneyness, options strategies, 74–77, 133
Morgan Stanley Retail Index ($RLX), 88
Mortgage refinancing, 13
Motley Fool, 262
Motorola (MOT), 25
Moving average (MA):
  defined, 48, 239
  implications of, 54–58, 68, 90, 222, 239–240
  standard deviation and, 67
Moving average convergence/divergence (MACD), 48, 224, 240–242
Multiple contracts, 299
Multiplier, stock options, 83
Mutual funds, 20–21

Naked options, generally:
  characteristics of, 130, 169–170
  credit spreads vs., 173–174
  puts, 165–168
Nasdaq Composite Index ($COMPQ), 23, 29, 52, 87–88
Nasdaq 100 index ($NDS), 30, 88
Nasdaq 100 Index Trust (QQQ), 32, 88–89, 116, 129, 250, 265–268
Nasdaq 100 Volatility Index (VXN), 114, 116–117, 127–129, 254–255
Nasdaq Stock Market, 21, 24–26, 97
National Association of Purchasing Management Index (NAPM), 272
National Association of Securities Dealers (NASD), 26
Natural disasters, economic impact of, 163
NDX, 116–119
Near-the-money options, 75, 151, 170, 172
Negative correlation, perfect, 68
Neill, Humphrey B., 224
Neutral strategies, 176
New accounts, options trading:
  index options, 88
  stock options, 86–87

New Concepts in Technical Trading Systems (Wilder), 45
New York Stock Exchange (NYSE), 21, 24, 26, 29, 39
New York Stock Exchange Composite Index, 29
Nifty Fifty, 15
9-day moving average, 57–58
Nixon, Richard, 15
Nondirectional strategies:
  defined, 148
  delta neutral, 64
Nonfarm Jobs Growth report, 271
Normal decline, defined, 20
Normal distribution, 58

Odd-lot short sellers, 263
OEF, 148, 149, 152
OHLC (open, high, low, close) charts, 45, 228–229
On-balance volume (OBV), 237–238
100-day historical volatility, 61, 63
Online brokerages, 86, 153
Opening price, 27
Opening transactions, 78
Open interest, 82–85
Optimism:
  economic impact of, 110, 122–124
  measurements, 225
Option codes:
  expiration month, 268
  strike price, 268–269
Option contracts:
  implied volatility and, 92
  index options, 88
  interest in, 94
  stock options, 72–73, 80, 88, 92
  value decline, 102
Optionetics.com, 40–41, 43, 45, 63, 69, 76, 80, 84, 95, 124, 153, 160, 212, 266, 291, 307, 310
Optionetics Platinum, 262
Option premiums (prices):
  call options, generally, 132
  determination of, 79–81
  implied volatility and, 93–95, 121
  influential factors, 131
  selling, 163–164
Option pricing models, 36, 80–81, 93, 95
Options chain, 153, 158, 211
Options Clearing Corporation (OCC), 75, 77–78, 85, 89
Options exchanges, 85–86
Options trading:
  buying options, 100–102
  greeks, 105–108, 152–153

Options trading *(Continued)*
  index options, 87–90
  popularity of, 90–91
  quick reference guide, 274
  selling options, 102–105
  stock options, characteristics of, 70–87
  strategy reviews, 281–308
  strategy summaries, 275–281
Option strategists, 70, 78, 83, 129, 132, 213
Option symbols, 82
Oracle Corporation (ORCL), 32, 246–247
Oscillators, 224, 244–245
Out-of-the-money (OTM) options:
  bear call credit spread, 173–174
  bull call spread, 151, 153
  butterfly spreads, 177–178
  calendar spreads, 208, 211
  call ratio backspread, 154–155
  calls, 103, 105, 133
  characteristics of, 74–76, 84
  credit spreads, 170–171, 173–174
  long iron butterfly spread, 178
  puts, 140, 147, 170–171
Overbought conditions, 54–55, 59–60,
    246–247
Oversold conditions, 54, 59–60, 111,
    246–247

Pacific Exchange (PCX), 77, 85
Panic, 54, 110, 119, 122
Passive investors, 20
Pennants, 233
Persian Gulf War, 16, 113
Personal Income and Consumption Expenditures
    report, 273
Pessimism:
  economic impact of, 110, 126–127
  measurements, 225
Philadelphia Stock Exchange (PHLX):
  Bank Index ($BKX), 31, 88
  Fiber Optics Index ($FOP), 89
  Gold and Silver Mining Index ($XAU), 31, 61,
    88
  Oil Service Index, 31
  performance of, generally, 77, 85–86, 124
  Semiconductor Index ($SOX), 30–31,
    88
Philip Morris (MO), 144–146, 148, 196,
    236–237
Political climate, economic impact of, 14, 16, 28,
    96, 113–114
Portfolio diversification, importance of, 19–20
Positive correlation, perfect, 68
Premiums, 3

Premiums, stock options, 3, 77–78, 103. *See also*
    Option premiums (prices)
Price, generally:
  label, 44
  options, *see* Option premiums (prices)
  significance of, 3
Price-to-earnings (P/E) ratio, 219
Price-to-earnings growth rate (PEG) ratio, 219
Producer Price Index (PPI), 272
Profit opportunities:
  Bollinger bands and, 59
  protective put, 101
  recognition of, 52
Profit taking, 232
Protective put strategy, 100–102, 131
Prudent investors, 3
Pullback, defined, 20, 218
Put butterfly spread, 183–186
Put options:
  buying, 96, 122, 140–143
  characteristics of, 72, 74–76, 79, 89
  naked, 165–168
  risk management, 100–101
  short, 167–168
Put ratio backspread:
  characteristics of, 156–159
  strategy, *see* Put ratio backspread strategy
Put ratio backspread strategy:
  review of, 295–297
  stock analysis template, 316
  summary of, 279
Put-to-call ratios:
  implications of, 121–124
  implied volatility and, 125–129
Put writer, 72

QQQ, *see* Nasdaq 100 Index Trust (QQQ)
QQV, 117–119, 254–255
Quotes:
  options, 82–85, 90
  stock, 27–28

Rampart Time Index, 263
Random Walk Down Wall Street, A (Malkiel), 16
Range trading, 176–177
Ratio backspreads:
  call, 157
  low-volatility environment, 154–156
  put, 156–159
Reagan, Ronald, 15
Recession, 14–15, 113
Red Herring Online, 262
Regional stock exchanges, 26
Relative Strength Index (RSI), 224, 244–245

Resistance:
  charting, 221
  long iron butterfly spread, 178
  moving averages and, 57
Restrictive monetary policy, 13
Retail Sales report, 272
Retirement accounts, 1
Return on assets (ROA), 219
Return on equity (ROE), 219
Reverse volatility skew, 175
Reversion to the mean, 54, 69, 131–132, 161,
    193, 206, 213
Risk-free rate, 112
Risk graphs:
  applications, generally, 265–267
  bullish diagonal spread, 203
  calendar spread, 209
  covered call, 165
  defined, 137
  iron butterfly, 179
  put butterfly spread, 184
  put ratio backspread, 158–159
  short put, 167
Risk management:
  in options trading, 130–131. *See also specific*
    types of options strategies
  significance of, 5
Risk/reward analysis, 50, 133, 206, 210, 216, 292
Risk/reward chart, 50
Root symbol, options, 82
Rumors, impact of, 93, 96–98, 198, 214
Russell 2000 Small Cap Index ($SOX), 30–31,
    88

S&P MidCap 400 index, 30–31
S&P 100 index ($OEX), 41–43, 88, 95, 111–116,
    119, 121, 125, 129, 133–138, 141–143, 157,
    162, 197, 247–248
Scandals:
  Arthur Andersen, 18
  Enron, 18
  Stewart, Martha, 19
  WorldCom, 18–19
Scholes, Myron, 36, 81, 92, 214
Secondary market, 84
Securities and Exchange Commission (SEC), 18
Securities Exchange Act (1934), 11
Sell signals:
  characteristics of, 57–58, 67–68, 127
  stochastics, 244
Semiconductor Equipment and Materials
    International (SEMI), 30–31
Sentiment analysis, 110–111, 119, 128, 224–227.
    See also Sentiment indicators

Sentiment indicators:
  media, 257–263
  put-to-call ratios, 255–257
  QQV, 254–255
  VIX, 95, 111–114, 118–121, 127–129, 253–254
  VXN, 254–255
Severe correction, 20
Short call strategy, summary of, 276
Short interest ratio, 264
Short put options:
  characteristics of, 167–168
  strategy, *see* Short put strategy
Short put strategy, summary of, 276
Short sellers, odd-lot, 263
Short stock strategy, summary of, 275
Short-term average, 63
Short-term trends, 69
Sideways-moving market, 20, 34, 38, 300, 302
Simple moving average, 222
Skews, *see* Volatility skews
Skilling, Jeffrey, 18
Slope, 196–197
Smiles, 193–194
Smith, Edgar Lawrence, 9
Speculation, 71, 90
Speculative bubbles, 12–13, 17, 24
Speculators, 1, 122
Spreads, options trading, 87, 121. *See also*
    specific types of spreads
Sprint PCS, 95–96
Standard & Poor's Corporation (S&P), 77
Standard & Poor's 500 (S&P 500):
  Cash Index, 259
  performance, 9–10, 12, 14–17, 19–20, 23,
    29–30, 50, 88, 114, 116
Standard deviation, generally:
  Average True Range *vs.*, 67–68
  Bollinger bands, 48
  statistical volatility, 40–42
Statistical volatility:
  characteristics of, 38, 40–43, 51, 90
  charting, 234–235
  computation of, 249
  implied volatility *vs.*, example of, 97–100
  time frames and, 53, 60–64, 69
  VIX, 120–122
Stewart, Martha, 19
Stochastics, 242–244
Stock(s), generally:
  characteristics of, 24–27
  market relationships, 220
  price decline, implications of, 36–37
  quotes, 27–28
  splits, 96

Stock analysis templates:
  applications, generally, 309–310
  bear call spread, 315
  bear put spread, 313
  bull call spread, 312
  bull put spread, 314
  calendar spread, 321
  call ratio backspread, 316
  covered call, 311
  diagonal spread, 322
  long butterfly spread, 319
  long iron butterfly, 320
  long straddle, 318
  put ratio backspread, 317
Stock charts:
  characteristics of, 40, 43–51
  consolidation, 231–232
  OHLC, 228–229
  patterns, 231–235
  trend lines, 229–230
  volatility, 230–235
Stock exchanges, 26, 70, 85, 90
Stock market crash(es):
  fear of, 96
  Great Depression, 9, 12–14
  mini-crash of 1989, 113
  October 1987, 22, 34, 36, 53, 163
Stock market declines, 8–9
Stock options:
  analysis of, *see* Stock analysis templates
  broker role, 86–87
  expiration, 77–78
  moneyness, 74–77, 133
  open interest, 82–85
  option prices, determination of, 79–81
  overview, 71–74, 89–90
  quotes, 82–85
  time decay, 73–74, 78–80
  trading, 85–86
Stock price decline, 36–37
Stop orders, 2
Straddles, characteristics of, 60, 64, 121, 131,
    143–146, 160. *See also specific types of*
    straddles
Strike price:
  bear call credit spread, 173
  bear put spread, 147–148
  bull call spread, 151
  butterfly spreads, 177
  call options, 132–134
  call ratio backspread, 155
  covered calls, 103–104
  diagonal spreads, 201
  implications of, 60, 72, 74–76, 80, 82, 88, 90,
    92, 112, 133

options chain, 153
  put options, 140–143
Supply and demand, 93
Support:
  charting, 221
  long iron butterfly spread, 178
  moving averages and, 57

Takeover rumors, 93, 96–98, 214
Tau, defined, 107. *See also* Greeks; Vega
Technical analysis:
  applications of, 220–221
  Average True Range (ATR), 247–248
  Bollinger bands, 245–247
  characteristics of, 57, 59
  moving average, 238–242
  Relative Strength Index (RSI), 244–245
  stochastics, 242–244
  stock charts, 228–235
  technical tools, overview, 221
  trading volume, 236–238
Technical Analysis of Stocks & Commodities
    (Gustafson), 67–68, 242, 260
Technical analysts, 43
Technology sector, 52, 114, 116
Television programs, as information resource,
    258–259
10-day period historical volatility, 63
10/90 Volatility System, 63–64
Terayon Communications (TERN), 231
Terrorist attacks, economic impact of, 8, 12, 18,
    114, 128, 135, 138, 162–163
Texas Instruments, 30
Theoretical value(s):
  market prices *vs.*, 95–97
  stock options, 80
TheStreet.com, 262
TheStreet.com Internet Index (DOT), 42–43,
    244–245
Theta, 107, 201
30-day time frames, 61
Ticker symbols, 82
Time, significance of, 3–5
Time decay:
  covered calls, 105
  stock options and, 73–74, 78–80
  theta and, 107
Time frame, significance of, 53, 60–64, 69
Time value, stock options, 75–79
Tops, Bollinger bands, 59
Trade Options Online (Fontanills), 261
Trader's journal, 282, 284, 287, 289, 292, 294,
    297, 299, 301, 303, 305, 308
Trading for a Living (Elder), 243
Trading signals, *see* Buy signals; Sell signals

Trading volume, 21, 221, 236–238, 263
Trend analysis, 54
Trend line, 221
True ranges (TRs), 64–65, 247–248
Truman, Harry S., 14
Tuition savings plans, 1
20-day moving average, 55–57
20-day time frames, 61
200-day moving average, 48, 55, 58, 239–240
Tyco International (TYC), 18, 191–192

UAL Corporation, 113, 198–199
Uncovered options:
   characteristics of, 130
   sales, 168–170
Underlying securities, 72–75, 79–80, 93, 106,
   133, 140, 148, 166
U.S. Total Market Index, 30
U.S. Treasury bills (T-bills), 79, 94

Value investors, 218
Vanguard S&P 500 mutual fund, 20
Variable deltas, 106, 270
Vega, 107–108, 152–153, 183, 186
Vixen, *see* Nasdaq 100 Volatility Index (VXN)
Volatility, *see specific types of volatility*
   breakout, 64
   crush, 160
   defined, 7
   identification of, 34–36
   impact of, 37
   market relationships, 220
   significance of, 3, 5–6
   skew, *see* Volatility skews
Volatility skews:
   defined, 189
   Dell Computer example, 189–193

   diagonal spreads, 201–206
   by expiration month (series), 197–201
   frown, 194–196
   horizontal/calendar spreads, 207–210
   implications of, generally, 92, 175,
      215–216
   price, 188–189
   slope, 196–197
   smiles, 193–194
   types of, generally, 187
Volume, *see* Trading volume

Wall Street Journal, 19, 25, 29, 259, 309
Walt Disney, 15
Wasting assets, 74
Watergate, 15
Wealth creation, 19
Web sites, as information resource,
   260–263
Wedge pattern, 233
Whipsaw, 57
Wholesale Trade Inventories report, 271
Wilder, J. Welles, Jr., 45, 64
Wilshire 4500 Index, 30
Wilshire 5000, 30
Wired, 260
WorldCom, 18–19
World Trade Center, terrorist attack, 8, 12, 114,
   135, 138, 169
Worth, 260
Writer, stock options, 72, 74, 103

Xerox, 18

Yahoo! Inc., 64–65

Zacks Investment Research, 263

FREE TRADING PACKAGE
From George Fontanills and Tom Gentile

$100 GIFT

Now that you've read George and Tom's book, wouldn't you like to keep up with their day-to-day trading strategies? We're going to make it easy to do by sending you a FREE Trading Package worth $100.

Their company, Optionetics, is one of the leading investment education and publishing companies in the trading industry today. Optionetics has grown to provide dozens of vital resources for stock and stock options traders. Using a simple yet effective philosophy of continued education and personal attention, George and Tom and their team of traders strive for excellence in all their trading products and services.

To receive your free trading package, complete and mail (or fax) the coupon below to:

Optionetics
P.O. Box 2409
Santa Rosa, CA 95405-2409
Fax: (650) 802-0900

You may also reach us by phone at (888) 366-8264, or (650) 802-0700 outside the United States, e-mail the authors at george@optionetics.com or tom@optionetics.com, or visit our web site at www.optionetics.com.

George Fontanills and Tom Gentile Trading Package

❏ I would like to learn more about George and Tom's trading secrets and strategies. Please send me the FREE trading package mentioned in *The Volatility Course*.

Name: _____

Address: _____

City, State, Zip: _____

Phone: _____ **Fax:** _____

E-mail: _____

I purchased this book from: _____